JAPAN AT WAR AND PEACE

Shidehara Kijūrō and the
Making of Modern Diplomacy

JAPAN AT WAR AND PEACE

Shidehara Kijūrō and the
Making of Modern Diplomacy

RYUJI HATTORI

PRESS

Published by ANU Press
The Australian National University
Acton ACT 2601, Australia
Email: anupress@anu.edu.au

Available to download for free at press.anu.edu.au

ISBN (print): 9781760464967
ISBN (online): 9781760464974

WorldCat (print): 1285332861
WorldCat (online): 1285332893

DOI: 10.22459/JWP.2021

This title is published under a Creative Commons Attribution-NonCommercial-NoDerivatives 4.0 International (CC BY-NC-ND 4.0).

The full licence terms are available at
creativecommons.org/licenses/by-nc-nd/4.0/legalcode

Cover design and layout by ANU Press

This book is published under the aegis of the Asia-Pacific Security Studies Editorial Board of ANU Press.

This edition © 2021 ANU Press

This book is based on Ryuji Hattori, *Zōhoban Shidehara Kijūrō: Gaikō to Minshushugi*, published 2017 by Yoshida Shoten, Japan. This English translation has been updated with a new introduction and other information.

Contents

Introduction … 1

Part I. Glory: The Meiji and Taishō Eras

1. Path to the Ministry of Foreign Affairs … 13
2. The Russo-Japanese War, World War I and the Washington Naval Conference … 21
3. Japan–US Relations and Chinese Nationalism … 103

Part II. Breakdown: The Prewar Shōwa Era

4. Japan's Intervention in China … 159
5. The London Naval Conference and the Manchurian Incident … 173
6. From the Second Sino-Japanese War to the Pacific War … 225

Part III. Recovery: The Postwar Period

7. Prime Minister of an Occupied Nation: The Emperor System and the New Constitution … 251
8. War Responsibility and Nonpartisan Diplomacy for Peace … 293
9. A Legacy beyond War and Peace … 325

Conclusion: Diplomacy and Democracy … 337
Appendix: Brief Chronology of Shidehara Kijūrō … 345
Index … 349

Introduction

Continuity of Diplomacy in the Democratisation Process

Harold Nicolson, a British diplomat who became a member of the House of Commons, argued in his classic work *Diplomacy*:

> The function of diplomacy is the management of the relations between independent States by processes of negotiation. The professional diplomatist is the servant of the sovereign authority in his own country. In democratic countries, that sovereign authority is represented, in the first place by a majority of the House of Commons, and in the second place by the Government or Cabinet to whom that majority accords executive powers.[1]

Diplomacy is a form of foreign policy, and while foreign policy includes defence policy and the use of military force, diplomacy is negotiations between nations. A state's diplomacy with foreign counterparts requires continuous policy and human interaction to ensure unwavering trust.

However, two factors threaten the consistency of diplomacy. First, diplomacy in a democracy is prone to inconsistency due to regime changes. Democracy in a modern state is an indirect one and takes the form of party politics. Opposition parties often criticise the ruling party's diplomacy as soft and against the national interest and try to change the diplomacy when they come to power. Today, with the development of diverse media, the phenomenon of populism is common even in developed countries. It is not infrequent for politicians to manipulate the media to incite the masses or pander to public opinion and appeal to extreme foreign policies. Second, in countries in the process of democratisation, the military often comes to power and intervenes in foreign affairs. In countries on the verge of democratisation, such as modern Japan and contemporary South-East

Asia, coups d'état have often occurred, and the military has taken over the reins of power. Since the military, which has taken control of the country, also meddles in diplomacy, changes in civil–military relations have a significant impact on foreign policy.

Thus, the question of how to maintain the continuity of diplomacy while developing democracy without military intervention is an old and new issue. The challenge can be described as a dilemma between democracy and diplomatic coherence. This dilemma is not unique to the twenty-first century; it has been a constant challenge to the development of democracy. In non-Western countries, democratisation originated in the nineteenth century and has had many successes and failures. After the Russo-Japanese War, political parties began to take power in Japan, replacing the military-backed forces represented by Army General Yamagata Aritomo (1838–1922). The president of the Rikken Seiyūkai, Hara Takashi (1856–1921), who became prime minister in 1918, formed the first full-fledged party cabinet by appointing all ministers from the party except for the ministers of war, navy and foreign affairs. In the late 1920s, party politics with the two major parties—the Rikken Seiyūkai and the Minseitō—reached its peak in Japan. However, party politics in prewar Japan did not last long, and the military dominated politics from the Manchurian Incident in 1931 until the defeat in the Pacific War in 1945. The rise of militarism in Japan in the 1930s and early 1940s led to the collapse of party politics, but democracy was restored in the late twentieth century.

Who Is Shidehara and Why Is He So Important?

The best embodiment of diplomacy in Japan's emerging democracy—the development of parliamentary democracy and mass-based democracy—is Shidehara Kijūrō (1872–1951), who served as foreign minister from 1924 to 1927 and from 1929 to 1931, and was prime minister from 1945 to 1946. As a diplomat from the Ministry of Foreign Affairs, Shidehara had long grappled with the issue of how to ensure diplomatic coherence in modern Japan, which was becoming increasingly democratic. Although Shidehara succeeded to some extent in promoting diplomacy in cooperation with the US and the UK under party politics, the rise of the military after the Manchurian Incident forced him to retire for a period.

'Manchuria' is the former name for China's north-eastern region, covering the three provinces of Liaoning, Jilin and Heilongjiang, and part of the Inner Mongolia Autonomous Region. However, after the Pacific War, Shidehara became prime minister of the US-occupied Japan and attempted to restore cooperative diplomacy under party politics. Shidehara came to the conclusion that the way to achieve both democracy and diplomatic coherence was through nonpartisan diplomacy towards peace. This book examines the tension between diplomacy and democracy, focusing on Shidehara's life and exploring modern Japan's footsteps.

Shidehara was undoubtedly one of Japan's most important diplomatic figures. Along with Mutsu Munemitsu (1844–1897) and Komura Jutarō (1855–1911), he is considered one of the representative foreign ministers of the nation's modern era. Even in the twentieth century as a whole, only diplomatic figures like Yoshida Shigeru (1878–1967) or Shigemitsu Mamoru (1887–1957) made comparable contributions. Today, 'Mutsu diplomacy' has become a household term. Yet, it was Shidehara who was the first to have his name associated with a particular form of diplomacy—'Shidehara diplomacy'. Such is the extent to which he drew both praise and censure.

Shidehara's diplomatic career began in the era of the Russo-Japanese War (1904–05). After an initial posting to Incheon, followed by Busan and London, Shidehara served as the vice-minister for foreign affairs and then as Japan's ambassador to the United States. From 1924 to 1927, as well as from 1929 to 1931, Shidehara served as foreign minister, and his policies were commonly referred to as 'Shidehara diplomacy'. Although he left office following the Manchurian Incident (1931), he served as prime minister during the US occupation of Japan, working to preserve the emperor system as well as helping draft the new constitution. Shidehara also appeared in court during the International Military Tribunal for the Far East or the Tokyo Trial. At the time of his death in 1951, he was serving as the speaker of the House of Representatives.

Shidehara was an internationalist who advocated cooperative diplomacy with the US and the UK. At the same time, he regarded the annexation of Korea in 1910 as a natural occurrence and was critical of China's abolition of unequal treaties. In this sense, Shidehara's diplomacy was a confluence of internationalism towards the West and imperialism towards Asia. Shidehara is attracting new attention today. The reason for this is the issue of whether Prime Minister Shidehara was the originator of

Article 9 of the Constitution of Japan, which stipulates the renunciation of war and the non-preservation of military power, as constitutional revision has become a real issue in Japan in recent years. Further, as speaker of the House of Representatives in his final years, Shidehara was more enthusiastic than Prime Minister Yoshida about maintaining the US military presence in Japan after independence. These facts indicate the necessity of following in Shidehara's footsteps when considering contemporary international security.

Literature Review

A significant amount of research has focused on Shidehara's time as foreign minister. I will examine this research in more detail in the following chapters. However, biographical research has lagged behind. Currently, the most reliable source is *Shidehara Kijūrō*, edited by the Shidehara Peace Foundation and published in 1955. It is a thorough work for its time and one that has retained its value as a historical resource. However, it does not utilise important documents, including the records of the Ministry of Foreign Affairs. It is also significantly limited by its laudatory approach.

Studies published in Japanese in recent years include the following: Taneine Syūji, *Shidehara Kijūrō* (Tokyo: Yoshikawa Kōbunkan, 2021); and Kumamoto Fumio, *Shidehara Kijūrō* (Tokyo: Chūō Kōron Shinsha, 2021). Although these make use of Japanese historical sources, they are aimed at a general readership rather than an academic audience. Hence, until now, properly rigorous biographical research has not been conducted. Only one biography of Shidehara has ever been published in English: Klaus Schlichtmann, *Japan in the World: Shidehara Kijūrō, Pacifism, and the Abolition of War*, 2 vols (Lanham: Lexington Books, 2009). However, it does not utilise important documents, including the original records of the Japanese Ministry of Foreign Affairs. Hence, until now, properly rigorous biographical research has not been conducted in English.

In addition to the records of the Japanese Ministry of Foreign Affairs, this study uses documents of the US (Record Group 59, 331, National Archives), the UK (FO 228, 371, 800, National Archives) and Taiwan (Record of the Foreign Ministry, 03.25.25.31.1). Besides the above-mentioned public documents, I also researched private papers.

INTRODUCTION

Aims and Scope

This work is not intended to serve only as a biography in the narrow sense. Can Shidehara's life and career be adequately traced without also depicting the historical trajectory of Japan in the twentieth century? Certainly, it must be noted that Shidehara died in 1951. Therefore, at the very least, he cannot be said to occupy a central position in twentieth-century history. In fact, the opposite could be argued: Shidehara is, in a way, a *peripheral* figure.

In support of the above claim, let us briefly consider the other leading figures in Japan's modern diplomatic history. Beginning with Ōkubo Toshimichi (1830–1878), we would proceed to mention Itō Hirobumi (1841–1909), Yamagata Aritomo, Inoue Kaoru (1836–1915), Mutsu Munemitsu, Komura Jutarō, Hayashi Tadasu (1850–1913), Hara Takashi and Tanaka Giichi (1864–1929). Moving forward, we would have to mention Hirota Kōki (1878–1948), Tōgō Shigenori (1882–1950), Shigemitsu Mamoru, Yoshida Shigeru, Kishi Nobusuke (1896–1987), Satō Eisaku (1901–1975), Fukuda Takeo (1905–1995), Ōhira Masayoshi (1910–1980) and Nakasone Yasuhiro (1918–2019). When comparing Shidehara with such diplomatic figures, we might say that one of his characteristics was a certain kind of weakness. That is to say, by Shidehara's time, a wide range of foreign affairs mechanisms were already in place, and Japan was increasingly receptive to democratic forms of governance. What this new era needed was talented officials; it was no longer the age of daring diplomatic officers.

For this reason, in this book I consider not only Shidehara's policies and general outlook on foreign affairs but also his personal relationships. I speak of his connections with figures such as Komura Jutarō, Henry Willard Denison (1846–1914), James Bryce (1838–1922), Sir Edward Grey (1862–1933), Katō Takaaki (1860–1926), Debuchi Katsuji (1878–1947), Saburi Sadao (1879–1929), Yoshida Shigeru, William Richards Castle (1878–1963), Shigemitsu Mamoru, Joseph Grew (1880–1965), the Shōwa emperor, Douglas MacArthur (1880–1964) and Ashida Hitoshi (1887–1959). In the presence of such strong personalities as these, Shidehara could not help but be overshadowed.

Such is the fate of a person whose life and career coincided with such tumultuous historic events. Yet, I would like to suggest that Shidehara's peripheral position in this period is itself symbolic of Japan's own trajectory. There are four reasons why Shidehara was a peripheral figure. First, although Shidehara was a vice-minister for foreign affairs during World War I, the Ministry of Foreign Affairs' position had declined because the Japanese army had led the Siberian Intervention. Second, in 1927–28, against Shidehara's policy, the Tanaka Giichi cabinet sent troops to the Shandong Peninsula, and the Japanese Kwantung Army assassinated Zhang Zuolin, a Mukden warlord. Third, in 1931, when Shidehara was a foreign minister, the Japanese army caused the Manchurian Incident, destroying Shidehara's diplomatic solution. Fourth, although Shidehara was prime minister from 1945 to 1946, it was not Shidehara who led the Japanese constitution's enactment, but the US occupation forces, who held absolute power. Therefore, while I make Shidehara the main focus of this book, I also provide a brief historical overview. More concretely, I divide the twentieth century into three periods, on which I overlay Shidehara's own steps. These periods are the Meiji and Taishō eras, the prewar Shōwa era and the postwar era.

In the Meiji and Taishō eras, Japan won the First Sino-Japanese War (1894–95) and the Russo-Japanese War (1904–05) and secured its position as a 'Great Power' through the Paris Peace Conference (1919) and the Washington Naval Conference (1921–22). This is also the period that saw the establishment of party-based politics in Japan and the formation of the Katō Takaaki cabinet in 1924 (the thirteenth year of Taishō). The Katō cabinet was a cross-party cabinet consisting of members of the Kenseikai, the Rikken Seiyūkai and the Kakushin Club ('Reformist Club'); it was also referred to as the 'three-party coalition cabinet of constitutional protection'. It was as part of the Katō cabinet that Shidehara first served as foreign minister.

However, prewar Shōwa-era Japan stumbled as a result of the China policies adopted by the cabinet formed by Tanaka Giichi of the Seiyūkai. Following the Manchurian Incident and the May 15 Incident, party-based politics collapsed. Japan was now on a path to catastrophe. After his reappointment as foreign minister in the cabinet formed by Hamaguchi Osachi (1870–1931), Shidehara also served as foreign minister in Wakatsuki Reijirō's (1866–1949) second cabinet. Subsequently, however, he became a forgotten figure. Shidehara's residence in Sendagaya was damaged in the Pacific War, a conflict that would lead to the collapse of Japan's entire empire.

Yet postwar Japan, undergoing a period of reform under the occupation of the Allied forces and a subsequent era of rapid economic growth, eventually grew into an economic power. Serving as prime minister during the occupation, Shidehara was directly involved in the reforms of the period, beginning with the establishment of the constitution. In fact, it was Shidehara who prepared the English version of the Shōwa emperor's 'Declaration of Humanity'. Shidehara also took to the witness stand at the Tokyo Trial and worked tirelessly to maintain the integrity of the Ministry of Foreign Affairs. In his final years, as speaker of the House of Representatives, he endeavoured to find a way to achieve reconciliation with foreign countries through nonpartisan diplomacy.

If we were to briefly summarise these three periods, it might be said that Japan experienced a time of glory during the Meiji and Taishō eras, rising to the status of a first-class power; a time of breakdown in the prewar Shōwa era, beginning with the Tanaka cabinet; and an eventual recovery with the reconstruction of the postwar period. As it happened, only Shidehara served as a cabinet minister during all three of these periods. Long-serving figures such as Yamagata Aritomo and Hara Takashi did not live to see the Shōwa years, while conversely, others such as Yoshida Shigeru and Shigemitsu Mamoru remained peripheral to the Ministry of Foreign Affairs until the end of the Taishō era. Put simply, when it comes to representing Japan internationally during these three periods, and while having a career that reflected and embodied the successive changes that took place in Japan, no one surpasses Shidehara.

If those long-running threads of Shidehara's career that influenced foreign diplomacy could be thought of as the 'warp', then it is the cross-threads, the 'weft', that constitute the central focus of the present book. In short, a look at Shidehara's career allows us to consider the age-old tension between foreign diplomacy and democracy. This work asks: how did Shidehara understand the relationship between foreign policy and party-based politics, and how did he act accordingly? During Shidehara's time as a diplomat, party-based politics took shape and then collapsed. In this historical context, Shidehara attempted to preserve a certain consistency in foreign policy by separating domestic politics from diplomacy. In this sense, Shidehara is the clearest embodiment of orthodox Kasumigaseki-style (i.e. Japanese government bureaucracy-style) diplomacy.

However, once Shidehara was forced into opposition with the formation of the Tanaka cabinet, he became involved in the development of the Minseitō's policies. Then, in the postwar period, political parties naturally started once more to shoulder diplomatic responsibilities. The Ministry of Foreign Affairs could no longer centrally manage foreign relations. These significant changes between the prewar and the postwar periods are also reflected in Shidehara's words and actions. Moreover, starting in the postwar period, Shidehara devoted himself to the restoration of party-based politics. Thus I suggest that Shidehara's arguments remain instructive for us even today, when looking at the relationship between diplomacy and democracy.

Structure and Arguments

This book consists of three main parts and an epilogue. The three sections correspond to the three periods outlined above: Part I covers the period of Meiji- and Taishō-era glory, Part II examines the breakdown of the prewar Shōwa period and Part III focuses on the postwar recovery.

Starting with Part I, Chapter 1 looks at Shidehara's background. Here I will outline the stages of his early life, from his birth in the town of Kadoma, where he was raised in a privileged environment, until he joined the Ministry of Foreign Affairs.

Chapter 2 covers Shidehara's early career as a member of the diplomatic service. I will trace Shidehara's initial posting to the consulate of Incheon as a consular assistant following the end of the First Sino-Japanese War; his rise to the position of consul at Busan during the Russo-Japanese War; his role as vice-minister for foreign affairs during World War I; and, finally, his performance at the Washington Naval Conference as the ambassador plenipotentiary to the US.

Chapter 3 focuses on Shidehara's first stint as foreign minister, from 1924 until 1927. As foreign minister, Shidehara played a crucial role in orienting Japan towards the US and handling a China that was moving towards reunification. This chapter concludes Part I and the Meiji and Taishō eras.

INTRODUCTION

Proceeding to Part II, and Chapter 4, I turn to Shidehara's status during his time in political opposition. He was ousted from office because his political stance differed from that of the Seiyūkai, which had secured executive power with the formation of the Tanaka Giichi cabinet. At this point, Shidehara aligned himself with Hamaguchi Osachi's party, the Minseitō, and even debated Prime Minister Tanaka during Diet sessions.

Chapter 5 covers Shidehara's second stint as foreign minister, from 1929 to 1931. While Shidehara's diplomatic efforts resulted in success at the London Naval Treaty Conference in 1930, they were eventually undermined by the fallout from the Manchurian Incident.

Chapter 6 looks at the period from the start of the Second Sino-Japanese War in 1937 to the outbreak of the Pacific War in 1941. This was a time when Shidehara was once more in political opposition. Nevertheless, as we shall see, he was able to make pertinent judgements on the unfolding global situation, and he called for a peace accord to bring an early end to the Pacific War. This chapter concludes Part II and the prewar Shōwa era.

Next, in Chapter 7 and the beginning of Part III, I discuss Shidehara's actions during the initial period of the US military occupation of Japan. At this time, Shidehara became the prime minister. His time in office was brief, lasting only half a year. Nevertheless, as prime minister, Shidehara had an extremely important role, working, for example, to secure the survival of the emperor system and establish the new constitution.

In Chapter 8 I outline some of the important details of Shidehara's career in the final years of his life. At this point, Shidehara was no longer prime minister, instead becoming a minister of state and cabinet minister without a portfolio in Yoshida Shigeru's cabinet. He finally became speaker of the House of Representatives. As well as appearing in the Tokyo Trial in this period, Shidehara searched both for a nonpartisan approach to conducting diplomacy and a way to secure the integrity of the Ministry of Foreign Affairs.

In Chapter 9, I review some of the criticisms and discussions of Shidehara that took place after his death, and look at Japan's path in the years following the signing of the Treaty of San Francisco in 1951. This chapter concludes Part III and my examination of the postwar era.

Finally, in the conclusion, I look back upon Shidehara's legacy and the currents of Japan's diplomatic history, while reflecting upon the nature of the relationship between diplomacy and democracy.

Thus, this book seeks to place the reader at the crossroads of Japanese diplomacy from the perspective of Shidehara, providing a view of his repeated attempts to negotiate the nature of the relationship between foreign affairs and party-based politics. What I aim to show is that, by looking at Shidehara's life and career, we can learn much about Japan's twentieth-century history, and about the interlinkage of democracy and diplomacy within that history.

Endnotes

1   Harold Nicolson, *Diplomacy* (Washington: Institute for the Study of Diplomacy, Georgetown University, 1988), 41.

Part I.
Glory: The Meiji and Taishō Eras

1
Path to the Ministry of Foreign Affairs

The Lineage of the Shidehara Family

The forty-fourth prime minister of Japan, Shidehara Kijūrō, was born in the village of Kadoma, Osaka, on 11 August 1872.[1] Today, the village of Kadoma has become a city. While it now flourishes as the home of the Panasonic Corporation, it was originally a wetland. Even today, there remain various places within the city limits where vestiges of lotus root fields can be seen. As a wetland area, Kadoma has long suffered from flooding. In fact, the flood of the nearby Yodogawa River in 1885 dealt the Shidehara family a particularly heavy blow.

These circumstances delayed the development of Kadoma considerably. It was not until 1910 that the Keihan Train Line opened between Tenmanbashi in Osaka and Gojō in Kyoto. By 1912 (the beginning of the Taishō era), however, electric lighting began to be installed, and the Great Consolidated Electric Company constructed a transformer substation at Osaka. Finally, in 1933, Panasonic opened its headquarters and factory at Kadoma.

The Shidehara household, which accrued its wealth through farming, became the most prosperous in the village. The family lineage could be traced back at least as far as the eighteenth century. It is said that they were originally located in nearby Kyoto and later moved to Kadoma.[2] Various records about the Shidehara household remain at the Kadoma City Historical Archive, comprising some 520 documents. These include crop production records, ledgers, notebooks, and other documents pertaining to village administration, household affairs, construction, family register (*koseki*) population, etc. The majority of these documents are from modern times. For this reason, there are not many that relate directly to Kijūrō. Nevertheless, these records on the Shidehara household remain valuable for understanding Kijūrō's roots.[3]

While the home of Kijūrō's birth no longer exists, a street corner of Kadoma City, Ichiban-cho, bears a plaque dedicated to Kijūrō's oldest brother, Taira, and to Kijūrō's siblings. The plaque is signed by Kijūrō's junior at the Ministry of Foreign Affairs—Yoshida Shigeru, another future prime minister. Given the lineage of the Shidehara household, Kijūrō's future life and career might seem quite surprising. Kijūrō, after all, came from a farming family in an underdeveloped area. How did such a child go on to reach the very top of Japanese politics?

Home Environment

The key to unlocking this mystery is Kijūrō's home environment. His father, Shidehara Shinjirō, had married into the family from the Ichikawa household of Shimoshima-gashira, also located in Kadoma. Kijūrō's mother was Shidehara Kuichirō's eldest daughter, Shizu. As Shizu was the only child of Kuichirō, a large landowner, Kuichirō adopted Shinjirō. Shinjirō was also the primary assistant of the head of the village. While responsible for managing a wealthy farming household, Shinjirō was also extremely committed to the education of his two sons, Taira and Kijūrō, and two daughters. In this regard, Shinjirō's wife, Shizu, was also supportive. Taira, who was two years older than Kijūrō, was a quiet, bookish child, regarded as intelligent from a young age. He would go on to study national history at the Imperial University of Tokyo. After becoming principal of the Yamanashi Prefectural Junior High School and a professor at the Higher Normal School in Tokyo, Taira would eventually be appointed as the library bureau director for the Ministry of Education.

Here I would like to speak about Taira in more detail. This is because he was the individual who eventually laid the foundations for the colonial education system in Korea and Taiwan. As a parliamentary councillor on educational policy for the Korean government, Taira strived to establish a system of education in Korea in the middle of the decade following

1900. When Taiping Imperial University was established in 1928, Taira was appointed the first president. After the war, during the US occupation of Japan, Taira also decided upon changes to the constitution in his role as privy councillor. As an individual who was highly conversant with issues surrounding national borders, he also argued in a 1951 paper titled 'Tsushima Mondai' (The Tsushima problem) that Tsushima Island 'was part of Japanese territory from long ago'.[4]

Taira also authored numerous publications on topics such as East Asian history and colonial education. One of these is titled *Daitōa no Seiiku* (The development of Greater East Asia). The preface to this text was written by Ishibashi Tanzan (1884–1973), the fifty-fifth prime minister of Japan. While Ishibashi was originally from Tokyo, he attended elementary and middle school in Yamanashi prefecture. According to the preface, when Ishibashi attended Yamanashi Prefectural Junior High School in Kofu City, 'my former teacher, Shidehara sensei', arrived to serve as school principal. Afterwards, Ishibashi would have the opportunity to meet with Shidehara Taira at the middle school alumni association known as the Tachibana Society. He writes that he found Taira's manner of speaking engrossing and that Taira displayed a deep knowledge of the various problems regarding Japan's overseas territories. Ishibashi, deeply impressed by these qualities, urged Taira to put together a lecture. This is how Ishibashi came to help Taira publish his book *Daitōa no Seiiku* through Tōyō Keizai Shinpōsha. At the time, Ishibashi was the president and chief executive officer of the company.[5]

Taira and Kijūrō also had two younger sisters, Misao and Setsu. Misao, who was a midwife, had her husband, a doctor, take her family name, and together they opened the Shidehara Clinic in Kadoma. Misao was also involved with social welfare. After her husband died, it was her younger sister, Setsu, who took over the Shidehara Clinic. Setsu was actually the first female doctor in Osaka Prefecture. However, it was not easy to be a female doctor in conservative Kadoma. Setsu eventually became disillusioned, left Kadoma, and set up a new clinic in Mikagekishimoto, in Kōbe City. Setsu's mother, Shizu, died young due to complications after giving birth. Setsu, therefore, treated her older sister Misao almost like a mother. Setsu never married, focusing instead on her work as a doctor and later adopting Misao's grandchild. After she died, the Shidehara Clinic closed.

The Diplomatic Service Exam

So, we come to Kijūrō himself. Compared to his older brother, Taira, young Kijūrō was an unruly child. According to their father, Shinjirō, while Taira would diligently study the Chinese classics, Kijūrō preferred 'the new subjects'. He wrote:

> The school principal also held out great hopes for their futures and expended a great deal of energy on their behalf. After graduating from elementary school, he helped Taira enter the junior and senior high school that was in Osaka Otemae at that time, at the recommendation of [Confucian scholar] Fujisawa Nangaku sensei.[6]

Kijūrō followed in his older brother's footsteps, attending Osaka Middle School.

Osaka Middle School was known for its English-language education. Matsui Keishirō (1868–1946), who would later serve as foreign minister, was Kijūrō's senior at the school. Eventually, Osaka Middle School would be renamed the Third Higher Middle School, one of the top-level schools in Japan at the time, which fed students into the Imperial University of Tokyo and careers in the bureaucracy. While Shidehara was still attending the school, it was relocated from Osaka to Kyoto. The future politician Izawa Takio (1869–1949) and future prime minister Hamaguchi Osachi (1870–1931) were also attending the school at this time.[7] Kijūrō would go on to study law at the Imperial University of Tokyo. Nevertheless, although Shinjirō was a wealthy farmer, it was remarkable that he sent both Taira and Kijūrō to university. Although today it is common to see parents so dedicated to their children's education, at the time he must have been regarded as quite odd.

There is an episode that illustrates Shinjirō's devotion to his children's education. In later years, when Kijūrō was appointed vice-minister for foreign affairs, a reporter for the *Osaka Asahi Shimbun* came to interview Shinjirō. As the reporter described it, the father made his appearance supported by Misao and Setsu. A bony-looking figure, he was already 70 years old at that time and spoke while stroking his white beard. As Shinjirō recalled, some around the family had been unsupportive of his efforts, saying that 'commoners didn't need a fancy education'. Shinjirō,

1. PATH TO THE MINISTRY OF FOREIGN AFFAIRS

however, 'was prepared to dedicate the entirety of his finances to the education of his four children, in the hope that they would be of use to the nation'.[8]

Being raised in such a fortunate environment, Shidehara Kijūrō 'had hoped, since his school years, that he could one day become a diplomat'. It so happened that, while he was at the Imperial University of Tokyo in 1893, an exam system for the diplomatic service was established by individuals including Hara Takashi, the head of the International Trade Bureau at the Ministry of Foreign Affairs and future tenth prime minister of Japan. However, Shidehara was diagnosed with thiamine deficiency in his fourth year of university and was unable to take the exam. Thus, following his graduation in 1895, Shidehara initially worked at the Bureau of Mining at the Ministry of Agriculture and Commerce. This work, however, did not reflect his real interests. The following year he took the fourth diplomatic service exam. He was one of only four individuals to pass the exam at that time. Thus, Shidehara realised his long-held ambition of entering the diplomatic service.[9]

Fellow successful candidates included Koike Chōzō, who would later become director-general of the Political Affairs Bureau at the Ministry of Foreign Affairs. In fact, there were numerous important diplomatic figures who passed the exam around this period. For example, the seventh cohort of successful candidates included Honda Kumatarō (1874–1948), Tanaka Tokichi (1877–1961), Hanihara Masanao (1876–1934) and Obata Yūkichi (1873–1947). Later, Matsudaira Tsuneo (1877–1949) and Debuchi Katsuji would pass the eleventh exam, Saburi Sadao and Satō Naotake (1882–1971) would pass the fourteenth exam, and Hirota Kōki and Yoshida Shigeru would pass the fifteenth exam. Arita Hachirō (1884–1965) and Shigemitsu Mamoru would pass the eighteenth and twentieth exams, respectively.

Thus, Shidehara graduated from the Imperial University of Tokyo in 1895—the twenty-eighth year of Meiji. His alumni association, the Nihachi-kai (literally the '2–8 Club'), borrowed the reign date of that year for their name. Members of the association included Izawa Takio, the political scientist Onozuka Kiheiji (1871–1944), future governor-general of Taiwan Kamiyama Mitsunoshin (1869–1938), bureaucrat and politician Shimooka Chūji (1870–1925), campaigner and social statistician Takano Iwasaburō (1871–1949), Tanaka Seijirō (1872–1954), future prime minister Hamaguchi Osachi and Shidehara himself.

17

Shidehara also took on the role of organising the association. These kinds of personal connections would become significant for Shidehara before long.[10]

It is said that Shidehara was devoted to his family and always made sure to attend the Buddhist memorial services held at Gantokuji temple in his hometown, even during his extremely busy years in the diplomatic service. How did such an individual start out as a diplomat? The following chapter outlines the first stages of Shidehara's career as a newly minted member of the diplomatic service, just before his initial appointment to the office of foreign minister.

Endnotes

1   The following discussion is based on the contents of a previously published essay. See Hattori Ryūji, 'Shidehara Kijūrō to 20 Seiki no Nihon' [Shidehara Kijūrō and 20th-century Japan], *Shosai no Mado*, no. 517 (September 2002): 19–23. See also Shidehara Peace Foundation, ed., *Shidehara Kijūrō* (Tokyo: Shidehara Peace Foundation, 1955), 7–21. I have compiled information on previous research on Shidehara and the status of historical materials in Hattori Ryūji, 'Shidehara Kijūrō', in *Kingendai Nihon Jinbutsu Shiryō Jōhō Jiten* [A reference book for historical material and information on modern-era Japanese figures], ed. Itō Takashi and Suetake Yoshiya (Tokyo: Yoshikawa Kōbunkan, 2004), 205–07.

2   'Shidehara Taira-shi no Ohanashi kara' [A word from Mr Shidehara Taira], date unknown, in 'Shidehara Heiwa Bunko' [Shidehara Peace Library], Reel 13, Modern Japanese Political History Materials Room, National Diet Library.

3   For further details, see 'Shidehara-ke Bunsho' [Documents relating to the Shidehara household], Kadoma Municipal History Museum. Important Shidehara family documents are collected in Kadoma City, ed., *Kadoma-shi-shi, Dai 3 Kan: Kinsei Shiryō Hen* [A history of Kadoma City, vol. 3: Early modern historical documents] (Kadoma: Kadoma City, 1997). Several texts on local government history have used this work as a primary historical source, including Kadoma Town History Editing Committee, ed., *Kadoma-cho Shi* [A history of the town of Kadoma] (Kadoma: Kadoma Town Office, 1962); Kadoma City, ed., *Kadoma-shi-shi, Dai 4 Kan: Kinsei Honbun Hen* [A history of Kadoma City, vol. 4: Overview of the early modern era] (Kadoma: Kadoma City, 2000). According to Kadoma City, *Kadoma-shi-shi, Dai 4 Kan*, in the Hōreki era, the Shidehara family rapidly increased their holdings and shifted from manual management to landowner management. The documents on inheritance and marriage proposals are contained in Kadoma City, *Kadoma-shi-shi, Dai 3 Kan*, and are also fascinating from a sociohistorical perspective.

4   Shidehara Taira, 'Tsushima Mondai' [The Tsushima problem], *Chōsen Gakuhō*, no. 1 (May 1951): 1. Taira also discusses the Tsushima problem from the perspective of Japanese–Korean relations in Shidehara Taira, *Chōsen Shiwa* [A discussion of Korean history] (Tokyo: Fuzanbō, 1924), 159–215.

5   Of course, all this must have been unexpected for Taira. In middle school, Tanzan was far from a model student. He had to repeat one year twice, so it took him seven years to finish middle school. Taira would have been quite surprised to be praised by, and even receive an offer of publication from, a student such as Tanzan. Human relationships are full of strange twists. In any case, *Daitōa no Seiiku* [The development of Greater East Asia] was published in 1941, three days before the attack on Pearl Harbor. Taira died in 1953 and did not live to see the formation of the Ishibashi cabinet three-and-a-half years later.

Alongside the aforementioned books, Shidehara Taira's numerous works include *Joshi Kyōiku* [Women's education] (Tokyo: Shūeidō, 1898); *Nantō Enkaku-shi Ron* [Discourse on the history of the southern islands] (Tokyo: Fuzanbō, 1899); *Kyōiku Manpitsu, Zen* [Some thoughts on education, complete ed.] (Tokyo: Kinkōdō Shoseki, 1902); *Nichi-Ro-Kan no Kankoku* [Korea between Japan and Russia] (Tokyo: Hakubunkan, 1905); *Kankoku Seisō-shi* [A chronicle of Korean political troubles] (Tokyo: Sanseidō, 1907); *Gakkō Ron* [A discourse on school] (Tokyo: Dōbunkan, 1909); 'Kantō Kokkyō Mondai' [The problem of the Kantō national border], in *Tōyōkyō-kai Chōsa-bu Gakujutsu Hōkoku* [The Oriental Association Investigation Department scholarly report], ed. Tōyōkyō-kai, vol. 1 (Tōyōkyō-kai, 1909), 207–36; 'Java oyobi "Borneo" Shisatsu Hōkoku' [Observation report on Java and 'Borneo'], *Imin Chōsa Hōkoku*, no. 6, (March 1911): 387–400; *Sekai Shōkan* [Small view of the world] (Tokyo: Hōbunkan, 1912); *Nikkan-Kankei yorino Taishū Kenkyū* [A study of Tsushima, drawing on the Japan–Korea relationship] (Hiroshima: Hiroshima Higher Normal School Geography and History Association, 1913); *Manshūkan* [My view on Manchuria] (Tokyo: Hōbunkan, 1916); 'Wakou nitsuite' [On the Japanese pirates of the middle ages], in *Zoku Shiteki Kenkyū* [Historical research, continued], ed. Society of Historical Research (Tokyo: Fuzanbō, 1916), 1–21; *Shōseinen no Hanzai Bōatsu Seisaku nitsuite* [On policy to prevent youth crime] (Tokyo: Ministry of Home Affairs Bureau for Regions, 1917); *Chōsen Kyōikuron* [Discourse on education in Korea] (Tokyo: Rokumeikan, 1919); *Sekai no Hensen wo Miru* [Examining global changes] (Tokyo: Fuzanbō, 1926); 'Taiwan niokeru Kin, Iō oyobi Sekitan no Tanken' [The search for gold, sulphur and coal in Taiwan], in *Ichimura Hakase Koki Kinen Tōyōshi Ronsō* [Dr Shimura's 70th birthday commemorative essay collection on Eastern history], ed. Publication Society for an Eastern History Essay Collection Commemorating Dr Ichimura's 70th Birthday (Tokyo: Fuzanbō, 1933), 395–434; 'Kokushi yori Mitaru 300 Nen Kinen' [Three-hundred-year commemoration as seen from the perspective of national history], in *Taiwan Bunka-shi Setsu* [A theory of Taiwanese cultural history], ed. Tainan Prefecture Mutual Prosperity Association (Tokyo: Tainan Support Association, 1935), 1–32; *Napō Bunka no Kensetsu e* [Toward the construction of a southern culture] (Tokyo: Fuzanbō, 1938); *Kyōiku Kentō: Dai 1, Kyōiku Gyōsei no Tokushitsu* [Investigations in education: 1, the special characteristics of education administration] (Tokyo: Shinkōsha, 1938); 'Honpōjin to Taiwan' [The Japanese and Taiwan], in *Andō Kyōju Kanreki Shukuga Kinen Ronbunshū* [Prof. Andō's 60th birthday commemorative essay collection], ed. Prof. Andō's 60th Birthday Commemorative Association (Tokyo: Sanseidō, 1940), 571–84; *Kōa no Shūyō* [The cultivation of Asian development] (Tokyo: Meisedō Shoten, 1941); 'Nanpō Kensetsu no Bunka Taisaku' [Cultural measures for southern construction], in *Nanpō Shin-Kensetsu Kōza* [Course for new construction in the southern region], ed. Southern Region Research Association (Tokyo: Osakayagō Shoten, 1943), 55–78; 'Oki no Awa' [The foam offshore], in *Okinawa Bunka Sōsetsu* [Theories on Okinawan culture], ed. Yanagita Kunio (Tokyo: Chuōkōronsha, 1947), 5–22; *Kyokutō Bunka no Kōryū* [Cultural exchange in the Far East] (Tokyo: Sekishoin, 1949); *Bunka no Kensetsu* [The construction of culture] (Tokyo: Yoshikawa Kōbunkan, 1953); Shidehara Taira, *Kokushi-jō Nanyō Hatten no Ichimen* [An aspect of the development of the South Sea in national history], ed. Konishi Tatehiko (Tokyo: Nanyō Keizai Kenkyūjo, 1941).

Of these, *Nichi-Ro-Kan no Kankoku* was reproduced in Literature on Korean Studies Research Institute, ed., *Kyūkanmatsu Nittei Shinryakyu Shiryō Sōsho IV: Seiji-hen 5* [Collected historical documents on the end of old Korea and the invasion of the Japanese empire IV: Politics volume 5] (Seoul: Aseamunkasya, 1984), 1–221. *Chōsen Kyōikuron* was also reprinted in Watanabe Manabu and Abe Hiroshi, eds, *Nihon Shokuminchi Kyōiku Seisaku Shiryo Shusei (Chōsen-hen)* [Compilation of historical documents concerning Japanese colonial education policy (Korean section)], vol. 25 (Tokyo: Ryūkei Shosha, 1989). *Gakkō Ron* was reprinted in Ishikawa Matsutarō, ed., *Kindai Nihon Gakkō Kyōiku-ron Kōza, 5: Gakkō-ron* [A course on modern Japanese school education discourse, 5: Discourse on school] (Tokyo: Kress Shuppan, 2001). A chronological list and bibliographic catalogue are presented at the end of *Bunka no Kensetsu*. Shidehara Taira was also the editor of *Naigai Jitsuyō Chizu, Nihon no Bu* [Domestic and foreign practical maps, Japanese section] (Tokyo: Kyōeiki Shōsha Shoten, 1897); *Naigai Jitsuyō Chizu, Sekai no Bu* [Domestic and foreign practical maps, world section] (Tokyo: Kyōeiki Shōsha Shoten, 1897).

See also Ishibashi Tanzan Complete Works Compilation Committee, ed., *Ishibashi Tanzan Zenshū* [The complete works of Tanzan Ishibashi], vol. 15 (Tokyo: Tōyō Keizai Shinpōsha, 1972), 12–14.

6   *Osaka Asahi Shimbun*, evening edition, 30 October 1915.

7   Izawa Takio Biography Compilation Committee, ed., *Izawa Takio* [Takio Izawa] (Tokyo: Haneda Shoten, 1951), 37–38.

8   *Osaka Asahi Shimbun*, evening edition, 30 October 1915.

9   Shidehara Kijūrō, *Gaikō 50 Nen* [Fifty years of diplomacy] (Tokyo: Chūōkōronsha, 1987), 225–27.

10 'Ni Hachi Dōsōkai Kiji' [2–8 club articles], in 'Shidehara Heiwa Bunko', Reel 7. Dr Asano Toyomi has kindly provided his assistance in this area. With respect to the *Ni Hachi-Kai*, details can be found in Suetake Yoshiya, *Taishō-ki no Seiji Kōzō* [The political structure of the Taishō era] (Tokyo: Yoshikawa Kōbunkan, 1998), 148–50. For further information, see Izawa Takio Biography Compilation Committee, *Izawa Takio*, 49; Izawa Takio Document Research Association, ed., *Izawa Takio Kankei Bunsho* [Documents relating to Izawa Takio] (Tokyo: Fuyō Shobō Shuppan, 2000), 478.

2
The Russo-Japanese War, World War I and the Washington Naval Conference

Towards the Commencement of the Russo-Japanese War

First Steps in the Diplomatic Service

After passing the diplomatic service exam, in September 1896, Shidehara was posted to the Japanese consulate in Incheon, Korea, where he served as a consular assistant.[1] Later, when the Russo-Japanese War erupted in February 1904, Shidehara was at the Busan consulate and even played a diplomatic role in the events that unfolded. After returning to Japan from Busan, he was appointed to roles such as the director of the Telegraph Division. Later, during and just after World War I, he assumed positions such as vice-minister for foreign affairs and ambassador to the US. His most important work at this time was his participation in the Washington Naval Conference as the plenipotentiary and ambassador to the US, which began in 1921 and stretched into the following year. During this period, therefore, Shidehara reached a position where the policies he enacted could potentially influence the direction of Japan's diplomatic efforts. This was also a time where he acquired the etiquette expected of a diplomat and developed his own principles.

There are four topics that I wish to focus on while giving an overview of this quarter century. The first regards the formation of Shidehara's own thinking. What is particularly important here is his understanding of an 'open door policy'. It is said that, in general, Shidehara proactively adopted an American-style open door policy. Certainly, Shidehara did accept an open door approach as a guiding principle. On the other hand, it should be recalled that, at this time, Japan had 'special interests' in Manchuria in north-eastern China. These special interests in China would have been on Shidehara's mind. We should ask, therefore, how these different considerations or orientations came together in Shidehara's diplomatic outlook. Further, what did having an economic 'open door' really mean to Shidehara? To begin with, it should be noted that the term 'open door' itself is ambiguous. For the original 'open door notes' issued by the US, there were actually two meanings. It is necessary, therefore, to clarify the specific nuance that this term held for Shidehara.

To state the conclusion to this line of questioning in advance, while Shidehara was enthusiastic about adopting an 'open door' approach as a general principle, he also attempted to restrict its practical application. He utilised this concept in a restricted sense and thereby was able to find a compromise regarding Japan's 'special interests' in China. In this chapter, I will explain this accommodation in Shidehara's thinking through analysis of his response to matters such as the New Four-Power Consortium and the Washington Naval Conference. As I shall show, Shidehara's commitment to the principle of 'open door' economics did not simply mean an adoption of US policy. Rather, he was initially receptive to these ideas in the context of agreements such as the Anglo-Japanese Alliance (1902–23) and the Franco-Japanese Treaty (1907).

Meanwhile, Shidehara saw Japan's annexation of Korea in 1910 as a natural development. This might appear to run counter to the perception that he was internationally minded. One anecdote about Shidehara holds that he used to sit with a copy of *Webster's Dictionary* at hand and memorise Shakespeare. Such accounts might tempt us to think of Shidehara as cut from a different cloth than other Japanese diplomats. However, it should be remembered that this was only one side of the man. Shidehara fully identified with the mindset the Japanese people had at that time. Like them, he worshipped the imperial household, and he was a great admirer of Count Nogi Maresuke (1849–1912), the Imperial Japanese Army general who participated in the capture of Port Arthur from China in 1894.

2. THE RUSSO-JAPANESE WAR, WORLD WAR I AND THE WASHINGTON NAVAL CONFERENCE

Following the above consideration of the formation of Shidehara's own thinking, the second topic I wish to examine with respect to this 25-year period is Shidehara's diplomatic style. Here, the impact of Henry Willard Denison—adviser to the Foreign Ministry when Shidehara was director of the Telegraph Division—was considerable.[2] Up until his time at the Busan consulate, Shidehara showed no discomfort with the use of diplomacy backed up by the threat of military force. Indeed, he went as far as to support the launching of the Russo-Japanese War. However, his encounter with Denison would become a turning point. From then on, Shidehara would become a member of the committee for revising Japan's unequal treaties with Western powers and would also become highly familiar with matters of international law. However, even while Denison initiated him in the subtler arts of diplomacy, Shidehara was no passive recipient. A clearer view of Shidehara's approach is available by looking at how he handled the abrogation of the Anglo-Japanese Alliance at the Washington Naval Conference.

It is also important to situate the handling of public relations with respect to the topic of Shidehara's diplomatic style.[3] Shidehara has been understood as having been largely indifferent to matters of public relations. His intense dislike of Japan's mass media emanates from the pages of his memoir, *Gaikō 50 Nen* (Fifty years of diplomacy). In reality, however, Shidehara also had his own form of public relations diplomacy. Here, too, the Washington Naval Conference provides an excellent opportunity for analysis.

The third topic that I will focus on for this period is Shidehara's personal relationships. As is well known, Shidehara and Katō Takaaki were brothers-in-law. Shidehara also had close relationships with individuals such as Komura Jutarō, Chinda Sutemi (1857–1929), Ishii Kikujirō (1866–1945) and Hara Takashi. Shidehara's personal connection with Komura is the most deserving of close attention. At first glance, it may seem as though Komura and Shidehara were polar opposites, given Komura's fierce promotion of continental policy aimed at Japan's domination of North-East Asia. However, Shidehara supported Komura in areas such as the revision of the unequal treaties and the annexation of Korea. This point will no doubt be instructive when comparing the Russo-Japanese War and the diplomacy of the 1920s.

What was actually problematic for Shidehara was when his brother-in-law Katō, then foreign minister, drafted the Twenty-One Demands issued to China in 1915. I will also consider Shidehara's relations with diplomats such as Moroi Rokurō (1872–1940), Kawashima Nobutarō (1880–1957), Saburi Sadao, Honda Kumatarō, Hirota Kōki, Debuchi Katsuji, Tani Masayuki (1889–1962) and Ishii Itarō (1887–1954).

The final topic concerning this quarter century is how the various nations of the time viewed Shidehara's statements and actions. Naturally, diplomatic negotiations are important for our purposes here. However, the role of the diplomat is not restricted to negotiations alone. The acquaintances and relationships of trust a person has formed also reveal much about them. Because Shidehara's time as ambassador to the US marked the point at which his position rapidly strengthened, my examination of this topic will focus mainly on this period. In particular, though, Shidehara formed a number of relationships during his time as the plenipotentiary and ambassador to the US, around the time of the Washington Naval Conference. These include Shidehara's relationships with figures such as Secretary of State Charles Evans Hughes (1862–1948), Plenipotentiary Elihu Root and John Van Antwerp MacMurray (1881–1960), the chief of the State Department's Division of Far Eastern Affairs. I have explored these relations in a previous work.[4]

For this reason, I also wish to touch on some other more practical and specialised individuals with whom Shidehara interacted. These include Stanley Washburn, Root's secretary at the Washington Naval Conference; Roland S. Morris (1874–1920), the US ambassador to Japan; Norman H. Davis (1878–1944), undersecretary of state; DeWitt Clinton Poole, chief of the State Department's Division of Russian Affairs; Nelson Trusler Johnson, official at the State Department's Division of Far Eastern Affairs; Eugene H. Dooman (1890–1969), first secretary at the US embassy in Japan; and Edward Thomas Williams (1854–1944), chief of the State Department's Division of Far Eastern Affairs during World War I.

The International Situation Following the First Sino-Japanese War

In September 1896, Shidehara passed the fourth diplomatic service exam. Alongside Shidehara, the four individuals who passed included Koike Chōzō, who would later participate in the issuing of the Twenty-One Demands during his time as director-general of the Political Affairs

2. THE RUSSO-JAPANESE WAR, WORLD WAR I AND THE WASHINGTON NAVAL CONFERENCE

Bureau. The following month, Shidehara was appointed consular assistant at Incheon, Korea. This was the first step of his initial diplomatic career, which would take him to locations such as London, Antwerp and Busan.

What was the international situation at that time? When Shidehara began his diplomatic career at the end of the nineteenth century, the reverberations of the 'Triple Intervention' still lingered. In 1895, when the Sino-Japanese peace treaty was signed at Shimonoseki, the three nations of Russia, France and Germany intervened. Although Japan was the supposed victor of the war, it was forced to return the Liaodong Peninsula to China. Naturally, the locus of East Asian international politics at this time was Korea. Following the conclusion of the First Sino-Japanese War, a series of influential figures served as Japan's ministers in Korea, including Inoue Kaoru, Komura Jutarō, Hara Takashi and Hayashi Gonsuke (1860–1939). While Incheon and Busan were not on the same level as Korea's capital Hanseong—then known in Japanese as 'Keijō' and today known as Seoul—they were nevertheless considered important. According to Hayashi Gonsuke, who served as consul at Incheon before the First Sino-Japanese War, 'even though it was the Incheon consulate, at the time it was akin to the consulate for the whole of Korea'.[5] It was surely no coincidence that Shidehara was sent to Incheon, given that he was expected to have a promising career.

When Shidehara arrived at his post in Incheon in January 1897, he earned the favour of the consul, Ishii Kikujirō. When Ishii finally transferred to Beijing, Shidehara assumed the role of the acting consul until the arrival of the new consul, Ijūin Hikokichi (1864–1924). Shidehara reflected that while Ijūin 'was not particularly skillful', he nevertheless 'possessed a certain kind of special magnetism that drew me to him'.[6] While it may sound surprising, from his time in Incheon onwards, Shidehara was a heavy drinker. The branch chief of a local mercantile company with whom he was on good terms would often appear with high-quality Nada-brand spirits, whereupon Shidehara would close the door of his official residence, and together they would drink the night away.[7]

At that time, Japan was seeking to preserve its policy of *Hokushu-Nanshin*, literally 'defend the north and advance to the south'. At the same time, it was attempting to establish a position in Korea that would put it on an equal footing with Russia. In May 1896, a memorandum between Japan and Russia was signed in Hanseong by Komura and Karl Ivanovich Weber (1841–1910). In June of the same year, the Yamagata–Lobanov

Agreement was signed in Moscow. The Komura–Weber Memorandum sought the return of the king of Korea, who had sought refuge in the Russian legation. The Yamagata–Lobanov Agreement stipulated that Japan and Russia would jointly provide assistance for Korea's public budget. The Komura–Weber Memorandum and the Yamagata–Lobanov Agreement were still of importance in 1901, when Shidehara returned to Korea to serve as consul in Busan. This was because they included a provision for the management of the telegraph lines between Hanseong and Busan that was advantageous to Japan. Further, the Nishi–Rosen Agreement, signed in Tokyo in 1898, recognised Korea's independence and declared that the respective parties would refrain from interfering in the internal politics of the country. Even Shidehara's memoirs feature an idyllic account of the Incheon of this period, with the warship captains of both nations sharing drinks.[8]

In May 1899, Shidehara was assigned to London. When he arrived at his post in August, he began to polish his English. The effort he put into this study would become an important asset in his future career. In December 1900, he was transferred once more, this time to the position of consul in Antwerp. Located in the north of Belgium, Antwerp was one of Europe's most important trading ports. However, not long afterward, in September 1901, Shidehara was ordered to return to Korea. This time, he assumed the office of consul in Busan. He remained in Busan until March 1904 and the beginning of the Russo-Japanese War. These events comprised Shidehara's formative experience as a diplomat.

During this period, Russia's foreign minister, Aleksei Borisovich Lobanov-Rostovskii, and its finance minister, Sergei Yulievich Witte, were making progress with their policies for containing Japan. In 1896, they signed a secret military alliance with the Chinese politician and general Li Hongzhang. On the basis of this pact between Russia and the Qing dynasty, work on the Chinese Eastern Railway began in 1898. The Chinese Eastern Railway would cross the length of Manchuria when completed. Another major incident at this time was the outbreak of the Yihetuan Movement (Boxer Rebellion) in China. The rebellion was suppressed in 1900 by a coalition army of eight nations, including Japan. In the following year, the European Great Powers, Komura Jutarō, and Li Hongzhang signed the Boxer Protocol. This agreement gave Japan reparations and the right to station troops in China. Regarding Komura Jutarō's performance at the Yihetuan Movement peace conference, Shidehara wrote: 'Komura-san's farsightedness was on display'.[9]

Komura Jutarō and Hayashi Tadasu

At that time, Komura Jutarō was the driving force in Japanese diplomacy. Komura successively filled the roles of ambassador to Korea, vice-minister for foreign affairs, ambassador to the US, ambassador to Russia and minister to China. In 1901, he became the foreign minister in the first Katsura Tarō cabinet.

The common view is that Japan at this time had two basic orientations or policies.[10] First, Katō Takaaki and Komura Jutarō promoted *Man-Kan Fukabun*, the position that Japan's interests in Manchuria and Korea could not be dealt with separately but were intertwined. Second, Itō Hirobumi, Inoue Kaoru and a number of other figures promoted *Man-Kan Kōkan*, the position that influence in Manchuria could be ceded to Russia in exchange for Japan having control over Korea. The first of these two positions favoured the obstruction of Russia's southward advance by strengthening Japan's relationship with the UK. The second promoted the formation of an entente between Japan and Russia. The first prevailed within Japan's diplomatic circles, and, as a result, negotiations towards an Anglo-Japanese alliance soon began.

The initial alliance was signed in January 1902. According to the first article of the Anglo-Japanese Alliance, both nations recognised each other's special interests in Qing-dynasty China, while the UK also recognised Japan's special interests in Korea. The second article stated that if either nation were to go to war, the other would maintain neutrality. The third article stated that if a third nation joined that conflict against the allied partner, the other partner would assist the ally. This was the birth of the defensive alliance.

It was Hayashi Tadasu who would directly experience from his postings the sequence of events that led from the Triple Intervention to the signing of the Anglo-Japanese Alliance. Hayashi's formative experience as a diplomat was the Triple Intervention of 1895. It was Hayashi who, as vice-minister for foreign affairs, received the Triple Intervention memorandum from the ministers of Russia, Germany and France.[11] On that occasion, Foreign Minister Mutsu Munemitsu had come down with tuberculosis and was receiving treatment in the town of Maiko, Hyogo Prefecture.[12] Under the command of Foreign Minister Mutsu, Vice-Minister Hayashi, the director-general of the Political Affairs Bureau, Katō Takaaki, and the director-general of the International Trade Bureau, Hara Takashi, were jointly referred to as the 'Mutsu Triumvirate'. Originally the governor of Hyogo Prefecture, Hayashi was summoned to the Ministry of Foreign Affairs by the previous foreign minister, Enomoto Takeaki (1836–1908), before he was promoted further by Mutsu.

Hayashi, shocked by the Triple Intervention, went himself as the minister to China to sign the Liaodong Peninsula Return Agreement and conclude the negotiations for the Sino-Japanese Treaty of Commerce and Navigation. This treaty, signed in July 1896, was a typically unequal treaty. Hayashi also attended the First International Peace Conference at The Hague as minister to Russia. Hayashi would go on to become Japan's minister to the UK, negotiating with Foreign Secretary Henry Petty-Fitzmaurice, Lord Lansdowne, and signing the Anglo-Japanese Alliance. Of course, Hayashi was also critical of Itō Hirobumi's promotion of a Russo-Japanese entente. Later, in 1905, the Second Anglo-Japanese Alliance would also be signed by Hayashi and Petty-Fitzmaurice.[13]

Naturally, Shidehara was also critical of the Triple Intervention. As he put it, 'the Triple Intervention amounts to a diplomatic conspiracy', with the secret treaty signed between China and Russia 'exposed during the course of the Washington Naval Conference of 1922'.[14] In Shidehara's view, it was necessary for Japan to 'endure the bitterness of the Triple Intervention, enduring hardship so that it might slowly develop its national power, and then within a decade push Russia out of south Manchuria'.[15] He added that, 'in the end, trickery will not determine the fate of the nation's next hundred years'.[16]

Towards the Beginning of the Russo-Japanese War

Shidehara left for his new position as consul in Busan in October 1901. Busan and Japan have a historically significant connection. In the Edo period, Busan contained a Japanese trading settlement called Waegwan (Wakan in Japanese), which covered some 330 square kilometres. Waegwan's internal affairs were originally managed by the head of the Tsushima domain and functioned as a gateway to Korea, which at that time was ruled—like Japan—according to a policy of national isolation.[17] With the opening of ports following the Japan–Korea Treaty of 1876, Busan would come to play an increasingly important role in events between the two countries. It was not only foreign settlements and boards of trade that shaped it. Busan was also of strategic importance for transport.

2. THE RUSSO-JAPANESE WAR, WORLD WAR I AND THE WASHINGTON NAVAL CONFERENCE

The year that Shidehara assumed this new posting saw the establishment of the Keifu Railway Company, with Shibusawa Eiichi (1840–1931) as the chairman. The Keifu Railway Company linked Hanseong and Busan together (the characters for 'Keifu' [京釜] mean 'Capital' and 'Busan') and opened at the height of the Russo-Japanese War. Meanwhile, the shipping company Nippon Yūsen had already expanded its sea routes to Busan and Incheon before the First Sino-Japanese War, concentrating its efforts on Korea. Nippon Yūsen had also acquired the coastal right of passage through Korean waters from the Korean government at the time of the First Sino-Japanese War.[18] Following the end of the Russo-Japanese War, another shipping company, Sanyō Kisen, commenced services from Shimonoseki to Busan. Once the Shimonoseki-Busan line was connected to the Sanyō railway line and the Keifu railway line, it became possible to travel from Tokyo to Hanseong within 60 hours.[19] Before long, the railway network of the Korean Peninsula was joined to the South Manchuria Railway, creating a main artery for operations on the continent. Alongside this development, Busan would develop into a major city, second in Korea only to Hanseong.

As it happened, as consul in Busan, Shidehara had an offer of marriage. His future wife, Masako, was the youngest of the four daughters of Iwasaki Yatarō (1835–1885). Iwasaki Yatarō was the founder of the Mitsubishi financial conglomerate (*zaibatsu*). In fact, Masako and Shidehara's relationship had already begun when Shidehara was stationed in London. They were married in Tokyo in January 1903. Their matchmaker (*nakōdo*) was Ishii Kikujirō, Shidehara's good acquaintance from his time in Incheon. Through his marriage with Masako, Shidehara become brother-in-law to Katō Takaaki. This was because Mrs Katō, Harumi, was the eldest daughter of Iwasaki Yatarō.[20]

Katō Takaaki would serve as Japan's foreign minister on several occasions: first in the fourth Itō cabinet and later in the first Saionji cabinet and the third Katsura cabinet. Each appointment, however, would last only a short time. It was his later service as foreign minister in the second Ōkuma cabinet that would put his name in the history books. In particular, the Twenty-One Demands he issued to China in 1915 are notorious. Eventually, Katō would come to lead the Kenseikai party, forming a government as prime minister in 1924. The foreign minister in this cabinet would be none other than Shidehara.[21] In any case, after the wedding, Shidehara returned to his post at Busan. In the fall of 1903, his first son, Michitarō, was born. Yet Shidehara had no time to enjoy the life of a newlywed because the Russian situation was becoming more and more serious. Japan and Russia exchanged alternative propositions regarding Manchuria's territorial integrity and the neutral zone in Korea. As negotiations bogged down, Japan began preparing for war. It would finally come in February 1904.

Hostilities began when the Japanese navy fired upon a Russian fleet outside of the port of Lushun. At the same time, the Japanese army also began to mobilise, advancing northwards through the Korean Peninsula, defeating the Russian army in a battle at Liaoyang and capturing Lushun. In March 1905, the Japanese army secured a victory at the battle of Mukden (present-day Shenyang) and the navy won a sea battle in May. In September that year, a peace treaty was signed near Portsmouth, New Hampshire, mediated by the US. Shidehara was no mere spectator during the Russo-Japanese War; he had his own role to play.

It was 6 February 1904. Leaving for work early in the morning as usual, Shidehara saw an unusual sight as he surveyed the port of Busan from the consulate. A Japanese warship had captured a Russian steamship, the *Mukden*, belonging to the Chinese Eastern Railway Company. This incident would draw a note of protest from the Russian consulate. According to international law, capturing an enemy nation's vessel was illegal if it was encountered in the territorial waters of a neutral country. Shidehara, however, rejected Russia's protest, commenting: 'Given the current discontinuation of diplomatic relations between Japan and Russia, I am in no position to enter into negotiations with the Russian consulate, regardless of the circumstances'.[22] Admittedly, this was quite an obstinate position for Shidehara to take. Certainly, war loomed in the atmosphere. The Katsura cabinet had cut off diplomatic relations on 4 February. However, it was not until two days after the capture of the steamship, on 8 February, that the Japanese navy would fire upon the Russian fleet at Lushun. The day after that, on 9 February, two Russian warships were sunk in a naval battle off the coast of Incheon. War was formally declared on 10 February.[23]

In fact, before the war began, Shidehara had received Foreign Minister Komura's permission to support the Japanese navy's occupation of the telegraph offices at Busan and Masan. As a result, the Russian consulate in Busan was unable to receive coded telegrams from its minister and was driven into a corner. Hayashi Gonsuke, Japan's minister to Korea based in Hanseong, also cooperated with Shidehara in closing down Russia's telegraph-based communication.[24] On 23 February, Hayashi signed the Japan–Korea Protocol, permitting the free movement of Japanese troops within Korea's borders. This paved the way for the annexation of Korea through the three Japan–Korea agreements.

Diplomacy in the Aftermath of the Russo-Japanese War

Shidehara's Encounter with Denison

Shidehara was ordered to return to Japan in March 1904, following the commencement of the Russo-Japanese War. His next appointment would be to oversee the Telegraph Division. The Telegraph Division was in charge of the drafting and decoding of encrypted telegrams, as well as the sending and receiving of various other telegram messages. The then director of the Telegraph Division, Ishii Kikujirō, was also put in charge of the International Trade Bureau, leaving Shidehara as the de facto Telegraph Division director.

In November 1905 Shidehara was officially promoted to director. He would continue in this role for some time, even after becoming the director of the Investigation Division and the director-general of the Investigation Bureau. The Investigation Division was established to examine domestic and foreign laws, as well as international law. Shidehara would continue to hold these two offices concurrently until his assignment in 1912 as a counsellor to Japan's embassy in the US.[25]

At that time, the individual who would train Shidehara in the writing of diplomatic telegrams was Henry Willard Denison, then adviser to Japan's Foreign Ministry. Denison had originally stayed in Japan as the assistant to the US consul general, who was based in Yokohama. He was then hired as an adviser to Japan's Foreign Ministry on the recommendation of US minister John A. Bingham. Denison would remain employed in Tokyo as an adviser for the Foreign Ministry from 1880 until his death from illness in 1914. It was rumoured that Denison had memorised all of Japan's diplomatic precedents since the period of the Meiji Restoration.[26] Shidehara's official residence was very close to Denison's lodgings. Almost every morning, Shidehara would take 30–40-minute walks with

Denison around the area of the Imperial Palace, learning much from their conversations. Denison was also an astute judge of politicians. When the Katsura cabinet was formed in 1901, Denison was inwardly pleased.[27]

Shidehara was particularly impressed by Denison's anecdotes about little-known episodes of diplomacy concerning the start of the Russo-Japanese War. According to Denison, in July 1903 Foreign Minister Komura ordered Denison to draft telegraphic instructions to be addressed to the Japanese minister in St Petersburg Kurino Shinichirō (1851–1937), which requested negotiations with Russia. For Komura, 'Russia's aggressive actions in the Manchurian and Korean regions had recently reached the stage where they could no longer be overlooked'. When Denison suggested to Komura that the instructions include the statement that 'we must recognize the importance of avoiding war at all costs', Komura replied: 'I have been told that whether it ends in war shall be determined by the results of the negotiation'. As Denison told Shidehara, 'I could tell that the [Japanese] government was determined … and so I was able to get right to work drafting the instructions'.[28]

Shidehara was not satisfied with this account. He asked Denison whether the instructions should not differ depending on whether the government was determined to go to war. Denison replied that if the policy was to avoid war then threatening the other party could still be a valid strategy. If, however, one was determined to go to war, then it was better to use as temperate language as possible, so that after hostilities commenced, the diplomatic papers could be made public in order to gain international sympathy. According to Shidehara, actions such as making diplomatic papers public after hostilities commenced was 'now something that practically all the great powers have done in order to gain support for their positions'.[29] It was also Denison who would teach Shidehara the various formats for writing such diplomatic papers as notes, verbal notes and memoranda.[30]

The Treaty of Portsmouth—the Ceding of South Sakhalin and the Korean Provision

The main theatre of the Russo-Japanese War was Manchuria, with Lushun and Mukden the scenes of hard-fought battles. There were no significant engagements in Korea. Around the time Shidehara returned to Japan from Busan, the Japanese navy was struggling to close off the entrance to Lushun harbor. Even after the Japanese army landed on the Liaodong

2. THE RUSSO-JAPANESE WAR, WORLD WAR I AND THE WASHINGTON NAVAL CONFERENCE

Peninsula, it was not until January 1905 that they managed to defeat the Russian forces holding Lushun fort. Third Army Commander Nogi Maresuke directed the assault on Lushun. The Japanese army would also go on to occupy Mukden in March. However, its forces in the area were exhausted, preventing it from decisively defeating the Russian army. While the navy later secured a victory in the Sea of Japan in May, Japan nevertheless felt compelled to seek an early peace. It was then that US President Theodore Roosevelt stepped forward as a peace mediator. This was when Foreign Minister Komura travelled to the US.

Following peace negotiations with Russia, Japanese Foreign Minister Komura and Minister to the US Takahira Kogorō (1854–1926) signed a peace treaty to conclude the Russo-Japanese War. The treaty was signed on 5 September 1905, near Portsmouth, New Hampshire. On the Russian side, the representative empowered to sign the treaty was former finance minister Witte and then Ambassador to the US Roman Romanovich von Rozen (1847–1921). The instruments of ratification were exchanged on 25 November. The Treaty of Portsmouth included a number of important articles for Japan, including the recognition of Japan's hegemony over Korea (Article 2); the devolution of the leaseholds of the Chinese ports of Lushun and Dalian to Japan (Article 5); the transfer to Japan of the rights to the South Manchuria Railway (Article 6); and the ceding to Japan of the southern part of Sakhalin Island, below the 50th parallel north (Article 9). Further, according to the first of the additional conditions, Japan and Russia would recognise their respective rights in Manchuria to station 15 soldiers per kilometre of railway as guards. This led to Japan stationing two divisions of troops under the command of the governor-general of the territory of Kwantung. This would eventually become the Kwantung Army. However, Japan was not able to receive reparations from Russia.

With respect to Article 9 and the ceding of the southern part of Sakhalin, Shidehara hints at something. According to his memoirs, the day before the meeting of the Imperial Council in the second half of August, another meeting was held at the official residence of the lord president of the council. A number of government leaders attended, including the lord president of the council himself, Itō Hirobumi; Prime Minister Katsura Tarō; Navy Minister Yamamoto Gonbē (1852–1933); Army Minister Terauchi Masatake (1852–1919); and Vice-Minister for Foreign Affairs Chinda Sutemi (1857–1929). Shidehara served as secretary of the proceedings. According to Shidehara, when Yamamoto argued in favour of the demand that Russia cede part of Sakhalin, Itō directed Shidehara to put together the diplomatic instructions accordingly.

As it happened, when Chinda returned to the Ministry of Foreign Affairs after attending the Imperial Council the following day, he unexpectedly ordered Shidehara to send a telegram instructing the diplomatic staff to remove the request for reparations and the ceding of territory on Sakhalin. Shidehara had no choice but to send the telegram as Chinda instructed. Just afterwards, some good news arrived from the UK. Claude M. MacDonald, the British minister to Japan, informed International Trade Bureau Director-General Ishii that the Russian emperor was open to accepting the cession of southern Sakhalin. Acting on this information, Shidehara 'took personal responsibility' and sent a telegraph requesting that the execution of the previous instructions be delayed.[31] After receiving this message, Komura made excuses in order to ask the Russian side to postpone the meeting. Prime Minister Katsura was then able to visit the Imperial Palace and receive permission to revise the previous instructions so that they would once more request that Japan demand the cession of southern Sakhalin. This was how Shidehara recalled these events.

If Shidehara's memory is correct, it would mean that his quick thinking in postponing the removal of the Sakhalin cession request allowed Japan to gain southern Sakhalin as territory. However, it is rather difficult to imagine Shidehara making such a request of his own accord, given that, at this time, he was only the surrogate director of the Telegraph Division. Rather, what is most important in this story is the role of International Trade Bureau Director-General Ishii. By relaying Russia's thinking as heard from MacDonald, he was able to propose to Prime Minister Katsura that Japan should not abandon its request for Sakhalin territory after all. Following his report to Vice-Minister for Foreign Affairs Chinda, Ishii had Shidehara send the telegram instructing that a demand be made for the ceding of southern Sakhalin.[32] The then director-general of the Political Affairs Bureau, Yamaza Enjirō (1866–1914), who also travelled to the US with Komura, attributed the acquisition of southern Sakhalin to Komura's skill.[33] However, while Yamaza was expected to succeed Komura and become foreign minister one day, this was not to be. In fact, Yamaza passed away suddenly in 1914 while he was Japan's minister to China. This was three years after Komura's death.

2. THE RUSSO-JAPANESE WAR, WORLD WAR I AND THE WASHINGTON NAVAL CONFERENCE

Of course, the Treaty of Portsmouth included more than just the cession of southern Sakhalin. Article 2 included the following clause with respect to Korea:

> The Imperial Russian Government, acknowledging that Japan possesses in Korea paramount political, military and economical interest, engages neither to obstruct nor interfere with measures for guidance, protection and control which the Imperial Government of Japan may find necessary to take in Korea.[34]

What did Shidehara think of this clause on Korea? In his own words, he wrote:

> Because at the time, our government sought to root out the source of trouble in the Far East, and foresaw that this could well necessitate the step of annexing Korea, but knew that it would not be appropriate to state so explicitly in the text of the treaty, it was necessary to use more abstract language and request that Russia recognise Japan's right to give 'guidance, protection, and control' to Korea.[35]

In other words, the section of the clause noting Japan's right to take measures to give necessary 'guidance, protection, and control' can be understood as having been included with an eye towards a future annexation of Korea by Japan.

In fact, it was Denison who had instructed Shidehara in the use of such language. Denison had told Shidehara that:

> It was a normal trend for measures to guide sooner or later becoming measures to protect, and for protection to sooner or later become an incentive for shifting towards control.[36]

In reality, Japan–Korea relations began with the Japan–Korea Protocol of February 1904, followed by three Japan–Korea agreements, and culminated in the conclusion of the Korea Annexation Treaty in August 1910. Watching over this process in the Ministry of Foreign Affairs, Shidehara thought that, 'at the time, his [Denison's] prediction in the case of Korea was coming true step by step'.[37] Shidehara also thought that the section in Article 2 of the Portsmouth Treaty on 'guidance, protection, and control' should be used in Article 3 of the Second Anglo-Japanese Alliance that was signed in August 1905. However, in the editing process, these terms were mistakenly transposed to read: 'guidance, control, and protection'. This error was not discovered until after the treaty was signed, much to Denison's regret.[38]

After signing the Treaty of Portsmouth, Komura suddenly fell ill and had to postpone his return to Japan.[39] When he finally returned in October 1905, Shidehara went to Yokohama to greet him. When the party arrived at Shinbashi Station, Prime Minister Katsura and Navy Minister Yamamoto boarded the train and supported Komura by both arms to help him dismount. The public mood in Japan was volatile. Yet, as Shidehara put it, Katsura and Yamamoto felt that 'if they would die, they would die together with Komura'.[40] What was on Shidehara's mind was the scene when Komura was dispatched to Portsmouth. At that time, crowds had come to cheer Komura as he departed as Japan's plenipotentiary representative. Komura, however, remained composed and whispered to Shidehara:

> The crowd that cheers our party departing today may in the future turn against us and become a cursing, violent mob. At the very least, then, we should cheerfully accept this demonstration of good will while it lasts.[41]

In other words, according to Shidehara, even before journeying to the US, Komura anticipated that the peace treaty would be poorly received by the Japanese public. And indeed, at the end of September 1905, tens of thousands of demonstrators in Tokyo's Hibiya Park protested the perceived shortcomings of the Treaty of Portsmouth, such as the lack of reparations. Moreover, mobs rampaged through Tokyo, attacking and setting fire to locations such as the Kokumin Shimbun Company, the official residence of the home secretary, and numerous police stations. The riots, which lasted two days, led to the deaths of 17 people, with hundreds wounded. This was known as the Hibiya Incendiary Incident. The government responded with a declaration of martial law. At one point, even the Ministry of Foreign Affairs was surrounded by a mob. Shidehara watched the police fighting the rioters from the ministry windows. Shidehara was clearly sympathetic to Komura. This incident may well have been a catalyst for his own understanding of the proper distance to be kept from popular sentiment when it came to diplomacy.[42]

Treaty Revision and Continental Policy—Supporting Komura Diplomacy

While public opinion had turned against Komura, Japanese politics itself entered a period of stability. The leading party in the Diet, the Seiyūkai, supported the Katsura cabinet's peace policy. The Seiyūkai was formed in 1900 by figures such as Itō Hirobumi and Hoshi Tōru (1850–1901) of the Kenseitō party. At the time of the Treaty of Portsmouth, Saionji Kinmochi (1849–1940) was the president of the Seiyūkai. However, the Seiyūkai's support of the peace treaty negotiated at Portsmouth came at a cost. In exchange, they received the promise that the Katsura cabinet would transfer administrative power to the Seiyūkai. Hara Takashi of the Seiyūkai conducted the manoeuvring to help secure this agreement. Hara had multiple meetings with Prime Minister Katsura during the course of the Russo-Japanese War. With the formation of the Saionji cabinet following the transfer of power, Hara himself was appointed minister of home affairs.[43] This development indicated that the Seiyūkai was increasingly being recognised as a political party in the establishment by the older domain-based (Hanbatsu or Meiji oligarchy) cliques of figures such as Yamagata Aritomo.

Political power was subsequently passed from the first Saionji cabinet to the second Katsura cabinet, the second Saionji cabinet, and to the third Katsura cabinet. This state of affairs continued until 1913 and the collapse of the third Katsura cabinet. Today, this era is referred to as the 'Kei-En' (桂園) era. The term 'Kei-En' combines the character for Katsura (桂) and the middle character of Saionji (西園寺). With the formation of the first Saionji cabinet in January 1906, Katō Takaaki, and later Hayashi Tadasu, became foreign minister. Nevertheless, Shidehara and Komura's relationship continued. When the second Katsura cabinet was formed in July 1908, Komura returned to the post of foreign minister. As director of the Investigation Division, Shidehara had been ordered to participate in the Treaty Revision Preparatory Committee. He would now play a role in supporting both the treaty revision and the continental policy advocated by Komura.

In October 1908, Foreign Minister Komura officially announced the formation of the Treaty Revision Preparatory Committee. Assuming the role of committee chairmen, Komura nominated Minister of Home Affairs Hirata Tosuke, Minister for Agriculture and Forestry Ōura Kanetake and Former Ambassador to Germany Inoue Katsunosuke (1861–1929) as vice-chairmen. From the Ministry of Foreign Affairs, Vice-Minister Ishii Kikujirō, Political Affairs Bureau Director-General Kurachi Tetsukichi (1871–1944), International Trade Bureau Director-General Hagiwara Shuichi (1868–1911), Counsellor to the Chinese Legation Abe Moritarō, Investigation Division Director Shidehara and Secretary Moroi Rokurō were appointed as committee members. The committee also contained a number of individuals from outside of the Ministry of Foreign Affairs, including Cabinet Legislation Bureau Director-General Yasuhiro Tomoichirō (1859–1951), Vice-Minister of Home Affairs Ichiki Kitokurō (1867–1944), Vice-Minister of Finance Wakatsuki Reijirō, and Secretary for the Ministry of Agriculture and Commerce Tsurumi Sakio (1873–1946).

Some readers may be puzzled at the participation of Finance Ministry bureaucrats in the process of treaty revision. However, this is not unnatural. Treaty revision has a significant impact on internal affairs. If, for example, Japan could succeed in restoring its own customs autonomy, then this would be of great interest to the Finance Ministry. This is why Prime Minister Katsura took the unusual step of also assuming the role of finance minister and assisting Foreign Minister Komura's initiative. Komura also nominated Vice-Minister of Finance Wakatsuki as the chairman of the special committee on general tariffs. For the chiefs of the special committees on conventional tariffs, land ownership and perpetual leases, he appointed Ishii, Yasuhiro and Ichiki, respectively. International Trade Bureau Director-General Hagiwara Shuichi, who was personally selected for this role by Hayashi Tadasu, was also engaged in revitalising trade with China while he was engaged in the work of treaty revision.[44]

Shidehara's role on the committee was to examine the issues of perpetual leases and land ownership rights for foreigners. He was also responsible for liaising with Denison. Under Shidehara, investigations were pursued by Moroi Rokurō, Kawashima Nobutarō and Itō Nobufumi.[45] Shidehara had a particularly close relationship with Moroi. Previously, Moroi had succeeded Shidehara's old posting in London and Antwerp. According to diplomat Kimura Eiichi, Moroi studied economics assiduously while assigned to the consular post in Antwerp. This diligence served him well after he returned to Japan, with Moroi becoming the manager of the Treaty Revision Preparatory Committee. Later in his life, Shidehara would propose a memorial for Moroi and sign the condolence book. Sitting with his desk alongside Moroi was Kawashima Nobutarō. Kawashima's presence was heartening for Shidehara, given his familiarity with international trade policy. In February 1911, with the conclusion of agreements such as the new Japan–US Commerce and Navigation Treaty, Japan regained its tariff autonomy.[46]

Other diplomatic issues included Japan's relationship with Korea. However, this issue would also gradually be resolved, as Japan received consent from the other world powers to turn Korea into a protectorate. In October 1909, the moderate-faction member and lord president of the council, Itō Hirobumi, was assassinated in Harbin by An Chung-gun, a member of the Korean independence movement. This incident had the effect of accelerating the annexation of Korea the following year. With this development, the locus of international politics in the region shifted from Korea to Manchuria. As noted above, Shidehara understood the clause on Korea in the Treaty of Portsmouth as already anticipating the future annexation of Korea. As Shidehara wrote:

> Our government has recognized that in order to reform the administration of Korea and establish peace in the Far East, it is necessary to take the decisive action of annexing Korea. Therefore, in August in 1910, the governments of both nations concluded the treaty of annexation.[47]

In other words, he saw the annexation of Korea as a natural outcome. In Shidehara's mind, internationalism and imperialism coexisted.

This view of foreign relations was hardly unique to Shidehara. For example, Kurachi Tetsukichi, who had previously served as private secretary to Itō Hirobumi when he was resident general in Korea, has left similar comments in his own written recollections of the time. According to Kurachi, when he was made director-general of the Ministry of Foreign Affairs' Political Affairs Bureau, under Foreign Minister Komura, Komura ordered the drafting of a basic policy with respect to Korean annexation. On the basis of this draft, the cabinet meeting of July 1909 decided to move ahead with Korean annexation when the appropriate time arose. Ishii Kikujirō reflected similarly that 'the annexation of Korea was absolutely unavoidable for the sake of establishing a general peace in the East'.[48]

Upon annexing Korea, the Japanese government announced that it would impose tariffs for a 10-year period. Nevertheless, it was not long before Japan removed the import duty on Korean rice. According to Kawashima Nobutarō, this was Shidehara's decision. In June 1911, Shidehara received a set of gold cups for his role in the annexation of Korea. Later, as vice-minister for foreign affairs, he naturally displayed no particular reaction when the Ministry of Home Affairs reported the imprisonment and other sentences against Korean independence activists.[49] When Komura's second term as foreign minister ended in July 1911, Shidehara was ordered to serve as director-general of the newly formed Investigation Bureau. Then-diplomat (and future prime minister) Ashida Hitoshi (1887–1959) would later reflect that 'at that time the Investigation Bureau was a new bureau that carried out the roles of today's Research Bureau and Treaties and Conventions Bureau'.[50]

Komura, who pursued a shrewd continental policy, is often considered to have had a style antithetical to Shidehara's, who was generally very rationalistic. Certainly, for their respective periods as foreign minister, this framing of their differences is understandable. From among the diplomats of that period, Honda Kumatarō's trajectory is instructive here. Previously, Honda had accompanied Foreign Minister Komura as a private secretary for the signing of the Treaty of Portsmouth. He deeply admired Komura. He would later be at the forefront of those criticising Shidehara's own diplomatic efforts and would assume the position of ambassador to China under the Wang Jingwei regime in 1940.[51] That said, it is not true that Shidehara was antagonistic towards Foreign Minister Komura. In fact, Shidehara lent Komura practical support. It must be added that Shidehara had his own critics within the department. According to Mushanokōji Kintomo (1882–1962), a group based in the Political Affairs Bureau, including Ariyoshi Akira, Yoshizawa Kenkichi (1874–1965), Hirota Kōki and Matsuoka Yōsuke (1880–1946), together with Nakamura Takashi of the International Trade Bureau and Honda Kumatarō of the secretary office, 'formed an increasingly passionate anti-Shidehara clique'.[52] In his view, their opposition to Shidehara was rooted in envy at his success.

Table 1: Prime ministers and foreign ministers, 1900–21

Prime Minister	Foreign Minister
Itō Hirobumi (1900–01)	Katō Takaaki
Katsura Tarō (1901–06)	Komura Jutarō
Saionji Kinmochi (1906–08)	Katō Takaaki Hayashi Tadasu
Katsura Tarō (1908–11)	Komura Jutarō
Saionji Kinmochi (1911–12)	Uchida Yasuya
Katsura Tarō (1912–13)	Katō Takaaki
Yamamoto Gonbē (1913–14)	Makino Nobuaki
Ōkuma Shigenobu (1914–16)	Katō Takaaki Ishii Kikujirō
Terauchi Masatake (1916–18)	Terauchi Masatake (temporary concurrent) Motono Ichirō Gotō Shinpei
Hara Takashi (1918–21)	Uchida Yasuya

Note: With the exception of the period of the Terauchi cabinet, I have omitted temporary periods during which the prime ministers also took on the role of foreign minister.

Japan–US Relations and the End of the Meiji Era

Denison's Will

In May 1912, Shidehara was transferred from director-general of the Investigation Bureau to the role of counsellor at the Japanese embassy in the US. At this time, Denison was going to the US for a vacation. Shidehara decided to travel with Denison as far as Washington, DC, and the two began preparing for their departure simultaneously.

When helping to clean out Denison's drawers in the office, he found several drafts of telegrams addressed to Minister Kurino, who worked under Foreign Minister Komura, relating to diplomacy surrounding the start of the Russo-Japanese War. Each of the telegram drafts was written in Denison's hand, and they amounted to 14 or 15 revisions of a single message. For Shidehara, 'those drafts amounted to a perfect model for studying the writing of diplomatic papers, while also being valuable historical documents for understanding Japan's diplomatic efforts'.[53]

For this reason, Shidehara asked if he could keep the drafts. Denison, after thinking it over for a moment, suddenly threw the documents into the fireplace and burned them.

Denison turned to a dumbfounded Shidehara and calmly explained. He had burned the documents because others might have the wrong impression after reading them. The success of the diplomacy surrounding the commencement of the Russo-Japanese War belonged to Foreign Minister Komura. However, these documents could be misread as indicating that Denison had masterminded the Russo-Japanese negotiations behind the scenes. Shidehara was greatly moved by Denison's words. Denison felt that the publicly released diplomatic documents of the Japanese government had helped improve Japan's international image. For Shidehara, Denison's consideration in this regard 'impressed upon me greatly the extent of his good character, such that I was struck silent'.[54]

There was another reason in the back of Denison's mind, however. He was 66, had served the Ministry of Foreign Affairs for over 30 years and was considering retirement. Shidehara had no way of knowing it, but Denison felt that he did not have much longer to live. Thus, in July 1912, he prepared his will. He bequeathed his golden cups, granted by the emperor, to Ishii Kikujirō. Moreover, he left his entire personal library, of which he was quite proud, to Shidehara. Denison kept the writing of his will a close secret, never mentioning it to Shidehara. This was the last thing he did for Shidehara, who had admired and followed him so earnestly. However, because of Denison's official duties, he was unable to depart for the US on the same boat as Shidehara. This would be their final parting, as Denison died less than two years later.[55]

The End of the Meiji Era—a Favourite Book: *Nogi*

At the end of July 1912, just before his visit to the US, Shidehara learned of the death of the charismatic Meiji emperor. When Shidehara arrived in Washington in mid-September, he learned of yet another shocking occurrence: the suicide of Nogi Maresuke and his wife following the funeral of the Meiji emperor (an old samurai practice known as *junshi*). Nogi had been to the frontline during the Russo-Japanese War as Third Army commander, and deeds such as his supervision of the capture of Lushun were still fresh in Shidehara's memory. In 1907 Nogi became the president of Gakushūin School and oversaw the education of young

2. THE RUSSO-JAPANESE WAR, WORLD WAR I AND THE WASHINGTON NAVAL CONFERENCE

Prince Hirohito. The suicide of Nogi, who had directed fighting in the Russo-Japanese War, seemed to symbolise the end of the Meiji era. As an entire era ended, hardly a soul in Japan was not deeply touched.[56]

Yet it was not only the Japanese who were shocked to hear of Nogi's suicide. One foreigner who was deeply affected by it was US journalist Stanley Washburn. Washburn had been attached to the Japanese army during the Russo-Japanese War as a freshly minted foreign correspondent. Nogi left a deep impression on young Washburn in that period. Upon hearing of Nogi's suicide, Washburn quickly began writing down his memories of Nogi. He completed a manuscript in English for a book that would simply be titled *Nogi*, recounting incidents such as the capture of Lushun and Mukden by the Third Army, under Nogi's command. Washburn's *Nogi* was published in New York in February 1913. The work depicted Nogi as a brave figure who remained resolute even in the face of his own son's death in battle. It could even be considered an elegy.[57]

There was one Japanese reader who deeply enjoyed reading *Nogi*, recommending its Japanese translation to his friends. That was Shidehara, then counsellor to the Japanese embassy in the US. How Shidehara came to read this book is quite interesting. One day in 1913, when Shidehara was visiting the US State Department, a surprise gift was waiting for him. A temporary employee at the State Department, Hamilton Wright, had given Shidehara a copy of *Nogi*, which had been written by his brother-in-law. Shidehara later stated that he 'devoured the whole thing all at once' and 'never tired of reading it'.[58] His own copy of *Nogi*, however, became misplaced at some point while on loan to one of his friends.

Several years later, Shidehara had the opportunity to meet with Washburn while serving as ambassador to the US. When participating in the Washington Naval Conference as Japan's ambassador plenipotentiary, Washburn was working behind the scenes as secretary to plenipotentiary representative Root. The member of the Japanese side who dealt with Washburn most directly was not Shidehara but plenipotentiary representative Hanihara Masanao. Shidehara was able to make contact with Root starting from before the conference.[59]

On his impression of Washburn, Shidehara wrote:

> His genius extended beyond the literary world. Both his ideals and his insight were remarkable. I realized that it was no coincidence that he came to admire General Nogi from his daily contact with that man.[60]

43

At that time Washburn presented Shidehara with a newly revised edition of *Nogi*. Shidehara 'kept that book beside him at all times, and after returning to Japan, showed it to his old schoolmate Mr. Meguro Masumi'.[61]

According to Meguro, Shidehara 'suggested that I try reading this book. He believed that young adults and students of our nation would benefit from it and that I too would surely find myself moved'.[62] After receiving permission from his publishing company to have the book translated, Washburn informed Shidehara via Hanihara, the then ambassador to the US. This is how Washburn's *Nogi* came to be translated into Japanese by Meguro and published in 1924. Shidehara himself supplied the foreword, which stated:

> In recent years there are many in our nation who are quite unreasonably infatuated with the latest ideas from abroad. Yet in foreign countries there are actually more than a few individuals who can interpret, understand, and respect the mind of one such as General Nogi, that model of the Japanese samurai of old … *Nogi* examines the tendencies of the minds of us modern people. It is a particularly fascinating work.[63]

Although Shidehara tends to be interpreted as an unemotional rationalist, he venerated Nogi's idealism. Shidehara and Washburn's relationship would continue until his second term as foreign minister.

The 1913 Alien Land Law

In the fall of 1912, Shidehara assumed the position of counsellor at the Japanese embassy in the US. What was the relationship between Japan and the US like at that time? To answer this question, I would like to return briefly to the period of transition represented by the Russo-Japanese War. Japan's victory over Russia in that conflict inevitably influenced the Japan–US relationship. When a developing nation seeks a bigger role on the world stage, it cannot help but attract more critical attention. As Japan's world prominence grew, some in the US sought to exclude Japanese immigrants. At the root of this was prejudice against Asians. In 1906, San Francisco passed a resolution that segregated Japanese schoolchildren. Meanwhile, the state legislature of California attempted to prohibit Japanese people from owning land, but this move was prevented by Republican President Theodore Roosevelt and William Howard Taft.

2. THE RUSSO-JAPANESE WAR, WORLD WAR I AND THE WASHINGTON NAVAL CONFERENCE

However, a turning point came under Democratic President Woodrow Wilson. Two alien land laws were passed in California. With the 1913 Alien Land Law, foreigners who were unable to naturalise as US citizens were forbidden from owning land. Despite the Japan–US Gentlemen's Agreement of 1908—which saw Japan voluntarily restrict the number of immigrants to the US—this law was clearly targeted at Japanese immigrants. Then the 1920 Alien Land Law prohibited even the leasing of land.

Japan did not simply remain silent when these laws were enacted. In fact, Shidehara was deeply involved in the reactions to both—as embassy counsellor in the case of the first law, and as ambassador to the US in the case of the second. Who were some of the key individuals staffing the Japanese embassy when the 1913 Alien Land Law was presented to the state legislature of California? Alongside then counsellor Shidehara was Ambassador Chinda Sutemi and Second Secretary Okabe Saburō, Third Secretary Ōta Tamekichi (1880–1956), Third Secretary Kawashima Nobutarō, Probationary Diplomat Okabe Nagakage (1884–1970), Probationary Diplomat Hiroshi Saitō and Embassy Clerk Imai Tadanao.[64]

Naturally, Ambassador Chinda and his colleagues protested the enactment of this law. President Wilson also dispatched Secretary of State William J. Bryan to California. However, they were not able to change the minds of the members of the state legislature. Nevertheless, Shidehara admired Ambassador Chinda and his willingness to engage Bryan in debate. Of Chinda, he wrote: 'His arguments were always perfectly reasonable, devoid of any disorder or anger, and expressed in inoffensive language. Yet the will he thereby expressed was extremely firm'.[65] Shidehara also thought of Chinda as a master of the English language. Conversely, Shidehara was much harsher in his assessment of Bryan, whom he considered an eloquent yet inexperienced diplomat, unaccustomed to writing official documents. This evaluation was very typical of Shidehara.

The Republican Party held the majority in California's state legislature. If the Wilson administration could not convince them, nothing could be done. Even after Shidehara left the US, Chinda remained as the ambassador. He continued his negotiations with Bryan in an effort to prevent the establishment of similar laws in other states. Meanwhile, with the coming of World War I, the Wilson administration began to have doubts about Japan's opportunistic politics with respect to China.[66]

The Influence of Ambassador Bryce

Shidehara's tenure as counsellor at the Japanese embassy in the US would last only a year and two months. Nevertheless, it was long enough for him to be influenced by James Bryce, a British historian and then ambassador to the US. Bryce was already in his mid-70s, yet he took the time while he was ambassador to the US to revise his 1888 work, *The American Commonwealth*, for which he was well known in the country.[67]

What left a particular impression upon Shidehara was how Bryce deliberately refrained from challenging the Panama Canal Passage Tax Bill as it made its way through the US Senate. This Bill was disadvantageous to the UK, yet Bryce foresaw that the US would eventually come to regret it. For the same reason, Bryce admonished Shidehara for persisting in his protests against the Alien Land Law. According to British Foreign Secretary Sir Edward Grey: 'At Washington the personal position of Mr. Bryce was less that of an Ambassador than of a distinguished man of letters and knowledge'.[68] With respect to the Panama Canal, Grey also seemed to have anticipated that sooner or later, the US would come to observe the agreements existing between the two nations and abolish the discriminatory canal passage tax.

According to the recollections of Ōta Tamekichi, then third secretary at the Japanese embassy in the US, Shidehara was also instructed about diplomatic affairs by individuals such as the counsellor at the British embassy. Upon hearing that 'the British do not have the practice of pushing their own countrymen to one side', Shidehara decided not to press strongly for the right of Japanese to naturalise as Americans.[69] In November 1913, Shidehara was relieved of his posting as embassy counsellor and ordered to a new posting in the UK. After spending time in a number of roles, including that of vice-minister for foreign affairs, he eventually returned to the US in November 1919, this time as Japan's ambassador.

In 1921, in Washington, Shidehara met Bryce again for the first time in several years. At this time Bryce was untitled. Shidehara took the opportunity to remark, somewhat wryly, that while the Panama Canal Passage Tax had been abolished, to the UK's benefit, the US's anti-Japanese laws did not appear to be going anywhere. Upon hearing this, Bryce glared at Shidehara, admonishing him once more not to be too eager for success. 'Do you not recognize', he asked, 'that the fate of nations is timeless?'[70] Shidehara understood Bryce to mean that it was important to be prudent and avoid excessive appeals, entrusting developments to the US's own reform efforts. As it happened, Bryce was visiting the US to give a series of lectures. The topic of those lectures was international relations, and, while cautious, they called for coexistence with what was then called the 'colored races' of the world.[71] Bryce would pass away the following year, making this exchange the last with Shidehara. It may also have been, I suggest, an exchange that Shidehara slightly misunderstood. In other words, Bryce's point was surely not to promote a straightforward attitude of forbearance.

Grey's Enlightenment, News of Denison's Death—Counsellor to Japan's Embassy in the UK

In December 1913, Shidehara arrived in London to assume his role as embassy counsellor. It had been 13 years since he was last in that country. By that point, the relationship between Japan and the UK had already begun to come under strain. The cause was Japan's railway policy in the Yangtze Valley.[72] The ambassador to the UK at that time was Inoue Katsunosuke. Other embassy staff included Second Secretary Yoshida Isaburō, Third Secretary Sawada Setsuzō, Third Secretary Okabe Nagakage and Probationary Diplomat Yano Makoto.

After being influenced by Bryce in the US, Shidehara was now positioned to be influenced even further by British-style diplomacy. In this case, the instructor was none other than Secretary of State for Foreign Affairs Sir Edward Grey. Although Shidehara stayed in London for only half a year, Grey's thinking had a profound impact. It would not be an exaggeration to say that, for Shidehara, Grey came to represent the ideal foreign secretary. Grey served as foreign secretary for over a decade, from 1905 until 1916. Thus, when Shidehara arrived in the UK, Grey had already been at that post for eight years.

What particularly impressed Shidehara was Grey's response to the murder of a British citizen in Mexico. Initially, the UK wanted to send a warship to the region. The US, however, adopting the viewpoint of the Monroe Doctrine—which held that the US and Europe should each refrain from intervening in the other's sphere of influence—was opposed to this action. In response, Foreign Secretary Grey decided not to take

47

any special action. The newspapers, rather than merely avoiding any criticism of Grey for this decision, actually praised him for preventing any worsening of the US–UK relationship. Shidehara was also surprised at the maturity of public opinion in the UK. He wrote: 'As can be seen from this one example, the average British citizen possesses a surprising degree of common sense, to an extent that would be unimaginable in Japan'.[73] Grey's influence also manifested in Shidehara's integrity as a politician and his aversion to deciphering coded messages.

Shidehara was not the only foreigner to be influenced by Grey. Another such individual was US diplomat William Phillips (1878–1968). Phillips was assigned the role of first secretary at the US embassy in the UK at practically the same time that Shidehara received his assignment. Phillips, who would soon become undersecretary of state, met Grey again in Washington after the conclusion of World War I. At that time, Grey was tasked with improving relations between the UK and the US, as ambassador to the US. Unfortunately, Grey's eyesight began to weaken starting in World War I and worsened during his time in the US. Phillips could only watch in despair as Grey became blind. Shidehara too must have been upset by this development when he became ambassador to the US in 1919. When he met Grey in Washington, the man's eyes were already clouded over. The one consolation was that Grey remembered the high-pitched sound of Shidehara's English.[74]

In July 1914, Shidehara—then still a counsellor at the embassy in the UK—received some distressing news. Denison had died of illness in Tokyo. Upon learning of Denison's death, Shidehara sank into a deep grief. Alongside the passing of the Meiji emperor and the suicide of Nogi and his wife, the loss of Denison truly impressed upon Shidehara that an era had come to an end. Yet Shidehara had to compose himself and search for a successor to Denison. In this task he was assisted by Second Secretary Yoshida Isaburō. Eventually it was decided that Denison's replacement as adviser to the Foreign Ministry would be Thomas Baty, the famed English expert in international law. Following his appointment, Baty, too, would go on to live out the rest of his life in Japan.[75]

World War I

Ultimatums and the Outbreak of War—Dual Minister to the Netherlands and Denmark

On the eve of World War I, Shidehara's career reached a significant turning point. This was his appointment as dual minister to the Netherlands and Denmark. Becoming an extraordinary and minister plenipotentiary meant a significant increase in responsibility. Previous occupants of this position included talented individuals such as Chinda Sutemi and Satō Aimaro (1857–1934). Chinda went on to receive a series of promotions, taking positions such as minister to Russia, vice-minister for foreign affairs, ambassador to Germany, ambassador to the US and ambassador to the UK. Satō, meanwhile, became Japan's ambassador to Austria-Hungary for the period leading up to World War I, before becoming ambassador to the US during the course of the war.

Shidehara was appointed dual minister to the Netherlands and Denmark in June 1914. Soon afterwards, on 28 June, gunshots rang out in Sarajevo, Bosnia. The presumptive heir to the Austro-Hungarian Empire, Franz Ferdinand, and his wife were assassinated by a young Serbian nationalist. The following month, when Shidehara arrived at his post in The Hague, World War I had already commenced. Meeting Shidehara at the Dutch legation was Second Secretary Matsuhara Katsuo, Probationary Diplomat Yokota Seiichirō and Legation Clerk Tokita Takurō.

In August, Japan declared war with Germany on the basis of the Anglo-Japanese Alliance. It was here that Shidehara had a bitter experience. Tasked with delivering Japan's ultimatum to Germany, Shidehara attempted to do so via Germany's minister to the Netherlands, with whom he was already familiar. This attempt was a failure.[76] Funakoshi Mitsunojō (1867–1942), who was serving as counsellor at the Japanese embassy in Germany, has left us some comments regarding this ultimatum to Germany. According to Funakoshi, the first to make contact regarding the ultimatum was Foreign Minister Katō, followed by the ambassador to Italy, Hayashi Gonsuke and the minister to Sweden, Uchida Sadatsuchi (1865–1942). To make sure that the ultimatum was delivered properly, Katō contacted not only Uchida in Stockholm but also Shidehara in The Hague. As Funakoshi wrote: '[Katō] sent a classified telegram, telling us that he was sending the ultimatum, and that we needed to prepare to deploy a secret messenger'.[77]

Upon receiving this message, Uchida judged that it would be difficult to send a secret messenger to Germany, given the tense circumstances. He therefore decided to reach out to a friend, the Brazilian minister to Sweden, requesting that he get in contact with the envoy in Brazil to arrange a coded telegram to be sent to Funakoshi in Germany. By the time Uchida's coded telegram reached Germany, however, Funakoshi had already received word of the ultimatum from Tokyo directly. Nevertheless, Funakoshi was deeply impressed by Uchida's resourcefulness. By contrast, Funakoshi was irritated by Shidehara, whom he perceived as dull-witted.

Leaving Germany, Funakoshi met with Shidehara in The Hague on his way back to Japan. Shidehara told Funakoshi that he had sent a telegram to Foreign Minister Katō, stating that he was unable to dispatch a secret messenger to Germany. According to Funakoshi, Shidehara apologised and said 'there was nothing else he could do'. Later in life, Funakoshi would remark: 'It is at times like these that you get to know a person's real merits'.[78] In any case, Foreign Minister Katō's preparations for the ultimatum to Germany were exhaustive. Even the Japanese embassy in Germany was surprised at how he ensured the ultimatum's delivery by sending it through multiple routes.[79]

In fact, in terms of its exhaustiveness, Foreign Minister Katō's ultimatum to Germany stood in contrast to his Twenty-One Demands issued to China. These demands were thrust at China by Japan in January 1915. Among other things, they required that Japan inherit Germany's interests in Shandong, and also that Japan's leaseholds over Lushun and Dalian, as well as its control over the South Manchuria Railway, be extended for a period of 99 years. Japan used an ultimatum in order to force China to accept the key demands. Shidehara, who was then residing in the Netherlands, was not at that time very familiar with the process by which the demands were formulated. Nevertheless, upon learning of the details of their contents, Shidehara submitted a detailed opposing opinion to Katō.[80]

On the above topic, Shidehara's subordinate, Probationary Diplomat Tani Masayuki, left some remarks. According to Tani, after serious consideration, Shidehara resolutely relayed his opposing opinion on the Twenty-One Demands to Katō. Just as Denison once did with him, Shidehara frequently took Tani out for meals and walks. Vice-Minister for Foreign Affairs Matsui Keishirō also mentioned Denison's absence as one of the causes of the disorder surrounding the issuing of the Twenty-One Demands. Shidehara presumably held the same opinion.[81]

Recalling his time in the Netherlands later in life, Shidehara mentioned China's minister to Belgium, Wang Rongbao. As Shidehara told it, given that China was not yet a belligerent in World War I, Wang was free to assist Kimura Eiichi, then secretary at the Japanese legation in Belgium, to wind up his own affairs. Shidehara was not yet acquainted with Wang; however, Wang would come to spend most of the 1920s as Chinese minister to Japan. In the course of that decade, they would come to develop a candid relationship. Shidehara also had the opportunity to observe Kimura Eiichi, whom he considered to be 'brilliant' at his work.[82]

Vice-Minister for Foreign Affairs—Concern for the Russo-Japanese Relationship

Under the second Ōkuma cabinet, Ishii Kikujirō was appointed foreign minister, succeeding Katō, who had stumbled with his issuing of the Twenty-One Demands. Ishii would summon Shidehara to come and work with him in the role of vice-minister for foreign affairs. When Shidehara departed Europe in September 1915, the tide of war still favoured Germany and Austria. When the war broke out, no one could foresee that it would drag on for four years. In October, Shidehara arrived back in Japan from the Netherlands and assumed his new appointment as vice-minister for foreign affairs.

The then director-general of the Political Affairs Bureau, Koike Chōzō, was, along with Shidehara, one of the four individuals who had passed the fourth diplomatic service exam. Koike had remained in office from the time of the first Yamamoto Gonbē cabinet, where he was appointed under Foreign Minister Makino Nobuaki (1861–1949). The director-general of the International Trade Bureau was Sakata Jūtarō (1868–1919). Sakata also had other important responsibilities that he had been carrying out for some time, since the period of the second Saionji cabinet and Foreign Minister Uchida Yasuya (1865–1936). Shidehara, meanwhile, had been director-general of the Investigation Bureau when Uchida was foreign minister. Given this similar background, we might wonder how Shidehara's own career trajectory compared. The vice-minister for foreign affairs who served under Foreign Minister Katō had been Matsui Keishirō. Matsui had been ahead of Shidehara at Osaka Middle School. Shidehara was four years younger than Matsui and was 43 years old when he took over as vice-minister for foreign affairs.

When Shidehara returned to Japan in high spirits, something unexpected awaited him: thousands of Denison's books, delivered by the executor of Denison's estate. Shidehara had the executor show him Denison's handwritten will. As Shidehara recalls: '[I] read it thoroughly, multiple times, my heart filled with grief'.[83]

Over the next four years, Shidehara carried out his duties as vice-minister for foreign affairs, supporting five successive foreign ministers: Ishii Kikujirō, Terauchi Masatake, Motono Ichirō (1862–1918), Gotō Shinpei (1857–1929) and Uchida Yasuya. Excluding Uchida, who served as foreign minister for five years, including in the Hara cabinet, each of these foreign ministers served no longer than a year and a half (including Motono, who was the longest serving of these four). Shidehara plunged into his responsibilities as vice-minister, frequently working long into the night for days on end. According to Nagai Matsuzō (1877–1957), then director of the Telegraph Division, whenever Shidehara eventually returned home, the ministry would become much quieter.[84]

During Shidehara's term as vice-minister for foreign affairs, the administration changed from the second Ōkuma cabinet to the Terauchi cabinet and then to the Hara cabinet. There were many important issues that Shidehara would be involved with during this period. These can broadly be divided into the categories of Russo-Japanese relations, Sino-Japanese relations, American–Japanese relations and the Paris Peace Conference. Of these, it was Japan's relationship with Russia following the end of World War I that became more involved. In particular, the Fourth Russo-Japanese Agreement of July 1916 was close to a military alliance. At this time, Japan and Russia were sending members of their respective imperial families on state visits in order to publicly display their friendship. Naturally, Shidehara devoted great care to Japan's relationship with Russia at this time.[85]

Just after his appointment as vice-minister, Shidehara began exchanging information with resident Russian Ambassador Nikolai A. Malevskii-Malevich regarding Germany's intentions. For example, as rumours swirled of a German plan to sabotage the Chinese Eastern Railway, Shidehara shared information with the Russian ambassador about a German individual behaving suspiciously. The Chinese Eastern Railway was located in north-east China and was originally built by Russia. Cooperating with Russia in this manner was an approach that Shidehara carried over from his predecessor as vice-minister for foreign affairs, Matsui

Keishirō. This approach was not unique to Shidehara. On the other hand, when Japan responded coldly to Yuan Shikai's imperial government plans, Malevich informed Shidehara that Russia would pursue the same policy. Incidentally, written communications between Russia and Japan were generally not in English but in French.[86]

What Russia dearly desired from the Japanese side was military supplies. However, the Ministry of War was not inclined to agree to the provisioning of Russia. Shidehara's solution was to work with the Ministry of War, the Ministry of Finance, and the Russian embassy to arrange for Russian treasury bonds to be paid in exchange for Japan's military supplies. Shidehara also worked to ensure that Japan's newspapers did not report sensitive news about Russia.[87]

On the economic front, fishing rights were regarded as particularly important. The Russo-Japanese Fishing Agreement, signed in July 1907, was for a period of 12 years. As early as 1916, however, the Fisheries Bureau of the Ministry of Agriculture and Commerce began surveying the Russian territorial coastline with an eye to the treaty's renewal three years later. Shidehara worked to accommodate these efforts by coordinating with Foreign Minister Ishii and the Russian embassy.[88]

Sino-Japanese and American–Japanese Relations during World War I

While Japan was strengthening its relationship with Russia, the situation in China was thrown into chaos as a result of the Chinese Revolution of 1911, which led to the overthrow of the Chinese Qing dynasty and the establishment of the Republic of China. In Manchuria and Inner Mongolia, there were even independence movements launched by parts of the Japanese army, and groups such as one led by Kawashima Naniwa (1865–1949), one of the so-called 'continental wanderers' who appeared in this period (independent Japanese who roamed continental Asia). Although the Ōkuma cabinet decided to attempt to remove Yuan Shikai in March 1916, his sudden death in June made it necessary to shift towards a policy of supporting President Li Yuanhong (1864–1928). This new policy meant ending earlier plans to assist independence movements in Manchuria and Inner Mongolia. Consequently, Shidehara supported the confiscation of weapons and ammunition in Changchun, working to obstruct the raising of independence armies.[89]

With respect to the new government in Beijing, there was the problem of China potentially participating in the conflict against Germany. While the UK, France and Russia had also asked the Chinese government to participate, Japan had opposed this move. Russian ambassador Vasilii N. Krupenskii pressed Shidehara as to why Japan opposed China's participation. Shidehara replied: 'It is hard to believe that China would be prepared to give up its neutral status to accept an offer from the Allies'. In other words, Shidehara responded that it was because China had not properly made up its mind about engaging in the war. In reality, however, Shidehara shared the same concern as Foreign Minister Ishii—that China might be able to improve its position by participating in the war. On the other hand, Shidehara was also anxious about China falling into a state of lawlessness and hoped that the forces in southern and northern China might reach 'a clear reconciliation'.[90]

In October 1916, the Terauchi Masatake cabinet was formed. General Terauchi, who had for many years served as governor-general of Korea, temporarily served as foreign minister alongside his duties as prime minister. However, this ministerial post was soon taken over by Motono Ichirō. Motono had become Japan's minister to Russia in 1906. In May 1908, the legation was upgraded to an embassy, and Motono continued to serve as ambassador to Russia until 1916. Motono was deeply involved in each of the four Russo-Japanese agreements. Therefore, while Motono was very familiar with the general state of affairs in Europe, he was less knowledgeable about the Sino-Japanese relationship. Thus, Shidehara was able to enjoy an enhanced position within the ministry with respect to Chinese policy.

That said, Shidehara did not have complete control over how Japan responded to the situation in China. The leading individual in this area was the China expert Obata Yūkichi (1873–1947). Obata had replaced Koike Chōzō as director-general of the Political Affairs Bureau. Having been critical of the Ōkuma cabinet's policy of intervention, Obata submitted a written opinion to Foreign Minister Motono that advocated the restoration of friendly relations with the other world powers. Shidehara assisted Obata in polishing the prose of this written opinion. Motono was able to receive private consent for this policy from figures such as Terauchi and Yamagata. The new policy direction, of establishing harmonious relationships with the world powers, was agreed upon in a meeting of the Terauchi cabinet on 9 January 1917.[91]

2. THE RUSSO-JAPANESE WAR, WORLD WAR I AND THE WASHINGTON NAVAL CONFERENCE

China's entry into World War I in August 1917 led to heightened tensions between Japan and the US. This was because the US had increased its involvement in China's internal affairs. US Minister Paul S. Reinsch took a leading role in pushing for this new approach. When the Wilson administration advised the Chinese government to put an end to that nation's internal conflicts, the Terauchi cabinet saw this as a form of interference. When Post Wheeler, the chargé d'affaires (the provisional ambassador) of the US embassy in Japan, visited the ministry to explain their position, Shidehara reminded him that 'the manner in which the Japanese were always particularly sensitive with regard to the problem of China was no different to Americans with respect to Mexico'.[92]

For this reason, Japan and the US needed to reach some form of consensus with respect to China policy. Japan's approach was to dispatch former foreign minister Ishii Kikujirō to the US. In November 1917, Ishii was able to conclude an exchange of notes with Secretary of State Robert Lansing (sometimes referred to as the Lansing–Ishii Agreement). In the agreement, the US recognised Japan's 'special interests' in China. Further, the accord stipulated that both nations would maintain equality of opportunity and open door policies as their ideals. It was a quintessentially ambiguous agreement. For the most part, however, its contents were regarded as satisfactory in Japan. After the accord was finalised, Ishii took over as ambassador to the US, and American–Japanese relations also improved regarding naval deployment in the Pacific.[93]

During this period Shidehara consulted with Foreign Minister Motono to help ensure that the negotiations between Ishii and Lansing proceeded as planned. Taking into consideration Shidehara's views, Motono had Satō, then ambassador to the US, deliver a memorandum to Lansing by hand. This memorandum cleverly included a passage stating that Japan had important political and economic interests in China. Shidehara took the additional step of showing this memorandum to Chargé d'Affaires Wheeler, indicating that Lansing 'expressed himself as quite in accord with the deep sense of the memorandum'.[94] However, Lansing would later angrily refute this claim. Apparently, Shidehara's attempts here were actually counterproductive. Nevertheless, the conclusion of the agreement between Ishii and Lansing helped to ease tensions between the US and Japan. The diary of Undersecretary of State William Phillips is particularly illuminating on this matter. While Phillips was initially suspicious of

Ishii, after some time they were able to speak candidly. Phillips wrote in his diary: 'The editorial comment this morning on the exchange of notes with Japan is very good, with the exception of the *New York Times*'.[95]

In the following year, 1918, a serious issue for Japanese diplomacy was the sending of troops to Russia in the wake of the Russian Revolution. The nations most enthusiastic about sending a coalition expeditionary force to quell the revolution were the UK and France. The Wilson administration in the US was more wary and hesitated to commit armed forces. In Japan, Foreign Minister Motono of the Terauchi cabinet strongly backed participating in the expedition. However, Shidehara's position was closer to the US's. He was cautious about the idea of sending troops. With Motono frequently ill at this time, Shidehara had the rare opportunity to freely present his own view to US Ambassador Morris, British Ambassador William Conyngham Greene, French Ambassador Eugène L. G. Regnault and Russian Ambassador Krupenskii.[96]

Nevertheless, the US gradually began to lean towards sending soldiers. Surprisingly, in July 1918 the Wilson administration proposed to Japan that they land a joint expeditionary force at Vladivostok. The pretext of this move would be to relieve the Czech army. In August, therefore, a Japanese–American joint military expedition was launched. However, Japan committed 73,000 soldiers, which the US saw as entirely too many. The Wilson administration and Undersecretary of State Phillips were also irritated at the actions of the Japanese army at that time.[97]

The end of September 1918 saw a change of government in Japan, with the formation of the Seiyūkai party's Hara Takashi cabinet. This was the first properly party-based cabinet. With the change in cabinet, Gotō Shinpei, who had served as the foreign minister for about five months towards the end of the Terauchi cabinet, was replaced by Uchida Yasuya. Uchida, who had once enjoyed the favour of Mutsu Munemitsu, had passed through the successive positions of director-general of the International Trade Bureau, director-general of the Political Affairs Bureau, minister to the Qing dynasty and ambassador to the US. In 1911, he became foreign minister in the second Saionji cabinet. He also served as the ambassador to Russia but had to return to Japan upon the outbreak of the Russian Revolution.

2. THE RUSSO-JAPANESE WAR, WORLD WAR I AND THE WASHINGTON NAVAL CONFERENCE

The Hara cabinet set to work, seeking to reduce the size of the military force that had been sent to Siberia, as well as placing geographical limits on how far the army could move. It must be added that Shidehara's diplomatic activity after troops were deployed to Siberia was not simply targeted at fostering cooperation with the UK and the US. In his negotiations with these two nations, he frequently had to assert Japan's agreed-upon special interests in Manchuria. In particular, Shidehara disapproved of the proposal to internationalise the management of the Chinese Eastern Railway under the guidance of the US. He cited 'Japan's special status' in Manchuria.[98]

That said, Shidehara showed a different face domestically. On 26 October 1918, he attended a meeting with the army, alongside Political Affairs Bureau Director-General Obata. Together, they succeeded in winning over Major General Hoshino Shōzaburō, chief of the Third Bureau of the Office of Army General Staff. (The Office of Army General Staff was one of two agencies that managed the Imperial Japanese Army at that time.) Hoshino also opposed the US proposal to place the Chinese Eastern Railway under international management. Shidehara responded to his concerns by asserting that 'there is absolutely no fear of the US going back on its word, given its national character'.[99]

Shidehara was also critical of the inclusion of the Baikal Cossack chief (*ataman*) Grigorii Mikhailovich Semenov (1890–1946) in the Office of Army General Staff. Instead, Shidehara sought to strengthen Japan's relationship with Aleksandr Vasil'evich Kolchak (1874–1920), the navy admiral who had taken over governance of the city of Omsk, which the UK and France were supporting. Omsk was the centre of the anticommunist government in Siberia, supported by other leaders of the white movement. In practice, this meant that Japan helped supply Omsk with munitions, while also dispatching Katō Tsunetada (1859–1923) as temporary ambassador plenipotentiary.[100] The government in Omsk was short-lived, however, collapsing in November 1919. Following the subsequent withdrawal of UK, French and US troops from Russia, the Japanese army became the last Allied forces in the former Russian Empire.

At this time another issue with the US began to emerge. The Wilson administration reached out to Japan, the UK and France about the possibility of the four nations jointly loaning money to the Chinese government. The syndicated loan that was established through this cooperation was known as the New Four-Power Consortium. Secretary of

State Lansing first brought the proposal for this consortium to Ambassador Ishii in July 1918. However, Shidehara had some doubts. In a Tokyo meeting held in October with Ransford S. Millar, who would go on to become the chief of the Division of Far Eastern Affairs of the US State Department, Shidehara emphasised that this development could be 'the first step toward the abolition of [Japan's] sphere of influence', making its 'execution extremely problematic [for us]'.[101] Behind the establishment of the New Four-Power Consortium was a plan by actors such as the Manchurian Railway Company to secretly expand the transcontinental railroad. Shidehara and Foreign Minister Uchida were well aware of this fact.

The Paris Peace Conference

January 1919 saw the commencement of the Paris Peace Conference, where the victorious powers set the terms for the conclusion of World War I. It was not until June that year that the Allied powers (including Japan) concluded a formal peace treaty with Germany: the Treaty of Versailles. At this conference, the Hara cabinet acted in concert with the UK while successfully negotiating Japan's inheritance of Germany's interests in the Shandong Peninsula. Japan was even able to establish the 'South Pacific Mandate', whereby Pacific islands north of the equator that had been part of the German Empire were placed under Japanese control. As vice-minister for foreign affairs, Shidehara showed his discomfort with the diplomatic ideals of President Wilson. This was visible in his response to Wilson's Fourteen Points and to Wilson's call for the establishment of the League of Nations.

Wilson had given a speech to the US Congress in January 1918 in which he presented his vision for a liberal world order. The Fourteen Points that Wilson outlined in this speech included a call for the abolition of secret diplomacy and the establishment of a League of Nations. According to Mushanokōji Kintomo (1882–1962), who was director of the second division of the Foreign Ministry's Political Affairs Bureau, Shidehara's opinion on this plan for a League of Nations was that:

> It is a great nuisance to have our fate decided at this kind of roundtable discussion, rather than through respective direct negotiations between countries that have an interest on a given matter.[102]

In fact, Shidehara opposed not only the League of Nations but also the later-established United Nations.

On the topic of the Paris Peace Conference, a fascinating anecdote about this period emerged after Shidehara became Japan's ambassador to the US. Secretary of State Lansing had criticised Japan in his memoirs for being so persistent in trying to secure interests in Shandong.[103] Lansing's account appeared aimed at warding off critiques that he compromised with Japan too much with the Lansing–Ishii Agreement and during the Paris Peace Conference. Lansing was considerate enough to send a copy of these memoirs to Shidehara.

Shidehara's strong sense of pride shows through in the letter of thanks he wrote for this gift, which bristles with sarcasm. Shidehara wrote that Lansing's memoirs were highly 'instructive to me'. He continued:

> It shows how little the actual situation and relevant history of the Far East are understood by even the foremost statesmen and scholars of this country, and how easily the best intentions and honest thinkings of one nation are liable to be misconstrued by another. I have, however, every confidence that Japan's position will someday be viewed in its truer and fairer perspective.[104]

Shidehara apparently encountered Lansing and his wife at a tea party shortly afterwards, leading to no small amount of awkwardness. Shidehara sent a copy of this letter of thanks addressed to Lansing to Makino Nobuaki, minister of the imperial household, via Vice-Minister for Foreign Affairs Hanihara Masanao (1876–1934). Substantially, Makino had been Japan's chief plenipotentiary at the Paris Peace Conference.

A Time of Trials for the Foreign Ministry—Katō Takaaki and Hara Takashi

So far, I have traced Shidehara's participation in events pertaining to Russo-Japanese, Sino-Japanese and American–Japanese relations, as well as with respect to the Paris Peace Conference. The reader may therefore have been left with the impression that Shidehara was practically the architect of Japan's diplomacy during World War I. However, this was not the case. It was not until the Washington Naval Conference that Shidehara would come to lead Japan's diplomatic efforts and make a name for himself. In fact, more generally, World War I was a time of trials for the Ministry of Foreign Affairs, which saw its status within the government deteriorate. There were five reasons for this state of affairs.

First was the intervention in foreign affairs by Japan's elder statesmen, the *genrō*. For example, the Fourth Russo-Japanese Agreement, concluded in July 1916, was advocated by two *genrō*: Yamagata Aritomo and Inoue Kaoru.

Second, the Extraordinary Foreign Diplomacy Investigation Committee was established in June 1917 by the Terauchi cabinet. Alongside figures such as Privy Councillor Itō Miyoji (1857–1934) and Makino Nobuaki, members of this committee also included presidents of two political parties: Seiyūkai President Hara Takashi and Kokumintō President Inukai Tsuyoshi (1855–1932). Together they would convene and deliberate upon Japan's diplomatic problems. We may regard this as the beginning of the direct involvement of political parties in Japanese diplomacy.[105]

A third reason was the existence of the army. Leading the army during its Siberian Intervention were individuals such as Vice Chief of Army General Staff Tanaka Giichi. After troops were dispatched to the continent, the Office of Army General Staff worked independently in assisting pro-Japanese factions.

Fourth, private citizens such as Nishihara Kamezō (1873–1954) were involved behind the scenes in Japan's China policy, promoting the lending of money to the Chinese government. The 'Nishihara Loans' were further supported by Finance Minister Shōda Kazue (1869–1948).

Finally, there was the problem of government organisation in Manchuria. The Resident Generals Office of Kwantung was abolished in 1919, with the Kwantung Territory Government established in its place. The Kwantung Territory Government had jurisdiction over a leased territory known as Guandong (usually known as Kwantung, in Japanese, *Kantō*), located on the south-western tip of the Liaodong Peninsula. It also functioned as the office for policing the Manchurian Railway. The head of the Kwantung Territory Government was the chief of the Kwantung Territory Government. The chief of the Kwantung Territory Government was a civil service employee who, according to regulations, was under the supervision of the foreign minister when it came to negotiations. At the same time, the military division that belonged to the former Resident Generals Office of Kwantung was turned into the independent Kwantung Army, headquartered in the city of Lushun.

2. THE RUSSO-JAPANESE WAR, WORLD WAR I AND THE WASHINGTON NAVAL CONFERENCE

What this meant was that, alongside the various consulates general and the South Manchuria Railway Company, there was now the Kwantung Territory Government and the Kwantung Army, turning Japanese governance in Manchuria into a four-pronged political structure. Long gone were the days when Japanese diplomacy in the region was based only on the Ministry of Foreign Affairs.

In such a situation, it was inevitable that Shidehara would want the Ministry of Foreign Affairs to enjoy greater power. Yet Shidehara rarely expressed these views in public directly. Shidehara's measured stance became all the more conspicuous when contrasted with that of Katō Takaaki, who, although occupying a different position within the government, frequently argued for the centralisation of diplomacy.

Previously, Katō had taken up his first cabinet posting as foreign minister in the fourth Itō cabinet, in which he argued forcefully for a hard line against Russia. Later, in the first Saionji cabinet, Katō would clash with the military over policy in Manchuria and quit his post as foreign minister. When he again became foreign minister in the third Katsura cabinet, he made centralisation of diplomatic power his condition for accepting the post. Further, as foreign minister in the second Ōkuma cabinet, Katō antagonised the *genrō* by blocking their access to confidential documents. Katō also refused to participate in the Extraordinary Foreign Diplomacy Investigation Committee, on the grounds that it went against his principle of diplomatic centralisation. Katō also worked vigorously towards the realisation of one more dream: the establishment of a two-party system.[106]

Before long, Shidehara and Katō's respective directions would overlap. The occasion was Katō's establishment, in 1924, of the three-party coalition cabinet of constitutional protection (Goken Sanpa), which he led as prime minister. Shidehara would become foreign minister in Katō's cabinet, although Shidehara had never sought to use Katō for his own gain. However, while Katō did attempt to promote the centralisation of diplomatic power within the government, his record as foreign minister was poor. Indeed, it was stained by the debacle of the Twenty-One Demands of 1915. For that reason alone, Katō would leave diplomatic matters to Shidehara once he assumed the position of prime minister. Assuming this new position, Shidehara would surely have been conscious of the difficult experiences his brother-in-law had undergone before him.

Compared to Katō, Shidehara's record as foreign minister was faultless. He was able to assist not only Ishii Kikujirō, Terauchi Masatake, Gotō Shinpei and Hara Takashi but also the group of individual personalities that was the *genrō*. Conversely, it is hard to avoid the conclusion that his time in office was somewhat unremarkable. Yet there was a reason for this. Simply put, the times were changing. With the gradual establishment of various diplomatic organisations and systems, alongside the emergence of truly party-led cabinets, what the Ministry of Foreign Affairs most needed was skilled officials. It was no longer the age of heroic diplomatic figures, as in the days of Mutsu Munemitsu or Komura Jutarō.

That said, skilled officials can still be particular when it comes to their acquaintances. Shidehara was fortunate to have his connection with Hara Takashi. When the Hara cabinet sought to scale back the excessive aid that had thus far been given to the Chinese warlord Duan Qirui (1865–1936), Shidehara lent his support. At the beginning, Hara and Shidehara's relationship was not exactly amicable. When Shidehara initially assumed the position of vice-minister for foreign affairs, Hara and Yamagata suspected him of being aligned with their rival, Katō Takaaki. Yet Hara found himself gradually trusting Shidehara more over time. Shidehara's selection as ambassador to the US reflected the seriousness with which Hara viewed Japan's relationship with that nation.[107]

The Washington Naval Conference

Japan's Embassy in the US

In modern terms, the elite diplomats of Japan's Ministry of Foreign Affairs can hope for no higher career achievement than to be assigned ambassador to the US, following a stint as vice-minister. In other words, the situation has hardly changed since the prewar era. Of course, in Shidehara's day, it was also possible for a government official to advance one step further and take on the position of foreign minister. At that point there were only six Japanese embassies around the world—in the UK, France, Russia, Italy, the US and Germany. The diplomatic establishments in places such as Belgium, the Netherlands and China were only legations.

2. THE RUSSO-JAPANESE WAR, WORLD WAR I AND THE WASHINGTON NAVAL CONFERENCE

Of the overseas diplomatic establishments of the earlier Meiji era, the most important would surely have been the British legation. Famous ministers to the UK included figures such as Katō Takaaki and Hayashi Tadasu. However, past ministers to the US were by no means inferior. Beginning with Mori Arinori (1847–1889), these distinguished individuals include Yoshida Kiyonari (1845–1891), Terashima Munenori (1832–1893), Mutsu Munemitsu, Hoshi Tōru (1850–1901), Komura Jutarō and Takahira Kogorō (1854–1926). At the end of the Meiji era, the legation was upgraded to an embassy, with Aoki Shūzō (1844–1914), Uchida Yasuya, Chinda Sutemi, Satō Aimaro (1857–1934) and Ishii Kikujirō successively serving as ambassador to the US. After Ishii left the post, embassy counsellor Debuchi Katsuji served as chargé d'affaires starting June 1919. In November of the same year, Shidehara would arrive in the US to fill the position. He was then 47 years old.

Just after Shidehara became ambassador, the US Congress made an unexpected decision. The Senate rejected the Treaty of Versailles. There was already a degree of conflict between Japan and the US surrounding the issue of Yap Island, which the League of Nations had decreed was now Japan's mandated territory, and it was feared that further fallout might result from the rejection of the treaty.[108] Yap Island is one of the western Caroline Islands, an island group located in the Western Pacific Ocean. It is also close to Guam, which was already US territory at that time. Previously, Yap Island was under the control of Germany, but Japan had occupied it by force in 1914, during World War I.

From the time when Debuchi transferred to the position of counsellor at the embassy in Germany, until the arrival of Furuya Shigetsuna in April 1920, the embassy in the US had no counsellor. Assisting Shidehara was First Secretary Saburi Sadao and Hirota Kōki. During this period Shidehara had to place his complete trust in Saburi. However, Saburi was still a young diplomat, and his reputation was poor. Though he possessed a keen intellect, Saburi was known to be so faithful to his duties that he came across as somewhat aloof. It would take time before Shidehara was able to speak with him frankly. By contrast, Hirota was a popular figure among other young diplomats, such as Third Secretary Ishii Itarō. Although Hirota was Saburi's junior by a year, there was something philosophical about his thinking, and he seemed to hold great promise.[109]

Other staff at the embassy included Third Secretary Shiratori Toshio (1887–1949) and probationary diplomats Ōhashi Chūichi and Morishima Morito. Ōhashi and Morishima disapproved of Shidehara, finding his instructions to his subordinates insufficient. However, Shidehara paid this no notice. To him, such complaints were only a reflection of overreliance upon others due to a lack of independence. What Shidehara wanted was talented subordinates such as Saburi who would faithfully carry out his commands. The military attaché to the embassy was Major General Inoue Kazutsugu. The naval attaché was Lieutenant Colonel Ueda Yoshitake, who was later succeeded by Colonel Nagano Osami (1880–1947). Lieutenant Commander Yamamoto Isoroku (1884–1943) was also in the US at that time, and Shidehara had already formed the opinion that he was an able individual.[110]

The Siberian Intervention Force and the Yap Island Problem

Many of the diplomatic problems facing Shidehara were inherited as part of the legacy of World War I. The most troublesome of these was the Siberian Intervention force. Although the Hara cabinet expressed a sincere intention to reduce the number of Japanese troops in Siberia, the Wilson administration remained suspicious of Japan.

In early January 1920, Japan was suddenly informed that American troops would be removed. Although the deployment of troops to Siberia was a joint US–Japan undertaking in name only, for Shidehara this sudden withdrawal amounted to a humiliation. First, the US announcement was made without prior consultation with Japan. Second, the announcement was directly relayed from the expeditionary force commander, William S. Graves, to the Japanese commander of the Vladivostok expeditionary force, General Ōi Shigemoto, bypassing Shidehara altogether.

The astonished Shidehara expressed his outrage at Lansing, writing:

> On what possible basis can the U.S. government decide upon the withdrawal of military forces and railway engineers and simply report this decision without any prior negotiation with the Japanese government?[111]

However, the withdrawal was a fait accompli. For the rest of his life, Shidehara was unable to set aside the memories of this humiliating event. It constituted the largest blemish upon his record as ambassador to the US.

It must be added that the Wilson administration was not united on the decision to withdraw from Siberia. Numerous officials supported a continuation of the expeditionary force. The central figure in this camp was the chief of the State Department's Division of Russian Affairs, Clinton Poole. Secretary of State Lansing was also of a similar mind. It should also be noted that Poole had a good relationship with the chief of the Division of Far Eastern Affairs, John MacMurray. However, as Poole himself explained, he did not call for the continuation of the expeditionary force in order to foster a harmonious relationship with Japan. Rather, Poole had previous experience in Russia and, as an anti-Bolshevik, he was concerned about the devastation taking place in the country. There is no evidence that Shidehara had properly understood this tendency among the Americans and used it to build a cooperative relationship.[112]

The legacy of World War I with respect to relations between Japan and the US extended beyond the issue of the Siberian Intervention force. When Japan entered World War I, it captured the German stronghold in Qingdao, effectively taking over Germany's interests on the Shandong Peninsula. Moreover, the territory occupied by Japan during the war was not limited to the Shandong Peninsula. Japan also took control of the South Sea Islands, a region of far more importance in relations with the US.[113] During the war, the Japanese navy occupied the Mariana Islands, the Caroline Islands, and the Marshall Islands (previously German territory), placing them under military administration. These South Sea Islands were turned into a mandated territory under Japanese control as a result of the Paris Peace Conference.

There were a number of mandated territories following World War I. This term referred to those former German and Ottoman territories that were governed by other nations under the mandate of the League of Nations. The form of governance to be deployed in these territories was categorised into Class A, Class B and Class C according to factors such as geographical location, economic status and living standards. Former Ottoman territories in the Middle East were categorised as Class A. Former German territories in East Africa and Central Africa were categorised as Class B. Former German territories in South-West Africa and the Pacific were categorised as Class C. Class A governance meant that the mandatory power had only limited authority. Class C, however, was more like outright annexation.

Of the Class C territories, the formerly German-controlled South Sea Islands that were north of the equator were entrusted to Japan, which had already placed them under military administration. There was one more Class C territory on the western edge of the Caroline Islands (located in the Western Pacific): the small island of Yap. The US was not pleased with Japan becoming the mandatory power for Yap Island. This is because it was in a critical area for the laying of submarine cables.[114]

Just before Shidehara left Japan for the US, he asked that the Japanese navy undertake a survey of the prescribed rights of foreigners in the South Sea Island, former German territories. After Shidehara left for his new posting as ambassador, the Special Micronesia Defense Corps completed the survey of the South Sea Islands.[115] Meanwhile, the US maintained that the Yap Island submarine cables should be placed under international administration. Shidehara would engage Undersecretary of State Norman Davis in a heated debate on this topic on 8 October 1920. There was also a Preliminary International Conference on Electrical Communications held in Washington, with Davis appointed as chairman. Shidehara was in attendance, along with Saburi. There the US attempted to have Yap Island removed from Japan's mandated territories. In February 1921, Secretary of State Bainbridge Colby (1869–1950) submitted a letter of protest to the Council of the League of Nations.[116]

In March 1921, Warren G. Harding was inaugurated as president of the US. His was the first Republican administration in eight years. The secretary of state was Charles Evans Hughes (1862–1948). The Harding administration was also reluctant to acknowledge Japan's mandate over Yap Island. Some form of resolution was necessary. It is here that Shidehara suggested a course of action to Foreign Minister Uchida. Shidehara's idea was for Japan to offer a proposal to the US; if it acquiesced to Japan's mandate over Yap Island, then Japan would open up submarine cable unloading and management to the other world powers. Upon hearing of this offer, Secretary of State Hughes, who had until then strongly opposed Japan's rights over the island, began to search for points of compromise.[117] After further negotiation, Shidehara and Hughes were finally able to conclude an agreement that included Japan's Yap Island mandate. The agreement was signed on 11 February 1922. In exchange for recognising Japan's mandate, the US received permission from Japan to unload and operate the submarine cable connecting Yap and Guam, as well as any future cables that would connect to Yap.[118]

During this period, Shidehara was visiting the State Department practically every day, which eventually took a toll on his health. He was initially diagnosed with kidney inflammation, but it turned out to be a kidney stone. When the Washington Naval Conference began in November 1921, Shidehara was largely confined to bed. The following year, when he became acting prime minister for a period during the Hamaguchi cabinet, he was still suffering badly from the condition. In any case, Japan abolished military administration on the South Sea Islands and, in April 1922, established the Government Office of the South Sea Islands (Nanyōcho), located on Koro Island, part of the Palau Island group, located on the western edge of the Caroline Islands. Branch offices were set up in six locations, including Yap and Saipan.[119] The South Sea Islands remained under Japanese administration until the end of the Pacific War, after which they became entrusted to the United Nations, which in turn delegated their administration to the US.

The Anti-Japanese Immigration Issue

Along with the Siberian Intervention force and the mandate of Yap Island, there was also the serious issue of the movement in the US to block Japanese immigration. Shidehara had to grapple with this problem once he became ambassador to the US during the Wilson administration. Shidehara was well versed in the immigration issue due to his past experience as embassy counsellor, where he lent support to the talks held in 1913 between Chinda Sutemi and William Jennings Bryan. First, Shidehara informed the US that Japan was voluntarily prohibiting its women from immigrating to the US to be brides in prearranged 'picture marriages'—a practice that inflamed anti-immigration sentiment among Americans. Then, in February 1920, Japanese labourers held a large-scale strike at a sugar cane farm in Hawaii. Here, too, Shidehara took the conciliatory move of informing Undersecretary of State Frank Lyon Polk that he had instructed the consul general to 'do all he could to restore order'.[120]

Despite Shidehara's best efforts, the state of California was moving towards the enactment of a Second Alien Land Law that would prohibit people of Japanese ethnicity from leasing land. Further, there was little hope that US Secretary of State Bainbridge Colby would offer any measures to counter this development. This was because Colby had only just taken over from Lansing in March 1920. It was at this time that Roland S.

Morris returned from his term as ambassador to Japan and was able to assist in resolving the issue. With the commencement of negotiations surrounding the immigration issue, which were suggested by the US, talks between Shidehara and Morris began to reveal a potential way forward.[121]

Shidehara and Morris began their series of talks in September 1920. By January 1921 they had met 23 times. Shidehara's position was that there should be a reform of the gentlemen's agreement between Japan and the US, so that anti-Japanese movements in the US could be mitigated. Because the talks with Morris were unofficial, Shidehara's role was all the larger. A difficult event that occurred in the middle of their discussions was the passing of the Second Alien Land Law in California. Despite this discouraging development, Shidehara persisted, continuing the negotiations with Morris until a new treaty draft was prepared. Yet progress on this front was foiled by a transition in the US government to the Harding administration, which was not willing to move forward with the treaty draft.[122]

Following his return to the US, Morris became the first honorary president of the America–Japan Society, which had been founded during World War I. Shidehara's name was also formally recorded as one of the people who initially proposed this society. Morris would later invite Shidehara to attend some of the lectures that he gave in the US. With Shidehara in the audience, Morris stated: 'There are no questions between Japan and the United States which, if approached in a generous spirit of confidence and candor, are not susceptible to a just and honorable solution'.[123]

Concerns Surrounding the Crown Prince's Visit to the US

During Shidehara's repeated talks with Morris, Prime Minister Hara Takashi was holding his own discussions in Tokyo with Yamagata Aritomo, the *genrō*. Their topic was the possibility that Crown Prince Hirohito Shinno might travel abroad. Hara and Foreign Minister Uchida supported the idea of the crown prince visiting not only Europe but also the US.[124]

Shidehara, however, was extremely apprehensive about this idea. Shidehara remembered what happened to Edward, the Prince of Wales (later King Edward VIII). When Edward had visited the US two years earlier, the trip had exhausted him, in part because of the 'bad manners' of the Americans. Given this concern, Shidehara wrote to Uchida:

> Even if His Highness, our crown prince, were to come to the U.S., because the state of our nations is so different, the crown prince would be placed in a position of having no option but to endure not only physical discomfort but also the rudeness of the ordinary people. For example, even if people of no standing approach His Highness and address him in a familiar manner, then His Highness is placed in a position in which he must nevertheless give an appropriate response, without which he may unavoidably give the impression of being rude.[125]

In other words, Shidehara felt that the national conditions of the US were simply too different, given that the country had nothing comparable to Japan's imperial household. Amplifying this sense of unease was the press reporting. Previously, Shidehara had personally witnessed a reporter disrespectfully asking Prince Edward directly for a copy of his prepared speech. At this already delicate time in US–Japan relations, it was not impossible for things to develop in unforeseen ways as a result of Japan's press reporting. Shidehara's warnings were heeded, and the crown prince's overseas trip was confined to Europe. While the Hara cabinet refused the invitation from the US president, they were able to settle the matter by having the Taishō emperor send a personal telegram.

The Washington Naval Conference

From November 1921 to February 1922, the Harding administration sponsored an international naval conference in Washington. Representatives from nine nations attended, including the UK, France, Italy, Japan, China and the US itself. The main topics of the Washington Naval Conference were naval restrictions and the situation in the Far East and the Pacific. Discussion of these issues led to the forming of three major treaties: Five-Power Treaty, Nine-Power Treaty and Four-Power Treaty.

Japan's chief delegate for the naval restrictions negotiations was Navy Minister Katō Tomosaburō (1861–1923). At the beginning of the conference, Secretary of State Hughes made the bold proposal that naval construction be prohibited for a 10-year period, with capital ship inventory between the US, the UK and Japan maintained at a ratio of 5:5:3. The originality of Hughes's proposal meant that it was received as a 'bombshell'. Some in the Japanese navy staunchly opposed it, such as Vice Admiral Katō Hiroharu (1870–1939), who sought a 70 per cent ratio vis-à-vis the US. However, Katō Tomosaburō accepted a 60 per cent ratio, taking into consideration the burden of naval expenditures as well as the fostering of a cooperative relationship with the US.

In February 1922, Japan, the US, the UK, France and Italy signed the Five-Power Treaty, which restricted navy armaments. In exchange, Katō Tomosaburō, as noted in Article 19 of the Five-Power Treaty, had the US admit that it would not construct any fortresses or naval bases on Pacific islands. However, as there were no armament restrictions on auxiliary vessels, it was not long before the world powers once more entered a warship-building race with respect to these smaller ships.

Shidehara's involvement in the Washington Naval Conference was primarily focused on discussions surrounding the 'Far East problem' and the 'Pacific problem'. Here, the 'Far East problem' referred to issues of international order relating to China and the interests in Shandong. The 'Pacific problem', meanwhile, concerned the continuation or termination of the Anglo-Japanese Alliance. To help deal with the related negotiations, Vice-Minister Hanihara Masanao and American and European Bureau Director-General Matsudaira Tsuneo were sent to Washington from the Ministry of Foreign Affairs in Tokyo. Hanihara, in particular, was invested with plenipotentiary and would in fact later become Shidehara's successor as ambassador to the US. Hiroshi Saitō (who Shidehara had referred to as a 'master of English') and Shiratori Toshio also attended.[126]

The Japanese government's underlying position was that they did not wish to have a debate on the Pacific or Far East problems. Shidehara's advice, however, was the opposite. According to Shidehara, because Secretary of State Hughes was not knowledgeable about the Pacific or Fast East problems, it would be advantageous for 'Japan, which has interests of vital importance at stake, to make the first move in setting the agenda for discussion'.[127] This difference in enthusiasm between Shidehara and Tokyo would be most visible with respect to discussions surrounding the termination of the Anglo-Japanese Alliance.

With respect to the Far East problem, in February 1922, the Nine-Power Treaty concerning China was signed at the Washington Naval Conference. It was criticised at the time for lacking any provisions for punishment in the event of non-compliance. However, what is probably even more important was the manner in which the open door policy clause was interpreted. The term 'open door' is quite ambiguous. In the open door policy notes issued by Secretary of State John Hay, there are two main types of open door policy. In the first open door policy note, dating to September 1899, Hay sought equality of opportunity in the sphere of commerce. On the other hand, in the second open door policy note of July 1900, Hay stipulated the territorial and governmental integrity of China.[128] Secretary of State Hughes also emphasised the importance of the open door policy as a basic principle.[129]

So, what did an open door policy mean for Shidehara? As his writing indicates, here too Shidehara was influenced by Denison. In the past, when Denison was drafting the First Anglo-Japanese Alliance at the instructions of Foreign Minister Komura, he 'avoided the ambiguous terminology of having an "open door"'. Instead, the preamble included the words: 'in securing equal opportunities in those countries for the commerce and industry of all nations'. This was the first time that the term 'equal opportunities' was used in a convention. Later, in the preamble to the Second Anglo-Japanese Alliance, Denison referred to 'the principle of equal opportunities for the commerce and industry of all nations in China'. The same term also made an appearance in the preamble of the Third Anglo-Japanese Alliance, as well as in Article 3 of the Treaty of Portsmouth. Shidehara also understood the 'principle of equal treatment' that appears in the Franco-Japanese Treaty of 1907 as being the same concept.[130]

Based on the above, we can assume that Shidehara understood the concept of an 'open door' policy as meaning the embracing of equality of opportunity—in other words, the sense shown in the first policy note issued by Hay. Further, given that the open door principle was also included in the terms of the Anglo-Japanese Alliance and the Franco-Japanese Treaty, it could hardly be regarded as an ideal that was unique to US diplomacy.

In the case of the Nine-Power Treaty, however, the first item utilises the term 'open door' in a sense that is closer to the second policy note issued by Hay: '[Signatories agree to] respect the sovereignty, the independence, and the territorial and administrative integrity of China'. Meanwhile, the third article of the same treaty uses this term in a sense closer to Hay's first policy note: 'With a view to applying more effectually the principles of the Open Door or equality of opportunity in China for the trade and industry of all nations'. Of these two sections of the treaty, it was the third article that Shidehara regarded as important. As he understood it, equality of opportunity was needed with respect to 'economic development' on the Chinese continent.[131] To put it another way, Shidehara was not inclined to interpret the open door clause in the sense of the second note, which would mean respecting China's territorial and governmental integrity.

Of course, this did not necessarily mean that he rejected the principle of China's territorial and governmental integrity. It was rather that, for Shidehara, the reality of the situation on the continent meant that this was not a useful guiding principle for diplomatic activity. One example of how Shidehara perceived this diplomatic reality was the discussion during the Washington Naval Conference of the international administration of the Chinese Eastern Railway, which was located in Manchuria. From the time of the Siberian Intervention, the Chinese Eastern Railway had been managed by the combined international efforts of nations including Japan, the US, the UK and France. At the Washington Naval Conference, the US wished to reinforce this state of affairs. Although Shidehara was initially inclined to agree to the international administration of the Chinese Eastern Railway, led by the US, he was later swayed by Foreign Minister Uchida's more cautious thinking and eventually rejected the proposal.

Even when Hughes attempted to establish an international investigative body that would look into open door principles, Shidehara ensured that it would be toothless. Shidehara was particularly opposed to any US political involvement in Manchuria. This attitude is also visible in the way in which, as foreign minister, he responded to the Sino-Soviet conflict in 1929. It appears that, in reality, Shidehara interpreted 'open door policy' in a narrow sense.[132]

Resolving the Shandong Issue—the US State Department's View of Japan

Of the various diplomatic issues regarding the Far East at that time, the most serious for Japan was the inheritance of the interests in Shandong Peninsula. During World War I, Japan seized Germany's interests on Shandong. Later, at the Paris Peace Conference, it succeeded in having its control of these interests recognised by other foreign powers. However, the Chinese representatives refused to sign the Treaty of Versailles, meaning that the issue of the interests in Shandong lingered and was later brought up at the Washington Naval Conference.

Shidehara was able to resolve the Shandong problem at the Washington Naval Conference, in part because he had worked to gain the support of figures such as John MacMurray, chief of the State Department's Division of Far Eastern Affairs. In a February 1922 treaty between Japan and China that concerned issues relating to Shandong, Japan redeemed the value of the railway assets through 15-year-term treasury bonds from China. The treaty also stipulated that during the redemption period for those bonds, the posts for chief of transportation and chief of accounting would both be filled by Japanese. Meanwhile, the local mines would be placed under joint Sino-Japanese management. Japan was largely satisfied with this compromise, in which, although it would eventually lose the Shandong railway to China, it would receive suitable repayment and, for the time being, the right to make appointments to the top management positions. In his memoirs, Shidehara wrote that 'China intended to make the [negotiations surrounding the] Shandong issue collapse'. However, he added that, with the intervention of the US and the UK, China 'saw that the situation was not developing in their favour, and hence completely changed their attitude'.[133]

Under Division of Far Eastern Affairs Chief MacMurray were two individuals responsible for China and Japan, respectively: Nelson Trusler Johnson and Edwin L. Neville. Johnson, who was highly knowledgeable about China, died suddenly in 1954. However, just before he died, he agreed to a lengthy interview about his experiences. In this interview, Johnson stated that, during the Washington Naval Conference, he felt that Japan, as well as the Anglo-Japanese Alliance, constituted a threat to US interests in the Far East.[134] Sympathy towards China was quite deeply rooted in the US State Department.

In that sense, Edward Thomas Williams (who would have been Johnson's senior if he were still at the State Department) was no exception. Following a long period of initially working in China, Williams went on to enter the Division of Far Eastern Affairs in 1913, where he remained for five years. In 1918, he became a professor at the University of California, Berkeley, and went on to write numerous books on China's foreign relations. During the Paris Peace Conference, Williams attended as an adviser on Far East issues and was also a State Department adviser at the Washington Naval Conference. For this reason, he was in a position to offer counsel to Secretary of State Hughes during the naval conference on matters such as Shandong. Williams was even capable of offering detailed opinions to MacMurray, the Division of Far Eastern Affairs chief, on topics such as the provision on Chinese tariff treaties.[135]

Though he now lived in Washington, Williams, who was fluent in Chinese, had near-daily conversations with Shi Zhaoji (Alfred Sao-ke Sze) (1877–1958), China's ambassador to the US. Shi would also confide in Williams and, on occasion, would privately show him telegrams sent to him from the government in Beijing. The two even went for drives together. Williams also tried to get MacMurray to inform him about Shidehara's diplomatic movements. Meanwhile, Williams was very suspicious of Saburi, who was effectively Shidehara's right-hand man. By this point, Saburi had already risen up the ranks to become embassy counsellor. Regarding the matter of Shandong, Williams also consulted thoroughly with Stanley K. Hornbeck, an old acquaintance and a member of the State Department's Division of Far Eastern Affairs.

Reflecting on his experiences with the Paris Peace Conference, Shidehara came to distrust Williams even more. He wrote:

> While occupying the post of advisor to the U.S. committee during the Paris Peace Conference, Williams would continually offer advice to the Chinese committee. Even worse, he would take actions in direct opposition to Japan. It is an undeniable fact that the extreme complications that emerged regarding negotiations involving China stemmed from the actions of Williams and his sympathizers.[136]

Meanwhile, from Williams's perspective, MacMurray's proposed solution for Shandong was too conciliatory. The thought of Japan being left with a foothold on the Shandong Peninsula kept Williams up at night. Instead of sleeping, he would type letters to MacMurray and Hughes, calling for a different course of action. Further, when topics came up on the agenda such as how to deal with the foreign troops stationed in China, or whether foreign post offices in China would continue to be permitted, here too Williams would show concern over Japan's movements.[137]

Finally, at the fifth general meeting on 1 February 1922, it was decided that foreign troops not stationed as part of a treaty needed to be withdrawn, and that foreign post offices had to be abolished. The Nine-Power Treaty was signed five days later. With respect to important matters such as Japan's interests in Shandong, there is little evidence that Williams's suggestions were adopted.[138] However, Williams's sympathy towards China was passed on to Johnson and Hornbeck. Given that both individuals would go on to become chief of the Division of Far Eastern Affairs, it can be said that pro-Chinese officials in the State Department held more sway than pro-Japanese ones. From the perspective of the pro-Chinese faction, it could hardly be said that a Japanese–American cooperative framework had been established at the Washington Naval Conference.

The Four-Power Treaty and the Termination of the Anglo-Japanese Alliance

At around this time, in December 1921, the Four-Power Treaty was concluded at the Washington Naval Conference. The signatories of the Four-Power Treaty promised to maintain the status quo in the Pacific, and its ratification simultaneously led to the termination of the Anglo-Japanese Alliance. Shidehara also played a decisive role in this development. The Third Anglo-Japanese Alliance, signed in 1911, was valid for 10 years. Opinion had been divided within the British Empire as to whether the alliance ought to be renewed. While Australia and New Zealand hoped to defend against any possible future invasion by keeping Japan within the alliance, nations such as Canada and South Africa saw the alliance as a hindrance to cooperative relations between the UK and the US. In the end, the Anglo-Japanese Alliance was ended as a result of the conclusion of the Four-Power Treaty at the Washington Naval Conference. The formation of the Four-Power Treaty and the formal termination of the alliance took place in three stages, outlined below.

The first stage was the drafting of a proposal by the UK's chief delegate, Arthur James Balfour. Balfour, who was prime minister at the time of the signing of the Second Anglo-Japanese Alliance, had also served as navy minister and foreign secretary. His proposal was the formation of a triple entente that would include the US as a third nation. With the Balfour proposal, care was taken to gain the approval of the US, while at the same time preserving the freedom for Japan and the UK to restore a military alliance in the future. In effect, therefore, the proposal amounted to an attempt to maintain the Anglo-Japanese Alliance. Balfour went on to present this proposal to Katō and Hanihara.

The next stage was a counterproposal by Shidehara. Referring to Balfour's proposal, he made significant revisions in order to make it more palatable to the US. A distinguishing feature of Shidehara's proposal was that it specified that the triple entente would take the place of the Anglo-Japanese Alliance altogether. In other words, it watered down the effective continuation of the alliance that was contained in Balfour's proposal. Shidehara also took the step of presenting this proposal to Balfour without first receiving instructions from Tokyo. Once Balfour had made his own adjustments, Shidehara personally delivered the revised proposal to Hughes.

The third stage was Hughes's own proposal. Having received the revised proposal from Shidehara, he proposed the inclusion of France. With China excluded, this meant a treaty that would be adopted between four powers.[139] The resulting Four-Power Treaty was signed on 13 December 1921. Article 4 of the treaty explicitly abolished the Anglo-Japanese Alliance.

Shidehara's solution with respect to this treaty has received occasional criticism. Some have argued that Shidehara made a mistake in judgement and that it should have been possible to avoid abolishing the Anglo-Japanese Alliance.[140] Certainly, if we look back over Japanese government policy at that period, we can see that it merely *accepted* the termination of the alliance only when the UK were to advance such a proposal. However, the Japanese government's preference was to maintain the alliance if possible. In contrast to the detailed instructions that were issued with respect to the Far East problem, Tokyo's policy on the continuation or termination of the Anglo-Japanese Alliance was fluid.[141]

For this reason, Shidehara had more room than usual to exercise discretion. But, in that case, was there a chance that the Anglo-Japanese Alliance could have been saved? If there was such a possibility, it would have been through Balfour's proposed triple entente between Japan, the UK and the US. Shidehara himself has emphasised that there were problems with communication concerning Balfour's proposal. That is to say, when Balfour suggested to Hughes that the three nations form an entente, Shidehara said, 'I was indisposed due to illness and was completely unaware that this had happened'.[142] It was actually Saburi who received word of the proposal from the US State Department.

When Shidehara then dispatched Saburi to speak with Balfour, it emerged that Balfour had already sounded out Plenipotentiary Tokugawa Iesato (1863–1940) with respect to the proposal. Yet, given that issues concerning the Pacific and the Far East—including the Anglo-Japanese Alliance—

were being managed by Shidehara, Tokugawa felt that Balfour needed to negotiate directly with Shidehara. The situation was complicated by the fact that the UK's secretary-general, Maurice Hankey, actually forgot to hand over the full text of the triple entente.[143]

However, while this is how Shidehara recollected the events of this period, the fact is that, as noted above, Balfour did directly submit his proposal to Katō and Hanihara. That means that Shidehara's claims of communication problems are somewhat exaggerated. What was more decisive for the eventual outcome were Shidehara's true intentions when he rewrote Balfour's initial proposal.

In Shidehara's recollections, he stated that, in Balfour's proposal, 'the triple entente between Japan, the U.K., and the U.S. was close to an alliance, being understood as though it existed for the purpose of creating a political confederation'. For this reason, Shidehara surmised that the US would not accept it, given its traditional reticence towards forming alliances. Further, Shidehara interpreted the instructions he received from Foreign Minister Uchida as indicating that 'if Japan were to press strongly for the continuation of the alliance, then it may end up simply troubling the British government; it might be fruitless, yet also undignified'.[144]

Following this understanding, Shidehara:

> Removed the provisions concerning the creation of a type of political confederation similar to an alliance from the triple entente proposal by the British chief delegate, and created a provision that stipulated the holding of conferences between the signatory nations whenever the need arose. What [I] created was a new proposal that replaced a treaty of alliance with something that more closely resembled a consultative pact.[145]

Although Shidehara was confined to his bed due to his sickness, he had this proposal shown to Balfour, who agreed to the basic approach before making his own revisions. Once Saburi showed this revised proposal to Hughes, Hughes argued that France should also be included in the pact.

Hughes invited Balfour, Shidehara and the French chief delegate to his private residence, where he showed them his revised proposal, along with an added preamble and a clause stating when it would come into effect. Due to circumstances such as the details of this proposal having been leaked to the Jiji Shinposha Shimbun newspaper company, the Four-Power Treaty would be quickly signed by the participating nations.

The French chief delegate, however, became flustered as a result of this haste. Because approval from his home government did not arrive in time for the signing ceremony, he had to put off adding his own signature until a later date. This was perceived as a slight to France's pride as a major power. According to Shidehara, Hughes added France to the treaty because he wished to exploit Americans' affinity with France; this feeling had been fostered with French General Ferdinand Foch's visit to the US.[146]

If the intention was to prioritise the easing of tensions between the US and Japan, then Shidehara's approach was not mistaken. And, indeed, this was exactly what Shidehara hoped for. Hughes had been on edge at the idea of a renewal of the Anglo-Japanese Alliance. And even the UK, if it came to a standoff between Japan and the US, would have been highly unlikely to have sided with Japan. Given this reality, the potential for continuing the Anglo-Japanese Alliance remained limited.[147]

Honest Diplomacy — Tranquil Public Relations

Yet, we might ask, would an ambassador of lesser talents have come to the conclusion that the US would not readily agree to a proposal that included the effective continuation of the Anglo-Japanese Alliance? In fact, I suggest, what we should focus on regarding the above process is what it tells us about Shidehara's diplomatic technique. It can be argued that Shidehara had a tendency to look too far ahead, due to the importance with which he viewed Japan's relationship with the US. When Shidehara made his alterations to the proposal, was he not actually putting into practice the method of 'honest diplomacy' as the first principle in building a relationship of trust? To put it differently, I suggest that Shidehara sought to anticipate the possible US reaction to such a degree that he ended up proposing something that was already a compromise. Supporting this interpretation are the memoirs of Ishii Itarō. According to Ishii, 'Shidehara's conviction was that the most important thing needed for diplomacy is sincerity'.[148]

In general, the art of diplomatic negotiation cannot simply be to proceed according to your anticipation of what another nation wants. There are also times when it is necessary to take the opposite tack, to argue from a position that is initially removed from a point of possible compromise. This is something that Shidehara should have learned from the experience that Denison shared with him concerning the start of the Russo-Japanese War. Apparently, a degree of cunning was a part of Denison's legacy that

2. THE RUSSO-JAPANESE WAR, WORLD WAR I AND THE WASHINGTON NAVAL CONFERENCE

Shidehara did not attempt to emulate. This is why the Four-Power Treaty was agreed upon so hastily. Even if the Anglo-Japanese Alliance was to be abolished, it should have been possible to do so using a different approach. By giving the impression, for example, that it was foreign pressure from the US that caused the end of the alliance, it may have been possible to instil in the minds of the citizenry that Japan and the UK were natural allies. Yet Shidehara decided not to take this route.

In any case, some noteworthy developments also occurred later regarding the Washington Naval Conference. First, Japan's diplomatic telegrams were decoded by the US. This fact was not revealed until 10 years after the conference, in 1931. In later years Shidehara would recall, 'I could not quite help smiling in satisfaction at the idea that because of the stolen codes, the U.S. must have taken Shidehara to be an unimaginative, honest man'.[149] Although Shidehara felt a degree of bitterness regarding this development, it was certainly true that he had faith in the importance of honest diplomacy.

Thus, the Anglo-Japanese Alliance, once the cornerstone of Japanese diplomacy, finally came to an end. At this time, Foreign Minister Uchida confessed that he was 'strongly missing the Anglo-Japanese Alliance and reminiscing about the past'.[150] It was not only the Japanese who regretted the termination of the alliance. Along with Balfour, UK Ambassador to Japan Charles N. E. Eliot, also deplored the alliance's passing. Meanwhile, George Sansom, then a commercial counsellor at the British embassy in Japan, later asserted that if the alliance had continued, Japan may well have avoided heading down the extreme path it took in subsequent decades. However, not everybody was displeased with this outcome. For one thing, it is true that for some time the UK's Foreign Office had many criticisms of the Anglo-Japanese Alliance.[151]

On the other hand, in the case of the US, a very interesting comment was made by Eugene H. Dooman, first secretary at the US embassy in Japan. Dooman expressed doubt as to whether, 'if the United States had not brought about the abrogation of the Anglo-Japanese Alliance, the character and temperament of the Japanese would have been what it was'. For Dooman, the Japanese 'resented very much the action of Great Britain in surrendering to American pressure in bringing that alliance to an end'.[152] This episode suggests that ending an alliance is more challenging than establishing one.

Yet, regardless of whether it was a necessary, a positive or a negative outcome, the Anglo-Japanese Alliance was abolished when the Four-Power Treaty was formed. It should also be noted that Shidehara was successful in excluding the Japanese home islands from the scope of the new treaty. The reason for this exclusion was that the Japanese citizenry broadly felt that applying the treaty to Japan itself would be a national disgrace. Therefore, following the receipt of new orders after the signing of the Four-Power Treaty, Shidehara drafted and received approval for an additional agreement to be attached to the original, which outlined the exception with respect to the Japanese home islands.[153]

The honest diplomacy that Shidehara envisioned would also appear in material read by the general public. Starting from his time as vice-minister for foreign affairs, Shidehara kept his distance from newspapers. According to Baba Tsunego, a journalist for the *Kokumin Shimbun*, 'even if [Shidehara] would sometimes meet with [the press], he would only answer one question in 10 posed to him by the newspaper reporters'. However, 'whenever he answered a question with a straight 'yes' or 'no', he would never lie'.[154]

This was not to say that Shidehara was entirely uninterested in communicating with the public. Meanwhile, a turning point in public relations and Japanese diplomacy took place during the Paris Peace Conference. Despite the fact that Japan had taken over Germany's former interests at the conference, a commonly expressed view was that Japan had lost to China in advertising. This negative experience was a major motive behind the eventual formal establishment, in 1921, of the Intelligence Department inside the head office of Japan's Ministry of Foreign Affairs. According to Ishii Kikujirō, however, 'if you try to look back at what kind of results the Intelligence Department actually achieved, there is nothing in particular that catches the eye'.[155]

In fact, while serving as ambassador to the US, Shidehara had established his own Intelligence Department within the embassy, in the period before the Washington Naval Conference. Shidehara also invited Frederick Moore to assist as adviser for public relations. Moore was recommended to Shidehara by Hiroshi Saitō.[156] Meanwhile, the press unit was also established at the time of the Naval Conference, and Counsellor Debuchi was dispatched from Germany to head the public relations section. From the beginning, Debuchi would be a plenipotentiary attendant, and Moore also later received this status. Shidehara himself once asserted to a Washington newspaper reporter—while referring to Article 4 of the Anglo-Japanese Alliance—that 'it is next to impossible that Japan and the U.K. would assist the other in a joint strategy if their opponent was the United States'.[157] On another occasion he explained Japan's position in a magazine owned by the *New York Times*. Shidehara also sought to foster a friendly relationship with Thomas William Lamont, who was US representative at the time of the New Four-Power Consortium.[158]

Nevertheless, Shidehara struggled when it came to dealing with Japanese newspapers. In his view, they were still far too underdeveloped and insincere compared to their counterparts in the UK and the US. He was particularly nervous when a draft proposal of the Four-Power Treaty was leaked to the *Jiji Shinpo*. In his memoirs, Shidehara asserted that the draft found its way into the hands of the papers' special correspondent, Itō Masanori. Although there was some suspicion that it was Plenipotentiary Tokugawa who shared the draft with the *Jiji Shinpo*, the truth of the matter was never revealed.[159]

Incidents such as the one above help cast light on how Shidehara understood public relations. For Shidehara, public relations did not constitute the axis of diplomacy. On the contrary, there was now so much propaganda being produced that it could only damage Japan's relationships with other nations. In his view, it was enough if Japan's true nature and intentions were 'correctly' conveyed. In other words, Japan needed to promote itself and its interests in a 'tranquil' manner. Even if China were content to pursue 'propaganda diplomacy', Japan should not follow suit. While Japan's subsequent efforts in creative public relations were more modest, Shidehara gradually came to appreciate their effectiveness.[160] Yet, he continued to believe that what was essential was not public relations but negotiations themselves and the relationships of trust upon which they relied. Any other approach, in Shidehara's opinion, was putting the cart before the horse.

Returning to Japan—the Great Kantō Earthquake

With the conclusion of the Washington Naval Conference, Shidehara returned to Japan for medical treatment in April 1922. Counsellor Saburi would serve as acting ambassador until February of the following year. Back in Japan, Shidehara spent his time in convalescence, reading and thought. Yet, this stay was interrupted by an unexpected disaster: the Great Kantō Earthquake of September 1923. Following the earthquake, a large amount of aid was sent to Japan from the US. Surprisingly, the US was concerned that the Japanese people might be insulted if they thought they were being treated as an object of charity. For this reason, banker Thomas W. Lamont, of J. P. Morgan & Co., reached out to Finance Minister Inoue Junnosuke (1869–1932) of the Yamamoto cabinet to impress upon the Japanese government that US aid to Japan was being given with no ulterior motive.[161]

On the day of the earthquake, Shidehara was in Osaka. In his reflections on this time, he stated that, while passing between Nagoya and Nagano on his way back to Tokyo, he helped some Koreans who were being harassed. Unfortunately, the residence that Shidehara had purchased in the Surugadai district, near central Tokyo, was lost in the fires that followed the earthquake. Most of the several thousand books from Denison's old library were turned to ash. Shidehara wrote that the few books that survived 'were later also destroyed when my residence in Sendagaya was damaged in bombing in the spring of the twentieth year of Shōwa [1945]. So [in the end] not a single volume remained'. He added: 'Whenever I think back on this loss, I am overwhelmed by emotion'.[162]

Following the earthquake, the Shidehara household received support from the Iwasaki family (who, it should be recalled, were the founders of the Mitsubishi financial conglomerate, and Shidehara's wife Masako's original family). The Iwasaki family bestowed on the Shidehara household the Rikugien garden in Komagome, which was to serve as a new residence. Rikugien was a famous garden in Tokyo from the Edo period. Shidehara moved there a few months before his appointment as foreign minister. At the time, however, Shidehara was not particularly looking forward to serving as foreign minister.

On this topic, we have testimony from Ishii Itarō. During Shidehara's time as ambassador to the US, Ishii once happened to sit beside him in a railway car. Ishii took the opportunity to attempt to draw Shidehara out a little concerning his upcoming appointment as foreign minister. Shidehara, however, responded curtly: 'No, no, I'm not fit to be foreign minister'. Reflecting upon his time as vice-minister for foreign affairs, he confided in Ishii that, because 'the Japanese political world is truly quite complicated, a person like me is simply not cut out to be foreign minister'. In particular, Shidehara considered the Privy Council and the political parties to be simply too difficult for him to handle. Yet, despite Shidehara's reservations, in June 1924 he became foreign minister.

The next time he met Ishii, Shidehara greeted him with a wry smile. 'I didn't want to become foreign minister; that's just when they went and made me one.'[163]

Four Points in a Quarter Century

This initial chapter has traced Shidehara's career path up to the moment that he assumed this important position. As noted earlier, this chapter sought to cover four main topics regarding this quarter century. Its findings are summarised below.

The first topic concerned the formation of Shidehara's thinking. Shidehara's ideal was British-style diplomacy. Here the influence of James Bryce and Sir Edward Grey was particularly significant. This does not mean, however, that Shidehara's policies were necessarily pro-British, as shown by Shidehara's initiative in abolishing the Anglo-Japanese Alliance.

While Shidehara also stayed in the US for a long time, he did not encounter an individual comparable in stature with Bryce or Grey. He was uncomfortable with the foreign policy ideals of President Wilson and considered Bryan a diplomatic novice. Shidehara's relationship with Lansing was also strained, as evidenced from the proceedings of the Paris Peace Conference and the manner in which the US withdrew its troops from the Siberian Intervention. Shidehara was further aware, along with Foreign Minister Uchida, that behind the scenes of the negotiations surrounding a New Four-Power Consortium was a plan to secretly expand railways such as the Manchurian Railway into a continental railway. In the final phase of the New Four-Power Consortium negotiations, Shidehara strove to do his utmost as ambassador to the US to protect Japan's interests in China.[164]

That said, more than a few of Shidehara's policies were actually favourable towards the US. As vice-minister for foreign affairs, Shidehara had worked to restrain the Japanese army during the Siberian Intervention, while at the Washington Naval Conference he proactively adopted open door policy positions. Therefore, while it is certainly the case that British-style diplomacy represented Shidehara's ideal, when it came to the concrete actions he took as a diplomat in this period, if anything, he was in closer alignment with the US. Shidehara understood that diplomatic ideals and the Japanese national interest were separate affairs.

As I have shown in this chapter, however, Shidehara's interpretation and application of an open door policy deserves closer scrutiny. Shidehara understood the open door provision of the Nine-Power Treaty in a restricted manner. For him, it referred primarily to equality of opportunity, that is, the sense of the term that Hay deployed in his first note. In other words, Shidehara was strictly opposed to any third nation intervening politically in China. This is why Shidehara, despite being on fairly congenial terms with Hughes, stood firmly against international management of the Chinese Eastern Railway. Meanwhile, when Hughes attempted to establish an open door policy investigative body, Shidehara ensured that it was as toothless as possible.

In summary, while Shidehara accepted a form of open door policy, he interpreted and applied that policy in a restricted sense to protect Japan's interests on the Chinese continent. By accepting an open door policy as an ideal, Shidehara was able to use it to protect the reality of a defence of national interests in China. It should be kept in mind that Shidehara did not think that having an open door policy was only an ideal of US diplomacy. According to Shidehara, Japan's pursuit of such a policy was a development that arose in the wake of the Anglo-Japanese Alliance, the Treaty of Portsmouth and the Franco-Japanese Treaty. This is another instance where the influence of Denison is visible. I have further noted in this chapter that Shidehara also saw the annexation of Korea as a natural development. It was also Shidehara who oversaw the removal of import duties on Korean rice after the annexation. We can see, therefore, how the open door principle was already understood in a restricted sense in this early period. If we also take into consideration the interpretation of the Korean provision in the Treaty of Portsmouth, then what emerges is a picture whereby pursuit of the open door principle, understood in a limited sense, actually helped to support the development of the Japanese empire.

We have also seen how the locus of Shidehara's direct experience of Asia was Korea and not China. It was not until his time as vice-minister for foreign affairs that he would need to seriously confront issues surrounding China. Later, as ambassador to the US, he would take the lead directly and demonstrate that he was as good as anyone in dealing with Chinese issues on a broad basis. Yet he tended to be overly theoretical. Later diplomats such as Yoshida Shigeru, Arita Hachirō and Shigemitsu Mamoru were frequently richer in experience with regard to China.

Finally, with respect to the formation of Shidehara's thinking, two more details should be kept in mind. First, I noted that Shidehara greatly admired Washburn's book *Nogi* and recommended its translation to an old school colleague. Second, I pointed out that Shidehara was apprehensive about the crown prince visiting the US.

The second main topic explored in this chapter was that of Shidehara's diplomatic style. If it could be said that Shidehara had a formative experience, then that would be his witnessing of the commencement of the Russo-Japanese War while stationed in Busan. It was there that he was baptised in the conduct of 'power politics', which is based on the deployment of military power. Shidehara was also not squeamish about gunboat diplomacy and its attendant use of force. His later meeting with Denison, however, would be a turning point. It was thereafter that Shidehara would acquire a thorough knowledge of international law. It was also from Denison that he would hear behind the scenes anecdotes about the diplomacy relating to the commencement of the Russo-Japanese War.

Yet, despite the inside knowledge Shidehara acquired of how to conduct diplomatic negotiations, he did not simply follow the model set for him by Denison. Rather, Shidehara tried to follow the path of 'honest diplomacy', which he saw as the first principle in building relationships of trust with other nations. Shidehara's thinking in this regard is shown in the way he handled public relations and the termination of the Anglo-Japanese Alliance at the Washington Naval Conference. At that conference, Shidehara even took the initiative in seeking a resolution to the Far East problem.

We can better understand Shidehara's 'honest diplomacy' by contrasting it with the approach of Katō Takaaki. In his Twenty-One Demands issued to China, Foreign Minister Katō included Group 5 (the last and most aggressive set of demands) as leverage for subsequent negotiation. It was included without the expectation that the Chinese would acquiesce to it. In other words, Katō was here pursuing British-style imperialist diplomacy. This method would also be deployed by figures such as Foreign Minister Komura. From Katō's perspective, therefore, the Twenty-One Demands must have seemed fairly reasonable at the time of their conception. Yet the Wilson administration sought a more moral approach to international relations and reacted negatively to the Twenty-One

Demands. Katō's approach therefore complicated affairs significantly for Japan.[165] It is reasonable to assume that Shidehara would have learned from the failure of Katō's diplomatic efforts here.

It was at just this time that the status of the European powers was beginning to decline, relative to the rise of the US. Shidehara's response to this new global reality was to take the initiative in abolishing the Anglo-Japanese Alliance and in pursuing an open door policy with respect to the Far East. This diplomatic style helped to establish Shidehara's name internationally. It was also a style that was particularly compatible with the US.

The third topic I examined was Shidehara's personal connections. I noted that, at first glance, Shidehara and Komura's personalities appear to have been diametrically opposed. However, Shidehara's concrete actions show that, along with individuals such as Moroi Rokurō, he actually supported Komura's efforts at treaty revision. It must be added that Shidehara was not a fervent adherent to the view that Japan ought to become the future leader of East Asia. In this sense, therefore, Shidehara certainly was not Komura's successor. I also pointed out that during his time as counsellor at the Japanese embassy in the US, Shidehara greatly respected Ambassador Chinda for his ability to go head-to-head in debating Secretary of State Bryan.

As vice-minister for foreign affairs, Shidehara flawlessly served five consecutive foreign ministers: Ishii Kikujirō, Terauchi Masatake, Motono Ichirō, Gotō Shinpei and Uchida Yasuya. It was under Foreign Minister Motono that Shidehara would take on the burden of formulating policy with respect to China. Shidehara's relationship with Hara Takashi, meanwhile, was not exactly good at the outset. Yet he was gradually able to earn Hara's trust.

As ambassador to the US, Shidehara made Debuchi Katsuji his right-hand man. Once Debuchi left the embassy for a new role, Shidehara would place greater trust in Saburi Sadao, rather than Hirota Kōki. I have suggested that when it came to dealing with important issues, Shidehara preferred to work with subordinates whom he could trust. Shidehara's close-knit relations with Debuchi and Saburi during his time as ambassador can actually be regarded as the origin of what would later be the 'Shidehara clique'. These connections would later come to the fore once he assumed the office of foreign minister, as we shall see in more detail at the beginning of Chapter 3.

The fourth and final topic for consideration was the impact that Shidehara had on how other foreign nations, and, in particular, the US, viewed Japan. Certainly, Shidehara gained a degree of international fame for his efforts during the Washington Naval Conference. A product of this conference was the formation of a cooperative international order that centred on Japan, the US and the UK. In academic circles this would be called the Washington System. The greatest personification of the diplomatic approach symbolised by the Washington System was Shidehara himself.

That said, the tide still did not turn fully in favour of the US cooperating with Japan. A tendency to favour China, visible in the speech and actions of Williams, was also adopted in the State Department by individuals such as Johnson and Hornbeck. It would not be until the conference in London to sign the Treaty for the Limitation and Reduction of Naval Armament—during Shidehara's second stint as foreign minister—that a pro-Japanese force would begin to form on the US side, making it possible for Japanese diplomats to begin exploring how to build a relationship with them.

Endnotes

1   This chapter is based on my previously published article. See Hattori Ryūji, 'Meiji Taishō-ki no Shidehara Kijūrō' [Shidehara Kijūrō in the Meiji and Taishō periods], *Chūō Daigaku Ronshū*, no. 25 (March 2004): 1–41.

2   Ōno Katsumi, 'Meiji Gaikō to Denison Komon no Kenshin' [Meiji diplomacy and the dedication of Advisor Denison], *Bungei Shunjū* 44, no. 11 (November 1966): 180–88; Ministry of Foreign Affairs Hundred-Year History Compilation Association, ed., *Gaimushō no 100 Nen* [A hundred years of the Ministry of Foreign Affairs], vol. 2 (Tokyo: Harashobō, 1969), 1341–47; Ichimata Masao, *Nihon no Kokusai Hōgaku wo Kizuita Hitobito* [The builders of Japan's international law] (Tokyo: Japan Institute of International Affairs, 1973), 58–59; Takeuchi Haruhisa, 'Denison-zō to Meiji no Omokage' [A portrait of Denison and the remnants of the Meiji era], *Gaikō Forum*, no. 171 (2002): 76–81; Takeuchi Haruhisa, 'Kieta Denison Shōzōga' [A vanished portrait of Denison], *Gaikō Forum*, no. 172 (2002): 82–87.

3   Valuable insights on this point are available in Matsumura Masayoshi, 'Washington Kaigi to Nihon no Kōhō Gaikō' [The Washington Naval Conference and Japanese public diplomacy], *Gaimushō Chosa Geppō*, no. 1 (June 2002): 47–76. See also Matsumura Masayoshi, *Shinpan Kokusai Kōryū-shi: Kingendai Nihon no Kōhō Bunka Gaikō to Minkan Kōryū* [History of international exchange: Modern Japanese public and cultural diplomacy and its connection with civilian exchange], 2nd ed. (Tokyo: Tajinkan, 2002).

4   Hattori Ryūji, *Higashi Asia Kokusai Kankyō no Hendō to Nihon Gaikō, 1918–1931* [Japanese diplomacy and East Asian international politics, 1918–1931] (Tokyo: Yūhikaku, 2001), 89–112.

5   Hayashi Gonsuke, *Waga 70 Nen wo Kataru* [Speaking of my 70 years], ed. Iwai Takahito (Tokyo: Daiichi Shobō, 1935), 65.

6   Shidehara Kijūrō, 'Senpai toshiteno Ijūin-Dan' [My senior, Baron Ijūin], in Ijūin Hikokichi-Dan, General Aoki Nobuzumi Tsuitō-roku [Tribute to Baron Ijūin Hikokichi and General Aoki Nobuzumi], ed. Memorial Service Initiator (Tokyo: Memorial Service Initiator, 1934), 28–30.

7   Shidehara Kijūrō, 'Senpai toshiteno Ijūin-Dan' [My senior, Baron Ijūin], in *Ijūin Hikokichi-Dan, General Aoki Nobuzumi Tsuitō-roku* [Tribute to Baron Ijūin Hikokichi and General Aoki Nobuzumi], ed. Memorial Service Initiator (Tokyo: Memorial Service Initiator, 1934), 28–30; Nagai Matsuzō, 'Shidehara Danshaku no Omoide' [Memories of Baron Shidehara], 16 June 1952, in 'Shidehara Heiwa Bunko', Reel 13; Shidehara, *Gaikō 50 Nen*, 35–36.

8   Shidehara, *Gaikō 50 Nen*, 13–15.

9   Tonedachi Masao, ed., *Nihon Gaikō Hiroku* [Confidential records of Japanese diplomacy] (Tokyo: Asahi Shimbunsha, 1934), 87.

10   For an overview of these doctrines along with a critique, see Chiba Isao, 'Man-Kan Fukabun-Ron = Man-Kan Kōkan-Ron no Keisei to Takakuteki Dōmei, Kyōshōmō no Mosaku [The formation of the Man-Kan Fukabun Doctrine as equivalent to the Man-Kan Kōkan Doctrine, and the search for a multilateral alliance or entente], *Shigaku Zasshi* 105, no. 7 (July 1996): 38–73; Chiba Isao, 'Nichi-Ro Senzen-ki [1900–04]: Gaikō-shi Kenkyū no Jōtai' [The pre-Russo-Japanese War era [1900–04]: The current state of diplomatic history research], *Shigaku Zasshi* 106, no. 8 (August 1997): 87–103.

11   Hayashi to Mutsu (in Maiko), 23 April 1895, in *Nihon Gaikō Bunsho* [Documents on Japanese foreign policy], ed. Ministry of Foreign Affairs, vol. 28, no. 2 (Tokyo: United Nations Association of Japan, 1963), 14–17.

12   Mutsu Munemitsu, *Shintei Kenkenroku* [A record of tribulations], 2nd ed., annotated Nakatsuka Akira (Tokyo: Iwanami Shoten, 1983), 302.

13   Hayashi Tadasu, *Nochi wa Mukashi no Ki, Hoka: Hayashi Tadasu Kaikoroku* [Records of the past, other: Memoirs of Hayashi Tadasu], ed. Yui Masaomi (Tokyo: Heibonsha, 1970), 66–83, 261–383.

14   Shidehara Kijūrō, 'Gaikō Kanken' [My views on diplomacy], 9 October 1928, in 'Shidehara Heiwa Bunko', Reel 7. See also Hattori Ryūji, 'Shidehara Kijūrō (lecture), "Gaikō Kanken"' [My views on diplomacy], *Sōgō Seisaku Kenkyū*, no. 13 (March 2006): 99–112.

15   Shidehara, 'Gaikō Kanken'.

16   Ibid.

17   Tashiro Kazui, *Wakan: Sakoku Jidai no Nihonjin-machi* [Wakan: Japanese town of the age of national isolation] (Tokyo: Bungei Shunjū, 2002).

18   Governor-General of Korea Railway Bureau, *Chōsen Tetsudō-shi* [The history of railways in Korea] (Seoul: Governor-General of Korea Railway Bureau, 1915), 61–112, 163–91; Nihon Yūsen, ed., *Nihon Yūsen Kabushiki Gaisha 50 Nen-shi* [A 50-year history of Nihon Yusen co.] (Tokyo: Nihon Yūsen, 1935), 133; Tani Hisao, *Kimitsu Nichi-Ro Sen-shi* [Secret history of the Russo-Japanese War] (Tokyo: Harashobō, 1966), 108; Kimura Kenji, *Zaichō Nihonjin no Shakai-shi* [The social history of Japanese residents in Korea] (Tokyo: Miraisha, 1989), 75, 81–83; Kokaze Hidemasa, *Teikokushugi-ka no Nihon Kaiun: Kokusai Kyōsō to Taigai Jiritsu* [Japanese shipping in the age of imperialism: International competition and independence from abroad] (Tokyo: Yamakawa Shuppansha, 1995), 229–58; Takahashi Yasutaka, *Nihon Shokuminchi Tetsudō-shi Ron* [Discourse on railways in the Japanese colonies] (Tokyo: Nihon Keizai Hyōronsha, 1995), 61–65.

19   Japanese National Railways, Hiroshima Railway Management Bureau, *Kanpu Renrakusen-shi* [A history of the ferry service between Shimonoseki and Busan] (Tokyo: Japanese National Railways, Hiroshima Railway Management Bureau, 1979), 18.

20   Iwasaki Yatarō, Iwasaki Yanosuke Biography Editing Association, ed., *Iwasaki Yatarō Den* [A biography of Iwasaki Yatarō], vol. 2 (Tokyo: Iwasaki Yanosuke Biography Editing Association, 1967), 619–21. For more detailed information on the beginning of the relationship between Shidehara and Masako, see Kishi Kuramatsu, *Ko-Shidehara Kijūrō-shi no Omoide wo Kataru* [Memories of Late Mr. Shidehara Kijūrō], 19 July 1952, in 'Shidehara Heiwa Bunko', Reel 13.

21   Shidehara is not the only example of a diplomat receiving a marriage offer in this manner. In fact, it was customary for diplomats to use marriage to align their families with those of powerful people and other diplomats. Examples include Sawada Miki—the wife of Japan's delegate to the United Nations in the postwar era Sawada Renzō—was the eldest daughter of Iwasaki Hisaya, who in turn was the eldest son of Iwasaki Yatarō. Diplomat Sawada Setsuzō—the elder brother of diplomat

2. THE RUSSO-JAPANESE WAR, WORLD WAR I AND THE WASHINGTON NAVAL CONFERENCE

Sawada Renzō—was the son-in-law of Ōyama Tsunasuke, Japan's ambassador to Italy. He would later occupy posts such as Japan's secretary general at the League of Nations. It is also well known that Yoshida Shigeru was the son-in-law of Makino Nobuaki. Saburi Sadao, who would eventually die under suspicious circumstances as Japan's minister to China, was the son-in-law of Komura Jutarō. Yoshizawa Kenkichi was the son-in-law of Inukai Tsuyoshi and served as the foreign minister in the Inukai cabinet. At the outset of the Pacific War, the counsellor to Japan's embassy in the US, Iguchi Sadao, became Yoshizawa Kenkichi's son-in-law. Okabe Nagakage—chief of the Department of Cultural Affairs with China—married Katō Takaaki's daughter. Debuchi Katsuji, who served as both vice-minister for foreign affairs and ambassador to the US, was Kikuchi Takeo's son-in-law; as a judiciary bureaucrat, he became both chairman for the Tokyo Bar Association and president of Chūō University. Debuchi's eldest daughter, Takako, married Asakai Kōichirō, who served as an ambassador to the US for five years and 10 months, exceeding Debuchi's tenure of five years and two months.

For further details, see the following works: Sawada Renzō, *Gaisenmon Hiroba* [Arch of Triumph Square] (Tokyo: Kadokawa Shoten, 1950), 85–57, 129–32; Sawada Renzō, *Zuikan, Zuihitsu* [Miscellaneous impressions] (Tokyo: Makino Shuppan, 1990), i; Iwasaki Family Bibliographical Publishing Association, ed., *Iwasaki Hisaya Den* [A biography of Iwasaki Hisaya] (Tokyo: University of Tokyo Press, 1979), 580; Sawada Toshio, ed., *Sawada Setsuzō Kaisōroku: Ichi Gaikōkan no Shōgai* [Memoirs of Sawada Setsuzō: The life of a diplomat] (Tokyo: Yūhikaku, 1985), 2, 16–18, 23, 26, 52, 127, 159, 218, 220, 221, 296; Kurogi Yūkichi, *Komura Jutarō* (Tokyo: Kōdansha, 1968), 948; Nakano Keishi, ed., *Yoshizawa Kenkichi Jiden* [The autobiography of Kenkichi Yoshizawa] (Tokyo: Jiji Tsūshinsha, 1964), 57–58, 61–62; Shōyū Society Incorporated, ed., *Okabe Nagakage Nikki: Shōwa Shoki Kazoku Kanryō no Kiroku* [The diary of Okabe Nagakage: Records of an early Shōwa-era aristocratic bureaucrat] (Tokyo: Kashiwa Shobō, 1993), 626–27; Arai Yōtarō, ed., *Kikuchi Sensei Den* [A biography of Kikuchi Sensei] (Tokyo: Ōzorasha, 1997), 2–3, 170–73; Takahashi Katsuhiro, ed., '"Debuchi Katsuji Nikki" (7) Kan: Kaikodan, Shuyō Chosaku Ichiran, Kankei Keizu, Shuyō Jinmei Sakuin' [The diary of Debuchi Katsuji (7) complete: Reminiscences, overview of major works, genealogical tables, index of major figures], *Kokugakuin Daigaku Nihonbunka Kenkyūjo Kiyō*, no. 90 (September 2002): 340–41; Asakai Kōichirō, *Tsukasamachi Kanwa: Ichi Gaikōkan no Kaisō* [Quiet talk in Tsukasamachi: Recollections of a diplomat] (Tokyo: Asakai Kōichirō Memoir Editorial Group, 1986), 300.

A few more examples are Inoue Katsunosuke—minister to Germany and ambassador to the UK—was the adoptive heir of Inoue Kaoru. Yamagata Isaburō, who served as governor-general of Kwantung, was the adoptive heir of Yamagata Aritomo. Satō Naotake, who became foreign minister in the Hayashi cabinet, was the adopted child of Satō Aimaro—ambassador to the US. Chinda Sutemi, who married Aimaro's younger sister, became ambassador to the US. In addition, Ishii Kikujirō was the adopted child of Mie prefectural governor Ishii Kunimichi. Kubota Kanichirō was the son-in-law of Ishii Kikujirō, while Shiratori Toshio was Ishii's nephew. Setsuko, eldest daughter of Matsudaira Tsuneo—who served as vice-minister for foreign affairs, ambassador to the US, ambassador to the UK and minister of the imperial household—married Yasuhito (Prince Chichibu), becoming Princess Chichibu.

For details on the above, see: Marquis Inoue Kaoru Biography Editing Association, ed., *Kōshaku Inoue Katsunosuke Kun Ryakuden* [A short biography of Marquis Inoue Katsunosuke] (Tokyo: Naigai Shoseki, 1934), 2; Tokutomi Iichirō, ed., *Sokū Yamagata Kō Den* [The biography of Duke Sokū Yamagata] (Tokyo: Duke Yamagata Biography Editing Association, 1929), 13; Tokutomi Sohō, ed., *Kōshaku Yamagata Aritomo Den* [The biography of Duke Yamagata Aritomo], vol. 2 (Tokyo: Harashobō, 1969), 1036; Satō Naotake, *Kaiko 80 Nen* [Looking back on 80 years] (Tokyo: Jiji Tsūshinsha, 1963), 56–57; Kikuchi Takenori, ed., *Hakushaku Chinda Sutemi* [Count Chinda Sutemi] (Tokyo: Kōmeikaku, 1938), 319; Kajima Peace Research Center, ed., *Ishii Kikujirō Ikō: Gaikō Zuisō* [The posthumous manuscripts of Ishii Kikujirō: Diplomatic reflections] (Tokyo: Kajima Research Center Press, 1967), prologue, 363; Tokyo PR News Service, *Matsudaira Tsuneo Tsuisōroku* [Recollections of Matsudaira Tsuneo] (Tokyo: Late Matsudaira Tsuneo Memorial Association, 1961), 7–8, 726.

Given such family connections, it was inevitable that these elite bureaucratic graduates of the Imperial University of Tokyo saw themselves as a special group within Japanese society. Similar to Sugimura Fukashi and Sugimura Yōtarō, there were also cases where both parent and child were diplomats. For example, Komura Jutarō and his eldest son, Komura Kinichi, were both diplomats, and Arita Hachirō's third son, Arita Keisuke, became vice-minister for foreign affairs in the latter half of the 1970s.

22 Shidehara to Foreign Minister Komura, 8 February 1904, in *Nikkan Gaikō Shiryo Shūsei* [Compilation of material concerning Japan-Korea diplomacy], ed. Kamikawa Hikomatsu and Kin Seimei, vol. 5 (Tokyo: Gannandō, 1967), 45; Shidehara Kijūrō, 'Busan Ryōji Jidai no Ōtegara' [The high achievements of the Busan Consul era], in *Sono Koro wo Kataru* [Recalling those times], ed. Tonedachi Masao (Tokyo: Tokyo Asahi Shimbunsha, 1928), 222–27.

23 Ministry of Foreign Affairs, ed., *Nihon Gaikō Nenpyō narabini Shuyō Bunsho* [Chronology and main documents of Japanese diplomacy], vol. 1 (Tokyo: Harashobō, 1965), 222; Komura to Shidehara, 10 February 1904, in Kamikawa and Kin, *Nikkan Gaikō Shiryo Shūsei*, vol. 5, 55–56.

24 Shidehara to Komura, 21 January 1904, in *Nihon Gaikō Bunsho: Nichi-Ro Sensō* [Documents on Japanese foreign policy: The Russo-Japanese War], ed. Ministry of Foreign Affairs, vol. 4 (Tokyo: Ministry of Foreign Affairs, 1960), 347; Komura to Shidehara, 21 January, ibid., 347; Shidehara to Komura, 9 February, ibid., 350–51; Shidehara to Komura, 20 February, in Kamikawa and Kin, *Nikkan Gaikō Shiryo Shūsei*, vol. 5, 67; Hayashi, *Waga 70 Nen wo Kataru*, 182–85.

25 Ministry of Foreign Affairs Hundred-Year History Compilation Association, *Gaimushō no 100 Nen*, vol. 1, 257.

26 'Hon-shō Yatoi Denison Yakujōsho' [Written contract employing Denison at this ministry], 1 March 1880, in 'Gaimushō Gaikokujin Yatoiire Ikken (Fu-Keiyakusho) Bessatsu "Denison"-shi Kankei' [Ministry of Foreign Affairs foreigner employment case (contract attached) separate volume, relating to Mr Denison], 3.9.3.7-1, Diplomatic Archives of the Ministry of Foreign Affairs of Japan; Toyabe Shuntei, 'Denison', *Taiyō* 11, no. 1 (January 1905): 35–38. According to Aoki Shūzō, Foreign Minister Ōkuma Shigenobu often relied on Denison to amend the unequal treaties. See Aoki Shūzō, *Aoki Shūzō Jiden* [The autobiography of Aoki Shūzō], ed. Sakane Yoshihisa (Tokyo: Heibonsha, 1970), 155–56.

27 Shidehara, *Gaikō 50 Nen*, 246–53; Kajima Peace Research Center, *Ishii Kikujirō Ikō*, 325–26.

28 Shidehara Kijūrō, 'Gaikō Bunsho no Buntai, Kisōsha no Kokoroe narabini Shoshu no Keishiki' [Writing style for diplomatic documents, important knowledge for drafters, different types of forms], April 1940, in *Kindai Gaikō Kaikoroku* [Modern diplomatic memoirs], ed. Hirose Yoshihiro, vol. 4 (Tokyo: Yumani Shobō, 2000), 83–94.

29 Ibid.

30 For example, in official documents, the address entry was normally followed by the sender's signature. When the document was intended to be friendly, senders referred to themselves in the first person. For more serious documents, third person might be used. For verbal notes, important proposals were directly delivered by hand. In such cases, there was no need for an address or for the sender to provide a signature, and the sender was referred to in the third person. Memoranda included detailed notes on facts related to the items being negotiated. Here, too, both the address and sender's signature were omitted, and the third person was used to identify participants in the negotiations. Later, Shidehara would record Denison's instructions so that other ministry staff could use them.

31 Shidehara Kijūrō, 'Kaisō no Paris Heiwa Kaigi' [My recollections of the Paris Peace Conference], *Kaizō* (February 1950): 72–74. See also Shidehara, *Gaikō 50 Nen*, 20–30.

32 Ishii Kikujirō, *Gaikō Yoroku* [Diplomatic unofficial record] (Tokyo: Iwanami Shoten, 1930), 82–84; Ishii Kikujirō, *Gaikō Kaisō Danpen* [Some recollections of diplomacy], ed. Izumino Seiichi (Tokyo: Kinseidō, 1939), 6–7.

According to Mushanokōji, 'Shidehara-san no Omoide' [Memories of Mr Shidehara], date unknown, in 'Shidehara Heiwa Bunko', Reel 13:

> Regarding this idea that Mr. Shidehara, of his own accord, decided to send a telegram regarding a matter that would have major significance for the nation, this is very difficult to believe, given Mr. Shidehara's personality, as well as the seriousness of the matter in question. I think it likely that Shidehara had misremembered this incident and that he had sent the telegram on the basis of instructions from his superior.

In fact, elsewhere Shidehara himself has been recorded as stating: 'With the southern half of Sakhalin Island, this was a result that followed from Mr. Ishii (and, of course, me) strongly urging Mr. Chinda to act'. See Shidehara Kijūrō, 'Nihon Gaikōkai no Omoide' [Memories of Japan's diplomatic world], ed. Kiyosawa Kiyoshi, 5 December 1944, in 'Shidehara Heiwa Bunko', Reel 7.

2. THE RUSSO-JAPANESE WAR, WORLD WAR I AND THE WASHINGTON NAVAL CONFERENCE

Further, the following message was presented from Katsura to Kodama Gentarō, chief of the Office of Army General Staff for the Manchurian Army based in Mukden, in Ministry of Foreign Affairs, *Nihon Gaikō Bunsho: Nichi-Ro Sensō*, vol. 5, 302–03:

> Because the government has received a secret report that the Russian Empire is prepared to transfer the southern half of Sakhalin, this information is to be urgently shared with the committee.

However, even Foreign Ministry records do not clarify the details of the corrections made to the telegram.

For more details on this, see Ministry of Foreign Affairs, ed., *Komura Gaikō-shi* [A history of Komura diplomacy] (Tokyo: Harashobō, 1966), 585; Okamoto Shumpei, *The Japanese Oligarchy and the Russo-Japanese War* (New York: Columbia University Press, 1970), 155; Shinobu Seizaburō and Nakayama Jiichi, eds, *Kaiteiban Nichi-Ro Sensō-shi no Kenkyū* [A study of the history of the Russo-Japanese War], 2nd ed. (Tokyo: Kawade Shobō Shinsha, 1972), 412–14; Raymond A. Esthus, *Double Eagle and Rising Sun: The Russians and Japanese at Portsmouth in 1905* (Durham: Duke University Press, 1988).

33   Yamaza Enjirō, 'Nichi-Ro Kowa ni Tomonau Manshū Mondai no Kyokusetsu' [Twists and turns of the Manchurian problem attending the Russo-Japanese peace settlement], August 1913, in Ministry of Foreign Affairs, *Nihon Gaikō Bunsho: Nichi-Ro Sensō*, vol. 5, 303–09. See also Hasegawa Takashi, *Tairiku Gaikō no Senku Yamaza Kōshi* [Minister Yamaza, pioneer of continental diplomacy] (Tokyo: Ikuseisha, 1938), 95–96.

34   Shidehara Kijūrō, 'Washington Kaigi no Rimen-kan Sonota' [Behind the scenes of the Washington Naval Conference and others], February 1939, in Hirose, *Kindai Gaikō Kaikoroku*, vol. 4, 132–35.

35   Ibid.

36   Ibid.

37   Ibid.

38   Ibid.

39   Takahira to Foreign Minister Katsura, 13 September 1905, in 'Nichi-Ro Kowa Jyōyaku Teiketsu Ikken (Komura Iin Byōki Kikoku) (Kōwa Seiritsu Shukuji) (Denpō Toriatsukai)' [Russo-Japanese Peace Treaty conclusion (representative Komura's homecoming for sickness) (congratulatory addresses for peace attainment) (handling of telegrams)], 2.2.1.3-2, Diplomatic Archives of the Ministry of Foreign Affairs of Japan.

40   Shidehara, 'Kaisō no Paris Heiwa Kaigi', 72.

41   Ibid.

42   Ibid. Shidehara's conversation outline (Komagome residence), 24 October 1933, in 'Shoshushi Kankei Zakken: Gaikō Shiryō Shūshū Kankei' [Miscellanea related to various historiography: Diplomatic relations materials collection], vol. 1, N.2.1.0.4-1, Diplomatic Archives of the Ministry of Foreign Affairs of Japan; with the same point found in Shidehara, *Gaikō 50 Nen*, 31–35. See also Komura Kinichi, 'Teito Kensō no Naka wo Chichi Kaeru' [The father returns in the bustle of Tokyo], in *Sono Koro wo Kataru* [Recalling those times], ed. Tonedachi Masao (Tokyo: Tokyo Asahi Shimbunsha, 1928), 246–52.

43   Hara Keiichirō, ed., *Hara Takashi Nikki* [The diary of Hara Takashi], vol. 2 (Tokyo: Fukumura Shuppan, 1981), 131–32, 143–45; Oka Yoshitake, *Oka Yoshitake Chosaku-shū* [The collected works of Oka Yoshitake], vol. 4 (Tokyo: Iwanami Shoten, 1993), 94.

44   Ministry of Foreign Affairs and Japan Society for the Promotion of Science, eds, *Jōyaku Kaisei Kankei: Nihon Gaikō Bunsho, Bessatsu, Tsushō Jōyaku to Tsūshō Seisaku no Hensen* [Relating to treaty revision: Documents on Japanese foreign policy, separate volume, changes in commercial treaties and international trade policy] (Tokyo: World Economic Investigation Foundation, 1951), 5; Kubota Kiyochika, ed., *Hagiwara Moriichi-shi Tsuikairoku* [Remembering Mr Hagiwara Moriichi] (Tokyo: Hakubunkan, 1913), 10–11, 231–37.

45   Kawashima Nobutarō, 'Shidehara Sōri heno Omoide: Jōyaku Kaisei' [Memories of Prime Minister Shidehara: Treaty revision], 1953, in 'Shidehara Heiwa Bunko', Reel 18. For Moroi's memorandum, see Moroi Rokurō, 'Jōyaku Kaisei Iken' [An opinion on treaty revision], in *Jōyaku Kaisei Ron Shiryō Shūsei* [Treaty revision discourse complication], ed. Inō Tentarō, vol. 6 (Tokyo: Harashobō, 1994), 29–90. Kawashima Nobutarō's main work was *Honpō Tsūshō Seisaku Jyoyaku-shi Gairon* [Introduction to the history of Japanese trade policy treaties] (Tokyo: Ganshodō Shoten, 1941). It was also Kawashima who wrote Ministry of Foreign Affairs et al., *Jōyaku Kaisei Kankei: Nihon Gaikō Bunsho, Bessatsu, Tsushō Jōyaku to Tsūshō Seisaku no Hensen*. See also Itō Nobufumi, 'Nihon no Shin-Gaikō to Shidehara-san' [Japan's new diplomacy and Mr Shidehara], date unknown, in 'Shidehara Heiwa Bunko', Reel 13.

46   Moroi Tadakazu, ed., *Moroi Rokurō Kun Tsuitō Ihō-roku* [In remembrance of Moroi Rokurō] (Tokyo: Moroi Tadakazu, 1941), 8–14, 23–31, 47–48.

47   Shidehara, 'Washington Kaigi no Rimen-kan Sonota', 135.

48   Kurachi Tetsukichi, 'Kankoku Gappei no Keii' [The circumstances of the annexation of Korea], November 1939, in Hirose, *Kindai Gaikō Kaikoroku*, vol. 2, 249–85; Ishii, *Gaikō Yoroku*, 95.

49   'Kankoku Gappei nikansuru Sengen' [Declaration concerning the annexation of Korea], *Kanpō*, special edition, 29 August 1910; Kawashima Nobutarō, 'Shidehara Sōri heno Omoide'; Vice-Minister of Home Affairs Kubota Kiyochika to Shidehara, 25 December 1915, in Ministry of Foreign Affairs, *Nihon Gaikō Bunsho, 1915*, vol. 1, 381–88.

50   *Asahi Shimbun*, 11 March 1951.

51   Honda Kumatarō, *Tamashii no Gaikō: Nichi-Ro Sensō niokeru Komura-Ko* [Diplomacy of the spirit: Lord Komura and the Russo-Japanese War] (Tokyo: Chikura Shobō, 1941). Meanwhile, Teramoto Yasutoshi asserted:

> Komura's imperialistic policies had the effect of further inflaming nationalistic sentiment in Qing-dynasty China. Conversely, Hayashi's policy of maintaining the status quo attracted domestic criticism from the elder statesmen [the genrō]. To put it differently, Japanese diplomacy after the Russo-Japanese War was trapped between demands of Japanese continental expansion on the one hand and the rise of Chinese nationalism on the other; it was unable to secure a stable foothold. This situation would similarly be reflected in later diplomatic troubles suffered under Foreign Ministers Tanaka and Shidehara.

See Teramoto Yasutoshi, *Nichi-Ro Sensō Igo no Nihon Gaikō: Power Politics no Naka no Man-Kan Mondai* [Japanese diplomacy after the Russo-Japanese War: The Manchuria–Korea Problem in the context of power politics] (Tokyo: Shinzansha, 1999), 533.

52   Mushanokōji, 'Shidehara-san no Omoide'. For Hirota, see also Hattori Ryūji, *Hirota Kōki* [Hirota Kōki] (Tokyo: Chūō Kōron Shinsha, 2008).

53   Shidehara, 'Gaikō Bunsho no Buntai, Kisōsha no Kokoroe narabini Shoshu no Keishiki', 90–91.

54   Ibid. See also Furuya Shigetsuna, 'Omoide Banashi Zai Sao Paolo' [Some recollections in Sao Paolo], *Kasumigaseki-kai Kaihō*, no. 240 (February 1966): 5.

55   'Gaimushō Gaikokujin Yatoiire Ikken (Fu-Keiyakusho) Bessatsu "Denison"-shi Kankei'; Shidehara Peace Foundation, *Shidehara Kijūrō*, 59.

56   One such example is related to diplomat Satō Naotake, who later became the foreign minister. At that time, Satō was still the third secretary at the Japanese embassy in Russia. In the summer of 1912, Satō returned to Japan for the first time. When he arrived via ferry at the Japanese town of Moji, he found a nation in mourning. Consequently, Satō was given the task of receiving members of the Spanish royal family. Satō attended the imperial funeral on 13 September at the Aoyama Parade Ground. At midnight, he solemnly watched the ox-drawn hearse depart. Returning to the Shiba Imperial Villa while reminiscing 'the great emperor's achievements', Satō received a copy of a newspaper extra, which reported that, when the casket was being transported, Nogi and his wife committed *jijin* (ritual suicide). Satō was stunned: 'I could not say a single word. It felt as though a strong force was pressing upon my heart'. After all, Satō had met with Nogi only a few days earlier. It was Nogi who appeared when Satō arrived at the entrance to the Shiba Imperial Villa. Nogi was

responsible for entertaining Prince Arthur of Connaught, representative of the royal household of the United Kingdom. Given this diplomatic responsibility, Satō had the opportunity to see Nogi in person. See Satō, *Kaiko 80 Nen*, 103–05.

Nogi's suicide is also described in Nakano, *Yoshizawa Kenkichi Jiden*, 73. See also Tsukada Seiichi, ed., *Nogi Taishō Jiseki* [The achievements of General Nogi] (Tokyo: Privately Printed, 1916), 365–74; Office of Nogi Shrine, *Nogi Maresuke Zenshū* [The complete works of Nogi Maresuke], vol. 2 (Tokyo: Kokusho Publishing Association, 1994), 520.

57   Stanley Washburn, *Nogi: A Man against the Background of a Great War* (New York: Henry Holt and Company, 1913); reminiscences of Stanley Washburn, 1950, Oral History Research Office, Columbia University.

58   Shidehara Kijūrō, 'Jobun' [Introduction], 24 December 1923, in Stanley Washburn, *Nogi* [Nogi], trans. Meguro Masumi (Tokyo: Bunkōin, 1924), 1–5. The same text was reprinted in Stanley Washburn, *Nogi* [Nogi], trans. Meguro Masumi (Tokyo: Sōgensha, 1941); Stanley Washburn, *Nogi Taishō to Nihonjin* [General Nogi and the Japanese people], trans. Meguro Masumi (Tokyo: Kōdansha, 1980). As Washburn authored these two volumes, I refer to them collectively when speaking of Washburn and his opinions.

Further, Hamilton Wright and his wife were involved in the US response to the opium problem. For more information on this topic, see William Phillips diary, 29 January 1919, William Phillips Papers, Box 1, Houghton Library, Harvard University; Gotō Harumi, *Ahen to Igirisu Teikoku: Kokusai Kisei no Takamari, 1906–43* [Opium and the British Empire: The tightening of international regulations, 1906–43] (Tokyo: Yamakawa Shuppansha, 2005), 30, 34, 36, 43, 61, 76.

59   Reminiscences of Washburn; Shidehara to Root, 6 August 1921, Elihu Root Papers, Box 139, Manuscript Division, Library of Congress; Root to Shidehara, 9 August 1921, Root Papers, Box 139.

60   Shidehara, 'Jobun', 1–5.

61   Ibid.

62   Meguro Masumi, 'Chogen' [Introduction], in Stanley Washburn, *Nogi* [Nogi], trans. Meguro Masumi (Tokyo: Bunkōin, 1924), 1, 10–13.

63   Meguro Masumi, 'Chogen' [Introduction], in Stanley Washburn, *Nogi* [Nogi], trans. Meguro Masumi (Tokyo: Bunkōin, 1924), 1, 10–13; Washburn to Hanihara, 27 November 1923, ibid., page numbers are not noted; Shidehara, 'Jobun', 3–4; reminiscences of Washburn; Shidehara to Root, 6 August 1921, Root Papers, Box 139.

64   Minister's Secretariat Personal Division, ed., *Gaimushō Nenkan* [Ministry of Foreign Affairs yearbook], *1913*, 60. A work that summarises the developments leading up to passing of the 1913 Alien Land Law is Ministry of Foreign Affairs, ed., *Tai-Bei Imin Mondai narabini Kashū Hai-Nichi Undo no Enkaku, Fu: Kashū Mondai Nichi-Bei Kōshō Tenmatsu* [The history of the US immigration problem and Californian anti-Japanese movement, supplement: An account of Japan–US negotiations concerning the California problem] (Tokyo: Ministry of Foreign Affairs, 1920). See also Minohara Toshihiro, 'Imin Mondai Kaiketsu eno Futatsu no Nichi-Bei Kōshō: 1913 Chinda–Bryan Kaidan to 1920 Shidehara–Morris Kaidan' [Two Japan–US negotiations for resolving the immigration problem: The 1913 Chinda–Bryan talks and the 1920 Shidehara–Morris talks], *Kobe Hōgaku Zasshi* 50, no. 1 (June 2000): 39–92.

65   Shidehara Kijūrō, 'Haku to Bryan-shi' [The Count and Mr Bryan], in *Hakushaku Chinda Sutemi-Den* [The biography of Count Chinda Sutemi], ed. Kikuchi Takenori (Tokyo: Kyōmeikaku, 1938), 138–40. See also Shidehara, *Gaikō 50 Nen*, 40–42, 316–18.

66   Bryan to Wilson, 2 October 1914, William Jennings Bryan Papers, Box 45, Manuscript Division, Library of Congress; Bryan to Wilson, 23 January 1915, Bryan Papers, Box 45.

67   James Bryce, *The American Commonwealth*, rev. ed., 2 vols (New York: Macmillan Company, 1911).

68   Edward Grey, *Twenty-Five Years, 1892–1916*, vol. 3 (London: Hodder and Stoughton Limited, 1935), 15–16, 24–25.

69 Edward Price Bell, World Chancelleries: Sentiments, Ideas, and Arguments Expressed by Famous Occidental and Oriental Statesmen Looking to the Consolidation of the Psychological Bases of International Peace (Chicago: Chicago Daily News, 1926), 138–39; Shidehara, Gaikō 50 Nen, 48–51; Ōta Tamekichi, 'Shidehara-san wo Kataru' [Speaking about Mr Shidehara], 13 January 1953, in 'Shidehara Heiwa Bunko', Reel 13.

70 Shidehara, Gaikō 50 Nen, 51–53. In the same text, it is stated: 'It was certainly in the year 1919'. However, I suggest that this exchange actually took place in 1921.

71 James Bryce, *International Relations: Eight Lectures Delivered in the United States in August, 1921* (New York: Macmillan Company, 1927), 126–29. Further, Bryce's final visit to the US is discussed in H. A. L. Fisher, *James Bryce*, vol. 2 (London: Macmillan Company, 1927), 280–87.

72 E. W. Edwards, 'China and Japan, 1911–1914', in *British Foreign Policy under Sir Edward Grey*, ed. F. H. Hinsley (Cambridge: Cambridge University Press, 1977), 380–81; Hattori, *Higashi Asia Kokusai Kankyō no Hendō to Nihon Gaikō, 1918–1931*, 23.

73 Shidehara, *Gaikō 50 Nen*, 254–56, 259–62.

In Mexico—where the incident took place—with the country falling into a state of civil strife, the more than 30-year rule of the dictator, Porfirio Diaz, ended. While Victoriano Huerta became the temporary president following a counter-revolutionary coup d'état, Grey knew that the Wilson administration was unfriendly towards Huerta. While he felt uncomfortable with US policies toward Mexico, Grey decided to turn a blind eye. In his opinion, there were no benefits to resisting US military intervention in Mexico. This was Grey-style realism, rather than a mere refusal to get involved. As it turned out, the civil strife continued until the early 1920s. See Grey, *Twenty-Five Years*, vol. 3, 26–29; Peter Calvert, *The Mexican Revolution, 1910–1914: The Diplomacy of Anglo-American Conflict* (Cambridge: Cambridge University Press, 1968), 163, 170, 187–88, 195, 200–01, 204, 209, 245–47; Lloyd C. Gardner, 'Woodrow Wilson and the Mexican Revolution', in *Woodrow Wilson and a Revolutionary World, 1913–1921*, ed. Arthur S. Link (Chapel Hill: University of North Carolina Press, 1982), 17–20.

Academic views on Wilson's diplomacy in the context of Mexico are also presented in Kusama Hidesaburō, *Wilson no Kokusai Shakai Seisaku Kōsō* [Wilson's conception for international society policy] (Nagoya: Nagoya University Press, 1990), 58–67.

74 Reminiscences of William Phillips, 1951, Oral History Research Office, Columbia University; Keith Robbins, *Sir Edward Grey: A Biography of Lord Grey of Fallodon* (London: Cassell and Company Limited, 1971), 321–24; Yoshida Shigeru, Shidehara Kijūrō and Sato Naotake, 'Gaikō Jūō-dan' [Diplomatic free talk], *Jiji Shinpo*, 3 January 1950.

75 Foreign Minister Katō to Ambassador to the US Inoue, 3 July 1914, in 'Gaimushō Gaikokujin Yatoiire Ikken (Fu-Keiyakusho) Bessatsu "Denison"-shi Kankei'; Inoue to Katō, 9 March 1915, in 'Honpō Koyō Gaikokujin Kankei Zakken: Honshō no Bu' [Miscellaneous cases relating to the hiring of foreigners in Japan: Regarding this ministry], K.4.2.0.1-5, Diplomatic Archives of the Ministry of Foreign Affairs of Japan; Inoue to Foreign Minister Ōkuma, 16 September, ibid.; Shidehara, *Gaikō 50 Nen*, 248.

For further information on Baty, see Thomas Baty, *Alone in Japan: The Reminiscences of an International Jurist Resident in Japan 1916–1954*, ed. Hasegawa Motokichi (Tokyo: Maruzen, 1959); Ichimata Masao, 'Thomas Baty Hakase Seikyo' [On the passing of Dr Thomas Baty], *Kokusaihō Gaikō Zasshi* 53, nos 1, 2 (May 1954): 86–97; Ichimata Masao, *Nihon no Kokusai Hōgaku wo Kizuita Hitobito*, 172–76; Uchiyama Masakuma, 'Thomas Baty Hakase no Ronkō' [The merits of Thomas Baty], *Kokusaihō Gaikō Zasshi* 65, no. 6 (March 1967): 35–50; Ministry of Foreign Affairs Hundred-Year History Compilation Association, *Gaimushō no 100 Nen*, vol. 2, 1347–53; Murase Shinya, 'Twilight no Mukō ni: Higeki no Kokusaihō Gakusha Thomas Baty' [On the other side of twilight: The tragic scholar of international law, Thomas Baty] (1) (2) (3), *Gaikō Forum*, no. 177 (April 2003): 70–77, no. 178 (May 2003): 72–79, no. 179 (June 2003): 78–85; Peter Oblas, 'Naturalist Law and Japan's Legitimization of Empire in Manchuria: Thomas Baty and Japan's Ministry of Foreign Affairs', *Diplomacy and Statecraft* 15, no. 1 (2004): 35–55, doi.org/10.1080/09592290490438051; Martin Gornall, 'Dr Thomas Baty, 1869–1954: Legal Adviser to the Japanese Foreign Ministry, 1916–41', in *Britain and Japan: Biographical Portraits*, ed. Hugh Cortazzi, vol. 5 (Kent: Global Oriental, 2005), 431–42.

76   Shidehara to Katō, 15 August 1914, in Ministry of Foreign Affairs, *Nihon Gaikō Bunsho, 1914*, vol. 3, 161; Inoue to Katō, 17 August, ibid., 165–66; Shidehara, *Gaikō 50 Nen*, 274.

77   Funakoshi Mitsunojō, 'Nichi-Doku Kaisen Tōji no Omoide: Furoku, Rakuyōshū (Zuihitsu)' [Memories of the commencement of the war between Japan and Germany: Supplement, fallen leaves collection (essays)], October 1938, in Hirose, *Kindai Gaikō Kaikoroku*, vol. 2, 305–06.

78   Ibid. We find the same observation in Shigemitsu Mamoru, *Shigemitsu Mamoru Gaikō Kaisōroku* [Shigemitsu Mamoru's diplomatic memoirs] (Tokyo: Mainichi Shimbunsha, 1953), 21.

In his memoirs, Uchida Sadatsuchi stated that he took permission to send a coded telegram to the US chargé d'affaires in Sweden. This request was refused, meaning that the Brazilian minister's mediation was required instead. See Uchida Sadatsuchi, 'Zaikin Kakuchi niokeru Shuyō Jiken no Kaiko' [Recollections of major incidents during postings at numerous locations], January 1939, in Hirose, *Kindai Gaikō Kaikoroku*, vol. 1, 185–86. See also Hayashima Akira, ed., 'Uchida Sadatsuchi Nisshi' [The journal of Uchida Sadatsuchi], *Shigaku Zasshi* 88, no. 8 (August 1979): 75–90.

79   According to Funakoshi:

> At the same time that our nation directly handed over its ultimatum to the German ambassador residing in Tokyo, the other related world powers were informed as to its contents. I cannot claim that this was good policy. Usually, when it comes to an ultimatum, it should be enough to deliver it to the respective nation and allow the massive significance of its contents to be understood.

See Funakoshi Mitsunojō, *Nichi-Doku Kokkō Danzetsu Misshi* [The secret history of the severing of diplomatic ties between Japan and Germany], ed. Sekino Naotsugu (Tokyo: Nittō Shoin, 1934), 101–03, 107–09, 123.

80   Horiuchi Tateki, *Chūgoku no Arashi no Naka de* [In the storm that was China] (Tokyo: Kengensha, 1950), 37; Shidehara, *Gaikō 50 Nen*, 81.

81   Tani Masayuki, 'Holland Kōshi Jidai no Shidehara-san' [Mr Shidehara during his time as minister to the Netherlands], date unknown, in 'Shidehara Heiwa Bunko', Reel 18; Matsui Keishirō, *Matsui Keishirō Jijoden* [The autobiography of Matsui Keishirō] (Tokyo: Kankōsha, 1983), 81–82.

82   Shidehara Kijūrō, 'Chūgoku Kōshi Wang Rongbao to Watashi' [Chinese Minister Wang Rongbao and me], in *Sekai no Kokoro to Sugata* [The mind and form of the world], ed. Kijūrō Shidehara et al. (Tokyo: Fushichōsha, 1949), 3–7.

83   Shidehara, *Gaikō 50 Nen*, 248.

84   Nagai, 'Shidehara Danshaku no Omoide'.

85   Itō Hirokuni, vice-grand master of ceremonies in the Ministry of the Imperial Household, to Shidehara, 20 January 1916, in Ministry of Foreign Affairs, *Nihon Gaikō Bunsho, 1916*, vol. 1, 392; Takayama Kimimichi, chief of staff at the office of the Governor-General of Kwantung, to Shidehara, 16 September, ibid., 411–15.

For further details on the relationship between Japan and Russia during World War I, see Yoshimura Michio, *Zōho Nihon to Russia* [Japan and Russia], 2nd ed. (Tokyo: Nihon Keizai Hyōronsha, 1991), 169–318.

86   Shidehara to Malevich, 4 November 1915, in Ministry of Foreign Affairs, *Nihon Gaikō Bunsho, 1915*, vol. 3, part 2, 1185–88; Shidehara-Malevich talks, 6 January 1916, in Ministry of Foreign Affairs, *Nihon Gaikō Bunsho, 1916*, vol. 2, 1–2.

87   Yamada Ryūichi, vice-minister of war, to Shidehara, 6 April 1916, in Ministry of Foreign Affairs, *Nihon Gaikō Bunsho, 1916*, vol. 3, 402–06; Shidehara to Sugawara Michiyoshi, vice-minister of finance, 25 April 1916, ibid., 413–14; Shidehara to Sugawara, 10 June, ibid., 429–30; Shidehara to Sugawara, 27 June, ibid., 439; Shidehara to Shekine, counsellor to the Russian embassy in Japan, 25 August, ibid., 444; Shidehara-Shekine's talks, 25 September, ibid., 449–51; Shidehara to Krupinski, 6 October, ibid., 454–55; Shidehara to Shōda Kazue, vice-minister of finance, 10 October, ibid., 455–56; Shidehara to Shekine, 16 October, ibid., 456–57; Shidehara to Shōda, 19 October, ibid., 458–59; Shidehara to Shōda, ibid., 464–65; Yamada to Shidehara, 25 November, ibid., 471–75.

88   Kamiyama Mitsunoshin, vice-minister of the Ministry of Agriculture and Commerce, to Shidehara, 9 May 1916, in Ministry of Foreign Affairs, *Nihon Gaikō Bunsho, 1916*, vol. 1, 253.

89   Shidehara to Shirani Takeshi, civil governor, office of the Governor-General of Kwantung, 3 August 1916, in Ministry of Foreign Affairs, *Nihon Gaikō Bunsho, 1916*, vol. 2, 898. For research into independence movements in Manchuria and Inner Mongolia, see Kurihara Ken, 'Daiichiji, Dainiji Man-Mō Dokuritsu Undō to Koike Gaimushō Seimukyoku-chō no Jinin' [The first and second Manchurian–Mongolian Independence movements and the resignation of Political Affairs Bureau Director-General Koike at the Ministry of Foreign Affairs], in *Tai-Man-Mō Seisaku-shi no Ichimen* [A partial history of policy on Manchuria and Mongolia], ed. Kurihara Ken (Tokyo: Harashobō, 1966), 139–61; Hatano Masaru, *Man-Mō Dokuritsu Undō* [The Manchurian and Mongolian independence movements] (Tokyo: PHP Institute, 2001).

90   Shidehara-Krupinski's talks, 12 August 1916, in Ministry of Foreign Affairs, *Nihon Gaikō Bunsho, 1916*, vol. 3, 601–03; Shidehara-Zhang Shizhao's talks, 14 October 1918, ibid., vol. 2, part 1, 49–50.

91   'Taigai Seisaku narabini Taido Kankei Zassan: Tai-Shina no Bu (Motono Daijin)' [Collection of miscellaneous issues regarding the foreign policy and position: Part relevant to China (Minister Motono), recorded by Matsumoto], 1.1.1.3-2-4, Diplomatic Archives of the Ministry of Foreign Affairs of Japan; Ministry of Foreign Affairs, *Nihon Gaikō Nenpyō narabini Shuyō Bunsho*, vol. 1, 421–27; Ministry of Foreign Affairs, *Nihon Gaikō Bunsho, 1917*, vol. 2, 2–6; Obata Yūkichi Biography Publishing Association, ed., *Obata Yūkichi* (Tokyo: Obata Yūkichi Biography Publishing Association, 1957), 190–204; Hatano Masaru, *Kindai Higashi Asia no Seiji Hendō to Nihon no Gaikō* [Political changes and Japanese diplomacy in modern East Asia] (Tokyo: Keio Tsūshin, 1995), 260–61.

A work that traces the orientation of the Political Affairs Bureau's First Division and minister to China Hayashi Gonsuke is Kumamoto Fumio, 'Daiichiji Taisen-ki niokeru Gaimushō no Tai-Chu Seisaku: "Keizai Teikei" kara "Bunka Teikei" eno Tenkan' [The Ministry of Foreign Affairs' policies regarding China during the period of World War I: The shift from 'economic partnership' to 'cultural partnership'], *Shikyō*, no. 45 (September 2002): 1–19.

92   Motono to Satō, ambassador to the US, 9 June 1917, in Ministry of Foreign Affairs, *Nihon Gaikō Bunsho, 1917*, vol. 3, 722–23; Wheeler to Shidehara, 11 June, ibid., 726–27.

93   Ministry of Foreign Affairs, *Nihon Gaikō Nenpyō narabini Shuyō Bunsho*, vol. 1, 439–40; Navy Vice-Minister Tochinai Sōjirō to Shidehara, 29 September 1917, in Ministry of Foreign Affairs, *Nihon Gaikō Bunsho, 1917*, vol. 3, 784; W. Reginald Wheeler, *China and the World-War* (New York: Macmillan Company, 1919), 124–25. For recent research on the agreement between Ishii and Lansing, see Takahara Shūsuke, *Wilson Gaikō to Nihon* [Wilson diplomacy and Japan] (Tokyo: Sōbunsha, 2006), 61–102.

94   Motono to Satō, 13 June 1917, in Ministry of Foreign Affairs, *Nihon Gaikō Bunsho, 1917*, vol. 3, 729–31; Satō to Motono, 15 June, ibid., 732; Sato to Lansing, 15 June 1917, in *Papers Relating to the Foreign Relations of the United States* [hereafter cited as *FRUS*], *1917*, ed. Department of State (Washington: Government Printing Office, 1926), 71–72; Wheeler to Lansing, 18 June, ibid., 259; Lansing to Wheeler, 6 July, ibid., 260–62.

95   William Phillips diary, 30 July, 22 August, 8 October and 7 November 1917, Phillips Papers, Box 1.

96   Morris to Lansing, 14 December 1917, in *FRUS, 1918, Russia*, ed. Department of State, vol. 2 (Washington: Government Printing Office, 1926), 7–8; Morris to Lansing, 7 January 1918, ibid., 20; from Morris to Lansing, 13 April, ibid., 121; J. Jules Jusserand (French ambassador to the US) to Lansing, 21 April, ibid., 128–29; Shidehara-Morris talks, 23 January 1918, in Ministry of Foreign Affairs, *Nihon Gaikō Bunsho, 1918*, vol. 1, 641; Shidehara-Green talks, 12 March, ibid., 701–04; Shidehara-Krupinski talks, 3 April, ibid., 513–16; Shidehara-Regnault's talks, 22 April, ibid., 785–86; Shidehara-Green talks, 19 April, ibid., 417–19.

97   William Phillips diary, 3 August 1918, Phillips Papers, Box 1; chief of staff of the Vladivostok Expeditionary Force, Lieutenant General Yuhi Mitsue, to Shidehara, 27 February 1919, in Ministry of Foreign Affairs, *Nihon Gaikō Bunsho, 1919*, vol. 1, 612–14.

98   Shidehara-Green's talks, 27 September 1918, in Ministry of Foreign Affairs, *Nihon Gaikō Bunsho, 1918*, vol. 3, 409–11; Shidehara-Morris talks, 28 October, ibid., 429–32.

99   Ministry of Foreign Affairs, Nihon Gaikō Bunsho, 1918, vol. 3, 423–28; Hattori, Higashi Asia Kokusai Kankyō no Hendō to Nihon Gaikō, 1918–1931, 48–49.

100   Shidehara to vice-minister of war, Lieutenant General Yamanashi Hanzō, 4 August 1919, in Ministry of Foreign Affairs, *Nihon Gaikō Bunsho, 1919*, vol. 3, 1291–92; Shidehara, *Gaikō 50 Nen*, 95–97.

For further details on the Kolchak government and Katō Tsunetada, see Kageura Tsutomu, 'Katō Tsunetada', in *Ehime no Senkaku-sha* [Pioneers of Ehime], ed. Ehime Prefectural Education Committee, vol. 4 (Takamatsu: Ehime Prefectural Education Committee, 1966), 210–14; Hosoya Chihiro, *Russia Kakumei to Nihon* [The Russian revolution and Japan] (Tokyo: Harashobō, 1972), 85–192.

101   Shidehara-Miller talks, 7 August 1918, in Ministry of Foreign Affairs, *Nihon Gaikō Bunsho, 1918*, vol. 2, 231–32. For representative research on topics from this period, such as the New Four-Power Consortium, see Mitani Taiichirō, *Zōho Nihon Seitō Seiji no Keisei: Hara Takashi no Seiji Shidō no Tenkai* [The formation of party-based politics in Japan: The development of Hara Takashi's political leadership], 2nd ed. (Tokyo: University of Tokyo Press, 1995), 321–52. For my own views on this matter, see Hattori, *Higashi Asia Kokusai Kankyō no Hendō to Nihon Gaikō, 1918–1931*, 4–6, 20–34.

102   Mushanokōji, 'Shidehara-san no Omoide'. I have covered the Paris Peace Conference in more detail in Hattori, *Higashi Asia Kokusai Kankyō no Hendō to Nihon Gaikō, 1918–1931*, 34–46. Therefore, I will treat the topic relatively lightly here.

103   Robert Lansing, *The Peace Negotiations: A Personal Narrative* (Boston: Houghton Mifflin Company, 1921), 243–67.

104   Shidehara to Lansing, 26 March 1921, in 'Makino Nobuaki Kankei Bunsho' [Documents relating to Makino Nobuaki], Correspondence Department, vol. 28, Modern Japanese Political History Materials Room, National Diet Library; Shidehara, *Gaikō 50 Nen*, 318–19.

105   Shidehara himself provided details on the feud with Itō Miyoji in the Extraordinary Foreign Diplomacy Investigation Committee in Shidehara Kijūrō (speaking), Kiyosawa Kiyoshi (transcribing), 'Inin-chi Tōchi-ryo Tōchi Keishiki' [The form of mandated governance for lands and territories], date unknown, in 'Shidehara Heiwa Bunko', Reel 18.

106   Katō Takaaki, 'Fusanka no Riyū' [Reason for non-participation], *Seinen* 5, no. 7 (June 1917): 37–42; 'Katō-shi no Benkai' [The self-justification of Viscount Katō], *Seiyu*, no. 208 (July 1917): 45–49; Yokoyama Katsutarō and Higuchi Hideo, eds, *Kenseikai-shi* [A history of the Kenseikai], vol. 1 (Tokyo: Harashobō, 1985), 70–73.

For recent studies of Katō Takaaki, see Sakurai Ryōjū, 'Katō Takaaki to Ei-Bei-Chu Sangoku Kankei' [Katō Takaaki and the tri-nation relationship between the UK, the US and China], in *Taishō-ki Nihon no America Ninshiki* [Japan's perception of the US in the Taishō era], ed. Hasegawa Yūichi (Tokyo: Keio University Press, 2001), 79–121; Naraoka Sōchi, 'Katō Takaaki no Seiji Shidō to Kenseikai no Sōritsu: 1915–1919' [Katō Takaaki's political leadership and the founding of the Kenseikai: 1915–1919], (1) (2), *Hōgaku Ronsō* 151, no. 2 (May 2002): 112–37, 152, no. 1 (October 2002): 114–35; Naraoka Sōchi, 'Katō Takaaki Naikaku no Seiji Katei: Katō Takaaki no Seiji Shidō to Ni-Daiseitō-sei no Seiritsu' [The political process of the Katō Takaaki cabinet: Katō Takaaki's political leadership and the formation of the two-major-party system], (1) (2), *Hōgaku Ronsō* 152, no. 3 (December 2002): 64–87, 153, no. 1 (April 2003): 122–43.

107   Hara, *Hara Takashi Nikki*, vol. 4, 68, 126, 140.

108   Shidehara to Uchida, 20 November 1919, in Ministry of Foreign Affairs, *Nihon Gaikō Bunsho, 1919*, vol. 3, part 1, 402–06, 771–72.

109   Ishii Itarō, *Gaikōkan no Isshō* [The life of a diplomat] (Tokyo: Chūōkōronsha, 1986), 70–71, 80–81. See also Hirota Kōki Biography Publishing Association, *Hirota Kōki* (Tokyo: Ashishobō, 1992), 61.

110 Ishii Itarō, 'Shidehara-Dan no Omoide' [Memories of Baron Shidehara], date unknown, in 'Shidehara Heiwa Bunko', Reel 13; Shidehara, *Gaikō 50 Nen*, 281–84.

111 Shidehara to Uchida, 24 October 1919, in Ministry of Foreign Affairs, *Nihon Gaikō Bunsho, 1919*, vol. 1, 693–94; Vladivostok Expeditionary Force Chief of Staff, Lieutenant General Inagaki Saburō, to Yamanashi, 8 January 1920, in Ministry of Foreign Affairs, *Nihon Gaikō Bunsho, 1920*, vol. 1, part 2, 837; Shidehara to Uchida, 11 January, ibid., 840–48; Hara, *Hara Takashi Nikki*, vol. 5, 199; Shidehara, *Gaikō 50 Nen*, 97–99.

112 Reminiscences of DeWitt Clinton Poole, 1952, Oral History Research Office, Columbia University. For further details on the issue of the removal of troops from Siberia, see Takahara, *Wilson Gaikō to Nihon*, 118–68.

113 For research related to Yap Island, see Paul H. Clyde, *Japan's Pacific Mandate* (New York: Macmillan Company, 1935), 45–62; Hirama Yōichi, *Daiichiji Sekai Taisen to Nihon Kaigun: Gaikō to Gunji to no Rensetsu* [World War I and the Japanese navy: The connection between diplomacy and military] (Tokyo: Keiō University Press, 1998), 131–45; Inada Shinjō, 'Nihon Kaigun no Micronesia Senryō to Yap-tō Mondai' [The occupation of Micronesia by the Japanese navy and the problem of Yap Island], *Waseda Daigaku Daigakuin Hoken Ronshū*, no. 90 (June 1999): 103–22.

114 Government Office of the South Sea Islands, *Nanyōchō Shisei 10 Nenshi* [A 10-year history of administration by the Government Office of the South Sea Islands] (Tokyo: Government Office of the South Sea Islands' Director General's Secretariat, 1932), 65–73.

115 Shidehara to Tochinai, 14 August 1919, in Ministry of Foreign Affairs, *Nihon Gaikō Bunsho, 1919*, vol. 3, part 1, 411; Tochinai to Vice-Minister for Foreign Affairs Hanihara Masanao, 15 September , ibid., 415–16; Provisional Micronesia Defense Corps, 'Nanyōgun-tō: Tō-sei Chōsa Hōkoku' [Micronesia: Island status investigative report], 1 October 1920, in *Gaichi Kokusei Chōsa Hōkoku, Dai 6 Shū: Nanyō Guntō Tōsei Chōsa Hōkoku* [Reports on the census of foreign lands, no. 6: Reports on the island census of the South Seas Islands], ed. Onuma Yoshishige, vol. 1 (Tokyo: Bunseishoin, 1999), 1–15.

116 Shidehara to Uchida, 8 October 1920, in Ministry of Foreign Affairs, *Nihon Gaikō Bunsho, 1920*, vol. 3, part 1, 469–71; Ishii Kikujirō, ambassador to France, to Uchida, 23 February 1921, ibid., vol. 3, part 1, 268–72. Minutes of various meetings are included in Davis, Norman H. Papers, Box 30, Manuscript Division, Library of Congress. Also see memorandum by Davis of a conversation with Shidehara, 28 February 1921, Davis Papers, Box 9.

117 Shidehara to Uchida, 2 May 1921, in Ministry of Foreign Affairs, *Nihon Gaikō Bunsho, 1921*, vol. 3, part 1, 359–63; Shidehara to Uchida, 20 August, ibid., 384–89; Hughes to Shidehara, 15 September 1921, in *FRUS, 1921*, ed. Department of State, vol. 2 (Washington: Government Printing Office, 1945), 297–99.

118 Shidehara to Uchida, 11 February 1922, in Ministry of Foreign Affairs, *Nihon Gaikō Bunsho, 1922*, vol. 3, 378–87; convention between the US and Japan, 11 February 1922, in *FRUS, 1922*, ed. Department of State, vol. 2 (Washington: Government Printing Office, 1945), 600–04.

119 Government Office of the South Sea Islands, *Nanyōchō Shissei Jyūnen-shi* [A 10-year history of administration by the Government Office of the South Sea Islands] (Tokyo: Government Office of the South Sea Islands' Director General's Secretariat, 1932), 38–53; Shidehara, *Gaikō 50 Nen*, 79–80, 143–44.

120 Memorandum by Long of a conversation with Shidehara, 13 December 1919, Breckinridge Long Papers, Box 183, Manuscript Division, Library of Congress; Lansing to Shidehara, 13 December 1919, Long Papers, Box 183; Polk to MacMurray, 20 February 1920, Frank Lyon Polk Papers, Box 28, Sterling Memorial Library, Yale University.

121 Shidehara to Uchida, 24 November 1919, in Ministry of Foreign Affairs, *Nihon Gaikō Bunsho, 1919*, vol. 1, 81–83; Uchida to Shidehara, 6 December, ibid., 101–02. See also Minohara, 'Imin Mondai Kaiketsu eno Futatsu no Nichi-Bei Kōshō', 62–77.

2. THE RUSSO-JAPANESE WAR, WORLD WAR I AND THE WASHINGTON NAVAL CONFERENCE

122 Ministry of Foreign Affairs, ed., *Nihon Gaikō Bunsho: Tai-Bei Imin Mondai Keika Gaiyō* [Documents on Japanese foreign policy: Overview of process of the US immigration problem] (Tokyo: Ministry of Foreign Affairs, 1972), 623–71; Ministry of Foreign Affairs, ed., *Nihon Gaikō Bunsho: Tai-Bei Imin Mondai Keika Gaiyō Fuzokusho* [Documents on Japanese foreign policy: Overview of process of the US immigration problem supplementary documents] (Tokyo: Ministry of Foreign Affairs, 1973), 561–679.

123 Speech by Morris before the Japan Society, 15 December 1920, Roland S. Morris Papers, Box 13, Manuscript Division, Library of Congress.

124 Hara, *Hara Takashi Nikki*, vol. 5, 339; Iimori Akiko and Hatano Masaru, 'Taishō 10 Nen Kōtaishi Hirohito: Maboroshi no Hōbei' [Crown Prince Hirohito's abandoned visit to the US in the 10th year of Taishō], *Ningen Kagaku Ronkyū*, no. 3 (February 1995): 233–43; Hatano Masaru, *Hirohito Kōtaishi Europe Gaiyū-ki* [Record of Crown Prince Hirohito's visit to Europe] (Tokyo: Sōshisha, 1998), 57–62.

125 Shidehara to Uchida, 31 January 1921, in 'Kōtaishi Hirohito Shinnō Heika Gotoō Ikken' [The matter of His Imperial Highness the Crown Prince Hirohito's visit to Europe], L.1.3.0.6, Diplomatic Archives of the Ministry of Foreign Affairs of Japan; Hara, *Hara Takashi Nikki*, vol. 5, 366. Later, while dining with the emperor and prime minister, Shidehara also spoke of the 'impoliteness' of Americans. See Ōta Kenichi, Okazaki Katsuki, Sakamoto Noboru and Nanba Toshinari, eds, *Tsugita Daisaburō Nikki* [The diary of Tsugita Daisaburō] (Okayama: Sanyō Shimbunsha, 1991), 93.

126 Shidehara, *Gaikō 50 Nen*, 72. Regarding the Washington Naval Conference, see Asada Sadao, *Ryō-Taisen-kan no Nichi-Bei Kankei: Kaigun to Seisaku Kettei Katei* [Japanese–American relations between the two world wars: The navy and the process of policy decision-making] (Tokyo: University of Tokyo Press, 1993), 51–148; Hattori, *Higashi Asia Kokusai Kankyō no Hendō to Nihon Gaikō, 1918–1931*, 89–112; Hattori, 'The Washington Conference and East Asia, 1921–1922', *Sōgō Seisaku Kenkyū*, no. 29 (March 2021): 1–20.

127 Shidehara to Uchida, 28 August 1921, in *Nihon Gaikō Bunsho: Washington Kaigi* [Documents on Japanese foreign policy: The Washington Naval Conference], ed. Ministry of Foreign Affairs, vol. 1 (Tokyo: Ministry of Foreign Affairs, 1977), 146–47; Shidehara to Uchida, 15 September, ibid., 160–61; Hara, *Hara Takashi Nikki*, vol. 5, 415.

128 Department of State, ed., *FRUS, 1899* (Washington: Government Printing Office, 1945), 131–3; Department of State, *FRUS, 1900*, 299. For classic studies of this topic, see A. Whitney Griswold, *The Far Eastern Policy of the United States* (New York: Harcourt, Brace and Company, 1938), 36–86; Iriye Akira, *Pacific Estrangement: Japanese and American Expansion, 1897–1911* (Cambridge: Harvard University Press, 1972), 66.

129 Charles E. Hughes, 'Some Aspects of Our Foreign Policy', 29–33, 29 December 1922, 500, A4/508, Record Group 59, National Archives.

130 Shidehara, 'Washington Kaigi no Rimen-kan Sonota', 125–26.

131 Shidehara Kijūrō (speaking), Kiyosawa Kiyoshi (transcribing), 'Washington Kaigi no Hanashi (zoku)' [About the Washington Naval Conference (continued)], 1944, in 'Shidehara Heiwa Bunko', Reel 18.

132 Japanese delegation to Uchida, 16 December 1921, in *Nihon Gaikō Bunsho: Washington Kaigi*, ed. Ministry of Foreign Affairs, vol. 2 (Tokyo: Ministry of Foreign Affairs, 1978), 386–88; Japanese delegation to Uchida, 5 February 1922, ibid., 414–18; Hattori, *Higashi Asia Kokusai Kankyō no Hendō to Nihon Gaikō, 1918–1931*, 97–99, 255–63.

133 Shidehara, Gaikō 50 Nen, 84, 88; Hattori, Higashi Asia Kokusai Kankyō no Hendō to Nihon Gaikō, 1918–1931, 99–102.

134 Johnson was also bitter about how the US and Japan opposed each other in the conference on Yap Island and Chinese communication services. The German-controlled Yap–Shanghai submarine cable had been transferred to Japan. From Johnson's perspective, it was impermissible for Japan to have monopolised control over wireless communication in China. Beginning before the conference, the US had supported the American Federal Company, attempting to enter the Chinese wireless

communications market. However, the issue of Chinese wireless communication was left unresolved at the Washington Naval Conference, leaving the opposition between Japan and the US on this front to linger. It was also typical of Johnson to evaluate the Nine-Power Treaty from the perspective of pursuing an open door ideal in China. According to Johnson, Japan unwillingly followed the US's lead in this area. Further, Johnson worried a great deal about how to secure the removal of Japanese soldiers from Siberia. See reminiscences of Nelson Trusler Johnson, 1954, Oral History Research Office, Columbia University.

For details on Japanese and US opposition regarding communication services in China, see Sunaga Noritake, 'Chūgoku no Tsushin Shihai to Nichi-Bei Kankei: Mitsui-Sōkyō Mudendai Shakkan to Federal Shakkan wo Megutte' [Control of Chinese communications and the Japan–US relationship: The Mitsui-Shuanqiao wireless station loan and the federal loan], *Keizai Shūshi* 60, no. 4 (January 1991): 157–87; Higuchi Hidemi, *Nihon Kaigun kara Mita Nicchū Kankei-shi Kenkyū* [A study of the history of the Sino-Japanese relationship from the perspective of the Japanese navy] (Tokyo: Fuyō Shobō Shuppan, 2002), 87–88; Hattori Ryūji, ed., *Manshū Jihen to Shigemitsu Chūka Kōshi Hōkokusho: Gaimushō Kiroku 'Shina no Taigai Seisaku Kankei Zassan "Kakumei Gaikō"' niyosete* [The Manchurian incident and the report by minister to China Shigemitsu: A Ministry of Foreign Affairs record 'miscellaneous collection relating to the Chinese foreign policy "revolutionary diplomacy"'] (Tokyo: Nihon Tosho Center, 2002), 171–72.

135 Williams to Hughes, 24 September 1921, Edward Thomas Williams Papers, Box 1, Bancroft Library, University of California at Berkeley; Williams to MacMurray, 5 December 1921, Williams Papers, Box 1.

136 Williams diary, 22–23 July, 23–24 August, 13 September and 24 October 1921, Williams Papers, Box 3; Shidehara to Uchida, 4 August 1921, in 'Washington Kaigi Ikken: Keihatsu Sonota Senden Zakken' [Washington conference: Enlightenment and other miscellaneous publicities], 2.4.3.55, Diplomatic Archives of the Ministry of Foreign Affairs of Japan. See Hu Shizhang, *Stanley K. Hornbeck and the Open Door Policy, 1919–1937* (Westport: Greenwood Press, 1995), 52.

137 Williams to MacMurray, 19 January 1922, Williams Papers, Box 1; Williams to Hughes, 24 January 1922, Williams Papers, Box 1; Williams to MacMurray, 7 January 1922, Williams Papers, Box 1.

138 Memorandum by the office of Hughes for the interview with Shidehara, 4 January 1922, Charles Evans Hughes Papers, Reel 126, Manuscript Division, Library of Congress.

139 Balfour to Lloyd George, 11 November 1921, in *Documents on British Foreign Policy 1919–1939* [hereafter cited as *DBFP*], ed. Rohan Butler and J. P. T. Bury, first series, vol. 14 (London: Her Majesty's Stationery Office, 1966), 466–70; Balfour to Lloyd George, 24 November, ibid., 505–11; Balfour to George N. Curzon, 29 November, ibid., 522–23; Japanese delegation to Uchida, 24 November 1921, in Ministry of Foreign Affairs, *Nihon Gaikō Bunsho: Washington Kaigi*, vol. 1, 547–50; Japanese delegation to Uchida, 29 November, ibid., 552–55; Japanese delegation to Uchida, 1 December, ibid., 564–66.

140 For example, according to Okazaki Hisahiko, *Shidehara Kijūrō to Sono Jidai* [Shidehara Kijūrō and his Era] (Tokyo: PHP Institute, 2000), 194–97, the Japanese government proceeded with a policy to 'secure the existence of the Anglo-Japanese Alliance by clarifying that it did not apply to the United States'. However:

> Shidehara, based on his own individual judgment, threw away the asset known as the Anglo-Japanese Alliance, which had been carefully built up over 20 years. He did this without proper discussion with the Japanese government or a clarification to Japan of the significance of what the alliance's termination would mean.

Further, according to Okazaki, what Shidehara should have done was present the Balfour proposal to the US as a proposal for Japanese–British cooperation:

> If the U.S. were to have rejected this proposal, then the U.K. would have to decide what is to be done. However, as a nation which prides itself on acting in a gentlemanly manner, it would be difficult for them to come forward with the proposal to end a 20-year alliance …

For Shidehara to end an alliance even when the U.K. had not made the offer itself, to put it bluntly, constituted a violation of orders ... Naturally, he could be criticized for attempting to be too clever with his application of diplomatic technique.

During a symposium, Mr Okazaki also stated: 'If Shidehara had attempted to maintain the alliance, then the alliance would have continued'. See Okazaki Hisahiko et al., 'Shidehara Gaiko no Zasetsu' [The failure of Shidehara diplomacy]', *Shokun* 35, no. 2 (February 2003): 241. Similar statements can also be found in Okazaki Hisahiko, *Nihon Gaikō no Jōhō Senryaku* [The information strategy of Japanese diplomacy] (Tokyo: PHP Institute, 2003), 28–35; Okazaki Hisahiko, *Dokode Nihonjin no Rekishi-kan ha Yugandanoka* [Where did the Japanese view of history become distorted?] (Tokyo: Kairyūsha, 2003), 139–43.

141 Uchida to Hara, 13 October 1921, in Ministry of Foreign Affairs, *Nihon Gaikō Bunsho: Washington Kaigi*, vol. 1, 181–218.

142 Shidehara, 'Washington Kaigi no Rimen-kan Sonota', 118–19. See also see Shidehara, *Gaikō 50 Nen*, 61–63.

143 Shidehara, 'Washington Kaigi no Rimen-kan Sonota', 118–19. See also see Shidehara, *Gaikō 50 Nen*, 61–63.

144 Shidehara, 'Washington Kaigi no Rimen-kan Sonota', 118–22. See also see Shidehara, *Gaikō 50 Nen*, 63–66.

145 Shidehara, 'Washington Kaigi no Rimen-kan Sonota', 118–22. See also see Shidehara, *Gaikō 50 Nen*, 63–66.

146 Shidehara, 'Washington Kaigi no Rimen-kan Sonota', 118–19. See also see Shidehara, *Gaikō 50 Nen*, 63–66.

147 Curzon to Auckland C. Geddes (British ambassador to the US), 29 June 1921, in Butler and Bury, *DBFP*, first series, vol. 14, 316–18; Geddes to Curzon, 6 July, ibid., 326; Curzon to Geddes, 9 July, ibid., 336–38; memorandum of a conversation between Hugh and Geddes, 23 June 1921, in Department of State, *FRUS, 1921*, vol. 2, 314–16.

148 Ishii, *Gaikōkan no Isshō*, 69.

149 Herbert O. Yardley, *The American Black Chamber* (New York: Blue Ribbon Books, 1931), 250–317; Herbert O. Yardley, *Black Chamber: Beikoku ha Ikanishite Gaikō Mitsuden wo Nusundaka?* [The black chamber: How did the US steal the secret diplomatic telegrams?], trans. Osaka Mainichi Shimbun (Osaka: Osaka Mainichi Shimbun, 1931), 303–90; Shidehara, *Gaikō 50 Nen*, 77.

150 Kurusu Saburō, *Hōmatsu no 35 Nen* [A fleeting 35 years] (Tokyo: Chūōkōronsha, 1986), 218–19.

151 Eliot to Curzon, 13 January 1922, in Butler and Bury, *DBFP*, first series, vol. 14, 606–08; Francis Stewart Gilderoy Piggott, *Broken Thread: An Autobiography* (Aldershot: Gale & Polden Limited, 1950), 144–45; reminiscences of Sir George Sansom, 1957, Oral History Research Office, Columbia University; Wellesley, Victor, 'Anglo-Japanese Alliance and Our Future Policy in the Far East', 1 September 1920, F 2200/199/23, FO 371/5361, National Archives; Hattori, *Higashi Asia Kokusai Kankyō no Hendō to Nihon Gaikō, 1918–1931*, 44–45.

152 Reminiscences of Eugene H. Dooman, 1962, Oral History Research Office, Columbia University.

153 Balfour to Curzon, 9 December 1921, in Butler and Bury, *DBFP*, first series, vol. 14, 546–47. See also Balfour to Curzon, 25 December, ibid., 576–77; note of a conversation between Balfour and Kato, 5 January 1922, ibid., 585–87; Uchida to Japanese delegation, 17 December 1921, in Ministry of Foreign Affairs, *Nihon Gaikō Bunsho: Washington Kaigi*, vol. 1, 616–18; Shidehara to Uchida, 21 February 1922, ibid., 677–80; Shidehara, *Gaikō 50 Nen*, 67–68.

154 Baba Tsunego, *Gendai Jinbutsu Hyōron* [A review of contemporary figures] (Tokyo: Chūōkōronsha, 1930), 275.

155 Ishii, *Gaikō Yoroku*, 417.

156 For details on how Saitō attempted to sway opinion in the US, see Sawada, *Zuikan, Zuihitsu*, 69–74.

157 Shidehara, 'Washington Kaigi no Rimen-kan Sonota', 106.

158 Shidehara Kijūro, 'A Frank Official Statement for Japan', *Current History,* vol. 15, no. 3 (1921): 394–97; Shidehara to Lamont, 6 December 1921, Thomas William Lamont Papers, Box 186, Barker Library, Harvard University. The same journal also included an essay by Chinese plenipotentiary Shi Zhaoji (Alfred Sao-ke Sze). See Sze, Sao-Ke Alfred, 'China at the World Council', *Current History*, vol. 15, no. 3 (1921): 397–99.

Moore later assumed a role at the head office of the Japanese Ministry for Foreign Affairs in March 1922. See Foreign Minister Uchida to Inoue Katsunosuke, Grand Master of Ceremonies, 3 November 1922, in 'Honpō Koyō Gaikokujin Kankei Zakken'. Also see Frederick Moore, *With Japan's Leaders: An Intimate Record of 14 Years as Counsellor to the Japanese Government, Ending December 7, 1941* (New York: Charles Scribner's Sons, 1942), 5, 9, 57–60, doi.org/10.1086/236683; Matsumura, 'Washington Kaigi to Nihon no Kōhō Gaikō', 47–76.

159 Uchida to Shidehara, 28 November 1921, in Ministry of Foreign Affairs, *Nihon Gaikō Bunsho: Washington Kaigi*, vol. 1, 550–51; Uchida to Shidehara, 29 November, ibid., 562–63; Uchida to Shidehara, 17 December, ibid., 616; *Jiji Shinpō*, 28 November 1921; Itō Masanori, *Shimbun 50 Nen-shi* [A 50-year history of newspapers] (Tokyo: Masushobō, 1943), 256–57; Shidehara, *Gaikō 50 Nen*, 65, 256–59; Ishii, *Gaikōkan no Isshō*, 102–04.

160 Shidehara to Uchida, 17 August 1921, in 'Washington Kaigi Ikken'.

161 Tsutsui Kiyoshi, 'Saigo no Gaikō' [The final diplomacy], *Kasumigaseki-kai Kaihō*, no. 305 (March 1971): 12; Lamont to Inoue, 10 October 1923, in 'Inoue Junnosuke Kankei Bunsho' [Documents relating to Inoue Junnosuke], Reels 7–11, Center for Modern Japanese Legal and Political Documents, the Faculty of Law, the University of Tokyo.

162 Shidehara, *Gaikō 50 Nen*, 248, 306–07.

163 Ishii, 'Shidehara-Dan no Omoide'.

164 Frank Lyon Polk diary, 2 March 1920, Polk Papers, Reel 3. This topic will be further covered in Chapter 2.

165 Kitaoka Shinichi, '21-kajō Saikō: Nichi-Bei Gaikō no Sōgo Sayō' [Reconsidering the 21 Demands: The mutual interaction of Japan–US diplomacy], *Nenpyō Kindai Nihon Kenkyū*, no. 7 (October 1985): 119–50; Takahara, *Wilson Gaikō to Nihon*, 31–60.

3

Japan–US Relations and Chinese Nationalism

The Policy Factions of the Ministry of Foreign Affairs

The Western Group and the Reformist Group

The second Yamamoto Gonbē cabinet, formed at the time of the Great Kantō Earthquake, would resign en masse in December 1923. The Yamamoto cabinet had taken responsibility for the assassination attempt on Crown Prince and Regent Hirohito, referred to as the Toranomon Incident.

Kiyoura Keigo (1850–1942), successor to the post of prime minister, was originally a government official and had been closely connected to the elder statesman Yamagata Aritomo, who had died in 1922. The Kiyoura cabinet's main members treated the 'Kenkyū-kai' (Study Group) of the House of Peers as its nucleus, with the governing party consisting only of the Seiyū Hontō. For this reason, the 'Goken Sanpa'—the name of a group comprised of three separate pro-constitution political factions: the Kenseikai, the Seiyūkai and the Kakushin Club—criticised the Kiyoura cabinet for being anachronistic. With the Goken Sanpa later achieving outright victory at the general election, a new cabinet was formed in June 1924, led by the president of the Kenseikai, Katō Takaaki.

Because the governing parties represented in the Katō cabinet included the Kenseikai, the Seiyūkai and the Kakushin Club, it was also referred to as the Goken Sanpa cabinet. The Katō cabinet was further known for actions such as its enactment of universal suffrage for men. As it happens, it was as part of the Katō cabinet that Shidehara would serve as foreign minister for the first time. Shidehara was 51 years old. Party-based cabinets would continue from that point until the attempted coup d'état of 15 May 1932 (known as the May 15 Incident). During this period, Shidehara would serve as foreign minister for a total of over five years in Kenseikai-aligned cabinets, including the Katō cabinet, the first Wakatsuki cabinet, the Hamaguchi cabinet and the second Wakatsuki cabinet.

Before covering Shidehara's time as foreign minister, I would like to clarify some of the personal relations within the Japanese Ministry of Foreign Affairs.[1] In general, Shidehara, Debuchi Katsuji, Satō Naotake and Hirota Kōki have collectively been referred to as the 'Western group', a clique oriented towards the major Western nations, due to the emphasis they placed on Japan's relationship with Europe and the US. This group's overall views initially dominated the Ministry of Foreign Affairs.

By contrast, when Arita Hachirō became director-general of the ministry's Asian Bureau in September 1927, he helped establish his own group, known as the 'Asia group' or the 'reformists'. Along with Arita, the reformists also included figures such as Shigemitsu Mamoru, Tani Masayuki and Shiratori Toshio. Of course, while we can speak of the 'Western group' or the 'reformists', neither was a monolithic entity. For example, as noted in Chapter 1 (Section 5: The Washington Naval Conference), when Shidehara served as ambassador to the US, he relied upon Saburi Sadao more than Hirota. Hirota, too, was close to the reformists.[2]

The reformists originated in a society within the Ministry of Foreign Affairs known as the Gaimushō Kakushin Dōshikai (Reform Association of Kindred Spirits of the Foreign Ministry). This was a society created by younger diplomats who had participated in the Paris Peace Conference—including Arita, Shigemitsu, Saitō Hiroshi and Horinouchi Kensuke—to work towards structural reform. The society had around 40 members. It should be noted that Shiratori, who played an important role in the reformists, maintained positive relations with Shidehara up until the Manchurian Incident of September 1931. After that incident, however, the reformists proceeded to take control over the direction of the ministry.

The reformists also had their own internal divisions, with a Shiratori clique facing off against Arita and his supporters. Individuals such as Arita, Shigemitsu and Tani became known as the 'traditionalists'.[3] The actions of the reformists are particularly instructive for understanding Japanese diplomacy in the 1930s. For it was they who would go to make up the core of the Ministry of Foreign Affairs in the years following the Manchurian Incident.

What about the Western group? It was in fact Shidehara who, as a member of the Western group, acted as a pivotal figure in the ministry in the 1920s. Extensive research has been conducted on Shidehara's two terms as foreign minister. That research characterises Shidehara as seeking cooperation with the US and the UK, and as a proponent of economism. With respect to China, Shidehara is portrayed as both a non-interventionist and someone who sought to foster the establishment of order. How prior commentators have evaluated Shidehara has depended upon which of these aspects they viewed as of greater significance.[4] How were these different aspects coordinated in Shidehara's thinking? Further, what kind of principle, if any, can we identify at the base of his policies? On these points, commentators have not yet arrived at a stable interpretation. One reason for this, I suggest, is the lack of analysis of his personal relations and of his policy process.

Among the Western group, it is particularly important to pay attention to the policy group that would best be referred to as the 'Shidehara clique'. Within this clique, we can trace a direct line of descent, as it were, from Shidehara to individuals such as Debuchi Katsuji and Saburi Sadao. It is they who would make up, for a time, the core actors in the Ministry of Foreign Affairs. Yet, as seen in the case of Shidehara not talking to Hirota, the Western group was not united in belonging to the Shidehara clique. These kinds of internal connections and divisions are, in my view, very important. Yet, for some reason, they have not previously been properly analysed. Thus, it would be valuable to shed some light on what kind of people Shidehara worked with and to achieve which goals.

The publication of Debuchi's diary is particularly significant in this respect, given his close relationship with Shidehara. As it happens, thus far, relatively little research has made substantial use of Debuchi's diary. In the case of Saburi, whom Shidehara relied upon so strongly, we see that research has merely emphasised the role he had to play in such matters as the Beijing Special Conference on Tariffs.[5] It can be said, therefore, that empirical research on the Shidehara clique has only now gotten underway.

To put it another way, investigations into the Shidehara clique are still insufficient compared with the research that has been carried out on the reformists. It seems that this has occurred because it was assumed that Shidehara simply took the initiative with respect to the actions of this clique. Yet if we are to deepen our understanding of Shidehara, we must not neglect more in-depth analysis of this personal connection and his policy process. There are five reasons for this, which I shall now outline.

First, Shidehara tended to advance his policies by coordinating with trusted subordinates. This approach was already evident during his time as ambassador to the US. Once he assumed the role of foreign minister as well, he preferred not to rely too much upon opinions from outside his own circle.

Second, Shidehara's experience of overseas postings was quite unbalanced. His longest posting abroad was in Korea. In all, Shidehara spent a little over five years at Incheon and Busan. His time in the US was also quite long, at nearly five years. In the case of the UK, Shidehara's posting lasted two years and a few months. He also spent some time in Belgium and the Netherlands. However, he never had any direct experience with China.

Third, the Ministry of Foreign Affairs underwent organisational expansion. Because the workload expanded significantly at the time of the Paris Peace Conference, the ministry first responded by establishing the Treaties and Conventions Bureau. Then, in 1920, the Political Affairs Bureau was divided up into the Asian Bureau and the American and European Bureau. The Asian Bureau was, in turn, formed of three divisions, in charge of general diplomacy, finance and economy, and Japanese expatriates, respectively. The American and European Bureau also had three divisions, in charge of Russia, Europe and the US, respectively. Given that Shidehara was a product of the diplomatic service exam and sought to act in the established framework of the ministry, understanding what kind of organisational changes occurred is important.

Fourth, the number of employees at the ministry increased sharply during this period. When Shidehara took the fourth diplomatic service exam, he was one of only four individuals who passed. Twenty years or so later, in the period following World War I, the number of successful candidates for the exam on a given occasion would grow to be more than 20. In 1920 and 1921, in particular, the number of incoming staff was closer to 40. Capable personnel were even recruited from outside the ministry. When Shidehara assumed the role of foreign minister, the total ministry staff had grown to more than 1,100. This indicates that, regardless of whether he was foreign minister, it would not be a simple task to steer the ministry as a whole in the direction he wanted it to go.[6]

Fifth, and finally, negotiations with institutions such as the army and the navy would be conducted by someone of at least the rank of director-general of bureaus. A classic example would be the Kiyoura cabinet's policy platform regarding China. This platform was deliberated over by Debuchi, who was then the director-general of the Asian Bureau. On this occasion Debuchi attempted to restrain the army's policy of advancement into northern Manchuria. This indicates the extent to which Shidehara relied upon the Asian Bureau staffs, and in particular Director-General Debuchi, on matters concerning policy on China.

Keeping these points in mind, I seek to clarify the nature of Shidehara's policy process and personal connections for his first term as foreign minister. An examination of what Shidehara left in the hands of his trusted subordinates, and of what was thereby achieved, allows us to better understand the reality of 'Shidehara diplomacy'. In some cases, actions that were thought to have arisen from Shidehara's own decision-making may turn out to have actually been cases of bottom-up policymaking. Therefore, in the discussion that follows, I will begin by tracing the formation of the Shidehara clique, before moving on to topics such as Shidehara's relationship with Prime Minister Katō, Shidehara's diplomatic ideals, the relationship between China and Japan, the US immigration problem, ministry personnel, economic diplomacy and policy on the Soviet Union.

The Formation of the Shidehara Faction

Our first step shall be to look at the formation of the Shidehara clique, by way of Shidehara's relationships with Debuchi and Saburi. For this reason, it is necessary to take a step backward and return to the era of Shidehara's service as the ambassador to the US. Shidehara arrived at his posting in Washington in November 1919. Of the various problems that exacerbated Japanese–American tensions during the Wilson administration, the primary one was opposition in the US to Japanese immigration. Naturally, Shidehara did his best to resolve this problem. Yet this was not the only issue. Japan and the US were also at odds over matters such as the Siberia expedition, the Shandong problem and the New Four-Power Consortium.[7]

When Shidehara became ambassador, the Wilson administration was already nearing its end. Moreover, the office of secretary of state was in transition from Lansing to Colby. This meant that the third undersecretary of state, Breckinridge Long, had to play a larger role, as he was frequently assigned to negotiations with Japan. Shidehara would make frequent use of Counsellor Debuchi for his negotiations with Long. Of the various issues discussed, it was that of the New Four-Power Consortium that saw the greatest progress.[8] Originally, it was Lamont, representative of the US bankers, who received attention for his role in the development of the New Four-Power Consortium. Certainly, Lamont displayed a willingness to go along with Japan's position and contributed significantly to the establishment of the consortium.[9]

Yet in the State Department, it was none other than Long who would collaborate with Lamont. This fact has been acknowledged by MacMurray, chief of the Division of Far Eastern Affairs. When in negotiations with Debuchi and others, Long wrote, in correspondence to Lamont, that 'it is necessary to get Japan to become a member of the Consortium'. He added, 'we are prepared to admit that Japan has certain specified vested interests in Manchuria, and that these be excepted from the operations of the Consortium'.[10] In other words, Long was more conciliatory with respect to Japan than even Lamont. Shidehara would have been made aware of this fact from Debuchi's group. This was why he was able to pressure Long further, as though he had seen through the intentions of the US side. In the words of Long, Shidehara:

> Spoke of the use of the word veto, and asked whether it was proposed by the use of it that Japan should not have the right to prevent those activities which might be aimed at her national interest.[11]

Here, too, Long replied in a way that seemed to accept Shidehara's wishes.

In this manner, Shidehara did his best to secure Japan's special interests in China. Meanwhile, Lamont, working through the commercial firm J. P. Morgan, sought to pressure Undersecretary of State Long and Polk to accept a settlement.[12] An agreement concerning the New Four-Power Consortium would finally be reached in May 1920. During this period, Debuchi was transferred to Germany to serve as an embassy counsellor. Shidehara therefore turned to his first secretary, Saburi Sadao, for help with negotiations with the US. As it happened, Saburi was originally known within the ministry as a specialist on France. His assignment to the embassy in the US, therefore, was due to the support he received from Shidehara. Back when Shidehara was serving as vice-minister for foreign affairs, Saburi had been serving as the French language instructor to Crown Prince Hirohito. He had 'no experience at all of the U.K. or the U.S.'. When Saburi heard that Shidehara 'would go to the US as the ambassador, he approached me with the request that he also go, because he wished to see the U.S.'.[13] Assenting to this request, Shidehara worked to ensure Saburi's assignment to the US.

In summary, Shidehara tended to advance his policy goals through coordination with his trusted subordinates. In particular, he relied heavily upon Debuchi and Saburi. At the Washington Naval Conference, Saburi would participate from the outset, while Debuchi also assisted as senior officer of the public relations section. Eventually, both Debuchi and Saburi supported Shidehara as the foreign minister, with Debuchi becoming the director-general of the Asian Bureau and Saburi the director-general of the International Trade Bureau. (See Table 2 on important ministry personnel in the 1920s.) Let us look at what roles Shidehara assigned Debuchi and Saburi to and what this says about his own diplomatic goals.

Table 2: Important personnel in Japan's Ministry of Foreign Affairs, 1920s

Prime Minister	Foreign Minister	Vice-Minister for Foreign Affairs	Director-General, Asian Bureau	Director-General, American and European Bureau	Director-General, International Trade Bureau	Director-General, Treaties and Conventions Bureau	Director-General, Intelligence Department
Hara Takashi (1918–21)	Uchida Yasuya	Shidehara Kijūrō	Yoshizawa Kenkichi	Matsudaira Tsuneo	Hanihara Masanao	Matsuda Michikazu	Ijūin Hikokichi
Takahashi Korekiyo (1921–22)	Uchida Yasuya	Hanihara Masanao	Debuchi Katsuji	Hirota Kōki	Tanaka Tokichi	Yamakawa Tadao	Tanaka Tokichi
Katō Tomosaburō (1922–23)	Uchida Yasuya	Tanaka Tokichi	Debuchi Katsuji	Hirota Kōki	Nagai Matsuzō	Yamakawa Tadao	Tanaka Tokichi
Yamamoto Gonbē (1923–24)	Ijūin Hikokichi	Matsudaira Tsuneo	Debuchi Katsuji	Hirota Kōki	Nagai Matsuzō	Yamakawa Tadao	Matsudaira Tsuneo
Kiyoura Keigo (1924)	Matsui Keishirō	Matsudaira Tsuneo	Debuchi Katsuji	Hirota Kōki	Nagai Matsuzō	Yamakawa Tadao	Matsudaira Tsuneo
Katō Takaaki (1924–26)	Shidehara Kijūrō	Matsudaira Tsuneo	Debuchi Katsuji	Hirota Kōki	Saburi Sadao	Yamakawa Tadao	Matsudaira Tsuneo
Wakatsuki Reijirō (1926–27)	Shidehara Kijūrō	Debuchi Katsuji	Kimura Eiichi	Hotta Masaaki	Saitō Yoshie	Nagaoka Harukazu	Debuchi Katsuji
Tanaka Giichi (1927–29)	Tanaka Giichi	Debuchi Katsuji Yoshida Shigeru	Kimura Eiichi Arita Hachirō	Hotta Masaaki	Saitō Yoshie Taketomi Toshihiko	Saburi Sadao Matsunaga Naokichi	Debuchi Katsuji Komura Kinichi Saitō Hiroshi
Hamaguchi Osachi (1929–31)	Shidehara Kijūrō	Yoshida Shigeru	Arita Hachirō	Hotta Masaaki	Taketomi Toshihiko	Matsunaga Naokichi	Saitō Hiroshi
Wakatsuki Reijirō (1931)	Shidehara Kijūrō	Nagai Matsuzō	Tani Masayuki	Matsushima Hajime	Taketomi Toshihiko	Matsuda Michikazu	Shiratori Toshio

Ambassador to the US	1919 (November): Shidehara Kijūrō
	1923 (February): Hanihara Masanao
	1925 (March): Matsudaira Tsuneo
	1928 (October): Debuchi Katsuji
Ambassador to the UK	1916 (July): Chinda Sutemi
	1920 (September): Hayashi Gonsuke
	1925 (August): Matsui Keishirō
	1929 (January): Matsudaira Tsuneo
Ambassador to France	1916 (February): Matsui Keishirō
	1920 (September): Ishii Kikujirō
	1928 (February): Adachi Mineichirō
	1930 (June): Yoshizawa Kenkichi
Ambassador to the Soviet Union	1925 (March): Satō Naotake (chargé d'affaires)
	1925 (July): Tanaka Tokichi
	1930 (December): Hirota Kōki
Minister to China	1918 (December): Obata Yūkichi
	1923 (July): Yoshizawa Kenkichi
	1929 (October): Saburi Sadao
	1931 (June): Shigemitsu Mamoru

Note: Sourced from the respective yearly editions of Minister's Secretariat Personal Division, ed., *Gaimushō Nenkan* (Ministry for Foreign Affairs yearbook).

The Spirit of the Washington Naval Conference

Shidehara and Katō

On 11 June 1924, the Goken Sanpa cabinet was formed, headed by Katō Takaaki. Informally, it was almost decided that the post of foreign minister would go not to Shidehara but to Ishii Kikujirō, who was then ambassador to France. At the very last minute, the position went to Shidehara.[14] Why did Shidehara ultimately become the foreign minister instead of Ishii? One interview provides Ishii's account of the circumstances:

> On one occasion, Mr. Katō (Takaaki) said that if he were to form his administration, he would very much like to give me the office of foreign minister. But I responded by refusing the offer. It could make things uncomfortable, given that Shidehara was a relative [of Katō]. But basically, I recommended him as the most suitable candidate. Later, during my second term as ambassador to France, Count Katō did actually get to form a government. I wrote a letter right away, just to state that my opinion was the same as before, and that I would prefer to not take on that position.[15]

In other words, Ishii declined the post of foreign minister and instead recommended Shidehara. Katō responded by appointing Shidehara, rather than Ishii or the previous foreign minister, Matsui. What was Katō's true intention here? Shidehara and Ishii did not have vastly different conceptions of foreign affairs. And, from the beginning, Shidehara had had a close relationship with Ishii. In fact, it was Ambassador to France Ishii who secured the role of vice-minister for foreign affairs in the second Ōkuma cabinet for Shidehara.[16] It was at that point that Ishii was internally thought to be the best candidate to succeed Katō as foreign minister.

Naturally, Ishii was therefore regarded as belonging to Katō's political faction. It was only appropriate that Ishii would go on to assume the role of foreign minister in Katō's own cabinet. Yet if Katō had made this decision, there would have been political complications. Hence, for the above reasons, it would ultimately be Shidehara who would become foreign minister in the Katō cabinet. In fact, Shidehara would be the very first foreign minister to enter the ministry through the diplomatic service exam. Until that point, foreign ministers were typically chosen more on the basis of their personal connections than the circumstances of their entry into the ministry.

The previous foreign minister, Matsui Keishirō, also exemplified this older way of doing things. Matsui stated:

> When I was thinking of securing a job that concerned foreign nations, I spoke with Mr. Hatoyama Kazuo [director-general of the Investigation Bureau and, simultaneously, a professor of law], because he seemed to have some status within the ministry. He was warm to the idea and said he would put in a word with Katō Takaaki, so I should go and introduce myself. When I went to visit him in Surugadai, he gave me his approval, so then it was decided that I would go work at the Foreign Ministry. All I had to do was wait for the summons after I graduated.[17]

By contrast, Shidehara, as a member of the generation who entered via the diplomatic service exam system, was a model official. Figures such as Hara Takashi and Yamagata Aritomo were initially cautious of Shidehara, whom they saw as belonging to the Katō clique. Yet despite being something of an arch-rival of Katō, Hara at least would gradually come to trust Shidehara. He would even go so far as to have Shidehara succeed Ishii for the role of ambassador to the US. This speaks to how Shidehara was regarded as less politically partisan than Ishii.

A talk by Nagai Matsuzō is instructive on this point. Nagai had a close relationship with Shidehara and served under him as vice-minister for foreign affairs during Shidehara's second term as foreign minister. This is what Nagai had to say:

> I have worked under Minister Ishii Kikujirō as well as under Minister Shidehara Kijūrō, and Viscount Ishii had the sharper mind. Mr. Shidehara was careful, but I am not sure he was particularly politically minded. Really, it was Uchida Yasuya who did not show much in the way of brilliance. However, he was good with people and quite a capable drinker. His personality like a rubber doll is well liked by everybody, I suppose.
>
> Katō Takaaki was not familiar with the U.S. At the time, I was director of the Immigration Division, around the time when the whole immigration problem was basically getting resolved. Then, when [Katō] became minister, he came around to our area, and

delivered his judgment of the whole thing right there on the spot: 'Those Americans can't be trusted. You can negotiate with them as long as you like, and it will not get you anywhere.'[18]

So why did Katō choose the less politically oriented Shidehara as the foreign minister? If we interpret his action logically, it would seem that, in considering his choices, Katō had his eye fixed on Saionji Kinmochi. Saionji was the last of Japan's *genrō* (elder statesmen). Certainly, it was no longer the golden age of the *genrō*, yet it was still they who approved the succeeding prime minister for leading the nation. To be able to decide who would head the cabinet was itself a great power.

The problem Katō faced was that he had a poor reputation in the wake of the Twenty-One Demands issued to China. For Katō, therefore, it was imperative that he take an action that could help eliminate Saionji's suspicion. For this reason, it was desirable for him to assign a more neutral figure such as Shidehara, rather than Ishii, who was more firmly in Katō's camp. Thus, Katō left diplomatic affairs to Shidehara in order to preserve some continuity in Japan's foreign policy.

The Diet held on 1 July 1924 seemed to hint at Katō's decision on this matter. This was Katō's first address to the Diet as prime minister. Contrary to expectations, he hardly addressed diplomatic issues at all. He merely expressed 'regret' that the US had passed the Japanese Exclusion Act, which was scheduled for enactment that very day. According to the preface of the influential journal *Gaikō Jihō* (Diplomatic review):

> It may seem that he had simply dropped the matter of the China problem as though he had forgotten it, yet this [omission] was actually reflective of Prime Minister Katō's administrative policy.[19]

In other words, perhaps Katō had intentionally avoided touching upon the China problem, given its controversial nature.

Shidehara was the next to take the podium after Katō. Shidehara asserted the need to 'maintain continuity in matters of diplomatic policy', claiming that this would also help 'preserve the dignity of the nation'.[20] Shidehara's approach towards diplomacy would eventually earn the trust of Saionji. While there may have been a mixed reception in general, Shidehara's more cordial relationship with Saionji was extremely valuable to the Kenseikai.

Shidehara and Debuchi

What kind of diplomacy did Shidehara initially pursue in the Katō cabinet? The longstanding issue at the time was how to deal with China. To better understand Shidehara's approach, it helps to look at his address to the Diet. As mentioned above, his initial address was given on 1 July 1924. The venue was the House of Peers. There Shidehara advanced the following position with respect to China:

> When it comes to the domestic political circumstances of China, we need to avoid getting overly involved. Furthermore, we need to avoid taking measures that appear to ignore China's reasonable positions. When it comes to China, for some time now, we have worked towards bringing Japan and China closer together economically, under the ideal of equal opportunity … As you are all well aware, at the time of the Washington Naval Conference, various treaties were signed that concern China … These prescribed policies are in complete accord with those policies we have sought to take. Therefore, the government's intention is to act in a manner that is consistent to the spirit of these treaties.[21]

In summary, Shidehara declared that Japan would not interfere in China's politics but would instead seek closer economic relations between the two countries on the basis of equal opportunity. The goal was to help forge an international order in accordance with the spirit of the Washington Naval Conference. This stance was naturally understood as constituting the essence of Shidehara diplomacy.

Yet it should be pointed out that, at the time, Shidehara's address was not necessarily warmly regarded. To quote once more from *Gaikō Jihō*:

> The address of Foreign Minister Shidehara was like something by a new editor of a provincial newspaper tasked with writing an editorial on diplomatic problems for the first time. It neither included any real aims nor had any clear central message.[22]

In other words, the journal harshly criticised Shidehara's address as not only unoriginal but empty of meaning.

How should such strong criticism be interpreted? It may help to consider the Diet address of former foreign minister Matsui:

> With regard to the peaceful unification of China, an improvement of the conditions of that country is a task that falls upon its citizens. It is they who need to awaken to the needs of the day, and apply their efforts. It is not the place of outsiders to overly interfere in their matters … We need instead to work towards a complete understanding between the peoples of Japan and China and be resolute in promoting further cultural and economic relations … In the case of the Washington Conference, we will honor the spirit of the various treaties and decisions made there, and on that basis, take necessary steps with respect to our policy on China.[23]

Matsui's address was given on 22 January 1924—only half a year before Shidehara's address. In this address, Matsui maintained that, while Japan ought to maintain its stance of non-intervention, in the hopes of promoting peace and national unity within China, it also needed to push forward with developing closer cultural and economic ties between the two nations, while also respecting the spirit of the Washington Naval Conference. There was no essential difference between Matsui's address and Shidehara's. Thus, the ideals expressed in Shidehara's speech can hardly be regarded as his own unique stance; instead, they were already identifiable within senior diplomatic circles from an earlier stage.

As to why Shidehara's and Matsui's speeches were so similar, the key here is Debuchi. As director-general of the Asian Bureau, Debuchi supported both Matsui and Shidehara during their respective terms as foreign minister. Debuchi, who had previously supported Shidehara during his time as ambassador to the US, went to Beijing in the period after the Washington Naval Conference to negotiate some of the details regarding the Shandong Treaty that had been signed at the conference. These negotiations began in June 1922 and were concluded in December. The committee chief of the Japanese side was Obata, then minister to China. Debuchi assisted Obata as a member of the committee, alongside Secretary-General Kimura Eiichi and others. The committee chief of the Chinese side, meanwhile, was Wang Zhengting.[24]

Debuchi would go on to become director-general of the Asian Bureau in May 1923. Debuchi was proud of the work he had done alongside Shidehara in successfully concluding the negotiations at the Washington Naval Conference. For this reason, he forcefully argued to Foreign Minister Ijūin and Vice-Minister Matsudaira of the Yamamoto cabinet that 'the Washington treaties be followed as our guiding principles'. However, Debuchi was dissatisfied with Ijūin. This was primarily due to their differences on policy on China. Debuchi sought to promote cultural undertakings with regard to China. In fact, Wang Zhengting, former Chinese foreign minister, even visited Debuchi once to discuss the issue of the lynching of innocent Chinese people in the aftermath of the Great Kantō Earthquake. Ijūin, meanwhile, had no interest in such matters. Further, from Debuchi's perspective, Ijūin tended to hire people on the basis of favouritism. For example, he declined to make former minister to China Obata the ambassador to Germany, instead choosing Honda Kumatarō.[25]

The Kiyoura cabinet was formed in January 1924. The position of foreign minister went to Matsui Keishirō. When he made the address quoted above, the section on China was actually written by Debuchi. The main points were the following:

> (1) The desirability of peace in China; (2) non-intervention in Chinese affairs; (3) cooperation between the citizens of the two nations; (4) the importance of cooperation conducted with a spirit of autonomy; (5) respect for the spirit of the Washington Naval Conference.[26]

These were principles, therefore, that predated Shidehara's promotion to foreign minister, and they were previously prepared by Debuchi. Moreover, it was also Debuchi who was able to impose an arms embargo on the warlord Zhang Zuolin.

With the beginning of the Katō cabinet in June of the same year, Shidehara, as foreign minister, internally shared an outline of his planned Diet address with the directors-general of the different ministry bureaus. Debuchi, after seeing a draft of the address, 'made substantial revisions to the section concerning China'.[27] The result was the kind of address seen in the excerpt above. This is all to say that the reason Matsui's and Shidehara's addresses were similar was that, in each case, Debuchi added his own, not inconsiderable changes. Of course, it was Shidehara himself who had influenced Debuchi considerably during his time as ambassador to the US. It was in this way that Shidehara's diplomatic ideals began to take hold within Japanese diplomatic circles in general, even before he became foreign minister.

In the autumn of 1924, a conflict erupted in China between the Zhili and Fengtian military cliques. This conflict is known as the Second Zhili–Fengtian War. At cabinet meetings at this time, Shidehara had to fight for his position without support. The Katō cabinet was leaning towards sending troops to China, urged on by the minister for agriculture and commerce, Takahashi Korekiyo. Nevertheless, Shidehara continued to argue against intervention. It should, of course, be kept in mind that Shidehara's non-interventionist stance was not at all arbitrary. Rather, he had his own underlying reasoning that supported his view of the situation.

At the cabinet meeting, Shidehara made the following statement:

> Even if Wu Peifu [of the Zhili clique] wins and enters Dongsan Province (the 'Three Northeast Provinces' that would later become subsumed within the puppet state of Manchukuo), his forces will be fully engaged, with no reserves for deployment elsewhere … Feng Yuxiang [also of the Zhili clique] is in Zhangjiakou; however, he is not well disposed towards Wu. He is not going to just sit back and watch Wu capture more territory.[28]

In response, Prime Minister Katō went so far as to criticise Shidehara's position as 'meaningless'.[29] After a furious debate, Shidehara submitted his resignation to Kato, but was appeased.

As it happened, the Second Zhili–Fengtian War played out as Shidehara predicted, with Japan managing to secure its interests in China without incident. However, behind the scenes, the Japanese army was lending support to Feng Yuxiang. It was at this time that Asian Bureau Director-General Debuchi lent his support to Shidehara's policy of non-intervention. Debuchi organised a three-party meeting with the Ministry of War and the Navy Ministry, whereupon 'it was decided that a basic policy of non-intervention would be followed'. Debuchi also 'emphasized the importance of a non-intervention policy' to the Seiyūkai and Seiyūhontō parties.[30]

It should be noted that Debuchi played a significant role in handling coordination with the army and navy during Shidehara's first term as foreign minister. Shidehara and Debuchi also shared similar ideals. Shidehara once argued, regarding international politics in the era after the Paris Peace Conference:

> We must speak of a future where the abuse of military force is swept away, where the ideology of invasion is rejected, where all international problems are resolved through cooperation based upon mutual respect of the parties involved, as well as upon an understanding that is shared between all the peoples of the world.[31]

In December 1924, Debuchi was promoted from Asian Bureau director-general to vice-minister for foreign affairs. This change also had an impact on Shidehara's policy of non-intervention. With Debuchi now extremely busy working as vice-minister for foreign affairs, coordination with the military became more difficult. It should be remembered that this situation was in the context of Japan's response to the 'Guo Songling Incident' of this period. The Guo Songling Incident was a rebellion launched in November 1925 by General Guo Songling against the Fengtian clique leader Zhang Zuolin. In response, Japan issued a warning and was able to force Guo Songling's army to retreat by increasing the size of the Kwantung Army.[32]

In August 1926, in the first phase of the 'Northern Expedition', Matsui Iwane, chief of the Second Bureau of the Office of Army General Staff, argued that peace should be recommended to the various armies of China. The Northern Expedition was a military campaign inside China. It was launched from Guangzhou by Chiang Kai-shek (Jiang Jieshi), leader of the National Revolutionary Army, for the purpose of defeating the Beiyang government. However, Matsui's proposal for promoting peace was rejected by Asian Bureau Director-General Kimura Seiichi. Kimura, as Debuchi's successor to the post, was also concerned about Japan's relations with the UK, the US and France, and wanted to maintain the course of non-intervention.[33]

Immigration and Personnel

Shidehara and Saburi

Along with Debuchi, another individual who was regarded as belonging to Shidehara's coterie was Saburi Sadao. As an embassy counsellor, Saburi had previously worked as a plenipotentiary attendant at the Washington Naval Conference, under Ambassador Shidehara to the US. In May 1924, Saburi was relieved of his position in the US. Upon returning to Japan, he became the director-general of the International Trade Bureau in September that year, following a brief period as acting director-general. The previous director-general of the bureau, Nagai Matsuzō, had required a period of convalescence.[34]

Traditionally, the International Trade Bureau had not been viewed as of particular importance within the ministry. One entry in Debuchi's diary even stated: 'In the vice-minister's office, we debated the matter of abolishing the International Trade Bureau'.[35] Horiuchi Tateki, who had long served in the bureau, was dissatisfied with its low position inside the ministry. This was because, in his view, 'from the perspective of Japan, within it lay the fate of economic diplomacy occupying a central position'.[36] Horiuchi was also in charge of handling practical affairs for the Gaimushō Kakushin Dōshikai.

So, what did Shidehara wish to promote through Saburi and the International Trade Bureau? The bureau was responsible for economic and immigration matters. The first issue that Shidehara and Saburi needed to engage with was the immigration problem in the US. Let us go back in time a little now to revisit the roots of this issue. In 1908, an informal agreement between Japan and the US ensured that, in exchange for a voluntary restriction in the number of vessels crossing over, Japanese individuals could still immigrate to the US. It should be noted that, at this time, the immigration of Asian people from countries other than Japan was already prohibited. However, towards the end of May 1924, the US Congress enacted a Japanese Exclusion Act. A clause in the new law forbade foreigners who were not eligible for naturalisation from entering the country. This effectively outlawed the immigration of all Japanese individuals. In reaction, anti-US protest movements spread across Japan. Japan was sensitive to matters of racial discrimination and had sought for its citizens the status of 'honorary whites'.

With the Japanese Exclusion Act passing in the US, Shidehara tended to be viewed as lacking any plan for dealing with the immigration problem. In reality, however, Shidehara had been deeply involved with this issue even before becoming foreign minister. While serving as ambassador to the US, Shidehara had been concerned about the influence of the 1920 Alien Land Law that had passed in California—the law that prohibited Japanese people from leasing land. In October 1920, immediately before the passing of the bill, Shidehara had put pressure on Secretary of State Colby. He urged Colby to speak out as a representative of the federal government 'for the purpose of allaying popular excitement in Japan'.[37] However, Colby believed he could not agree to Shidehara's request. Taking into account matters such as the situation in California, he was very cautious about issuing any government statement.

As mentioned earlier, Saburi left his posting in the US in 1924. On his way back to Japan, he visited the West Coast of the US to investigate the immigration problem. Undersecretary of State Phillips, after being informed by Saburi of his findings, wrote in his diary that Saburi 'has done much during the last few years to help good relations between the two countries'.[38]

Of those individuals in Japan at that time who made proposals on what to do about the Japanese Exclusion Act, one was Sakatani Yoshirō, member of the House of Peers. Sakatani discussed the issue with Foreign Minister Matsui, as well as the director of the Immigration Division of the International Trade Bureau, Akamatsu Hiroyuki. After returning to Japan, Saburi reached out to Sakatani. Meanwhile, Shidehara had returned earlier than Saburi and was waiting for his new posting. Saburi and International Trade Bureau Director-General Nagai provided detailed explanations on the developments behind the passing of the Japanese Exclusion Act to Shidehara and financier Shibusawa Eiichi.[39]

Around March 1924, the Kiyoura cabinet examined the possibility of sending Shibusawa, along with the privy councillor and chairman of the America–Japan Society, Kaneko Kentarō, to the US to help alleviate anti-Japanese sentiment. Shidehara, still waiting for his next posting, was invited by Kiyoura to the Prime Minister's Office where he discussed the matter with individuals such as Foreign Minister Matsui, Kaneko, Shibusawa, Uchida Yasuya and Chinda Sutemi. According to Matsui, 'Viscount Kaneko got very hot under the collar while debating, while by comparison, Shidehara primarily sought to discuss the matter by putting himself into the shoes of his interlocutors'.[40] Shidehara did his best to calm down Kaneko, who was very much in favour of the expedition. However, Matsui and Ambassador to the US Hanihara believed that such an expedition might complicate matters further. In the end, therefore, the plan was scuttled.

Later, towards the end of May, the Japanese Exclusion Act was formally enacted into law in Washington. In response, several protesters in Japan committed suicide in various public areas, including in front of the US embassy. At the National Sports Hall in Ryōgoku, a Kokumin Taibei Taikai (People's Meeting against the US) was held as a protest rally. Individuals involved in the organising of such gatherings included Ioki Ryōzō, Hatoyama Ichirō, Nagaoka Gaishi, Umeya Shōkichi, Shiroiwa Ryūhei, Mochitsuki Kotarō, Tōyama Mitsuru, Ogawa Heikichi, Nagai

Ryūtarō, Uesugi Shinkichi, Kuzū Yoshihisa, Miki Bukichi, Tomizu Hiroto, Okazaki Kunisuke, Tachibana Koichirō, Baba Tsunego, Nishihara Kamezō, Uchida Ryōhei and Shinobu Junpei.[41]

It was within this broader context that, on 31 May, Ambassador Hanihara personally delivered his letter of protest to Secretary of State Hughes. While the Kiyoura cabinet decided on the delivery of the letter, it was Shidehara who actually wrote it. According to Shidehara's memoirs, at the request of Foreign Minister Matsui, he:

> Drafted the letter of protest to the U.S. in English. When I read it over, I personally felt that it was an extremely polished piece of work. Matsui then read it out word for word during the cabinet meeting … Whereupon it was passed.[42]

Shidehara himself was quite unenthusiastic about the idea of formally issuing a protest with the US. When Matsui consulted him about the letter, Shidehara stated: 'Whatever form of protest is carried out, it will ultimately not succeed in changing the mind of the US government'.[43] Because International Trade Bureau Director-General Nagai was unwell, the Ministry of Foreign Affairs assigned Akamatsu, director of the Immigration Division, and Ministry Adviser Baty to handle this matter. Shidehara continued to view the formal protest as 'ill-advised'. Nevertheless, Shidehara entrusted the final decision to Foreign Minister Matsui: 'As I am not the individual responsible, the one who must decide whether to submit it [the letter] is Minister Matsui'.[44] Although Matsui did have the letter delivered to the US government, the content ended up largely reflecting Shidehara's own views. Soon afterward, when Shidehara assumed the post of foreign minister, he would discontinue Japan's protests over the immigration issue.

Publication of Diplomatic Documents and the Immigration Committee

Shidehara became foreign minister on 11 June 1924. Half a month had already passed since the Japanese Exclusion Act was enacted into law by the US Congress. Shidehara's view at that time was that actions needed to be taken to help restore relations between Japan and the US, while at the same time domestic and foreign popular opinion needed to be taken into consideration. His first step was to make public the diplomatic documents that had been used for negotiations between Japan and the

US. In response to this decision, Hanihara, Japan's ambassador to the US, sought to make sure that the classified documents handed to Hughes in December 1923 and January 1924 were not made public without the consent of the US government.[45]

Despite Hanihara's submission, in July 1924, the Ministry of Foreign Affairs went ahead and published two collections of official documents. These were titled, respectively, *1924 Nen Beikoku Imin-hō Seitei oyobi Kore nikansuru Nichi-Bei Kōshō Keika* (The US Immigration Act of 1924 and the process of Japan–US negotiations) and *1924 Nen Beikoku Imin-hō Seitei oyobi Kore nikansuru Nichi-Bei Kōshō Keika Kōbunsho Eibun Fuzokusho* (The US Immigration Act of 1924 and the process of Japan–US negotiations, supplementary English-language official documents). Both monographs exceeded 200 pages. It was unprecedented for Japan to publish a collection of diplomatic documents relating to an ongoing issue in this manner. According to the foreword in these publications, they 'were swiftly compiled in the hopes that they would be released before the end of the current special session of the Diet'.[46] While Ambassador Hanihara was concerned about the publication of the classified documents that were sent to Hughes, these monographs nevertheless included sections of those documents. Apparently, the ministry itself had pushed for their inclusion.

The Ministry of Foreign Affairs widely distributed this publication. Four hundred copies were sent to the House of Peers, and there were a further 500 copies for the House of Representatives, 50 copies for the Privy Council, 12 copies for the Ministry of Home Affairs, 50 copies for various Tokyo newspapers, 112 copies for the prefectural governments, 232 copies for overseas government establishments, 63 copies for the banks, 99 copies for the regional newspapers and so on. However, the major newspapers did not report on the published documents to any significant degree.[47]

Meanwhile, Shidehara was being prudent concerning further protests from Japan on the Japanese Exclusion Act. Given that the US was then in the middle of a presidential election, Shidehara believed that pressing Japan's case further would only 'uselessly inflame the sentiments of the citizens of the two nations'.[48] Finally, in mid-September, he had a protest sent to Hughes. Even so, this protest was made privately and only once. Shidehara also wished to prevent any cooperation between Japanese residents in the US and anti-US movements in Japan pushed by ultranationalist groups such as the Kokuryūkai (Black Dragon Society). Saburi, director-general of the International Trade Bureau; Akamatsu, director of the Immigration Division; and Ishii Itarō, of the section staff, debated what measures ought to be taken in response to the Japanese Exclusion Act. Yet there were no easy solutions. Saburi was hopeful, however, that 'rather than the president rejecting the act and overturning it, it would be better if he first won the general election, so that a new approach could be found'.[49]

With no solution in sight to the immigration problem in the US, Shidehara formed an immigration committee at the end of August 1924. This committee was to meet every Thursday under the supervision of the foreign minister. Shidehara chose individuals such as Bureau Director-General Saburi to serve as members of the committee. The secretary was Section Chief Akamatsu. The Ministry of Finance, the Ministry of Agriculture and Commerce, and the Ministry of Communication also appointed the bureau-director-general-level staffs to the committee. The immigration committee concluded that immigration to Brazil was to be encouraged. As Ishii wrote, 'Mr. Shidehara was particularly interested in Brazilian immigration'.[50] The committee also deliberated on the possibility of immigration to the South Sea Islands.

Edward Price Bell

How did Foreign Minister Shidehara and Prime Minister Katō view Japan–US relations at this time? At the end of May 1925, in the twilight of his life, Katō was interviewed by Edward Price Bell, a reporter for the *Chicago Daily News*. Katō spoke with great fervour. As he said: 'To the peace of the Pacific we Japanese are devoted'. Bell subsequently interviewed Shidehara. On the topic of Japanese immigration to the US, Shidehara explained the situation, beginning with his previous discussions with the former ambassador to Japan, Roland Morris. Shidehara then went on to quote the British ambassador to the US, James Bryce, stating: 'The American people may make mistakes. They may commit injustices. But in the end, they always of their own will put them right. It is their history'.[51] Bell appeared receptive to Katō's and Shidehara's message. In his article, they were depicted as true statesmen.

A closer look at Bell's article, however, raises questions. Why did Bell present Katō and Shidehara in such favourable terms? After all, the echoes of the Japanese Exclusion Act were still lingering. To present Japan in such positive terms, therefore, feels somehow unconvincing, even unnatural. A key to this mystery lies in Bell's personal documents, as well as in the records of the Ministry of Foreign Affairs. According to these sources, in December 1924, Bell had put in a request to Yoshida Isaburō, Japan's acting ambassador to the US, to interview Prime Minister Katō. At that stage, Bell had already interviewed the heads of the UK, France, Germany, Italy and the US. His hope was to have a meeting with Katō and to bring all of these interviews together in a booklet.

Upon learning of Bell's plan, Shidehara sounded out Katō on the idea and secured his consent. The interview was to be held after April 1925, thereby avoiding the extremely busy period when the Diet would be in session. Shidehara also informed Katō that Bell had already undertaken various fact-finding activities such as 'speaking with pro-Japanese and anti-Japanese Americans' in San Francisco. Meanwhile, Bell sent some correspondence to Katō in advance, informing him that he wished to ask him about the 'Pacific problem'.[52] From the above facts, we can surmise that, at the very least, Shidehara prepared the broad outlines that would guide Katō and Bell's interview. It is important to understand that, from Katō and Shidehara's perspective, this was no mere interview. In particular, for Shidehara, it amounted to something close to a message that Japan would be sending to the US. Thus, Bell's interview eventually took place at the end of May. Bell quickly had the minutes of the meeting sent to Katō and Shidehara, receiving their approval. For his background research Bell also went further, referring to sources such as Katō and Shidehara's Diet addresses. His pro-Japan article was published in various newspapers in the US and the Philippines. Shidehara would have received the impression on this occasion that US public opinion towards Japan was improving.

During his time in Japan, Bell also contacted US Ambassador Edgar A. Bancroft. Therefore, Bell's reporting efforts can be considered in some respects close to a joint Japan–US effort to shape US public opinion. Bancroft had also been concerned about the influence of the Japanese Exclusion Act for some time and had previously exchanged his opinions on the matter with Shidehara. Further, Bancroft had given detailed reports in private correspondence with Hughes as to the content of his meetings with Shidehara. It should be noted that Bancroft's background was as a lawyer who was familiar with issues concerning race. It was for this very reason that he was appointed US ambassador to Japan in November 1924. However, Shidehara and Bancroft were careful not to discuss the Japanese Exclusion Act in public. Unfortunately, Bancroft would pass away suddenly at Karuizawa at the end of July 1925.[53]

As it happened, Bell would eventually be nominated for the Nobel Peace Prize for his reporting. He was nominated by none other than Shidehara. In his letter to the Nobel Committee, Shidehara wrote: 'I admire his knowledge of international affairs, and not least those of the Far East; and especially his untiring efforts to promote peace among the nations'.[54] This is rare praise from Shidehara, given his distaste for the mass media. It seems that Bell had gained Shidehara's trust by faithfully reproducing the contents of the meetings and by showing the draft to Shidehara beforehand. In the end, Bell did not receive the Nobel Peace Prize. Nevertheless, he would continue to communicate with Shidehara thereafter.

Personnel

Following the passing of the Japanese Exclusion Act in Washington, Ambassador Hanihara relinquished his position, which was temporarily filled by Acting Ambassador Yoshida Isaburō. Meanwhile, Shidehara and Katō sought to install Mutsu Hirokichi as Hanihara's successor. Hirokichi was the eldest son of Mutsu Munemitsu and had also become a diplomat. However, Hirokichi declined the posting as US ambassador due to health reasons. Shidehara responded by appointing Vice-Minister for Foreign Affairs Matsudaira Tsuneo to the post. Matsudaira also had a close relationship with Debuchi; the two were originally classmates. It should be noted that, following his departure from the US, Shidehara and Debuchi recommended Hanihara for the job of ambassador to Italy. However, Hanihara himself turned down the suggestion.[55]

The appointment of Vice-Minister Matsudaira as US ambassador led to a further reshuffling of personnel within the ministry. In December 1924, Shidehara appointed Asian Bureau Director-General Debuchi as the new vice-minister. From this period, therefore, there are further references to personnel matters in Debuchi's diary. Debuchi held Saitō Yoshie in high esteem and considered making him the director-general of the Treaties and Conventions Bureau. In the end, Saitō was assigned the role of the International Trade Bureau instead. Concerning who would succeed him as vice-minister, Debuchi would later confide in his diary:

> I cannot necessarily say that Saburi is best suited to becoming the next vice-minister. If one day I were to become minister, I would want my vice-minister to be Saitō Yoshie.[56]

Debuchi was critical of the fact that Shidehara had recommended Tanaka Tokichi for the position of ambassador to the Soviet Union and believed that Obata Yūkichi would be suitable as Japan's minister to China. Thus, there were some differences of opinion between Shidehara and Debuchi when it came to staffing. Nevertheless, Debuchi's diary still offers a window on the personal networks of the Shidehara clique. For example, Shidehara removed Honda Kumatarō from the post of ambassador to Germany at Debuchi's recommendation.[57]

In any case, what was particularly important at this time was the question of who would succeed Debuchi as director-general of the Asian Bureau. Debuchi's idea was for Arita Hachirō to take on the role. In general, Arita was regarded as a representative of the reformist group. However, at this point he had not come out in opposition to Shidehara and Debuchi. Shigemitsu, meanwhile, was viewed as behaving too obsequiously towards Debuchi. In the end, it was not Arita but Kimura Eiichi who became Asian Bureau director-general. Previously, Kimura had attended the Washington Naval Conference as first division director of the Asian Bureau. Moreover, although he was invited by Horinouchi Kensuke, he did not join the Gaimushō Kakushin Dōshikai.[58]

Thus, the Asian Bureau would be headed by Kimura, with the role of first division director going to Tani Masayuki. At the time, the Asian Bureau was regarded as the leading bureau of the ministry. It was also said of the bureau that it had its own internal 'Monroe Doctrine'. So the critique went: 'A certain clique has consolidated its grip on the Asian Bureau, keeping non-clique members out and ensuring that its own bureau staff receive good positions when sent abroad'.[59] As director-general of the Asian Bureau, Kimura would support Shidehara's economic diplomacy and his policies on Manchuria and Mongolia. Further, proceeding from the correct assumption that warlord Zhang Zuolin would decline and that the authorities in north-eastern China would compromise with the Nationalist Party, Kimura began to plan for a future improvement in Sino-Japanese relations. In time, Shidehara, then in his second term as foreign minister, would send Kimura to direct the South Manchuria Railway.

Meanwhile, there is the question of what became of Tani, the chief of the first division in the Asian Bureau. He was generally seen as a member of the reformists. Later, upon advancing to the position of Asian Bureau director-general, he promoted a policy of Sino-Japanese cooperation.

Nevertheless, until the time of the Manchurian Incident, it seems that the personal relationship between Shidehara and Tani was not an overly poor one.⁶⁰

The real problem for Shidehara was Hirota, the director-general of the American and European Bureau. Debuchi and Shidehara felt that Hirota was too different from them, and they even wanted to have him removed from his position as bureau director-general. That was not to say Hirota was on a completely different wavelength when it came to foreign affairs.⁶¹ Yet, he was shunned by Shidehara and Debuchi. Why? The first reason concerns Hirota's relationship with the Gaimushō Kakushin Dōshikai. According to Arita Hachirō:

> One of the very first to join the [reformists] association was Mr. Hirota Kōki, who was then first secretary at the embassy in Washington. At that time, he already had something of the politician about him, not to mention the air of a member of Genyōsha [the Dark Ocean Society, a nationalist group from northern Kyūshū].⁶²

It should be noted that the Gaimushō Kakushin Dōshikai received internal support from a number of other figures, including Sawada Setsuzō, director of the Telegraph Division; Kawashima Nobutarō, director of the First Division of the Treaties and Conventions Bureau; and Sugimura Yōtarō, director of the Second Division of the Treaties and Conventions Bureau. There are indications that Hanihara may also have been involved. Arita, for example, wrote that 'there was something about Vice-Minister Hanihara that just did not sit well with me'.⁶³

Hirota had returned to Japan from Washington in December 1920, earlier than Shidehara, who at that point was still serving as ambassador. The following year, Hirota became director of the Second Division of the Intelligence Department before later rising to the post of vice director-general of the Intelligence Department. It is worth pointing out that Hirota and Shidehara were not far apart when it came to policy. For example, as division director, Hirota also supported the Four-Power Treaty that was concluded at the Washington Naval Conference. While House of Peers member Egi Tasuku criticised the termination of the Anglo-Japanese Alliance as deplorable, Hirota argued that 'the empire [Japan] has taken the best and only possible approach in shifting from the Anglo-Japanese Alliance to the Four-Power Treaty'.⁶⁴ Recall that it was

Shidehara who had recommended the abrogation of the Anglo-Japanese Alliance at the Washington Naval Conference. In this regard, Hirota was close to Shidehara.

Nevertheless, once Hirota became director-general of the American and European Bureau in September 1923, he began to show his colours more—and in a manner unbefitting a bureaucrat. On this matter, there is testimony from Horinouchi Kensuke. Horinouchi was second division director in the bureau, under Bureau Director-General Hirota. According to Horinouchi, Hirota's office was 'frequented by people such as Diet members, industrialists, independent patriots, and the like, lending the bureau quite a lordly atmosphere'. He added: 'From early on he [Hirota] had the air of a politician about him'.[65] Such accounts help explain why Shidehara and Debuchi felt uncomfortable with Hirota. Their distrust resulted less from his policies than from his behaviour. Hirota would subsequently be transferred to the position of minister to the Netherlands, with Hotta Masaaki succeeding him as American and European Bureau' director-general.

The Fate of Economic Diplomacy

The Beijing Special Conference on Tariffs

Above I have provided an outline of the situation with respect to ministry personnel. With this broader human context fleshed out, we can now consider what kind of policies Shidehara pursued as foreign minister. Particularly important here is the concept of 'economic diplomacy'. In Beijing, in the autumn of 1925, an international conference was held to discuss China's tariffs. Shidehara's early policy with respect to this conference was to limit the discussion to a 2.5 per cent tax, as was previously agreed upon at the Washington Naval Conference, and then proceed to examine how the increased revenue might be used. However, nations such as the US turned out to be more sympathetic towards China than anticipated, forcing Shidehara to rethink his policy.

At around the same time, the Ministry of Foreign Affairs, together with the Ministry of Finance, the Ministry of Commerce and Industry, and the Ministry of Agriculture and Forestry, held a joint committee for the purpose of preparing for a tariff conference. This committee included bureau-general-ranked bureaucrats from the respective ministries of the Japanese government. From the Ministry of Foreign Affairs, Shidehara sent Saburi Sadao, director-general of the International Trade Bureau. The committee secretary was Asaoka Ken, director of the First Section of the International Trade Bureau. There were other participants from the ministry as well. These included Asian Bureau Director-General Kimura, Asian Bureau First Division Director Tani, Secretary Horiuchi Tateki and Secretary Hidaka Shinrokurō. The committee met almost every day to discuss such matters as the conditions and impact of a 2.5 per cent tax. The committee also investigated the various conditions that could potentially arise if China were granted tariff autonomy.[66]

As it happened, Shidehara himself had not yet decided to recognise China's tariff autonomy. An indication of his stance appears in the record of the cabinet decision made on 13 October 1925. The Katō cabinet was, above all, concerned with keeping the discussion limited to an additional tax of 2.5 per cent, with any additional tax collection to be conditional on the use of a graduated tax rate and China's use of the increased revenue to service its foreign loans. On the topic of tariff autonomy, if it were granted depending on how events unfolded at the conference, the Katō cabinet intended for that autonomy to only extend as far as the setting of the period of transition.

The Special Tariff Conference in Beijing commenced in late October. The Japanese delegation to Beijing was headed by chief plenipotentiary Hioki Eki, assisted by deputy plenipotentiary Yoshizawa Kenkichi, who at that time was envoy to China. International Trade Bureau Director-General Saburi was also dispatched to Beijing, to act as the delegation's secretary-general. Other members of the delegation included Shigemitsu Mamoru, Horiuchi Tateki and Hidaka Shinrokurō. Surprisingly, at the commencement of the conference, Hioki began with an address stating that Japan was prepared to accept, as a basic principle, China's right to tariff autonomy. This move was actually a proposal of Saburi and Shigemitsu. While it had taken Shidehara by surprise when he read the speech in advance, he trusted Saburi's judgement and approved its content. The focus of the conference was therefore shifted towards what provisional measures would need to be taken in the lead-up to China gaining tariff autonomy.

The US and the UK wanted to recognise a high tariff rate. This was a problem for the Japanese delegation. Even as late as January 1926, Shidehara was instructing the attendees to not allow the additional tax rate to exceed 2.5 per cent for 'regular goods'. In March, a graduated tax rate of 2.5–22.5 per cent was jointly agreed upon by Japan, the US and the UK. Following this agreement, the central topic of discussion shifted to whether China would be required to use its increased tax revenue to service its foreign loans. It was at this stage that British Foreign Secretary J. Austen Chamberlain proposed an unconditional recognition of a 2.5 per cent additional tax. While an agreement on the topic of loan servicing had not yet been reached, each participating nation was on the verge of going ahead with an initial agreement on the tariff. However, Shidehara thought this would lead to a delay with respect to loan servicing and rejected the plan to go ahead with an agreement on the tariffs. Thus, the conference dragged on until July, whereupon it was indefinitely postponed without any clear resolution.

By sticking to the requirement of a clear economic benefit, Shidehara missed an opportunity for a more flexible give and take policy to be implemented. What the China tariff problem indicates is that, generally speaking, Shidehara's conception of the international order remained stuck within the framework established at the Washington Naval Conference. If Shidehara had taken the plunge of joining the UK and the US in recognising China's right to collect additional taxes, it may well have helped the government in Beijing to stabilise its financial base. However, it seems that on the ground in Beijing, Saburi had interpreted Shidehara's intentions as favourable to China and relayed this information to the Chinese side. This at least led to Saburi developing more friendly ties with Chinese plenipotentiary Huang Fu.

Beijing also hosted an international conference on extraterritorial rights that foreign nations had within China. While Shidehara favoured a resolution to conflicts over extraterritorial rights, arguing that it was 'conducive to the furtherance of our economic benefit', he also felt that the time was not yet ripe for their full termination.[67] At the same time, he also expressed his opposition to the international management of China and to foreign interference in China's domestic politics. All in all, the discussions conducted during this conference did not engender much progress on the problem of extraterritorial rights. It should also be noted that Shidehara accepted the October 1926 proposal of the Beijing government to revise the Sino-Japanese Trade Agreement.

Fragmentation of Conceptions of the Washington System

During this period, Prime Minister Katō entrusted diplomatic matters to Shidehara. That said, as someone who himself had served as foreign minister four times, Katō was by no means uninterested in diplomatic affairs. At the Beijing Special Conference on Tariffs, he spoke with 'surprising frankness' to the UK's ambassador to Japan, Charles Eliot. Eliot said it was Katō's view that the:

> Conference would last [a] long time and [the] result would be small. This, he said, would be to the advantage of Japan, for she would be [the] chief loser if China received tariff autonomy.[68]

Katō's stance, as revealed in this statement, presumably had a strong influence on Shidehara's policy.

It is worth briefly dwelling on Eliot. He was the UK's ambassador to Japan from 1920 and had regretted the termination of the Anglo-Japanese Alliance. An individual who was deeply familiar with the history of Buddhism, Eliot had attempted to secure the continued cooperative relationship of Japan and the UK. However, Katō and Eliot's relationship was not sufficient to cement the Anglo-Japanese bond. On the contrary, at this time the two nations were becoming increasingly estranged from each other over policy on China. Foreign Secretary Chamberlain acknowledged this fact in private correspondence to Eliot, writing: 'there is a less intimate friendship between our two nations since the termination of the Anglo-Japanese Treaty'.[69] Chamberlain had lamented the departure of Hayashi Gonsuke from his post as ambassador to the UK.

At the end of January 1926, Prime Minister Katō died due to illness. As expected, his successor was Wakatsuki Reijirō, new president of the Kenseikai party. Wakatsuki had never shown a particular interest in foreign affairs. With his advancement to the position of prime minister, therefore, responsibility for directing Japan's diplomatic efforts would fall even more upon Shidehara.

Another significant development would occur in February, when Eliot was replaced by John A. C. Tilley as the UK's ambassador to Japan. Ambassador Tilley was not as passionate as his predecessor; Eliot's research on Japan was instead taken up and carried on by the commercial counsellor, Sir George Bailey Sansom. Nevertheless, there were periods in which Tilley expended considerable efforts in his new role. In January and February 1927, for example, he visited the Japanese Ministry of Foreign Affairs almost every day. The reason was the commencement in China, in July of the previous year, of the aforementioned Northern Expedition. In response, Tilley sought to sound out Japan on a joint Anglo-Japanese deployment of troops to Shanghai. However, Shidehara did not acquiesce to the UK's request for a military deployment.[70]

One document that gives us a direct indication of the gap that had opened up between the UK and Japan is known as the 'December Memorandum'. The Stanley Baldwin cabinet unexpectedly sent this memorandum to China on 18 December 1926. Its contents included the immediate recognition of the additional taxation that had been agreed upon at the Washington Naval Conference. According to Matsui, Japan's ambassador to the UK at that time: 'Mr. Wellesley [assistant to the foreign vice-secretary] offered the excuse that because Foreign Secretary Chamberlain had suddenly made this decision afterwards, there was no time to let me know in advance'.[71]

After receiving the December Memorandum from Ambassador Tilley, Vice-Minister Debuchi went so far as to state: 'I have no choice but to admit that Britain ignores the spirit of the Washington Treaty and does not want to cooperate with Japan'.[72] Shidehara also criticised the December Memorandum on the basis of discussions such as the one that had been held between Saburi and Eugene Chen, foreign minister of the Nationalist government. He took the additional step of proposing to Tilley that an unofficial tariff conference be held, with representatives attending from northern and southern China. Perhaps he was out of patience, but Shidehara apparently warned Tilley while holding a copy of a book by former foreign secretary Grey.

So much for the situation with the UK. What about Japan's diplomatic relations with the US at that time? On this topic, the reminiscences of Eugene H. Dooman, first secretary to the US embassy in Japan, are instructive. According to Dooman, because of the US's misplaced benevolence, the Chinese had begun to trample upon the interests of various foreign nations. In Japan this weakened the political fortunes of Shidehara and Wakatsuki, who had sought to uphold the spirit of the Nine-Power Treaty and helped promote militarists. In summary, once Secretary of State Hughes was no longer leading the process, the US failed to explore systematically the premises of its own East Asia policy.

In this manner, the three nations of Japan, the US and the UK, while remaining within the Washington System, were each developing their own alternative conceptions of the international order in East Asia. Ultimately, they were not to converge. In other words, the diplomatic efforts of the powers in this period can be interpreted as representing a fragmentation of the Washington System.[73]

The Diversification of Trade

A well-known example of Shidehara's economism in action would be the aforementioned Beijing Special Conference on Tariffs. However, this was not the full extent of the economic diplomacy he pursued through the mediation of assistants such as Saburi. In fact, it would be in the domain of Franco-Japanese relations where Saburi would prove to be more adept.

An unsolved problem between Japan and France was the development of trade connections, specifically with French Indochina. Because of high tariffs, exports from Japan had stagnated. The governor-general of Indochina, Martial H. Merlin, had previously visited Japan in May 1924. At that time Saburi had observed the meeting that took place between Merlin and Foreign Minister Matsui.[74] After taking over as foreign minister, Shidehara organised the dispatch of a delegation to Indochina to discuss the tariff issue. He also sounded out the central French government on the matter, via Ishii, Japan's ambassador to France. The special envoy to Indochina was headed by privy councillor Yamagata Isaburō. Other accompanying personnel from the ministry included Saburi and Secretary Matsushima Shikao. Thus, in February 1925, Yamagata and Saburi were both in Indochina, negotiating tariffs. Of course, to begin with, there was no reason to believe that these negotiations would bear fruit. Nevertheless, Ishii would continue to negotiate with France on the matter in the period after the delegation's visit. It was around this time, in July 1925, that Japan and the UK concluded a supplementary treaty to the original Anglo-Japanese Treaty of Commerce and Navigation.[75]

In April–May 1926, the Near East Trade Conference was held in Constantinople (today Istanbul), Turkey. The chairman was Obata Yūkichi. Shidehara had appointed Obata as Japan's very first ambassador to Turkey. The conference was also attended by individuals such as Okuyama Seiji, Japan's minister to Greece, and Mushanokōji Kintomo, minister to Romania. The goal of the conference was to promote trade between Japan and the Near East, with resolutions made on topics such as the opening of direct sea routes, the establishment of suitably sized diplomatic establishments, the dispatching of commercial secretaries and the holding of trade fairs.[76]

It would be Nippon Yusen that would open up the Near East sea route. While Nippon Yusen is a member of the Mitsubishi group (recall that Shidehara had married a daughter of the head of the Mitsubishi group), there are no historical records showing a close relationship between the company and Shidehara. In fact, the proposal for the Near East Trade Conference originated not from Shidehara but from the International Trade Bureau. The bureau director-general at that time was Saitō Yoshie. It should be noted that the conference was not an international conference; the ministry only sent secretary Yamamoto Kumaichi from Japan (the other Japanese attendees were already in the region).[77]

Meanwhile, the First Trade Conference was also held in the House of Representatives in September 1926. This conference was organised to foster trade and investment opportunities in the regions south of Japan and was generally referred to as the South Sea Trade Conference. Representatives from numerous branches of government and sections of industry were in attendance, including the Ministry of Foreign Affairs, the Ministry of Home Affairs, the Ministry of Finance, the Ministry of Agriculture and Forestry, the Ministry of Commerce and Industry, the Ministry of Communication, the governor-general of Taiwan, the Government Office of the South Sea Islands, various Chambers of Commerce and Industry, the cotton spinning industry, and the banking and shipping industries.[78]

In the opening address of the conference, Shidehara asserted that it was principally oriented towards not only the 'promotion of foreign trade, but also the encouragement of overseas business investment by Japanese people'. Shidehara continued:

> We begin this conference with the view that commercial intercourse will absolutely change for the better and that, from the beginning, it must be free of any form of political motivation … The essence of the matter, and also our goal, must be that other nations will equally benefit at the same time as our own.[79]

Shidehara stated that 'the development of international commerce must be the principal focus'. He added:

> The strenuous efforts and cooperation of assembled businesspeople are to be anticipated, and the government must conduct itself in such a manner so as to fundamentally avoid interfering in this domain.[80]

Here we have a conception of free trade, to be opened up in the region of the South Sea. Shidehara's comments can also be read as an expression of Japan's orientation towards trade diversification and towards becoming a maritime nation. According to Ishii Itarō, who was then Third Division director under International Trade Bureau Director-General Saitō:

> My understanding of Shidehara's fundamental idea, upon which he based his international trade policy, was that Japan should, beginning with its closest neighbor, China, gradually expand [its trade connections] into Southeast Asia, thereby laying the foundations for building an economic powerhouse.[81]

On the topic of the South Sea Trade Conference, he added: 'I believe it was Saitō Yoshie's suggestion, which Shidehara then gave the OK to'.[82]

It should be noted that the aforementioned trade conferences were one-time events. It was not the case, therefore, that Shidehara and Saitō's plans quickly led to fruition. It was not until 1928 that the South Seas Unit was finally established within the International Trade Bureau, to investigate the economic conditions of the region, including the availability of resources. The South Seas Unit was quickly abolished, before being restored in 1929. The establishment of the South Seas Bureau to the Ministry of Foreign Affairs would have to wait until November 1940.[83]

Japan–Soviet Relations

Shidehara's diplomatic efforts had a weak spot. On Manchuria, he was unable to develop a policy that rose to the challenges presented by the region. At that time, the foreign affairs mechanisms in the region were diverse and were quite vulnerable to the intervention of other organisations, such as the army and the South Manchuria Railway Company. There were also further complications arising from the rise of the Soviet Union. The army and the South Manchuria Railway Company's policies with respect to Manchuria and Mongolia were partially directed at addressing this shift in regional power. Later, with the first Tanaka Giichi cabinet, the Ministry of Overseas Affairs would be established. This ministry was placed in charge of colonial administration and the supervision of the South Manchurian Railway Company. The relationship with the railway company would become more regulated under Foreign Minister Tanaka than it was under Shidehara.

At the same time, the policies Shidehara pursued in this region, with respect to Manchuria, Mongolia and the Soviet Union, serve to throw his ideals into sharp relief. Here I am referring not only to Shidehara's desire, as discussed earlier, to centralise Japan's diplomacy, placing it firmly under the control of the Ministry of Foreign Affairs. As seen earlier, Shidehara was also a firm believer in non-intervention and economism and was not particularly suspicious of communism. Hence, he helped to establish diplomatic relations between Japan and the Soviet Union in January 1925.

The agreement reached between the two parties (referred to in English by the lengthy title 'The Convention Embodying Basic Rules of the Relations between Japan and the Union of Soviet Socialist Republics') was signed in Beijing. It was generally seen as beneficial to Japan, and not only within Japanese circles. For example, this view was also expressed in the correspondence of Bancroft, the US ambassador to Japan. In a private letter to the US's minister to China, Jacob Gould Schurman, Bancroft wrote: 'The Treaty strikes me as distinctly advantageous to Japan'.[84] The reason for this perception was that the Japan–Soviet convention contained provisions such as the continuation of the Treaty of Portsmouth, the revision of the fishery treaty, an agreement of reciprocal non-intervention and the granting to Japan of rights over certain resources in the Soviet Union. Two protocols produced as a result of the convention set a May 1925 deadline for Japanese military withdrawal from northern Sakhalin Island, while promising Japan rights over the development of oil fields in that area. The final details of the revision of the fishery treaty and Japan's oil field rights would be left to be worked out in subsequent negotiations.

In February 1925, in private correspondence to Secretary of State Frank B. Kellogg, Bancroft further expressed the opinion that 'the Japan-Russian Treaty was wisely and advantageously made by Japan'. He added:

> The first crisis in the Far East, I suspect, will arise in China as a result of the activities of [the] Russian Ambassador in the dissemination, through purchased agents, of the destructive side of Sovietism.[85]

It should be noted that, at this point, the US had not yet officially recognised the Soviet Union. As though substantiating Bancroft's judgement, a large-scale strike soon took place at Zaikabō in Shanghai; Zaikabō were cotton spinning mills established in China with Japanese capital. Following this development, Bancroft wrote: 'Baron Shidehara told me that the Soviet[s] [were] the sole cause of that strike; that the workers had no grievances [sic] against their Japanese employers'.[86]

Prime Minister Katō and Foreign Minister Shidehara would have multiple meetings with Bancroft on this topic. Concerning the situation in China, Katō believed that 'the Powers must act together'.[87] Shidehara had the same opinion. Katō also indicated that he understood why the US continued to avoid recognising the Soviet Union, while at the same time implying that Japan's policy on the matter was different. Shidehara would provide further details on this topic at a later date, writing that 'the Japan-Russia Treaty was necessary in order to carry out the public declaration of Prime Minister Katō before he took office that Japanese troops should be promptly withdrawn from Saghalien [sic]'.[88] That said, the Soviet policy of the Katō cabinet did not amount to a Japan–Soviet partnership. Shidehara himself wrote to Bancroft that public rumours of Japan teaming up with the Soviet Union or with Germany 'lack common sense'.[89]

Even after the establishment of diplomatic relations between Japan and the Soviet Union, tensions between the two powers would continue with respect to problems such as the railways in northern Manchuria and political propaganda directed at Japan. It was in this context that the Soviet Union proposed the signing of a Japan–Soviet nonaggression pact. For Shidehara, however, the maintenance of good relations with the UK and the US ruled out such possibilities. Instead, he placed more emphasis upon economic relations between the two powers, prioritising the signing of the fisheries agreement and commercial treaties. To put it differently, Shidehara's policy regarding the Soviet Union was to separate political and economic concerns. Further, it is clear that Shidehara was not yet particularly concerned about the spread of communism in China. By contrast, Tanaka, who would later serve as both prime minister and foreign minister, was concerned about political propaganda aimed at Japan and alarmed about the influence of the Soviet Union on China.[90]

The Northern Expeditions and the Nanjing Incident of 1927

In southern China at this time, the National Revolutionary Army, led by Chiang Kai-shek, was continuing its advance in the name of reunifying China. As mentioned above, in Chinese history, this event is referred to as the Northern Expedition. On 24 March 1927, as the National Revolutionary Army of China advanced northwards, it attacked foreigners and Japanese and British consulates in Nanjing. It also damaged the US-affiliated Jinling University (also known as the University of Nanjing). During the 'Nanjing Incident' of 1927, UK and US warships fired upon the city. Partly at the request of Japanese residents in the city, Japan did not retaliate. Shidehara also had a favourable impression of Chiang Kai-shek and was opposed to punishing China. As a result, however, Shidehara was criticised domestically for his 'weak diplomacy'.[91]

Shidehara's policy during the Nanjing Incident of 1927 was to 'cooperate with the U.K. and the U.S. in negotiating' with Chiang Kai-shek. However, in the past, such cooperative diplomacy with the UK and the US was not particularly effective. For example, in such matters as the problem of treaty revision, the UK and the US would head in a different direction and attempt to earn the favour of China, throwing the joint efforts into disarray. This issue was on display with the aforementioned December Memorandum by the UK, as well as Secretary of State Kellogg's January 1927 declaration. Kellogg declared that the US would be adopting a new policy whereby it would be willing to act alone, if necessary, to help revise China's unequal treaties.

In the case of the Nanjing Incident of 1927 as well, while Japan initially issued a joint note with the US, the UK and France, cooperation with the other powers soon ran into trouble. The central point of contention was with respect to issuing a fresh warning. While the UK favoured such a move, the US staunchly opposed it. This disagreement caused negotiations with China to fragment, with each nation undertaking its own approach.[92]

A direct impression of Shidehara's understanding of the situation at that time can be gained from the discussion he held with Tilley, the UK's ambassador to Japan. On 2 April 1927, Shidehara warned Tilley that a hardline policy, such as issuing an ultimatum, needed to be avoided and that Chiang Kai-shek's 'position' was not to be undermined.

Even if a hardline approach was resorted to, Shidehara believed that 'the communist-aligned mobs, disorderly soldiers, and so forth who constituted the core of the anti-foreign rioting would hardly be affected'.[93] That is to say, Shidehara's understanding was that the cause of the Nanjing Incident of 1927 was not Chiang Kai-shek and his immediate clique, but the 'communists'. From the perspective of assisting the development of order in China, Shidehara believed that a 'peaceful diplomatic method' needed to be deployed, one that would enable 'a central figure such as Chiang Kai-shek' to deal with the situation.

At the basis of such a judgement lay Shidehara's perspective on the national interest, which prioritised economic benefits. Shidehara told Tilley that, while he did not think China would become communist, he did think that:

> Even if the communists were to take control, within the span of two or three years foreigners would be able to trade in China once again, so I do not think it is an overly dangerous situation.[94]

In other words, even in the unlikely event of a communist takeover of China, Japan could live with and trade with China, just as it could with the Soviet Union. In summary, Shidehara believed that, provided economic benefit could be gained, the national interest could be protected.

Shidehara's perspective on foreign affairs contrasts sharply with Hara Takashi's or Tanaka Giichi's. This is because Hara and, from some time earlier, Tanaka too saw the relationship Japan had with the government of the Manchurian warlord, Zhang Zuolin, as of particular importance. Conversely, Shidehara foresaw the eventual unification of China and therefore preached a policy of non-intervention and the prioritisation of markets and commerce. In this regard, Shidehara was exceptional for the era. Shidehara's view on the Northern Expedition was not unfounded. One justification for his stance was the field survey conducted by Saburi. When the Beijing Special Conference on Tariffs ended, Saburi headed to southern China under Shidehara's orders on a special mission to conduct a survey of the region. With the Northern Expedition underway, Saburi was able to contact leading figures of the Nationalist Party and hear their opinions on trade and the removal of China's unequal treaties. It seems that through Saburi's efforts, Shidehara was able to gain a window on the direction the leaders of the Northern Expedition would seek to take China.[95]

Was Shidehara correct, however, to interpret the Nanjing Incident of 1927 as the result of Chinese Communist Party intrigue? Current scholarly research on the topic has not returned any conclusive judgement. That said, the theory of a Communist Party conspiracy is not unfounded. There are comments, for example, by Yang Jie, commander of the 17th Division of the Sixth Army. On 25 March, Yang visited Morioka Shōhei at Japan's Nanjing consulate. There Yang expressed his regret for the events of the Nanjing Incident of 1927. According to Morioka, Yang stated that:

> The pillaging was the result of agitation directed by Communist Party members in Nanjing or by bad soldiers and that he would directly take strict control of the situation and respond to negotiations for reparation alongside China's Ministry of Foreign Affairs.[96]

Yang's claim—that responsibility for the Nanjing Incident of 1927 lay with the Communist Party—was relayed to Shidehara via a telegram from Morioka and would have influenced Shidehara's perspective on the situation in China. Further, Chiang Kai-shek, through his representative, Huang Fu, had also begun to indicate to the Japanese that the Nanjing Incident of 1927 was the result of the machinations of the Communist Party. Shidehara's response was to instruct Yada Shichitarō of the Shanghai consulate general to impress upon Chiang Kai-shek and his associates the importance of 'deep reflection and determination'.[97] In other words, Shidehara wanted Chiang Kai-shek to covertly take firm measures against the Communist Party. In fact, on 12 April, Chiang Kai-shek carried out an anti-communist coup d'état in Shanghai. On 3 April, an incident also occurred in Hankou: a Chinese mob attacked Japanese marines in the Japanese concession. Japan responded by deploying the land forces of the navy. This was known as the Hankou Incident, and Shidehara's response led to increased domestic criticism of his 'weak diplomacy'.

Another aspect of Shidehara's policies on Soviet Russia and Manchuria–Mongolia deserves attention. This is his approval of the construction of the Taoang (Japanese: Tōkō) Railway. The Taoang Railway was part of a strategy by the Japanese army and the South Manchuria Railway Company to advance into northern Manchuria and thereby counter the influence of the Soviets. This plan ran counter to the earlier agreement reached with the New Four-Power Consortium. In this case, it seems that Shidehara gave higher priority to the expansion of Japanese national interest in China along existing lines than to his principle of pursuing an open door policy. Victor L. Kopp, the Soviet ambassador to Japan, would issue a protest in response to this decision.

The original promoter of the Taoang Railway was Matsuoka Yōsuke, then director of the South Manchuria Railway. In a December 1925 correspondence to Prime Minister Katō, Matsuoka wrote that:

> Needless to say, the construction of the Taoang Railway would serve to push back against the sphere of influence that Russia established following the conclusion of the First Russo-Japanese Agreement; it would constitute a challenge to Russia['s regional dominance].[98]

Even during negotiations with the Dongsan Province Regime, Matsuoka stated that, 'with planning going ahead for the construction of the Taoang Railway, we are determined to do our very best to assist Zhang Zuolin and eliminate Russian resistance'.[99] It is clear that during Shidehara's term as foreign minister, the South Manchuria Railway was planning great advances, even when compared with the relationship it enjoyed with the Ministry of Foreign Affairs during the era of the Hara cabinet.

Diplomacy and Party Politics

Shidehara's Miscalculation

We now have some understanding of Shidehara's policies and personal connections during his first term as foreign minister. I would like to elaborate upon this topic further, while considering the connection that existed between Shidehara's diplomacy and Japanese party politics. At this time, and against the backdrop of the establishment of a 'four-bureau system', the rise of the generation of diplomats who had entered the ministry through the examination system can be seen in the Ministry of Foreign Affairs. For that reason alone, Shidehara was able to pursue his policies through close coordination with his trusted subordinates. In particular, he placed considerable trust in Debuchi and Saburi. However, he also had positive relations with other individuals in the ministry, such as Matsudaira, Kimura, Obata, Nagai and Ishii. Conversely, Shidehara

3. JAPAN–US RELATIONS AND CHINESE NATIONALISM

tended to ignore opinions from overseas agencies of the ministry. In this respect he contrasted sharply with the subsequent foreign minister, Tanaka Giichi.[100]

If we are to refer to this group of individuals with Shidehara at its centre as the 'Shidehara clique', then this clique was already germinating during his time as ambassador to the US. Meanwhile, Shidehara's first term as foreign minister was characterised not so much by this clique's opposition to the reformists as it was by aversion to Hirota, who was at least superficially closer with respect to his conception of foreign affairs. To put it another way, the Shidehara clique was extremely critical of Hirota's politician-like behaviour. Presumably, it was for the same reason that Shidehara did not like Yoshida Shigeru, who would become vice-minister under Foreign Minister Tanaka. Yoshida also differed from Shidehara in that he would not renounce state intervention in his policies on Manchuria and Mongolia.

What about Japan's relationship with the League of Nations? Shidehara and the other leaders of the Ministry of Foreign Affairs were not particularly interested in engaging with this organisation. Individuals who were more enthusiastic about the league included Ishii Kikujirō, ambassador to France; Sugimura Yōtarō, under-secretary-general of the League of Nations Permanent Secretariat; and individuals who worked in branches of the ministry, such as Satō Naotake, director-general of the League of Nations' Imperial (Japanese) Secretariat. Though Shidehara and Satō were together regarded as leaders of the 'Western group' in the ministry, their attitudes differed when it came to the league. Indeed, Satō was quite annoyed with the ministry's passive attitude towards the league.[101] If we then also consider the relationship between Hirota and Shidehara's circle, it becomes clear that the 'Western group' was far from monolithic in its composition.

Therefore, even if Shidehara, Hirota, Satō, Yoshida and others are collectively referred to as the 'Western group', this grouping only goes so far towards explaining the dynamics of the ministry. This is why I have instead used the concept of the Shidehara clique. Shidehara, Debuchi and other members of this clique sought to follow the spirit of the Washington Naval Conference, promoting non-interventionist and economic-centric policies. Further, even though they attempted to separate diplomacy from Japan's domestic politics, they were cool towards the activities of the

League of Nations. As is the case with all kinds of policy-oriented groups, the key to understanding the Shidehara clique is the human relations that comprised it.

The core of the Shidehara clique was made up of Shidehara himself, Debuchi and Saburi. However, figures such as Matsudaira, Kimura, Nagai and Ishii were in the periphery. Many of these individuals shared the same formative experience in the Washington Naval Conference, while much of the reformist group, by contrast, had experienced the Paris Peace Conference. That said, as the Shidehara clique occupied the dominant position within the Ministry of Foreign Affairs, they did not pursue the same centripetal force as the reformists. It was this closed-off elitism that led over time to an increasingly strong backlash.

Given the dominance of his clique within the ministry, what did Shidehara manage to achieve with the help of Debuchi, Saburi and the other members? First, he carried out a policy of non-intervention with regard to China, which he hoped would become unified and increasingly stable. In this regard, he respected the spirit of the Washington Naval Conference. The cliques' debt to Debuchi here was significant, with respect to both their guiding ideal and the practical implementation of that ideal. However, it should be remembered that this was an ideal that was originally developed by Shidehara himself during earlier occasions such as the Washington Naval Conference. Debuchi also took on the burden of coordinating ministry efforts with the army and navy. Meanwhile, Kimura too followed the non-interventionist path, planning the future of Sino-Japanese relations after the defeat of Zhang Zuolin.

Second, there was the problem of Japanese immigration to the US. Shidehara tends to be viewed as lacking a policy for dealing with this issue. In reality, however, Shidehara deftly navigated the complexities of this area, beginning with his time as ambassador to the US. When, for example, Foreign Minister Matsui requested that Shidehara write a letter of protest, he followed through with the request, while at the same time softening the contents. He also succeeded in calming down Kaneko, who strongly supported sending a special delegation to the US. Later, when Shidehara became foreign minister himself, he was cautious about launching further protests, while at the same time publishing two collections of public documents for a domestic audience. Further, Shidehara took the step of sending a group led by Saburi to an immigration committee and promoted Japanese immigration to Brazil. It should also be remembered that Shidehara utilised the reporting of Edward Bell as a way to convey Japan's position to the US, thereby working to improve US public opinion. Finally, because Shidehara was so familiar with the details surrounding the problem of Japanese immigration to the US, he was able to avoid overly relying on the International Trade Bureau. His policy process was close to a top-down model.

Third, there was Shidehara's economic diplomacy. A prime example of Shidehara responding with an economy-centred approach would be the Beijing Special Conference on Tariffs. For the most part, Shidehara's conception of regional order remained within the framework established at the Washington Naval Conference. He also displayed enthusiasm for the diversification of trade. On matters of economic diplomacy, Shidehara would take into account the opinions of his advisers such as Saburi, as well as Obata and Saitō. While the final decision on such matters may have rested with Shidehara, in this area his policy process was closer to a bottom-up model. We may say that through economic diplomacy, Shidehara raised the relative position within the ministry of the International Trade Bureau, which during this period would be alternately headed by Saburi and Saitō.

Shidehara's response to the Northern Expedition can be treated as an encapsulation of his diplomatic style. As pointed out above, following the spirit of the Washington Conference, Shidehara asserted to the UK's ambassador that, even if the Chinese mainland were to go communist, Japan's focus would remain on economic benefits such as rights of residency and access to trade. Shidehara therefore avoided the kind of ideological response later demonstrated by Tanaka Giichi.

Supporting Shidehara's interpretation of the Northern Expedition was Saburi's survey of southern China. Here again, Shidehara relied heavily upon Saburi. However, this reliance was also at the root of his miscalculation. When Saburi attended the Beijing Special Conference on Tariffs, he was influenced by the discourse on the 'Sino-Japanese partnership' promoted by figures such as Shigemitsu. Saburi would also take a more favourable attitude towards the Nationalist Party following his observations of the situation in southern China. The rationally minded Saburi would have found himself wavering between the positions of Shidehara and Shigemitsu. As it happens, this foreshadowed Saburi's mysterious death some years later.

Finally, there was also a side to Shidehara that sought to expand Japan's interests in China. We see this aspect of him on display when he gave approval to the construction of the Taoang Railway, despite the fact that it ran counter to the stance of the New Four-Power Consortium. Here we have a glimpse of how even Shidehara was not entirely free of the tradition of Japanese diplomacy.

Diplomacy and Party Politics

This chapter has shown how Shidehara utilised his connections with others to further his diplomatic goals. Yet it is worth re-emphasising that he did not have complete control over Japanese foreign policy. As indicated by the existence of the army and the South Manchuria Railway, Japan's diplomatic apparatus remained as pluralistic as ever. Shidehara worked within the framework of the Ministry of Foreign Affairs and did not pay much attention to the political background of Japan.

Nevertheless, Shidehara was fully entrusted with diplomatic matters by the Kenseikai-led cabinet, and his policies succeeded in earning the trust of the elder statesman Saionji. At the time of the Beijing Special Conference on Tariffs, Saionji even went so far as to state: 'Foreign Minister Shidehara's approach today really hit the mark. First off, I want to praise him for developing into a capable minister of foreign affairs'.[102] Shidehara also expressed his respect for Saionji as a politician. One incident is particularly symbolic of the relationship of trust that developed between Shidehara and Saionji. In December 1926, when the Taishō emperor was critically ill, Saionji was searching for accommodations closer to the Hayama Imperial Villa. Meanwhile, Shidehara had a holiday residence in the village of Kotsubo, in present-day Zushi city. As this residence was far closer to the Imperial Villa in Hayama, Shidehara lent it to Saionji. Thus, Shidehara and Saionji were able to 'become better acquainted and gained the opportunity to frequently meet'.[103]

There are two possible ways of evaluating the decision by the political-party-run cabinet to leave diplomatic decision-making to Shidehara. First, there is the interpretation that, by leaving diplomacy to Shidehara, the Kenseikai cabinet was able to gain the trust of Saionji. This decision also coincided with Shidehara's ideal of centralising Japan's diplomatic efforts. However, while Shidehara sought to separate Japan's domestic politics from its foreign policy, this does not mean that his diplomatic efforts were devoid of political implications. On the contrary, the consolidation of party-based cabinet rule could be said to constitute the domestic political significance of Shidehara diplomacy. Katō's Kenseikai party had already begun to absorb the spirit of the Washington Naval Conference from its time in opposition. With the coming of the Katō and Wakatsuki cabinets and Saionji's positive evaluation of Shidehara's diplomacy, the Kenseikai began to be viewed as the establishment party. Thus the Kenseikai developed into a proper governing party, and, together with the other major party, which was Seiyukai, helped to thereby establish party-based politics in Japan.[104]

Second, we have a somewhat different interpretation, whereby overreliance on Shidehara by the Kenseikai led to the general neglect of party-based guidance of Japanese diplomacy. Even if leaving foreign affairs to Shidehara had the positive effect of gaining Saionji's trust, should not the next stage have been the pursuit of a system where the governing political party had a hand in guiding diplomatic decision-making? In fact, this approach towards diplomacy would be undertaken by a later prime minister, Hamaguchi Osachi, when he guided Japan's participation in the London Naval Treaty Conference on Disarmament in 1930. However, the second Wakatsuki cabinet was unable to adequately respond to the international situation in the aftermath of the Manchurian Incident, and prewar party-based politics ultimately collapsed. The greatest tragedy of Taishō democracy was that the Manchurian Incident occurred before the institutionalisation of party-based guidance of Japan's diplomacy.[105]

How did Shidehara himself view diplomacy and party politics in Japan? On 10 June 1925, in a letter to Izawa Takio, the governor-general of Taiwan, Shidehara wrote:

> At least with respect to simple ideals, it seems that there are areas where the position of foreign minister is similar to that of the governor of a colony. In order to achieve continuity in diplomatic matters, it may be appropriate to create a custom whereby the foreign minister does not act in line with the cabinet. Nevertheless, such things are extremely difficult under the present political conditions.[106]

In other words, from the perspective of diplomatic continuity, the foreign minister should not share the same career path as the cabinet. Yet Shidehara understood that the party politics of Japan at that time meant that it was impossible for the foreign minister's position to not be tied to the cabinet in some manner. In fact, it could even be said that Shidehara's life work was this very problem of how to maintain diplomatic continuity, given that a party-based political system entails periodic changes in the governing party.

It would not be long before Shidehara himself would cede the position of foreign minister to the president of the Seiyukai party, Tanaka Giichi, in the wake of the collapse of the first Wakatsuki cabinet in 1927. The militaristic diplomacy of the Tanaka cabinet would be dubbed 'Tanaka diplomacy'. With the irregular course of Tanaka diplomacy, Shidehara's sense of impending crisis grew stronger. It was at that very time that, in June 1927, the Constitutional Democratic Party (the Rikken Minseitō) was formed, with Shidehara's old friend Hamaguchi Osachi as its president. This development would lead Shidehara to deepen his involvement in party-based politics. This is a topic that I wish to explore in more detail in Part II.

Endnotes

1   Chapters 3, 4 and 5 (Sections 1 and 3) of this book are based on my previous work: Hattori Ryūji, 'Shidehara Kijūrō no Seisaku to Jinmyaku' [Shidehara Kijūrō's policies and personal connections], *Chūō Daigaku Ronshū*, no. 27 (March 2006): 21–57.

2   Usui Katsumi, *Chugoku wo Meguru Kindai Nihon no Gaikō* [Modern Japanese diplomacy concerning China] (Tokyo: Chikuma Shobō, 1983), 128–29.

3   The reform faction movements have been thoroughly researched. See Tobe Ryōichi, 'Shiratori Toshio to Manshū Jihen' [Shiratori Toshio and the Manchurian Incident], *Bōei Daigakkō Kiyō*, no. 39 (September 1979): 77–130; Tobe Ryōichi, 'Shiratori Toshio to "Kōdō Gaikō"' [Shiratori Toshio and 'benevolent imperial diplomacy'], *Bōei Daigakkō Kiyō*, no. 40 (March 1980): 77–143; Tobe Ryōichi, 'Gaikō niokeru "Shisōteki Rikyo" no Tankyū: Shiratori Toshio no Kōdō Gaikō-ron' [The search for an 'intellectual approach' in diplomacy: Shiratori Toshio's theory of benevolent imperial diplomacy], *Kokusai Seiji*, no. 71 (August 1982): 124–40; Tobe Ryōichi, 'Gaimushō "Kakushin-ha" to Gunbu' [The 'reform faction' in the ministry of foreign affairs and the military], in *Shōwa-shi no Gunbu to Seiji* [The military and politics in Shōwa-era history], ed. Miyake Masaki, vol. 2 (Tokyo: Dai-ichi Hōki Co., 1983), 89–122; Tobe Ryōichi, 'Gaimushō Kakushin-ha no Tai-Bei-Saku' [The approach to the US advocated by the reform faction in the Ministry of Foreign Affairs], *Gaikō Jihō*, no. 1273 (November 1990): 66–80; Tobe Ryōichi, 'Gaimushō Kakushin-ha to Shin-Chitsujo' [The reform faction in the Ministry of Foreign Affairs and the new order], in *Nihon no Kiro to Matsuoka Gaikō* [Japan's crossroads and Matsuoka diplomacy], ed. Miwa Kimitada and Ryōichi Tobe (Tokyo: Nansōsha, 1993), 117–38; Sakai Tetsuya, '"Ei-Bei Kyōchō" to "Nicchū Teikei"' ['UK–US cooperation' and 'Japanese–Chinese partnership'], *Nenpyō Kindai Nihon Kenkyū*, no. 11 (October 1989): 61–92; Sakai Tetsuya, *Taishō Democracy Taisei no Hōkai: Naisei to Gaikō* [The collapse of the Taishō democracy system: Domestic politics and diplomacy] (Tokyo: University of Tokyo Press, 1992); Shiozaki Hiroaki, '"Pax Anglo Saxonica" to Gaimushō Kakushin-ha: Kokusai Chitsujo no "Kakushin" Ka wo Megutte' ['Pax Anglo Saxonica' and the reform faction in the Ministry of Foreign Affairs: On the 'reform' of the international order], in *Kindai Nihon no Seiji Kōzō* [The political structure of modern Japan], ed. Arima Manabu and Mitani Hiroshi (Tokyo: Yoshikawa Kōbunkan, 1993), 206–33; Shiozaki Hiroaki, *Kokunai Shin-Taisei wo Motomete: Ryō-Taisen ni Wataru Kakushin Undō, Shisō no Kiseki* [In search of a new national system: The trajectory of the reform movement and its thought between the two world wars] (Fukuoka: Kyūshū University Press, 1998), 61–108; Takeda Tomoki, *Shigemitsu Mamoru to Sengo Seiji* [Shigemitsu Mamoru and postwar politics] (Tokyo: Yoshikawa Kōbunkan, 2002); Hattori, *Manshū Jihen to Shigemitsu*

Chūka Kōshi Hōkokusho; Koike Seiichi, *Manshū Jihen to Tai-Chūgoku Seisaku* [The Manchurian Incident and policy regarding China] (Tokyo: Yoshikawa Kōbunkan, 2003); Takahashi Katsuhiro, 'Gaimushō Kakushin-ha no Shisō to Kōdō: Kurihara Tadashi wo Chūshin ni' [The actions and thoughts of the reform faction in the Ministry of Foreign Affairs: Focusing on Kurihara Tadashi], *Shoryō-bu Kiyō*, no. 55 (March 2004): 35–55.

4   For research on Shidehara's first period as foreign minister, see Iriye Akira, *After Imperialism: The Search for a New Order in the Far East, 1921–1931* (Cambridge: Harvard University Press, 1965), 57–145; Usui Katsumi, *Nihon to Chūgoku: Taishō Jidai* [Japan and China: The Taishō era] (Tokyo: Harashobō, 1972), 191–269; Bamba Nobuya, *Japanese Diplomacy in a Dilemma: New Light on Japan's China Policy, 1924–1929* (Kyoto: Minerva Press, 1972), 225–82; Goto-Shibata Harumi, *Japan and Britain in Shanghai, 1925–31* (London: Macmillan Press, 1995), 13–54, doi.org/10.1057/9780230389830; Nishida Toshihiro, 'Higashi Asia no Kokusai Chitsujo to Shidehara Gaikō: 1924–1927 Nen' [The international order in East Asia and Shidehara diplomacy: 1924–1927] (1) (2), *Hōgaku Ronsō* 147, no. 2 (May 2000): 51–69, 149, no. 1 (April 2001): 99–121; Katō Kiyofumi, 'Shidehara Gaikō niokeru Man-Mo Seisaku no Genkai: Gaimushō to Mantetsu Kantoku-ken Mondai' [The limits of Manchuria–Mongolia Policy in Shidehara diplomacy: The Ministry of Foreign Affairs and the problem of the power of supervision over the South Manchuria Railway], *Waseda Daigaku Daigakuin Bungaku Kenkyūka Kiyō*, no. 46 (February 2001): 47–58; Yu Hong, 'Shidehara Gaikō niokeru "Keizai Chūshin Shugi": 1925 Nen no Qingdao Rōdō Sōgi to 5/30 Jiken no Gaikō-teki Taiō wo Megutte' [The 'economic centrism' of Shidehara diplomacy: Considering the Qingdao labor dispute of 1925 and the May 30 Incident], *Ningen Bunka Ronsō*, no. 3 (March 2001): 1–11; Seki Shizuo, *Taishō Gaikō: Jinbutsu ni Miru Gaikō Senryaku-ron* [Taishō diplomacy: Theories of diplomatic strategy as represented by figures] (Tokyo: Minerva Shobō, 2001), 197–244; Furuse Hiroyuki, 'Austin Chamberlain no Higashi Asia Seisaku: 5/30 Jiken, Tokubetsu Kanzei Kaigi, Kanton Fukazei wo Chūshin ni' [Austin Chamberlain's East Asian policy: Focusing on the May 30 Incident, the Special Tariff Conference and the Canton additional tax], *Joho Bunka Kenkyū*, no. 16 (October 2002): 189–212.

5   Takahashi Katsuhiro, ed., '"Debuchi Katsuji Nikki" (1): Meiji 32 Nen, 34 Nen' [The diary of Debuchi Katsuji (1): Meiji 32, 34], *Kokugakuin Daigaku Nihon Bunka Kenkyū-jo Kiyo*, no. 84 (September 1999): 227–70; Takahashi Katsuhiro, ed., '"Debuchi Katsuji Nikki" (2): Taishō 12 Nen–15 Nen' [The diary of Debuchi Katsuji (2): Taishō 12–15], *Kokugakuin Daigaku Nihon Bunka Kenkyū-jo Kiyo*, no. 85 (March 2000): 373–530; Bamba Nobuya, 'Pekin Kanzei Tokubetsu Kaigi ni Nozomu Nihon no Seisaku Kettei Katei' [The Japanese policy decision-making process in the case of the Beijing Special Conference on Tariffs], in *Taigai Seisaku Kettei Katei no Nichi-Bei Hikaku* [A comparison between Japan and the United States with regard to the foreign policy decision-making process], ed. Hosoya Chihiro and Jōji Watanuki (Tokyo: University of Tokyo Press, 1977), 375–417; Hattori, *Higashi Asia Kokusai Kankyō no Hendō to Nihon Gaikō, 1918–1931*, 149–89.

6   'Taishō 14 Nen 4 Gatsu 16 Nichi Sesshōkan no Omeshi ni Yori Shidehara Daijin ga Nashitaru Shinkō no Sōkō' [Draft of the lecture to be presented to the emperor by Minister Shidehara, following his summoning by the regent official on 16 April, the 14th year of the Taishō Era], in 'Gaimushō Kansei oyobi Naiki Kankei Zakken' [Various incidents concerning the organisation and inner regulations of the Ministry of Foreign Affairs], vol. 1, M.1.2.0.2, Diplomatic Archives of the Ministry of Foreign Affairs of Japan. For a copy of the draft, see 'Goshinkō Kankei Zakken' [Various incidents relating to lectures for the emperor], L.1.0.0.6, Diplomatic Archives of the Ministry of Foreign Affairs of Japan. See also Minister's Secretariat Personal Division, *Gaimushō Nenkan*, 1926, 221–27; Ministry of Foreign Affairs Hundred-Year History Compilation Association, *Gaimushō no 100 Nen*, vol. 1, 752–55.

7   From Shidehara to Uchida, 5 November 1919, in Ministry of Foreign Affairs, *Nihon Gaikō Bunsho, 1919*, vol. 2, part 1, 371–75.

8   Long diary, 23 December 1919, Breckinridge Long Papers, Box 2, Manuscript Division, Library of Congress; memoranda by Long of conversations with Debuchi, 23 December, Long Papers, Box 183.

9   Mitani Taiichirō, 'Wall Street to Kyokutō: Washington Taisei niokeru Kokusai Kinyū Shihon no Yakuwari' [Wall Street and the Far East: The role of international finance capital under the Washington system], *Chūōkōron* 90, no. 9 (September 1975): 165–67.

10 Long to Lamont, 20 December 1919, Long Papers, Box 180.

11 Memorandum by Long of a conversation with Shidehara, 30 April 1920, Long Papers, Box 180; MacMurray to Long, 2 November 1920, Long Papers, Box 161. See also Long to Morris, 6 February 1920, Morris, Roland S. Papers, Box 3, Manuscript Division, Library of Congress; Shidehara to Uchida, 30 April 1920 in Ministry of Foreign Affairs, *Nihon Gaikō Bunsho*, 1920, vol. 2, part 1, 275–80.

12 Lamont to Morgan, 26 March 1920, Thomas William Lamont Papers, Box 185, Baker Library, Harvard University.

13 Shidehara Kijūrō, 'Wasureenu Hitobito: Kōyū Kaisōki' [Those I will never forget: Memoirs of comradeship], *Bungei Shunjū* 29, no. 1 (January 1951): 57–58.

14 Takahashi, 'Debuchi Katsuji Nikki (2)', 411. See also Murai Ryōta, *Seitō Naikaku-sei no Seiritsu, 1918–27 Nen* [The establishment of the party cabinet system, 1918–27] (Tokyo: Yūhikaku, 2005), 206–07.

15 Kubota Kanichirō, ed., 'Ishii Shishaku Kandan-roku' [Record of a chat by Viscount Ishii], *Kokusai Mondai*, no. 65 (August 1965): 61.

16 Kubota Kanichirō, ed., 'Ishii Shishaku Nikki' [Diary of Viscount Ishii], *Kokusai Mondai*, no. 67 (October 1965): 62–63.

17 Matsui, *Matsui Keishirō Jijoden*, 12.

18 Kiyosawa Kiyoshi, *Ankoku Nikki: Shōwa 17 Nen 12 Gatsu 9 Nichi–20 Nen 5 Gatsu 5 Nichi* [Diary of darkness: 9 December, Shōwa 17, to 5 May, Shōwa 20] (Tokyo: Nihon Hyōronsha, 1979), 459.

19 *Kanpō*, extra edition, 2 July 1924; Kantōgen [foreword], 'Shushō Gaishō no Enzetsu' [Speech by the prime minister and the foreign minister], *Gaikō Jihō*, no. 471 (July 1924): n.p.

20 *Kanpō*, extra edition, 2 July 1924; Kantōgen [foreword], 'Shushō Gaishō no Enzetsu' [Speech by the prime minister and the foreign minister], *Gaikō Jihō*, no. 471 (July 1924): n.p.

21 *Kanpō*, extra edition, 2 July 1924.

22 Kantōgen, 'Shushō Gaishō no Enzetsu', n.p.

23 'Dai 48 Kai Teikoku Gikai Kizokuin Giji Sokkiroku' [Shorthand record of the proceedings of the 48th Imperial Diet House of Peers], no. 2, 22 January 1924, in *Teikoku Gikai Gijiroku* [Proceedings of the Imperial Diet], Reel 46, Tokyo: Yūshōdō, date unknown, 28.

24 Institute of Modern History, Academia Sinica, ed., *Zhong Ri guanxi shi liao: Shandong wenti, 1920-6* [Documents on Sino-Japanese Relations: Shandong Question], vol. 1 (Taipei: Institute of Modern History, Academia Sinica, 1987), 489–93.

25 Takahashi, 'Debuchi Katsuji Nikki (2)', 375, 377–79, 381, 383–86, 389, 403–04, 462–63. See also Kawashima Shin, *Chugoku Kindai Gaikō no Keisei* [The formation of modern Chinese diplomacy] (Nagoya: Nagoya University Press, 2004), 532.

26 Takahashi, 'Debuchi Katsuji Nikki (2)', 390–96.

27 Ibid., 412–13.

28 Shidehara Kijūrō (speaking), Kiyosawa Kiyoshi (notation), 'Daiichiji Gaishō Jidai no Omoide' [Memories from my first period as foreign minister], date unknown, in 'Shidehara Heiwa Bunko', Reel 7.

29 Ibid.

30 Takahashi, 'Debuchi Katsuji Nikki (2)', 421–34.

31 Shidehara Kijūrō, 'Kokusai Seikyoku no Suii to Gaikō no Konpon-gi' [Shifts in international politics and the foundational significance of diplomacy], *Gaikō Jihō*, no. 500 (October 1925): 20.

32 Takahashi, 'Debuchi Katsuji Nikki (2)', 488–89.

33 Ministry of Foreign Affairs, *Nihon Gaikō Bunsho, 1921*, vol. 2, 126–35.

34 From Secretary Yamazaki to Yamakawa, 17 February, year unknown, in 'Yamakawa Tadao Kankei Bunsho' [Documents relating to Yamakawa Tadao], Reel 1, Modern Japanese Political History Materials Room, National Diet Library; Takahashi, 'Debuchi Katsuji Nikki (2)', 405; Nagai, 'Shidehara Danshaku no Omoide'.

35 Takahashi, 'Debuchi Katsuji Nikki (2)', 522.

36 Horiuchi, *Chūgoku no Arashi no Naka de*, 44.

37 Colby to Wilson, 4 October 1920, Bainbridge Colby Papers, Box 3B, Manuscript Division, Library of Congress; Ōta Tamekichi, consul general in San Francisco, to Foreign Minister Uchida, 11 October 1920, in Ministry of Foreign Affairs, *Nihon Gaikō Bunsho, 1920*, vol. 1, 256–57; Ōta to Uchida, 30 October ibid., 295–96; Shidehara to Uchida, 1 November, ibid., 300–01. For studies of the Japanese Exclusion Act of this period, see Hirobe Izumi, *Japanese Pride, American Prejudice: Modifying the Exclusion Clause of the 1924 Immigration Act* (Stanford: Stanford University Press, 2001); Minohara Toshihiro, *Hai-Nichi Imin-hō to Nichi-Bei Kankei* [The Japanese Exclusion Act and Japan–US relations] (Tokyo: Iwanami Shoten, 2002).

38 William Phillips diary, 31 January 1924, William Phillips Papers, Box 2, Houghton Library, Harvard University.

39 'Sakatani Yoshirō Nikki' [The diary of Sakatani Yoshirō], 16, 17, 24 March, 25 April and 24 May 1924, in 'Sakatani Yoshirō Kankei Bunsho' [Documents relating to Sakatani Yoshirō], Document Department, no. 698, Modern Japanese Political History Materials Room, National Diet Library; Nagai to Shidehara, 14 January 1924, in 'Beikoku niokeru Hai-Nichi Mondai Ikken—1924 Nen Imin Hōan Seiritsu Keika: Shibusawa Shishaku-tō ni Tsūchi no Ken' [An incident relating to the anti-Japanese problem in the US—the process of the establishment of the Immigration Act of 1924: The incident relating to the informing of Viscount Shibusawa, etc.], 3.8.2.339-6-1-4, Diplomatic Archives of the Ministry of Foreign Affairs of Japan; Saburi, proxy for the Chief of the International Trade Bureau to Shibusawa, 20 May, ibid.

40 Matsui, *Matsui Keishirō Jijoden*, 135–36; Matsui to Hanihara, 15 March 1924, in Ministry of Foreign Affairs, *Nihon Gaikō Bunsho, 1924*, vol. 1, 124–25.

41 'Beikoku niokeru Hai-Nichi Mondai Zakken—1924 Nen Imin Hō: Seiritsu to Kakushu Jiken' [Miscellaneous incidents relating to the anti-Japanese problem in the US—the Immigration Act of 1924: Its establishment and various incidents]. 3.8.2.339-6-1-5, Diplomatic Archives of the Ministry of Foreign Affairs of Japan; Kokumin Tai-Bei Taikai Kaisai Shusseki-gan [Request to attend the citizens vs. the United States meeting], 2 June 1924, in 'Yamakawa Tadao Kankei Bunsho', Reel 1.

42 Kiyoura cabinet meeting decision, 28 May 1924, in 'Beikoku niokeru Hai-Nichi Mondai Zakken: 1924 Nen Imin Hō nitaisuru Kōshō oyobi Kōgi' [Miscellaneous incidents relating to the anti-Japanese problem in the US: Negotiations and protests regarding the Immigration Act of 1924], 3.8.2.339-6-6, Diplomatic Archives of the Ministry of Foreign Affairs of Japan; Hanihara to Matsui, 1 June 1924, in Ministry of Foreign Affairs, *Nihon Gaikō Bunsho, 1924*, vol. 1, 190–202; Shidehara, *Gaikō 50 Nen*, 47–48.

43 Kawashima Nobutarō, 'Shidehara Sōri heno Omoide: Jyoyaku Kaisei (zoku)' [Memories of Prime Minister Shidehara: The revision of the unequal treaties (continued)], July 1953, in 'Shidehara Heiwa Bunko', Reel 18.

44 Ibid.

45 Hanihara to Shidehara, 28 June 1924, in Ministry of Foreign Affairs, *Nihon Gaikō Bunsho, 1924*, vol. 1, 217–18.

46 Ministry of Foreign Affairs, ed., *1924 Nen Beikoku Imin-hō Seitei oyobi Kore nikansuru Nichi-Bei Kōshō Keika* [The US Immigration Act of 1924 and the process of Japan–US negotiations] (Tokyo: Ministry of Foreign Affairs, 1924); Ministry of Foreign Affairs, ed., *1924 Nen Beikoku Imin-hō Seitei oyobi Kore nikansuru Nichi-Bei Kōshō Keika Kōbunsho Eibun Fuzokusho* [The US Immigration Act of 1924 and the process of Japan–US negotiations, supplementary English-language official documents]

(Tokyo: Ministry of Foreign Affairs, 1924); Ministry of Foreign Affairs Research Department, Section 1, 'Gaikō Shiryō Hensan Jigyō nitsuite' [Regarding the task of editing diplomatic historical material], April 1939, in Hirose, *Kindai Gaikō Kaikoroku*, vol. 1, 44; Takahashi, 'Debuchi Katsuji Nikki (2)', 412.

47   '"1924 Nen Beikoku Imin-hō Seitei oyobi Kore nikansuru Nichi-Bei Kōshō Keika" Kobunsho Haifu-Saki' [The US Immigration Act of 1924 and the process of related negotiations' official document distribution destination], in 'Teikoku niokeru Gaikō Bunsho Kohyō Kankei Zakken' [Miscellanea related to the publication of diplomatic documents in Japan], N.1.7.1.2, Diplomatic Archives of the Ministry of Foreign Affairs of Japan.

48   Shidehara to Yoshida Isaburō, temporary acting ambassador to the US, 11 September 1924, in Ministry of Foreign Affairs, *Nihon Gaikō Bunsho, 1924*, vol. 1, 221–23; Shidehara to Ōyama Ujirō, consul general in San Francisco, 3 August 1924, ibid., 313.

49   Saburi Sadao, 'Beikoku Shin-Imin Hōan nitsuite' [Regarding the new Immigration Act in the US], *Kensei* 7, no. 7 (July 1924): 45.

50   Shidehara to Foreign Minister Katō, 26 August 1924, in 'Zoku Kakugi Kettei-sho Shūroku (Sōkō)' [Continued compilation of cabinet decision (draft)], vol. 3, Z.1.3.0.1, Diplomatic Archives of the Ministry of Foreign Affairs of Japan; 'Imin Iinkai Giryō Jiko nikansuru Ken' [The matter relating to the discussed items of the immigration committee], 21 November 1924, 1-4E-018-00-zatsu-03205-100, National Archives of Japan; Ministry of Foreign Affairs, International Trade Bureau, 'Dai 50 Kai Teikoku Gikai Setsumei Sankō Shiryo' [Explanatory reference material for the 50th Imperial Diet], January 1925, in 'Teikoku Gikai Kankei Zassan: Bessatsu, Setsumei Shiryō (Tsūshō-kyoku)' [Miscellanea related to the imperial diet: explanatory materials (international trade bureau)], vol. 6, 1.5.2.2-6-2, Diplomatic Archives of the Ministry of Foreign Affairs of Japan; Ishii Itarō (speaking), 'Shidehara-dan no Keizai Gaikō nitsuite' [On the economic diplomacy of Baron Shidehara], date unknown, in 'Shidehara Heiwa Bunko', Reel 13; Ishii, *Gaikōkan no Isshō*, 141–50.

51   Edward Price Bell, with an introduction by Calvin Coolidge, *World Chancelleries: Sentiments, Ideas, and Arguments Expressed by Famous Occidental and Oriental Statesmen Looking to the Consolidation of the Psychological Bases of International Peace* (Chicago: Chicago Daily News, 1926), 119–43. See also James D. Startt, *Journalism's Unofficial Ambassador: A Biography of Edward Price Bell, 1869–1943* (Athens: Ohio University Press, 1979), 112; Minohara, *Hai-Nichi Imin-hō to Nichi-Bei Kankei*, 224; Murai, *Seitō Naikaku-sei no Seiritsu, 1918–27 Nen*, 232–33.

52   Yoshida to Shidehara, 10 December 1924, in 'Gaikoku Shimbun Tsushin Kikan oyobi Tsushin-in Kankei Zakken: Tsushin-in no Bu, Beikokujin no Bu' [Miscellaneous matters concerning foreign news communication media and communication staff: On communication staff, US individuals], vol. 1, 1.3.2.50-2-2, Diplomatic Archives of the Ministry of Foreign Affairs of Japan; Shidehara to Katō, 18 April 1925, ibid.; Bell to Kato, 5 May 1925, Edward Price Bell Papers, Outgoing Correspondence Box 1924–1930, Newberry Library; Bell to Kato, 30 May 1925, Bell Papers, Outgoing Correspondence Box 1924–1930.

53   Remarks of Edgar A. Bancroft at the Japan–American Society's dinner, 12 December 1924, Edgar A. Bancroft Papers, Box 5, Seymour Library, Knox College; Bancroft to Hughes, 5 January 1925, Bancroft Papers, Box 4; Bancroft to Bell, 8 May 1925, Bancroft Papers, Box 4; Bell to Bancroft, 6 June 1925, Bell Papers, Outgoing Correspondence Box 1924–1930; *New York Times*, 29 July 1925.

54   Shidehara to the Nobel Peace Prize Committee, 11 December 1930, in J. L. Garvin Papers, Folder: Recipient: Bell, Edward Price, Harry Ransom Humanities Research Center, University of Texas at Austin; Shidehara to Makino Nobuaki, 5 May 1933, in 'Makino Nobuaki Kankei Bunsho', Correspondence Department, vol. 28. See also Shidehara to Mrs Bell, 11 December 1930, Bell Papers, Incoming Materials Box Scraq-Sn; Startt, *Journalism's Unofficial Ambassador*, 159, 230.

55   Katō Takaaki to Mutsu Hirokichi, 29 August 1924, in 'Katō Takaaki Bunsho' [Katō Takaaki documents], 85, Modern Japanese Political History Materials Room, National Diet Library; Takahashi, 'Debuchi Katsuji Nikki (2)', 408, 418, 438–40, 454, 514–15; Mutsu Ian, 'The Mutsu Family', in *Britain and Japan: Biographical Portraits*, ed. Ian Nish, vol. 2 (Richmond, Surrey: Japan Library, 1997), 161.

56   Takahashi, 'Debuchi Katsuji Nikki (2)', 438, 441, 487, 509–10, 512–13, 521.

57   Ibid., 456, 458–61, 463, 473, 475, 500, 502–04.

58   Ibid., 392, 438–41; Horinouchi Kensuke, *Horinouchi Kensuke Kaikoroku: Nihon Gaikō 50 Nen no Rimen-shi* [The memoirs of Horinouchi Kensuke: A behind the scenes history of 50 years of Japanese diplomacy] (Tokyo: Sankei Shimbunsha, 1979), 24.

59   Ishii, *Gaikōkan no Isshō*, 158; Hattori, *Higashi Asia Kokusai Kankyō no Hendō to Nihon Gaikō, 1918–1931*, 43, 164, 197, 236, 309, 312; for a work that relays the collected information on the material section of the Manchurian Railway negotiations division, see Manchurian Railway Negotiations Division, Material Section, 'Shōwa 5 Nendo Sōgo Shiryō (Kimura Riji-yō)' [Comprehensive documentation for the fifth year of Shōwa (for use by Director Kimura)], 6 June 1931, in Kimura Eiichi Papers, Box 1, Hoover Institution, Stanford University; Manchurian Railway Negotiations Division, Material Section, 'Shōwa 6 Nendo Sōgo Shiryō (Kimura Riji-yō)' [Comprehensive documentation for the sixth year of Shōwa (for use by Director Kimura)], date unknown, Kimura Papers, Box 1. See also Satō Motoei, *Kindai Nihon no Gaikō to Gunji: Keneki Yōgō to Shinryaku no Kōzō* [Modern Japan's diplomacy and the military: The structure of interest protection and invasion] (Tokyo: Yoshikawa Kōbunkan, 2000), 287–88.

60   Tani Masayuki, 'Holland Kōshi Jidai no Shidehara-san'. See also Kawamura Shigehisa, 'Kasumigaseki Taiheiki: Jinei Ijyō Ariya Nakiya' [Record of the great peace of Kasumigaseki: Was there disorder in the camps or not], 11 November 1932, in 'Kawamura Shigehisa Kankei Bunsho' [Documents relating to Kawamura Shigehisa], 3–7, Diplomatic Archives of the Ministry of Foreign Affairs of Japan; Hattori, *Higashi Asia Kokusai Kankyō no Hendō to Nihon Gaikō, 1918–1931*, 311–12; Kobayashi Michihiko, 'Tanaka Seiyūkai to Santō Shuppei' [The Tanaka-led Seiyūkai and the sending of troops to Shandong], 1927–1928 (1), *Kita Kyūshū Shiritsu Daigaku Hōsei Ronshū* 32, no. 2–3 (December 2004): 26.

61   Takahashi, 'Debuchi Katsuji Nikki (2)', 407, 438, 453, 470, 510, 521, 523.

62   Arita Hachirō, *Bakahachi to Hito ha Iu: Ichi Gaikōkan no Kaiso* [Some people call me 'Bakahachi': The recollections of a diplomat] (Tokyo: Kōwadō, 1959), 29.

63   Ibid., 29.

64   Hirota Kōki, 'Egi Tasuku-shi no "Shikoku Jōyaku to Beikoku Ryūho" wo Yomu' [Reading Mr Egi Tasuku's 'The Four-Power Treaty and the US suspense'], *Gaikō Jihō*, no. 423 (June 1922): 1–13.

65   Hirota Kōki Biography Publishing Association, *Hirota Kōki*, 600–01.

66   Chūgoku Kanzei Tokubetsu Kaigi Jūnbi Uchiawase-kai Dai 1 Shouiinkai Hoka Gijiroku [Proceedings of the Chinese Tariff Special Conference, preliminary meeting, first subcommittee and others], 29 August – 29 September 1925, in 'Shina Kanzei narabini Chigai Hōken Teppai Mondai Pekin Kaigi Ikken: Shina Kanzei Tokubetsu Kaigi Junbi Uchiawase-kai' [Beijing conference on China's customs tariffs and elimination of extraterritoriality: Preparatory meeting for the special conference on customs tariffs in China], vol. 2. 2.9.10.13-12, Diplomatic Archives of the Ministry of Foreign Affairs of Japan.

67   Chinese Ministry of Foreign Affairs to Chinese Minister to the US Shi Zhaoji (Alfred Sao-ke Sze), 30 January 1926, in Diplomatic Archives, 03.25.25.31.1, Institute of Modern History, Academia Sinica; Shen Yunlong, ed., *Huang Yingbai xiansheng nianpu changbian* [Long chronicle of Mr Huang Yingbai] (Taipei: Lianjing chuban shiye gongsi, 1976), 252, 258, 259; Shidehara to Hioki, 15 December 1925, in Ministry of Foreign Affairs, *Nihon Gaikō Bunsho, 1926*, vol. 2, part 2, 871–72; Wang Rongbao, Chinese minister to Japan, to Shidehara, 20 October 1926, ibid., vol. 2, part 1, 385–87; Shidehara to Yoshizawa, 9 November, ibid., 400–02; Japanese legation in China to Chinese Ministry of Foreign Affairs, 13 November 1926, in *Zhong Ri guanxi shi liao: Shangwu jiaoshe, 1918–27* [Documents on Sino-Japanese relations: Commercial negotiations], ed. Institute of Modern History, Academia Sinica (Taipei: Institute of Modern History, Academia Sinica, 1994), 608–09; Hattori, *Higashi Asia Kokusai Kankyō no Hendō to Nihon Gaikō, 1918–1931*, 163–69.

68   Eliot to FO, 4 November 1925, 10813/25/30, FO 228/2791, National Archives; Hattori, *Higashi Asia Kokusai Kankyō no Hendō to Nihon Gaikō, 1918–1931*, 167.

69   Chamberlain to Eliot, 17 December 1924, FO 800/255, National Archives; Chamberlain to Eliot, 23 July 1925, FO 800/255, National Archives.

70 Reminiscences of Sansom; Charles Eliot, *Japanese Buddhism*, ed. G. B. Sansom, with a memoir of the author by Sir Harold Parlett (Richmond: Curzon Press, 1994). See also Shidehara to Matsui, ambassador to the UK, 3 February 1927, in Ministry of Foreign Affairs, *Nihon Gaikō Bunsho*, Shōwa Era I, part 1, vol. 1, 435–36; Etō Shinkichi, *Higashi Asia Seijishi Kenkyū* [Study of the political history of East Asia] (Tokyo: University of Tokyo Press, 1968), 160; Harumi Goto-Shibata, 'Sir John Tilley, 1869–1951: British Ambassador to Japan, 1926–31', in *Britain and Japan: Biographical Portraits*, ed. Hugh Cortazzi, vol. 4 (London: Japan Library, 2002), 78–88.

71 Matsui, *Matsui Keishirō Jijoden*, 143–44.

72 Takahashi, 'Debuchi Katsuji Nikki (2)', 529; Shidehara to Matsudaira, 30 December 1926, in Ministry of Foreign Affairs, *Nihon Gaikō Bunsho, 1926*, vol. 2, part 2, 1219–23.

73 Reminiscences of Dooman; Hattori, *Higashi Asia Kokusai Kankyō no Hendō to Nihon Gaikō, 1918–1931*, 167–69.

74 Ministry of Foreign Affairs, *Nihon Gaikō Bunsho, 1924*, vol. 2, 216–19, 222–25. Another source is Ministry of Foreign Affairs et. al., *Jōyaku Kaisei Kankei: Nihon Gaikō Bunsho, Bessatsu, Tsushō Jōyaku to Tsūshō Seisaku no Hensen*, 614–21. However, the above source does contain some inaccuracies. See also Unno Yoshirō, 'Nihon to Indochina no Bōeki Masatsu' [Trade friction between Japan and Indochina], in *Taiheiyō Asia-ken no Kokusai Keizai Funsō-shi* [A history of international economic disputes in the Pacific and Asia region], ed. Hosoya Chihiro (Tokyo: University of Tokyo Press, 1983), 41–64.

75 Shidehara to Ishii, 1 October 1924, in Ministry of Foreign Affairs, *Nihon Gaikō Bunsho, 1924*, vol. 2, 237; Katō cabinet meeting decision, 20 January 1925, ibid., *1925*, vol. 1, 254–55; Ministry of Foreign Affairs proclamation, 31 July 1925, ibid., 237–49. Regarding Yamagata, see Tokutomi, *Sokū Yamagata Kō Den*, 433–83.

76 Ministry of Foreign Affairs, International Trade Bureau, First Section, 'Kintō Bōeki Kaigi Gijiroku narabini Hōkoku-sho' [Near East Trade Conference minutes and report], date unknown, in 'Kintō Bōeki Kaigi' [Near East Trade Conference], vol. 3, 3.2.1.41, Diplomatic Archives of the Ministry of Foreign Affairs of Japan; Obata Yūkichi Biography Publishing Association, *Obata Yūkichi*, 340–59.

77 Permission Proposal, 'Honpō to "Balkan" Kokkai Engan Kantō oyobi Egypt Hōmen to no Bōeki Sokushin notame Gaimushō Kankei-kan Kaigi Kaisai-gata nikansuru Ken' [Matter concerning the holding of a conference with officials connected to the Ministry of Foreign Affairs, for the purpose of facilitating trade between Japan, the 'Balkan' Black Sea coast, the Near East, and Egypt], 28 December 1925, in 'Kintō Bōeki Kaigi', vol. 1; Shidehara to Obata, 29 December, ibid.; Nihon Yūsen, *Nihon Yūsen Kabushiki Gaisha 50 Nen-shi*, 410.

78 'Dai 1 Kai Bōeki Kaigi Ikken: Sankasha Kankei: 1' [First Trade Conference: Participants]. 3.2.1.40-5, Diplomatic Archives of the Ministry of Foreign Affairs of Japan.

79 'Dai 1 Kai Bōeki Kaigi Sōkai niokeru Gaimu Daijin Aisatsu (Taishō 15 Nen 9 Gatsu 13 Nichi)' [Opening address by the minister for foreign affairs at the First Trade Conference general meeting (13 September, 15th year of Taishō)], in 'Dai 1 Kai Bōeki Kaigi Ikken: Gidai nikansuru Ikensho (Ko) Kanchō oyobi Zaigai Kōkan' [First Trade Conference: View about subjects (section a) government office and diplomatic establishments abroad], 3.2.1.40-3-1, Diplomatic Archives of the Ministry of Foreign Affairs of Japan. For more details on the South Sea Trade Conference, see Shimizu Hajime, '1920 Nendai niokeru "Nanshin-Ron" no Kisuu to Nanyō Bōeki Kaigi no Shisō' [The trend of 'Nanshin-ron' ('advance to the south' theory) in the 1920s and the thought behind the South Sea Trade Conference], in *Ryō-Taisen-kan-ki Nihon, Tōnan Asia Kankei no Shosō* [Various aspects of the relationship between Japan and South-East Asia during the era between the two world wars], ed. Shimizu Hajime (Tokyo: Asian Economic Research Center, 1986), 3–46.

80 'Dai 1 Kai Bōeki Kaigi Sōkai niokeru Gaimu Daijin Aisatsu'.

81 Ishii Itarō (speaking), 'Shidehara-dan no Keizai Gaikō nitsuite'.

82 Ibid.

83 Permission Proposal, 'Tsusho-kyoku ni Nanyō-gakari Secchi nikansuru Ken' [Matter concerning the establishment of a South Sea section in the International Trade Bureau], drafted 7 November 1929, in 'Gaimushō Kansei oyobi Naiki Kankei Zakken', vol. 2. I also received insight on this topic from Koike, *Manshū Jihen to Tai-Chūgoku Seisaku*, 104. See also Ministry of Foreign Affairs Hundred-Year History Compilation Association, *Gaimushō no 100 Nen*, vol. 2, 7.

84 Perhaps for this reason, Bancroft's evaluation of the establishment of diplomatic relations between Japan and the Soviet Union was that: 'Of course this is not the end of their controversies, but rather an adjustment of some'. See Bancroft to Schurman, 25 January 1925, Bancroft Papers, Box 4.

85 Bancroft to Kellogg, 25 February 1925, Bancroft Papers, Box 4.

86 Bancroft to Kellogg, 5 March 1925, Bancroft Papers, Box 4.

87 Bancroft to Kellogg, 19 March 1925, Bancroft Papers, Box 4.

88 Ibid.

89 Ibid.

90 Hattori, *Higashi Asia Kokusai Kankyō no Hendō to Nihon Gaikō, 1918–1931*, 150–56, 229–34.

91 'Sasaki Tōichi Chūjō Dan' [A talk with Lieutenant General Sasaki Tōichi], 15 November 1942, in *Manshū Jihen no Rimen-shi* [The inside story of the Manchurian Incident], ed. Mori Katsumi (Tokyo: Kokusho Kankōkai, 1976), 437–38; Sasaki Tōichi, *Aru Gunjin no Jiden* [The autobiography of a soldier] (Tokyo: Futsūsha, 1963), 140.

For research on the Nanjing Incident, see Etō, *Higashi Asia Seijishi Kenkyū*, 149–76; Usui Katsumi, *Nicchū Gaikō-shi* [Sino-Japanese diplomatic history] (Tokyo: Hanawashobō, 1971), 30–47; Tochigi Toshio and Banno Ryōkichi, *Chūgoku Kokumin Kakumei: Senkanki Higashi Asia no Chikaku Hendō* [The Chinese national revolution: Tectonic shifts in East Asia during the inter-war period] (Tokyo: Hōsei University Press, 1997), 259–62.

92 Shidehara to Yoshizawa, 28 March 1927, in Ministry of Foreign Affairs, *Nihon Gaikō Bunsho*, Shōwa Era I, part 1, vol. 1, 521–22; Yoshizawa to Shidehara, 22 April 1927, ibid., 601–03; Iriye, *After Imperialism*, 97–109.

93 Ministry of Foreign Affairs, *Nihon Gaikō Bunsho*, Shōwa Era I, part 1, vol. 1, 542–45.

94 Ibid.

95 Yada Shichitarō, consulate general in Shanghai, to Shidehara, 4 December 1926, in 'Kakkoku Naisei Kankei Zassan: Shina no Bu, Chihō' [Miscellaneous collection relating to the internal affairs of various nations: China, regions], vol. 52, 1.6.1.4-2-3, Diplomatic Archives of the Ministry of Foreign Affairs of Japan; Takao Tōru, consul general in Hankou, to Shidehara, 16 December, in 'Shogaikoku Gaikō Kankei Zassan: Ei-Shi-Kan' [Miscellaneous diplomatic relations of various countries: Between the UK and China], vol. 2, 1.2.1.10-8, Diplomatic Archives of the Ministry of Foreign Affairs of Japan; Shidehara to Matsudaira, 2 February 1927, in Ministry of Foreign Affairs, *Nihon Gaikō Bunsho*, Shōwa Era I, part 1, vol. 1, 435; Horiuchi, *Chūgoku no Arashi no Naka de*, 62–63; Tsutsui Kiyoshi, 'Saigo no Gaikō' [The final diplomacy] (3), *Kasumigaseki-kai Kaihō*, no. 310 (December 1971): 12; Liu Jie, 'Nicchū Teikei no Mosaku to Man-Mō Mondai: Shigemitsu Mamoru to Wang Zhengting' [The Manchuria–Mongolia problem and the search for a Japanese–Chinese Partnership: Shigemitsu Mamoru and Wang Zhengting], in *Nihon Rikken Seiji no Keisei to Henshitsu* [The formation and deterioration of Japanese constitutional politics], ed. Toriumi Yasushi, Mitani Hiroshi, Nishikawa Makoto and Yano Nobuyuki, (Tokyo: Yoshikawa Kōbunkan, 2005), 303.

96 Morioka to Shidehara, 27 March 1927, in Ministry of Foreign Affairs, *Nihon Gaikō Bunsho*, Shōwa Era I, part 1, vol. 1, 518.

97 Shidehara to Yada, 31 March 1927, ibid., 532–33.

98 Matsuoka Yōsuke Biography Publishing Association, *Matsuoka Yōsuke: Sono Hito to Shōgai* [Matsuoka Yōsuke: The man and his life] (Tokyo: Kōdansha, 1974), 171–72; Katō Kiyofumi, 'Matsuoka Yōsuke to Mantetsu: Washington Taisei eno Chosen' [Matsuoka Yōsuke and the south Manchuria railway: Challenging the Washington system], in *Kindai Nihon to Mantetsu* [Modern

Japan and the south Manchuria railway], ed. Kobayashi Hideo (Tokyo: Yoshikawa Kōbunkan, 2000), 64–107; Hattori, *Higashi Asia Kokusai Kankyō no Hendō to Nihon Gaikō, 1918–1931*, 153, 230–32, 308–10.

99 Matsuoka Yōsuke Biography Publishing Association, *Matsuoka Yōsuke*, 171–72.

100 Hattori, *Higashi Asia Kokusai Kankyō no Hendō to Nihon Gaikō, 1918–1931*, 196.

101 Satō Naotake, ed., *Kokusai Renmei niokeru Nihon* [Japan in the League of Nations] (Tokyo: Kajima Research Center Press, 1972), 453–54.

For further details on the League of Nations, see Unno Yoshirō, *Kokusai Renmei to Nihon* [The League of Nations and Japan] (Tokyo: Harashobō, 1972); Usui Katsumi, *Manshūkoku to Kokusai Renmei* [Manchukuo and the League of Nations] (Tokyo: Yoshikawa Kōbunkan, 1995); Hattori, *Higashi Asia Kokusai Kankyō no Hendō to Nihon Gaikō, 1918–1931*, 35–42, 45, 54, 65, 76, 209, 260, 279, 281, 285–86; Hattori, *Manshū Jihen to Shigemitsu Chūka Kōshi Hōkokusho*; Gotō, *Ahen to Igirisu Teikoku*.

102 Oka Yoshitake and Hayashi Shigeru, eds, *Taishō Democracy-ki no Seiji: Matsumoto Gōkichi Seiji Nisshi* [Politics in the era of Taishō democracy: The political journal of Matsumoto Gōkichi] (Tokyo: Iwanami Shoten, 1959), 447.

103 Shidehara, 'Wasureenu Hitobito', 55. See also 'Gaimu Daijin Danshaku Shidehara Kijurō Shucchō no Ken' [The matter of Foreign Minister Baron Shidehara Kijurō's trip], 18 December 1926, 1-2A-019-00-nin-B1336-100, National Archives of Japan; Oka and Hayashi, *Taishō Democracy-ki no Seiji*, 331, 413, 457, 471, 545, 547.

104 Kobayashi Michihiko, 'Tairiku Seisaku to Jinkō Mondai: 1918–31' [Continental policy and the population problem: 1918–31], in *Kan-Taiheiyō no Kokusai Chitsujo no Mosaku to Nihon: Daiichiji Sekai Taisen-go kara 55 Nen Taisei Seiritsu* [The Search for an International Order in the Greater Pacific and Japan: From the Aftermath of World War I to the Establishment of the 1955 System], ed. Itō Yukio and Kawada Minoru (Tokyo: Yamakawa Shuppansha, 1999), 207; Murai, *Seitō Naikaku-sei no Seiritsu, 1918–27 Nen*, 229–34.

105 See also Hattori, *Higashi Asia Kokusai Kankyō no Hendō to Nihon Gaikō, 1918–1931*, 178, 313–14.

106 Izawa Takio Document Research Association, *Izawa Takio Kankei Bunsho*, 265.

Part II.
Breakdown:
The Prewar
Shōwa Era

4

Japan's Intervention in China

Japan and the Northern Expedition

The Shandong Expedition

The Seiyūkai party, led by Tanaka Giichi, formed a government in April 1927. At that time Prime Minister Tanaka also took on the role of foreign minister. Freed from his ministerial responsibilities, Shidehara spent a period of convalescence due to appendicitis at his coastal residence in Kotsubo, in the Zushi region south of Yokohama. This residence had been given the name 'Shūen-sō' (Shūen villa) by Saionji Kinmochi. After Shidehara recuperated from his illness, he visited Saionji in Okitsu to express his thanks. On this occasion he asked Saionji why he had given the residence the name of 'Shūen-sō'. Saionji told him that the meaning of the character 'for "en" (遠) was to convey the sense of "world", and means that you [Shidehara] are gathering together the hopes of the world'.[1] Saionji wanted to remind Shidehara that, although he was no longer the foreign minister for the time being, a great deal of responsibility rested upon his shoulders. I also note that from January of the previous year (1926), while Shidehara was still foreign minister, he had been nominated by the imperial household for a position in the House of Peers. Of the factions that constituted the Diet, he would go on to associate with the relatively neutral Dōwakai.[2]

In the political world, the formation of the Tanaka cabinet was the occasion for the Kenseikai and Seiyūhontō parties to merge. This development led to the birth of the Rikken Minseitō (the Constitutional Democratic Party, hereafter simply referred to as the Minseitō) in June 1927. The first president of the Minseitō was Hamaguchi Osachi. In fact, it was Shidehara who had persuaded Hamaguchi to assume the responsibility of party president. Although Hamaguchi then offered him the role of vice-president, Shidehara declined.

During this period, the Tanaka cabinet authorised the deployment of Japanese troops to the Shandong Peninsula in China. The impetus was the further advancement of the Northern Expedition, led by Chiang Kai-shek. Under the official justification of protecting local Japanese residents, the Tanaka cabinet authorised the first Shandong deployment in May 1927. The Tanaka cabinet authorised a second deployment in April of the following year. This move led to a clash with China's National Revolutionary Army in Jinan, west of Qingdao. The occurrence of the 'Jinan Incident' (in Japanese, the 'Sainan Incident') led to the Tanaka cabinet responding by committing even further, with the third Shandong deployment. Then, in June, Zhang Zuolin of the Mukden clique was assassinated when the train he was travelling in was bombed. In time, it was learned that the perpetrators of the assassination plot were actually the Kwantung Army (the branch of the Japanese army stationed in Kwantung-leased territory on the Liaodong Peninsula). The details of this 'Huanggutun Incident' (or, in Japanese, the 'Zhang Zuolin Explosion Death Incident') were not widely known in Japan; government documents simply referred to 'A Certain Important Incident in Manchuria'.[3]

The situation in China at the time of Chiang Kai-shek's Northern Expedition was therefore one of rapid change, while at the same time, the Tanaka cabinet's policy was characterised by dependency on military force. What did Shidehara think of these developments? Shidehara expressed his view in a private June 1927 letter to Adachi Mineichirō, Japan's ambassador to Belgium:

> Now that the upheaval in China is at its height, it is a great nuisance for the world's powers. Yet there is little doubt that for the citizens of China, the trend in thinking after the world war is towards a gradual political awakening, particularly in light of the examples of what occurred in Turkey and Egypt. Calls for the termination of unequal treaties or the overthrow of imperialism are now being recognized as a reflection of true national self-consciousness.

I believe that attempts by external forces to apply force in order to prevent these shifts are not only doomed to failure but may actually provoke matters further.[4]

In other words, according to Shidehara, not only was it impossible to prevent China's 'awakening' and 'national self-consciousness' with 'external forces' but also such measures could actually exacerbate the situation.

That is not to say that Shidehara thought Japan had to acquiesce to China's demands and renounce its interests in China. For example, when Belgium declared that it would return its foreign concessions in Tianjin, in the hopes that it could thereby develop its relations with China, Shidehara asked Adachi: 'Is this not a mistake on their part in judging the political situation in China?'[5]

'Overview of the Chinese Problem'

Although Shidehara was still in poor health, he would gradually become more active. The cause was the general election of February 1928. This was the first election in Japan with universal suffrage for male citizens. During the lead-up to the election, the Seiyūkai criticised the previous Wakatsuki cabinet for their policies on China. In reaction, Shidehara embarked upon trips to cities such as Nagoya and Osaka to present his views in public speeches. Newspapers from the period reported:

> Former foreign minister Mr. Shidehara Kijūrō fears that the Tanaka cabinet's handling of China policy may incur international misunderstanding and place the empire [Japan] in an unfavorable position. On this occasion, he has spoken forcefully on various aspects of his diplomatic approach, appealing to the citizens of the nation.[6]

Shidehara gave his speeches in order to convince his fellow citizens of the benefits of his diplomatic ideals, rather than to support any particular candidate in the general election. Their contents were conveyed in newspaper print, alongside photos. The *Tokyo Asahi Shimbun*, for example, reported:

> Expressing his regret that [the ideals of] Shidehara diplomacy had been trampled upon by the current cabinet, former foreign minister Baron Shidehara Kijūrō has made his way down to the Kansai area, via Nagoya, in order to publicly critique the government's approach to China policy.[7]

Although the governing Seiyūkai party would narrowly come in first place in the election, the Minseitō was able to close the gap to a single seat. In this political context, Shidehara published an essay titled 'Shina Mondai Gaikan' (Overview of the Chinese problem) in the April 1928 issue of *Gaikō Jihō*. This essay was a vehicle for Shidehara to discuss his own recommended policy on China. In the essay, Shidehara wrote:

> Today's China is no longer the China of the past. If you believe that it is still possible to recklessly use military force and pressure in order to achieve your goals through confrontation, you will fail to apprehend how the times have changed.[8]

On the other hand:

> If the citizens of China believe that they themselves can use violence and threats in order to subdue the great powers, ignoring their responsibilities and rigidly thinking only of their rights, then this would in turn be their mistake.[9]

In the same essay, Shidehara quoted his own Diet address to discuss China's communism, arguing:

> The question of how many people should be in control of political power, and what kind of domestic policies would be appropriate for China, is, of course, a matter that must be resolved by the citizens of that country.[10]

On the topic of the Wakatsuki cabinet's China policy, Shidehara repeated the following four points from his Diet address:

1. Respect the sovereignty and territorial integrity of China and abide by the principle of absolute non-interference in internal conflicts.
2. Pledge to promote a relationship of prosperous coexistence and economic cooperation between the two nations.
3. Respond to reasonable requests from the citizens of China with sympathy and goodwill and work resolutely toward a cooperative resolution.
4. While taking as patient and tolerant an attitude as possible with respect to current conditions in China, use all available reasonable methods to protect our legitimate and important rights and interests.[11]

According to 'Shina Mondai Gaikan', Sino-Japanese relations improved from the time of the Washington Naval Conference to the mid-1920s:

> Since the turning point of the Washington Conference, the relationship between our two nations gradually improved. In particular, our [ministry] staff played a central role in the Chinese Tariffs Special Conference and the Extraterritorial Rights Committee convened in Beijing last year. They worked in an impartial and temperate manner, thereby concretely demonstrating to China our sympathetic attitude. This, alongside our approach of absolutely not interfering in China's domestic conflict, served to bring the citizens of our two nations significantly closer together and improve mutual understanding.[12]

Shidehara was clearly proud of how his policies served to reform Japan's relations with China.

In the essay, Shidehara also set forth his thinking, albeit in an indirect manner, on whether it was correct to deploy troops to Shandong. In his view, when dispatching troops, it was important to carefully consider the possible outcomes, including any negative impacts on business dealings. Military intervention should only ever be an 'emergency measure'. For Shidehara, 'suddenly sending soldiers without first working out some form of preliminary measures must be regarded as gravely unfortunate for the nation'.[13] Finally, Shidehara touched upon his own speech at the Washington Naval Conference:

> Our nation feels most urgently a concern for the speed at which peace and unity may be restored to China, as well as for the economic development of both nations' rich natural resources … We must acknowledge that our own nation has particularly important interests in China, far more so than any geographically distant foreign land … What we seek is a footing for economic activity whereby both nations may benefit, under the principles of an open door policy and equal opportunity. I believe that at the time [of my speech] the above points received unanimous support.[14]

In the above manner, Shidehara asserted that Japan should avoid interference in China's affairs, in the interest of promoting peace and economic commercial activity in that nation. Further, even though Japan had special interests in China, it ought not to attempt to shut out other nations from economic participation. Publicly expressing this position was also Shidehara's way of attempting to reign in the Tanaka cabinet. He concluded the essay with the following words:

> It is my earnest desire that we might cut through present-day publicity stunts and various forms of emotional discord and, from the vantage point of pure concern for the nation, reach our judgements following earnest and calm consideration of the problem at hand.[15]

When viewed over the long-term, it would seem that Shidehara's opinion was correct. Yet what about the short-term? It is difficult to see what concrete policies could be drawn up to protect Japanese interests and residents. It is also doubtful as to whether this approach convinced the Japanese populace. It may well be that from Shidehara's perspective, politicians, the media and even the citizenry were immature, yet the fact remains that Shidehara received a significant degree of criticism from these quarters. One example is an essay by Honda Kumatarō titled 'Tai-Shi Gaikō no Hatan' (The bankruptcy of diplomacy towards China). After being forced out of his position by Shidehara, former diplomat Honda had become a commentator on Japanese diplomacy. On the topic of the previous Wakatsuki cabinet, Honda wrote:

> Time and again it led us to unstable situations, due to a lack of understanding as to the complex nature of China's revolutionary movement, and a failure to establish any foundational policies.[16]

'My Views on Diplomacy'

When Shidehara aired his views publicly in the manner outlined above, he was not simply giving his advice as a bureaucrat. Rather, in the context of a two-party political system, he was effectively siding with the Minseitō against the Seiyūkai. Shidehara also engaged with the Minseitō in other ways. For example, he participated in the formulation of a Minseitō statement on Chinese policy, alongside figures such as Hamaguchi Osachi, Egi Tasuku, Kobashi Ichita, Nagai Ryūtarō and Adachi Kenzō. He also spoke with Hamaguchi and other members of the party on the occasion of his speech on Chinese policy to the Japan–China Economic Association in Osaka. Further, Shidehara even consulted Hamaguchi on the topic of the Kellogg–Briand Pact.[17] The Kellogg–Briand Pact, which outlawed war, was signed in Paris in August 1928. Through such discussions, Shidehara's position would also influence Hamaguchi's thinking. We see this influence in Hamaguchi's view that 'we must give sufficient opportunity for peace and unity to take hold in China' and that diplomacy had to avoid becoming entangled in political strife.[18]

Shidehara would also publish a dialogue transcript in the Minseitō organ magazine, *Minsei*. As suggested by the title, 'Yashiteki Tanaka Gaikō' (The charlatanry of Tanaka diplomacy), it was a severe criticism of Tanaka's diplomatic approach. Shidehara attacked the Tanaka cabinet for its role in the Jinan Incident, writing that 'to pretend you can do something that is impossible is to act no differently than a street-side conjurer'.[19] In the past, when still foreign minister, Shidehara had also published his Diet address in the organ magazine of the Kenseikai (which, it should be recalled, was one of the two parties that merged to become the Minseitō). In having reached this point, however, we can see that Shidehara's deep sense of crisis with regard to Tanaka diplomacy had pushed him even further towards alignment with the Minseitō.

We can get a clearer sense of this more partisan Shidehara from the speech he gave on 19 October 1928 at Keiō University entitled 'Gaikō Kanken' (My views on diplomacy). In this speech, Shidehara argued forcefully that 'the essence of diplomacy does not lie in scheming'.[20] That is to say, diplomacy conducted through scheming had little to offer a nation in the long-term. This was because:

> As the life of a nation is to be eternal, those who would scheme for the purpose of a temporary benefit must prepare themselves for the serious calamities that would one day occur as a result.[21]

What did Shidehara mean here by diplomacy conducted through scheming? He mentioned the Triple Intervention as one such 'example of scheming diplomacy in the Far East'. (In the Triple Intervention of 1895, Russia, Germany and France intervened following Japan's victory over Qing-dynasty China.) 'Needless to say, the Triple Intervention was a diplomatic conspiracy, a serious international crime.' Yet, even though Japan was forced to return the Liaodong Peninsula to China as a result of the Triple Intervention, 'it was China itself who was the first to suffer poetic justice'. This was because:

> China was betrayed by the two governments of Russia and Germany, which it once regarded as its friends. Not only was China deprived of the benefits it hoped to gain through the Triple Intervention, but it ended up losing all of Manchuria, along with Shandong province, with no choice but to allow Russia and Germany to carry out their invasion strategies unimpeded.[22]

Shidehara stated:

> Diplomacy is not a conjurer's trick. Those who seek to deceive the eyes of onlookers, producing hundreds of feet of paper, a dove of peace, or the national flag expressing the dignity of the nation from the interior cavity of an empty box, in order to receive the praise of the masses, are not politicians but magicians.[23]

Shidehara's conviction was that diplomacy must be based upon honesty and begin by establishing a relationship of trust.

With this speech, Shidehara offered an explanation for his response in March the previous year to the Nanjing Incident of 1927, alongside a criticism of the Tanaka cabinet. He wrote:

> These days, there are those who view the Nanjing Incident as a product of the weak diplomacy Japan and other powers had pursued in the past with respect to China. Further, they may say that it followed from the Japanese government at that time following a path of absolute non-resistance. This kind of false speculation is circulating in our society even now. One cannot help but be shocked, however, at the sight of ministry officials of the present government openly disseminating such falsities.[24]

On the other hand, Shidehara also made demands of China's diplomacy. As he argued:

> The methods that the Chinese side are utilizing today, for the purpose of abolishing its unequal treaties, differ quite significantly from how our own nation dealt with the very same problem.[25]

That is to say, in the case of Japan:

> Rather than blame the great powers, we first blamed ourselves. Rather than calling for the overthrow of imperialism and so on, we first quietly put all our energy into reforming our national political affairs.[26]

However, in the case of China, 'the present situation is that it is unwilling to wait for an improvement in domestic governance, instead directly pressing for the revision and termination of currently existing treaties'.[27] In reality, however, there had been many reforms and attempts at self-strengthening in China, which Shidehara underestimated.

That being the case, what kind of policies should Japan adopt with respect to China? Shidehara argued for a combination of non-intervention and the protection of national interests. By 'non-intervention', Shidehara meant that:

> With various parties opposing each other in China's political world, it is essential to absolutely avoid lending any form of unfair aid to one side, or to work towards removing another side.[28]

His reason for taking this stance was that 'our rights and interests [in China] were certainly not bestowed by any one political faction'.[29] Shidehara then turned to the 'idea that the carrying out of a policy of non-intervention nevertheless requires some discrete intervention for the purpose of protecting our rights and interests'. However, he added: 'Such thinking actually looks down upon our benefits, our position [in China]'.[30]

By advancing this view, Shidehara criticised the Tanaka cabinet's deployment of troops to Shandong. He concluded his speech by making a final point on the importance of economic diplomacy:

> Our government must not stop at merely protecting our economic rights within a particular region of China. Rather, it must adopt a much bigger perspective and endeavor to promote greater economic ties between Japan and the entirety of China.[31]

Here Shidehara was direct in his criticism of the Tanaka cabinet. The bluntness of this speech is quite conspicuous when compared with his 'Overview of the Chinese Problem' essay of half a year earlier. Perhaps he felt more confident in sharing his real thoughts before a more limited audience. Certainly, having witnessed the fallout of the Jinan Incident and the assassination of Zhang Zuolin, Shidehara had an even stronger conviction as to the importance of non-intervention and economic diplomacy.

The Argument with Prime Minister Tanaka

Shidehara would have been anxious not only about the effects of Tanaka diplomacy abroad but also about how Ministry of Foreign Affairs personnel were faring. There were two significant shifts with respect to personnel during the era of the Tanaka cabinet, both of which would later have an impact on Shidehara's second term as foreign minister. First, there was the rise of reformists such as Arita Hachirō and Shigemitsu Mamoru. Arita became the director-general of the Asian Bureau, while Shigemitsu became the consulate general in Shanghai. Alongside Arita's appointment as Asian Bureau director-general, Shidehara's confidant Kimura Eiichi was made minister to Czechoslovakia. Second, Yoshida Shigeru became vice-minister for foreign affairs, replacing Debuchi Katsuji. Yoshida was not originally a member of the central clique within the ministry. It was due to his closeness to figures such as the Seiyūkai's Mori Tsutomu, the parliamentary vice-minister for foreign affairs, that he was able to secure this position. Thus, some referred to Yoshida as 'the uninvited vice-minister'. Debuchi, meanwhile, was made ambassador to the US.

Mori Tsutomu, parliamentary vice-minister for foreign affairs, had been critical of Shidehara's policy of non-intervention. He was also behind the move to push Shidehara's confidants, Vice-Minister Debuchi and Asian Bureau Director-General Kimura, out of their respective positions. Mori looked down upon career diplomats but saw Yoshida Shigeru and Shiratori Toshio as exceptions. While Tanaka initially resisted making these extensive changes in personnel, he apparently relented and accepted Yoshida as vice-minister following the assassination of Zhang Zuolin of June 1928 and the impasse that had been reached with Japan's China policy.

Given the circumstances, Shidehara could not have been particularly enthusiastic about Yoshida's appointment as the vice-minister. In fact, Yoshida had also disliked Shidehara for some time. When Shidehara was vice-minister for foreign affairs, Yoshida was acting director of the Document Section. A strong-willed individual, he did not get on well with Vice-Minister Shidehara. Even when Shidehara summoned him, he was apparently not quick to respond. Later, when the Manchurian Incident occurred during Shidehara's second term as foreign minister, Yoshida was also critical: 'He is not skilled at handling unexpected incidents'.[32]

Nevertheless, the most problematic individual for Shidehara was Prime Minister Tanaka himself. Tanaka's Manchuria policy began to stagnate following the Huanggutun Incident. Japan was unable to get China to recognise its right to lease land in southern Manchuria, which had long been a contentious issue between the two countries. Further, Zhang Zuolin's successor, his eldest son Zhang Xueliang, would not acknowledge Japan's right to begin constructing the Jihui or Zhangda railways. At this time, Shidehara was residing in Rikugien. One day he received some disturbing information. It was details on the 'Seiyūkai cabinet's latest hardline policy'. To strengthen Japan's hand in securing both land leasing and railway construction rights in Manchuria, the Tanaka cabinet were 'ready to carry out the mobilization of several divisions'.[33] Fearing the worst, Shidehara relayed this information to the lord keeper of the privy seal, Makino Nobuaki.

Shidehara felt it necessary to use his position as a member of the House of Peers in order to speak at the plenary session on 2 February 1929. Upon the podium, Shidehara addressed Tanaka, asking him to clarify just what was meant by a 'so-called hardline policy, and by an aggressive policy'. According to Shidehara, from the time of the Tōhō Kaigi (Eastern Summit) held in Tokyo in the summer of 1927, the Tanaka cabinet had inflamed the 'indignation of the [Chinese] people against our nation', triggering an anti-Japanese movement. Shidehara also argued that when Tanaka had previously spoken of rendering Manchuria 'into a peaceful land', he should have stopped at the protection of Japan's interests.[34] Shidehara was also critical of how the Tanaka cabinet had advised Zhang Xueliang to delay reaching an understanding with the Nationalist government.

Further, Shidehara asserted that the deployment of troops to Shandong was also a policy failure, given that they did not prevent a considerable loss of life among local Japanese residents. In his view, the Japanese government should have negotiated with the National Revolution Army and evacuated Japanese residents before deciding to send troops. He pointed out that not a single Japanese life was lost in the Nanjing Incident of 1927, when he himself had been foreign minister, despite the fact that no troops were deployed. Finally, Shidehara criticised the Tanaka cabinet's announcement that the Chinese policies of the previous cabinet had reached a dead end. Rather, the situation was exactly the opposite. In fiery language he handed down his damning verdict:

> The foundation of friendly Sino-Japanese relations, the achievement of diligent effort during our time in charge of the ministry, has during the current cabinet been, for the most part, tragically destroyed.[35]

In response, Tanaka spoke evasively of the need for diplomacy to be tough and aggressive. He also claimed that use of military force was a last resort and that he was doing his utmost to avoid it. According to Tanaka, if troops had not been deployed to Shandong, the situation would have certainly grown much worse. Of course, this line of reasoning would never have convinced Shidehara.[36]

Therefore, on 5 February 1929, Shidehara stood to ask questions at the House of Peers. Again, he pressed the issue, asking whether troops would be dispatched to Manchuria for the sake of maintaining stability. He also repeated his doubts as to the wisdom of the advice given to Zhang Xueliang, and the deployment of troops to Shandong. He also expressed his regret that Japan was now behind the other powers when it came to reaching a tariff agreement with China.

In the end, however, the Tanaka cabinet would not last out the year. The cause of its undoing was their handling of the assassination by bomb of Zhang Zuolin. Tanaka had asserted that the perpetrators would face harsh punishment. However, pressure from the army ensured that the chief conspirator, Kōmoto Daisaku, only faced suspension from office. This led to the Shōwa emperor reprimanding Tanaka, and the subsequent resignation of the entire cabinet in July 1929.

Years later, when questioned at the Tokyo Trial by international prosecutors, Shidehara would say emphatically: 'One cause of the collapse of the Tanaka cabinet was clearly the dispatch of troops to Jinan, along with other failures of its China diplomacy'.[37] From Shidehara's perspective, he had worked hard to establish both the tradition of Japanese diplomacy and international trust in Japan. Yet the policies of the Tanaka cabinet had disrupted these efforts. How would he manage to overcome these setbacks during his second term as foreign minister, commencing in the Hamaguchi cabinet?

Endnotes

1   Shidehara, *Gaikō 50 Nen*, 277–80.

2   Itō Takashi and Hirose Yoshihiro, eds, *Makino Nobuaki Nikki* [The diary of Makino Nobuaki] (Tokyo: Chuōkōronsha, 1990), 278; Oka and Hayashi, *Taishō Democracy-ki no Seiji*, 607; 'Kizokuin Giin Kakuha-betsu nikansuru Chosa' [Survey of respective factions among the House of Peers members], date unknown, in 'Kondō Hideaki Kankei Bunsho' [Documents relating to Kondō Hideaki], no. 70, Modern Japanese Political History Materials Room, National Diet Library; 'Kizokuin Giin Kakuha-betsu: Ji Meiji 34 Nen 12 Gatsu, Shi Shōwa 7 Nen 3 Gatsu' [Respective factions in the House of Peers, from December of Meiji 34 to March of Shōwa 7], in 'Kondō Hideaki Kankei Bunsho', no. 96; House of Representatives and House of Councilors, eds, *Gikai Seido 70 Nen-shi: Seitōkai-ha Hen* [A 70-year history of the Diet system: Volume on party-based factions] (Tokyo: Ministry of Finance Printing Bureau, 1961), 60; House of Representatives and House of Councilors, eds, *Gikai Seido 70 Nen-shi: Kizokuin, Sangiin Giin Meikan* [A 70-year history of the Diet system: House of Peers, House of Councillors, Diet members directory] (Tokyo: Ministry of Finance Printing Bureau, 1961), 124.

3   Shidehara, *Gaikō 50 Nen*, 145–49. For details on Chinese policies of the Tanaka cabinet, see Satō Motoei, *Shōwa Shoki Tai-Chūgoku Seisaku no Kenkyū: Tanaka Naikaku no Tai-Man-Mo Seisaku* [A study of policy regarding China of the early Shōwa era: The Tanaka cabinet's policies regarding Manchuria and Mongolia] (Tokyo: Harashobō, 1992); Hattori, *Higashi Asia Kokusai Kankyō no Hendō to Nihon Gaikō, 1918–1931*, 191–251; Kobayashi Michihiko, 'Tanaka Seiyūkai to Santō Shuppei: 1927–1928 (1) (2)', *Kita Kyūshū Shiritsu Daigaku Hōsei Ronshū* 32, no. 2–3 (December 2004): 1–33; 33, no. 1 (June 2005): 1-52; Shao Jianguo, *Beifa zhanzheng shiqi de Zhong Ri guan xi yan jiu* [A study of Sino-Japanese relations during the Northern Expedition War] (Beijing: Xinhua chubanshe, 2006).

4   Shidehara to Adachi, in 'Adachi Mineichirō Kankei Bunsho' [Documents relating to Adachi Mineichirō], 7 June 1927, Correspondence Department, no. 302, Modern Japanese Political History Materials Room, National Diet Library.

5   Ibid.

6   *Tokyo Asahi Shimbun*, 14 February 1928.

7   *Tokyo Asahi Shimbun*, evening edition, 16 February 1928.

8   Shidehara Kijūrō, 'Shina Mondai Gaikan' [Overview of the Chinese problem], *Gaikō Jihō*, no. 560 (April 1928): 9.

9   Ibid., 10.

10 Ibid., 10.

11 Ibid., 11.

12 Ibid., 12.

13 Ibid., 15.

14 Ibid., 17, 18.

15 Ibid., 18.

16 Honda Kumatarō, 'Tai-Shi Gaikō no Hasan' [The bankruptcy of diplomacy towards China], *Gaikō Jihō*, no. 538 (May 1927): 19–38.

17 Ikei Masaru, Hatano Masaru and Kurosawa Fumitaka, eds, *Hamaguchi Osachi Nikki, Zuikanroku* [Hamaguchi Osachi diary, record of reflections] (Tokyo: Misuzu Shobō, 1991), 19, 41, 44, 45, 46, 54, 56, 61, 65, 67, 74, 83, 109, 124, 134, 143, 158, 166. Murai Ryōta has also provided me with valuable insights on this topic.

The presentation given in Osaka is also contained in Shidehara Kijūrō, 'Tai-shi Gaikō nitsuite' [On the matter of diplomacy towards China], *Minsei* 2, no. 11 (November 1928): 4–17. See also 'Hamaguchi Shidehara Ryo-shi no Tanaka Gaikō Hihan' [Critiques of Tanaka diplomacy as advanced by Mr Hamaguchi and Mr Shidehara], date unknown, in 'Shidehara Heiwa Bunko', Reel 18.

18 Hamaguchi Osachi, 'Yukizumareru Kyokumen no Tenkai to Wagatō no Shuchō' [The development of the current impasse and the position of my party], *Minsei* 2, no. 10 (October 1928): 6–17; 'Hamaguchi Sōsai no Ketsui Kataku' [The strong determination of President Hamaguchi], *Minsei* 2, no. 10 (October 1928): 86–93. Murai Ryōta has also provided me with valuable insights on this topic.

19 Shidehara Kijūrō, 'Yashi-teki Tanaka Gaikō' [The charlatanry of Tanaka diplomacy], *Minsei* 2, no. 10 (October 1928): 18–20; Shidehara Kijūrō, 'Gen-Naikaku no Gaikō Hōshin' [The diplomatic policy of the present cabinet], *Kensei* 7, no. 8 (August 1924): 5–9; Shidehara Kijūrō, 'Teikoku Gaikō no Kichō' [The basic theme of Japanese diplomacy], *Kensei* 8, no. 2 (February 1925): 11–12; Shidehara Kijūrō, 'Jishu-teki Gaikō no Kiso Kakuritsu' [Establishing the foundations of autonomous diplomacy], *Kensei Kōron* 6, no. 2 (February 1926): 13–20; Shidehara Kijūrō, 'Waga Kuni Genka no Kokusai Kankei' [Our nation's contemporary international relations], *Kensei Kōron* 7, no. 2 (February 1927): 21–27.

For further details on Diet speeches given during Shidehara's second appointment as foreign minister, see Shidehara Kijūrō, 'Kokusai Heiwa nikansuru Sekai no Taisei' [The global situation on international peace], *Minsei* 3, no. 12 (December 1929): 9–13; Shidehara Kijūrō, 'Genjitsu Nihon no Kokusai Kankei' [Japan's international relationships at the present moment], *Minsei* 4, no. 2

(February 1930): 27–35; Shidehara Kijūrō, 'Genzai Nihon no Kokusai Kankei' [Japan's current international relationships], *Minsei* 4, no. 5 (May 1930): 16–19; Shidehara Kijūrō, 'Shiryoku wo Tsukushite Keirin no Jitsugen ni Manshin' [Pushing forward to the utmost of our ability to realise governance], Minsei 5, no. 2 (February 1931): 4–6; Shidehara Kijūrō, 'Wagakuni Saikin no Kokusai Kankei' [Our nation's recent international relationships], *Minsei* 5, no. 2 (February 1931): 15–18.

20   Shidehara Kijūrō (lecture), 'Gaikō Kanken' [My views on diplomacy], 9 October 1928, in 'Shidehara Heiwa Bunko', Reel 17. For discussion on the full text, see Hattori Ryūji, 'Shidehara Kijūrō kōen, "Gaikō Kanken"' [Shidehara Kijūrō (lecture), 'My Views on Diplomacy'], *Sōgō Seisaku Kenkyū*, no. 13 (March 2006): 99–112.

Further, the majority of 'Gaikō Kanken' is included in Shidehara Kijūrō, 'Gaikō no Honshitsu to Waga Tai-Shi Gaikō' [The essence of diplomacy and my diplomacy towards China], (1) (2) (3) (4) (5) (6), *Minsei* 3, nos 2, 3, 4, 5, 6, 7 (February–July 1929): 102–07, 100–03, 96–101, 88–93, 102–07, 96–101.

21   Shidehara, 'Gaikō Kanken'.

22   Ibid.

23   Ibid.

24   Ibid.

25   Ibid.

26   Ibid.

27   Ibid.

28   Ibid.

29   Ibid.

30   Ibid.

31   Ibid.

32   Miyake Kijirō, 'Yoshida-san wo Shinobite Omou Kotodomo' [Reminiscences of Mr Yoshida] (2), *Kasumigaseki-kai Kaihō*, no. 285 (November 1969): 12–13; Tsutsui Kiyoshi, 'Mori Tsutomu no Seikaku' [The personality of Mori Tsutomu], *Kasumigaseki-kai Kaihō*, no. 289 (March 1970): 7–10; Yamaura Kanichi, ed., *Mori Tsutomu* (Tokyo: Harashobō, 1982), 552–53; Yoshida to Makino Nobuaki, 7 June 1932, in *Yoshida Shigeru Shokan* [The letters of Yoshida Shigeru], ed. Yoshida Shigeru Memorial Project Foundation (Tokyo: Chuōkōronsha, 1994), 630–33. See also Shibata Shinichi, *Shōwa-ki no Kōshitsu to Seiji Gaikō* [The imperial household in the Shōwa era and political diplomacy] (Tokyo: Harashobō, 1995), 11–14.

33   Shidehara to Makino, 17 February 1929, in 'Makino Nobuaki Kankei Bunsho', Correspondence Department, vol. 28, no. 476–2. See also Itō and Hirose, *Makino Nobuaki Nikki*, 338–39, 341.

34   *Kanpō*, extra edition, 3 February 1929.

35   Ibid.

36   Ibid.

37   *Kanpō*, extra edition, 6 February 1929; a question to Minister of State Shidehara and its reply, 31 May 1947, in 'Shidehara Heiwa Bunko', Reel 7.

5

The London Naval Conference and the Manchurian Incident

China and the Soviet Union

The Hamaguchi Cabinet and Shidehara's Personnel

July 1929 marked the beginning of the Minseitō party cabinet, led by Hamaguchi Osachi. When the imperial order to form a cabinet was issued, Hamaguchi's reply to the throne included the names of Ugaki Kazushige, Inoue Junnosuke and Shidehara Kijūrō as cabinet minister nominees. Ugaki, Inoue and Shidehara would take over the positions of war minister, finance minister and foreign minister, respectively. Shidehara had anticipated that he would be able to return to the position of foreign minister at this time. Shidehara and Hamaguchi were old friends from school days; their school, what would become the Third Higher Middle School, had been relocated from Osaka to Kyoto while they were in attendance. Shidehara was also 56 years old and now reaching the end of middle age. The Hamaguchi cabinet announced that it would pursue a platform of 10 major policies, including the reform of Chinese policy, a reduction in the size of the military, a curtailment of public finance and a lifting of the gold embargo.

Now that he was once again serving as foreign minister, what kind of diplomatic efforts did Shidehara initially undertake? Let us answer that question by first looking at the matter of ministry personnel. The shift that is generally referred to as 'Shidehara personnel' would begin at the end of the following year, 1930. At that time, Shidehara installed Nagai Matsuzō and Matsuda Michikazu as vice-minister and Treaties and Conventions Bureau director-general, respectively.[1] That is to say that, for a period of over a year following his return to office, Shidehara avoided making any significant personnel changes. Presumably, Shidehara could have conducted an early reshuffle of individuals such as the Tanaka-cabinet-aligned vice-minister Yoshida Shigeru. However, Shidehara decided that he 'could not consent to administrative-level staffing changes directly following the assumption of office'.[2] This meant that Vice-Minister Yoshida and the various bureau directors-general retained their positions for a time.

Debuchi Katsuji, who had supported Shidehara during his first term as foreign minister, had already become ambassador to the US by this point. Meanwhile, his other trusted subordinate, Saburi Sadao, was now a counsellor at the British embassy. There, Saburi undertook actions such as visiting the Chamber of Commerce and Industry in Manchester to discuss trade with China.[3]

Before long, Saburi was internally selected to serve as ambassador to the Soviet Union. However, Shidehara instead sent him to China as Japan's minister. Unfortunately, this decision led to tragedy. Only a short time after becoming the minister to China, Saburi returned to Japan in November 1929 to discuss with Shidehara the future direction of Chinese policy. Just after these discussions, on 29 November, Saburi was discovered dead in his hotel in Hakone in suspicious circumstances. He had been minister to China for only one month. Upon receiving this shocking news, Shidehara decided that Saburi's death must have been a murder. This was because 'he held a pistol in his right hand. As it happens, the pistol bullet entered his head from the left temple and exited on the right'. Nevertheless, a theory spread widely that he committed suicide due to anguish over his wife's death and Sino-Japanese relations. Shidehara strongly rejected this theory, stating: 'Our discussions had concluded positively, and he had departed in good spirits, intending to enjoy himself [Hakone is a town popular for its recuperative hot springs]. This is an absolute fact'.[4]

Was Saburi murdered, as Shidehara asserted? Certainly, the suggestion that the bullet entered through his left temple lends some weight to this interpretation. However, this was an early rumour. An autopsy later found that the bullet entered not from the left temple but from the right. The police also determined that it was suicide. Shidehara would have been aware of these facts. Perhaps Shidehara simply did not want to admit that Saburi could have killed himself.[5]

Within the diplomatic corps, there were others who, unlike Shidehara, believed the suicide thesis. Shigemitsu Mamoru was one such individual. At the time, Shigemitsu was consul general in Shanghai. Shigemitsu and Saburi had a friendly relationship from the time of the Paris Peace Conference. In the past, on the occasion of the Beijing Special Conference on Tariffs, the two had worked on the announcement that Japan was prepared to recognise China's tariff autonomy. Together they had sought to lead policy on China from the front lines. The Nationalist government therefore welcomed the news that Shidehara was appointing Saburi as Japan's minister to China. According to Shigemitsu, when he temporarily returned to Japan, Saburi had attempted to convince Shidehara that 'for Japan the true problem of essential importance is the China problem'. Yet the leadership of the Ministry of Foreign Affairs was buried in work dealing with other matters, such as reductions in the size of the military. Saburi apparently complained to Shigemitsu that 'they simply won't consider the matter seriously'.[6] Given that Saburi's wife had already passed away, Shigemitsu saw his death as a suicide arising from loneliness. Horinouchi Kensuke, counsellor to the Japanese legation in China, had a similar interpretation of Saburi's death.[7]

In any case, Saburi's death must have been a serious blow to Shidehara. At the same time, however, he now had to decide who would replace Saburi as minister to China. In December 1929, he selected Obata Yūkichi for the role. Obata had previously headed the Political Affairs Bureau when Shidehara was vice-minister. The Chinese side, however, indicated that it was not inclined to reach an *agrément* on Obata. In diplomatic language, an *agrément* is the acknowledgement a nation gives before the appointment of a minister or similar dignitary who would be dispatched there. The reason the Chinese were concerned about Obata was that he had worked as first secretary at the Japanese legation in China at the time of the Twenty-One Demands. Further, China's foreign minister, Wang Zhengting, had issued a surprising condition: China would only give its *agrément* if the legation was upgraded to an embassy. There was no way that Shidehara would accept what he considered to be a preposterous demand. In his opinion, the promotion to the embassy should have had nothing to do with the *agrément*. In the first place, Obata had worked at the legation for some time following the Twenty-One Demands from 1918 to 1923. In the end, the Nationalist government refused to issue an *agrément* for Obata.[8]

China and the Soviet Union

During this period, some significant shifts occurred within China. When Shidehara returned to the position of foreign minister, a dispute broke out between China and the Soviet Union regarding the Chinese Eastern Railway. Located in north-eastern China, this railway was jointly managed by the Soviet Union and China. In July 1929, however, China attempted to regain full control over the railway. In response, the Soviet Union cut off diplomatic relations with the Chinese government. Events then escalated, with the Soviets launching a military incursion into Chinese territory in November. The north-eastern border towns of Manzhouli and Hailar were overrun. This Sino-Soviet conflict of 1929 ended in total victory for the Soviet side, and, in December, the two nations signed a protocol returning the Chinese Eastern Railway to its former state.

Shidehara's policy on responding to the Sino-Soviet conflict had two major features. First, he had Japan directly mediate negotiations between China and the Soviet Union. Believing that the Chinese policy of retaking the Chinese Eastern Railway was 'a plan to retake Russia's interests under the pretense of anti-Bolshevization', Shidehara closely questioned China's minister to Japan, Wang Rongbao. In this sense, Shidehara's response can be considered somewhat favourable towards the Soviet Union, even if only slightly. Second, Shidehara avoided adding Japan's voice to the multilaterally negotiated mediation by US Secretary of State Henry L. Stimson. Shidehara, who was assisting the unofficial negotiations between China and the Soviet Union, believed that Stimson's plan 'would only further inflame the feelings of the nations involved and could not be expected to yield positive results'.[9] Hence, although closely involved in the talks between the two nations, Shidehara kept the details of those talks secret. Later, he would boast that this kind of secret diplomacy was effective.

Around this time, there was another issue with implications for Sino-Japanese relations. A document of dubious origin known as the 'Tanaka Memorial' was circulating within China. The Tanaka Memorial purported to be a report by Prime Minister Tanaka Giichi to the Shōwa emperor. The contents were a plan for the invasion of China based upon the discussions held during the aforementioned Tōhō Kaigi (Eastern Summit). However, the details of the document differed significantly from the actual discussions held at the summit, and it is highly likely that it was forged in north-eastern China in the first half of 1929. On 16 September 1929, the acting minister to China, Horinouchi Kensuke, sent a telegram to Shidehara. According to this telegram, Cheng Liting, chief secretary for the Shanghai YMCA, planned to read the Tanaka Memorial aloud at the Kyoto conference of the Taiheiyō Mondai Chōsakai (Investigative Committee for the Pacific Problem). This civil international investigative committee was established for the purpose of mutual understanding; it was also known in English as the Institute of Pacific Relations (IPR).[10] IPR members included experts from Japan, the US and China, and the IPR had previously convened in Honolulu in 1925. Along with the general secretary of the YMCA in China, Yu Rizhang, Cheng Liting was a central figure in the IPR.[11]

At the time of the Honolulu conference, Shidehara displayed a cooperative attitude towards the IPR. He once stated to a US associate of the group that he thought 'this kind of unofficial conference can help to foster mutual understanding between the citizens of the various [Pacific] nations'.[12] However, at the Kyoto conference of the IPR, held in the autumn of 1929, the Asian Bureau and Intelligence Department of Japanese Ministry of Foreign Affairs stepped in to prevent the reading out of the Tanaka Memorial. Regardless, the Tanaka Memorial became widely distributed within China in pamphlet form, and even Chinese newspapers and magazines published its contents. This development led Shidehara to issue warnings in February 1930 to the various consuls general stationed in China. Guiding Japan's Chinese policy in the field at this time was Shigemitsu, acting minister to China. Shigemitsu's response to the problem represented by the Tanaka Memorial was to ask the Chinese government to crack down on its circulation. On this occasion, Shigemitsu also took the opportunity to thoroughly point out the fundamental mistakes visible in the document, and the Foreign Ministry of the Nationalist government showed signs that they would indeed take steps to deal with the matter. This appears to indicate that the Chinese side knew that the document was a forgery.

It is also worth noting that, during this period, Shidehara became the chairman of an arbitration committee established according to the guidelines of a treaty signed between the US and Germany. This arbitration committee would be tasked with helping the two nations reach an amicable settlement in the event of a conflict. While the US and Germany each selected two members to sit on the committee, the chairman was to be selected from a third nation that was trusted by both. Their agreed-upon choice was Shidehara. However, given the lack of a conflict, the role did not involve much work.[13]

The London Naval Conference on Disarmament

Party Politics and Japan–US Relations

Shidehara's greatest achievement during his second term as foreign minister was the London Naval Conference on Disarmament.[14] The aim of this international conference, held in London in the first half of 1930, was to limit the number of auxiliary warships among the participating nations. Before looking at the strategy Shidehara deployed, let us first review the circumstances leading up to the conference. Naturally, the precursor to the London Naval Conference was the Washington Naval Conference. As mentioned earlier, the Washington Naval Conference was held from November 1921 to February 1922. The naval disarmament agreed upon at this conference only limited the number of capital ships that participants could have. This led to an auxiliary ship construction race between the major powers in the years following the conference. Later, in the summer of 1927, a naval disarmament conference was held in Geneva to place limits on auxiliary ships as well. However, due to disagreements, including a confrontation between the UK and the US, the Geneva Conference was a failure. This was the background leading up to the 1930 London Naval Conference.

The London Naval Conference was attended by Japan, the UK, the US, France and Italy. Leading Japan's delegation, the Hamaguchi cabinet sent former prime minister Wakatsuki Reijirō and Navy Minister Takarabe Takeshi. The policy of the Hamaguchi cabinet included the goal of securing an auxiliary warship ratio of 70 per cent relative to the US in terms of total tonnage. This goal made compromise between Japan and the US quite difficult. Nevertheless, the representatives of the two nations reached an understanding whereby, among other things, the total tonnage of Japanese vessels would be permitted to reach 69.75 per cent relative to the US. Although the Japanese navy were unhappy with a number that was lower than their initial goal, the Hamaguchi cabinet accepted this compromise. The resulting treaty, the London Naval Treaty, was signed in April 1930. It can be considered a success for Japanese diplomacy.

The figures who were ultimately responsible for leading the conference to its successful conclusion were Foreign Minister Shidehara and Prime Minister Hamaguchi. The ratification of the London Naval Treaty as a result of their political guidance marked a high point for cooperative diplomacy in the history of modern Japanese party politics. Nevertheless, prewar party politics in Japan was fated for an early end. Strictly speaking, the period of party politics began with the formation of the Katō cabinet in June 1924 and ended with the May 15 Incident of 1932. As was revealed by the Manchurian Incident, an indirect cause of the collapse of party politics in Japan was that the political parties did not clearly define a system for guiding the nation's diplomatic efforts.

In this sense, the London Naval Treaty was a turning point. That is to say, while the Hamaguchi cabinet was certainly proactive in politically guiding the outcome, it led to another problem: the problem of supreme command interference. The concept of supreme command refers to the highest authority over the military, and, according to the Meiji Constitution, this highest authority was the emperor. Following the conclusion of the London Naval Treaty, the Seiyūkai opposition party was, therefore, able to accuse the Hamaguchi cabinet of supreme command interference—a problem that could potentially undermine the foundation of party politics.

The London Naval Conference was also quite important for relations between Japan and the US. As it happened, a group more familiar with, and sympathetic towards, Japan was beginning to take shape in the US State Department.[15] It should be noted that, because it was conflict between the UK and the US that had led the earlier Geneva Conference to run aground, both nations had had detailed consultations before the main event. The UK had also succeeded in decoding important telegrams from the Japanese Ministry of Foreign Affairs. Meanwhile, the Japanese navy continued in its tradition of viewing the US as a hypothetical enemy. It was therefore anticipated that the debate surrounding naval disarmament would be most contentious between Japan and the US. And, indeed, the Japanese–American relationship dominated the conference.[16]

Keeping these facts in mind, we can now consider the details of the London Naval Conference, which has been viewed as a high point in prewar Japanese democracy. In this overview I will consider not only Shidehara's perspective but also that of the US ambassador to Japan, William R. Castle, Jr. This approach will be of assistance for considering the maturity of party politics in Japan. There are three major points to consider.

This first is the internal processes in the Japanese Ministry of Foreign Affairs and, in particular, the relationship between Foreign Minister Shidehara and Vice-Minister Yoshida. From the time Yoshida was consul general in Mukden, his and Shidehara's policies on China began to diverge. Yoshida became vice-minister through his close association with the Tanaka cabinet, yet he was left in the role by Shidehara with the beginning of the Hamaguchi cabinet. This meant that the relationship between the two individuals was somewhat delicate. However, during the London Naval Conference, Yoshida would take Shidehara's opinions on board with respect to US policy, while making every effort to coordinate with Castle, the imperial court and the military.

Second, we need to consider Castle's actions and his perspective on Japan. As the US ambassador to Japan, Castle was a representative figure of the pro-Japanese faction in the State Department. Along with diplomatic telegrams, Castle also left behind documentation such as a detailed diary, correspondence and speech drafts.[17] If we examine these sources, we find, at times, unexpected evaluations of Japan's Ministry of Foreign Affairs, its political parties, the imperial household and other subjects. I suggest that such resources can not only serve as a guide to Castle's relationship with Shidehara but also may be helpful for considering contemporary Japanese party politics.

Third, we need to consider the possibilities and limits of any new order that could be reached through Japanese–American cooperation. The London Naval Conference was not an isolated phenomenon. It also included attempts to expand Japan–US cooperation to matters such as the 'China problem', as well as the immigration problem. This means that there was a latent possibility that international politics in this period could head towards the construction of a more stable global order, with the London Naval Conference serving as a foothold. While Shidehara is my main focus regarding this topic, I will also examine the actions of Castle, Secretary of State Stimson, State Department Division of Far Eastern Affairs Chief Hornbeck, ambassador to the US Debuchi and others. In this way, I aim to shed further light on barriers to the construction of a new international order, as well as the nature of the relationship between naval disarmament on the one hand and both the China and immigration problems on the other.

Shidehara and Castle

Before Castle was sent to Japan as the US ambassador at the time of the London Naval Conference, he worked for nearly three years as assistant secretary of state. Shidehara welcomed Castle's appointment as US ambassador, as Castle learned from Ambassador Debuchi. Castle had also thought for some time that Shidehara was trustworthy.[18] The personal relationship between Castle and President Herbert Hoover was also generally positive.[19] Conversely, there was some discord between Castle and Secretary of State Stimson at the time of the Sino-Soviet conflict in the second half of 1929.[20] While attending the London Naval Conference, Stimson requested that Undersecretary of State Joseph P. Cotton serve as acting secretary of state.

Meanwhile, in the lead-up to the London Naval Conference, the Hamaguchi cabinet made a number of planned attendees plenipotentiaries. These attendees included former prime minister Wakatsuki Reijirō as chief delegate; he would be accompanied by Navy Minister Admiral Takarabe Takeshi, ambassador to the UK Matsudaira Tsuneo and ambassador to Belgium Nagai Matsuzō. Further, Admiral Abo Kiyokazu and Admiral Sakonji Seizō were appointed as adviser and chief attendant, respectively. On 26 November 1929, the cabinet further decided upon three fundamental principles for the conference: auxiliary warship tonnage at 70 per cent of the US total, large cruisers at 70 per cent of the US total and the preservation of the current number of submersibles.[21]

Following the precedent of the Washington Naval Conference, Hamaguchi assigned multiple individuals to help the navy minister with his administrative responsibilities. These were the vice-minister of the Navy Ministry; Vice Admiral Yamanashi Katsunoshin; the chief of Bureau of Naval Affairs, Major General Hori Teikichi; and, as their assistant, senior aide Colonel Koga Mineichi. I also note that, at that time, the chief of the Naval General Staff was Admiral Katō Hiroharu, the vice chief was Vice Admiral Suetsugu Nobumasa and the chief of the First Bureau was Rear Admiral Katō Takayoshi. On the US side, the plenipotentiary delegation was headed by Secretary of State Stimson. The delegation also included the US ambassador to the UK, Charles G. Dawes; Secretary of the Navy Charles Francis Adams; a Democratic senator, Joseph T. Robinson; a Republican senator, David A. Reed; the ambassador to Belgium, Hugh S. Gibson; and the ambassador to Mexico, Dwight W. Morrow. The British representatives, meanwhile, were led by Prime Minister J. Ramsay MacDonald, who also chaired the conference. They included Foreign Secretary Arthur Henderson and Secretary for the Navy Albert Victor Alexander. Meanwhile, the French and Italian chief delegates were Prime Minister André P. G. A. Tardieu and Foreign Minister Dino Grandi di Mordano, respectively. On 9 January 1930, Japan's three representatives, Wakatsuki, Takarabe and Matsudaira, visited MacDonald at the prime minister's residence for informal talks.[22]

Castle, meanwhile, arrived at Yokohama via Honolulu on 20 January. Shidehara immediately received him as a visitor. Castle's task was to take over from acting US ambassador Neville.[23] On 24 January, Shidehara and his wife dined with Castle. They were joined by former ambassador to the US Hanihara Masanao, Vice-Minister for Foreign Affairs Yoshida Shigeru and Asian Bureau Director-General Arita Hachirō. The Shideharas were apparently in good spirits that evening. On the same day, Castle also met Nelson T. Johnson, the US consul to China, who was then visiting Japan. In his diary, Castle wrote: 'Nelson and I agree very largely on Far Eastern Questions, although I am not sure that he would agree that Japanese friendship is more important than Chinese'.[24]

It might also be asked how Shidehara appeared to Castle. In correspondence with President Hoover, dated 27 January, Castle relayed his first impressions of the Hamaguchi cabinet:

> Shidehara is really a statesman, farseeing and broad minded, and Hamaguchi, the Prime Minister, is a man of high integrity. It would be difficult to find another man as Finance Minister as able, courageous and experienced as Inoue.[25]

Castle added: 'We cannot ignore the fact that Japan as truly has special interests in Manchuria as we have in Cuba'.[26]

'Certain Thoughtful Japanese' — Foreign Minister Shidehara

Thus, Shidehara had the opportunity to strengthen his relationship with Castle. In a telegram sent on 14 February to Secretary of State Cotton, Castle reported that 'certain thoughtful Japanese' regretted that a 70 per cent tonnage ratio had been adopted as a critical target.[27] By 'certain thoughtful Japanese', Castle presumably meant the leaders of the Ministry of Foreign Affairs, beginning with Shidehara. In fact, Castle had met with Shidehara on that day and had informed him that even if Japan were limited to a 60 per cent tonnage ratio, the US navy would not regard an attack on Japan as viable. According to Castle, the US public worried that a build-up of the Japanese navy might lead to a future invasion of the Philippines. Shidehara replied that even if Japan initially succeeded in occupying the Philippines, 'it would be the beginning only of a war which in the end must be the ruin of Japan'.[28]

What was disturbing for Castle was the gap between Shidehara, who had extensive knowledge of the realities of international affairs, and public opinion in both Japan and the US, which was dominated by fear of possible conflict. For example, Hirata Shinsaku published an essay in the journal *Nihon oyobi Nihonjin* (Japan and the Japanese) titled 'Beikoku Taishi Sai-Kaiken-ki' (Records of another meeting with the US ambassador). The essay included a depiction of military commentator Hirata directly pressing Castle and First Secretary Dooman. According to this depiction, when speaking with Shidehara, Castle once threatened that the US Air Force would be capable of bombing Tokyo.[29] However, Castle did not actually threaten the bombing of Tokyo, and Shidehara and Castle got on quite well.

Shidehara and Castle were troubled by these trends in public opinion. Nevertheless, on 20 February, they received some positive news: the Minseitō had achieved an outright victory in the general election. This meant that the Hamaguchi cabinet was now in a position to carry out some bolder policies. Further, there was also a change in government in France with the formation of a cabinet led by G. Camille Chautemps. Until then, France had been holding back the proceedings at the London Naval Conference, and other participants hoped that a new French government would lead to greater progress. At this time, Castle sounded out Shidehara on the possibility of excluding France and Italy and reaching a tripartite agreement with the US and the UK. Shidehara gave a favourable response.[30]

On 26 February, the London Naval Conference split into the 'European Group' of the UK, France and Italy, and the 'High Seas Group' of the UK, the US and Japan.[31] To ensure that the preliminary negotiations of the latter would be smooth, Japan and the US in turn began with their own unofficial talks, held between Matsudaira and Reed. Likewise, Japanese–British negotiations were held between Saitō Hiroshi, director-general of the Intelligence Department of the Japanese Ministry of Foreign Affairs, and Robert Leslie Craigie, chief of the American Department of the British Foreign Office. Of these, it was the talks between Matsudaira and Reed that began to show signs of reaching a breakthrough. Shidehara himself was inclined to accept the US proposal regarding cruisers. However, he was concerned about opposition from the Japanese navy. In the end, Castle convinced him that it was now Japan's turn to make a compromise.[32]

On 13 March, Japan and the US agreed on a compromise proposal: Japan's auxiliary vessel tonnage would be set to 69.75 per cent of that of the US, and submarine tonnage between Japan, the UK and the US would be set at the same level. The following day, seeking approval of the proposal from the government at home, the Japanese delegation to London sent a telegram stating that 'the U.S. side has for all practical purposes already agreed to a general 70 per cent principle'.[33] Castle had also emphasised to Shidehara that this proposal would be the US's final concession. On 15 March, Shidehara visited Hamaguchi with this telegram in hand. Upon receiving it, Hamaguchi summoned Navy Vice-Minister Yamanashi and ordered him to sound out the general opinion of the naval leadership. Meanwhile, military affairs adviser Admiral Okada Keisuke (who had previously served as navy minister under the previous Tanaka cabinet) had already been coordinating with Vice-Minister for Foreign Affairs Yoshida in an effort to bring the Naval General Staff on board.[34]

The Hamaguchi cabinet also received support from a group affiliated with the imperial court. This group included the elder statesman Saionji Kinmochi, who was then suffering from pneumonia, Lord Keeper of the Privy Seal Makino Nobuaki, Minister of the Imperial Household Ichiki Kitokurō, Grand Chamberlain Suzuki Kantarō, Deputy Grand

Chamberlain Kawai Yahachi and Okabe Nagakage, who was concurrently serving as both chief secretary to the lord keeper of the privy seal and as deputy grand master of the ceremonies. At around this time, Castle wrote in his diary:

> The London situation looks a lot better as between the Americans and the Japanese because the Japanese are apparently realizing that if the conference is to succeed they cannot have everything they want.[35]

Despite the progress that had been made, three problems remained. First, there was criticism from the Naval General Staff and from Fleet Admiral Tōgō Heihachirō. To deal with this criticism, Shidehara enlisted the support of Yamanashi, a fact that Castle learned from Yoshida.[36]

Second, there was the problem of the Japanese media. Of particular concern were articles that appeared in the evening editions of the *Tokyo Asahi Shimbun* and the *Tokyo Nichinichi Shimbun* on 17 March. These articles contained figures from the compromise proposal between Japan and the US that had been leaked by Vice Chief Suetsugu and were published alongside a dissenting opinion from the navy. This event greatly irritated Shidehara, Hamaguchi and the Japanese delegation.[37]

Third, France, which had proven difficult in its negotiations with the UK, attempted to avoid becoming isolated by arguing that Japan should not be permitted more submarines than it already had. There were also those in the delegation, such as Representative Takarabe, who thought that Japan ought to join forces with France and push back against the UK and the US. However, Shidehara and Wakatsuki reacted coldly to France's proposal. Shidehara did not want the conference to founder upon the submarine problem. This, too, was relayed to Castle by Yoshida.[38]

To try to bring the navy around, Shidehara enlisted the cooperation of the governor-general of Korea, Saitō Makoto, who had temporarily returned to Japan. Shidehara also took into consideration the opinion of Okada Keisuke. However, it was thought that a direct meeting between Shidehara and Saitō might be misinterpreted by others. For this reason, Shidehara sent Yoshida as a messenger, after receiving approval from Hamaguchi. Meanwhile, Stimson was increasingly irritated at the delay in any formal instructions from the Hamaguchi cabinet to the Japanese delegation.[39]

'A Silent Man' — Prime Minister Hamaguchi

On 20 March, having grown tired of waiting for a response, Stimson sought to push through the apparent impasse by asking Castle to seek a meeting with Prime Minister Hamaguchi. However, Castle was against seeking such a meeting. He understood that it might give the Japanese public the impression that the US was directly applying pressure on Japan.

As Castle puts it, Hamaguchi was 'a silent man' and not necessarily the sort of politician who could exercise leadership in such matters. Rather, Castle suggested that within the cabinet it was Shidehara who had more initiative, asking rhetorically: 'Could anyone be stronger than Shidehara has proven himself to be?'[40] Castle's proposal was for Hamaguchi to be awakened to the reality of the situation in London through Shidehara. To put it another way, for Castle, it was Shidehara who was ultimately the real negotiating partner. He did not have a high opinion of Prime Minister Hamaguchi. The British ambassador to Japan, John Tilley, had the same impression. The message from Prime Minister MacDonald to Hamaguchi was also entrusted to Shidehara, as Castle was aware. Similarly, Shidehara was also concerned that if Castle were to meet directly with Hamaguchi, it could lead to sensationalistic reporting in the Japanese media.[41]

There was another individual who concurred with Shidehara on the issue of Castle directly speaking with Hamaguchi. This was Yoshida Shigeru. Speaking with Castle, Yoshida agreed that 'it would have been most unwise to approach Hamaguchi'.[42] Such a meeting, in his view, would only have furnished Japanese hardliners with an excuse to push their own agenda. In response to this feedback, Stimson began to change his stance. If Shidehara himself was against the idea, then he would not insist upon having his confidential message presented directly to Hamaguchi. On 24 March, Shidehara received a visit from Castle, who had come to discuss the message from Stimson to Hamaguchi. The message itself contained a great deal, including the argument that the US, the UK and Japan ought to cooperate with each other, given that they were the world's three great naval powers. As for how the message to Hamaguchi was to be handled, this Castle left entirely to Shidehara's discretion. The result was that Stimson's message was handed to Hamaguchi via Shidehara, as had taken place with the message from MacDonald.

5. THE LONDON NAVAL CONFERENCE AND THE MANCHURIAN INCIDENT

Shidehara was also kept informed of Castle's movements through Yoshida. For example, Yoshida informed Shidehara of a 23 March visit from Castle. At that time, to try to avoid the impression that the US was applying 'undue pressure', Castle had even sought to prevent Shidehara from passing Stimson's message on to Hamaguchi.[43] On another occasion, Castle informed Yoshida through Secretary Dooman that Stimson was concerned about potentially inciting the Japanese public. Certainly, the US diplomats were being extremely cautious. Shidehara, of course, was aware of their concern. He himself took great pains with the handling of these messages.

Throughout this period of negotiations, Shidehara met numerous times with Hamaguchi. Finally, on 1 April, the Hamaguchi cabinet decided to respond to the Japanese delegation's request with instructions to accept the Japanese–American compromise proposal. Half a month had already passed since the delegation had sent its request. Prior to the cabinet meeting, Hamaguchi invited Military Affairs Adviser Okada, Naval General Staff Director Katō and Navy Vice-Minister Yamanashi to his residence. For an hour he attempted to bring them on board with respect to the delegation instruction draft, giving reasons for accepting the compromise from the perspectives of diplomacy and finance. Despite Hamaguchi's efforts, when Shidehara met with Castle after the issuing of the instructions, Castle interpreted this outcome as the result of Shidehara's efforts and sought to assist Shidehara further. In fact, since before the cabinet meeting, Castle had foreseen that the Hamaguchi cabinet would approve of the terms of agreement reached in London, thanks to information shared by Vice-Minister Yoshida and Lord Keeper of the Privy Seal Makino.[44]

Meanwhile, from 31 March to 1 April, Naval General Staff Director Katō sought permission to issue a report to the throne. However, the report was delayed by Grand Chamberlain Suzuki Kantarō until 2 April. Nara Takeji, chief aide-de-camp to the emperor, was critical of Suzuki for this obstructionism, writing in his diary: 'I believe the grand chamberlain's actions were extremely improper'.[45] On 1 April, Hamaguchi issued his report to the throne on the delegation instructions draft, which was then approved by the emperor.

On 2 April, Katō had an audience with the Shōwa emperor and presented the following report:

> The proposal by the U.S. contains content that threatens to cause serious strategic ramifications for the Imperial Navy … The adoption of the agreement proposed by the U.S. would require,

> for all intents and purposes, a reduction in military capacity as well as the ratio [of our forces relative to other nations], as argued for by the other imperial powers. Because this [reduction] would bring about serious changes to our strategic planning, based upon the national defense policy that was adopted in the 12th year of Taishō [1923], it is my belief that it requires serious deliberation.[46]

Although unaware of the specific details of the report, on 3 April, the *Times* stated that it contained a severe critique of the Japanese government.

However, while Naval General Staff Director Katō did present his report to the emperor on 2 April, it was not the case that he sought to prevent the acceptance of the agreement outright. The formal reason was that the Shōwa emperor had already approved the delegation instructions the previous day. Katō himself stated that the true motive of the report was 'only to have my concerns heard'. The emperor, too, 'was only of the opinion that he should at least hear [what I wished to say]'. Nara, chief aide-de-camp to the emperor, similarly wrote in his diary: 'As for the handling of this report to the emperor, even if it had been submitted prior to the issuing of the instructions, there was nothing to be done except to listen [to Katō's concerns]'.[47] In other words, although it was a formal report, Katō, the emperor and Nara all felt that it should be treated only as an opinion to be taken into consideration.[48] Even so, Katō ought to have received support by Vice Chief Suetsugu. Yet Suetsugu's imprudent behaviour was counterproductive in this regard.[49]

On 13 April, a luncheon party was held at the Imperial Palace. The Shōwa emperor had invited British Ambassador Tilley, with Shidehara and Prince Takamatsu Nobuhito also attending. The task of interpreting for the emperor fell to Sawada Renzō, director of the Telegraph Division. While the luncheon party was being held prior to Prince Takamatsu's planned visit to Europe, the discussion also ranged over the London Naval Conference. It was here that the Shōwa emperor addressed Ambassador Tilley with the following words:

> Incidentally, on the topic of the Naval Disarmament Conference that is presently taking place in London, I am extremely pleased to hear that a satisfactory result may now be anticipated, thanks to the cooperation of the three nations of Japan, the U.K., and the U.S. … Along with the success of this conference, it is also my hope that cooperation among the participatory nations, and in particular between Japan, the U.K., and the U.S., will help to further the advancement of world peace.[50]

In front of both Shidehara and Prince Takamatsu, the emperor expressed his pleasure that negotiations at the London Naval Conference appeared to be concluding with a compromise agreement. Understandably, Sawada was nervous interpreting the emperor's words on this occasion. Although the Japanese delegation had already received instructions from the Hamaguchi cabinet to accept the Japanese–American compromise agreement, the treaty had yet to be signed in London. There were also disquieting moves being made by the navy and the Seiyūkai. Given the delicate nature of the situation, which was after the issuing of the instructions but before the signing of the final treaty, it may well have been better if the emperor's statement was more reserved. Although Sawada was unsure whether to interpret everything the emperor was saying, he was effectively left with no choice but to render his words into English.

Pleased with the emperor's comment, Tilley stated that he would relay it to London. The manner in which the emperor expressed his thoughts on this occasion was therefore fully capable of leading to unforeseen events. That being said, Shidehara, who, as noted above, was also in attendance, was not overly nervous about the possible ramifications of the emperor's statement. Moreover, when he returned to the Ministry of Foreign Affairs, he attempted himself to relay the details of the emperor's comment to the Japanese delegation. Although the emperor had already granted his approval of the delegation instructions, Shidehara's actions on this occasion appear to have been somewhat careless. It was Yoshida who realised the possible danger. Taking into account the wishes of Ichiki, the minister of the imperial household, he made his own addition to Shidehara's telegram: 'Request that particular care be taken to prevent this news leaking to the newspapers, etc'.[51] Yoshida was aware that the emperor's words, if leaked, would have a massive impact.

Shidehara's Diet Address and Castle's Departure

In the end, the London Naval Treaty on Disarmament was formally signed on 22 April.[52] Right afterwards, the 58th Imperial Diet commenced in Japan. This Diet would soon become the setting for an unfolding debate regarding the problem of supposed supreme command interference. Article 11 of the Meiji Constitution stipulates that supreme command over the navy rests with the emperor and not with the ministers of state. On the other hand, Article 12 states that supreme power over military organisation is a state affair to be determined by the advice of the cabinet.

At the convening of the House of Representatives on 25 April, Shidehara made an address directly after Prime Minister Hamaguchi. He stated: 'Through a comparative analysis of the various positives and negatives for the empire [Japan], we have confirmed that it is absolutely advisable to participate in this agreement'. Shidehara was immediately showered with criticism from the attending members of the Seiyūkai opposition. The president of the Seiyūkai, Inukai Tsuyoshi, then responded with a counterargument based upon a declaration by Naval General Staff Director Katō. In the same fashion, Hatoyama Ichirō aligned himself with the Naval General Staff, angrily arguing: 'I believe that Foreign Minister Shidehara's position is entirely that of an administrator and not the serious argument of a politician. (Applause.)'[53]

From today's perspective, we may find it hard to fault Shidehara's address. It cannot be denied, however, that, given the circumstances at the time, Shidehara did not show sufficient concern for how the opposition and the navy would react. In his diary, Naval General Staff Director Katō wrote that 'Shidehara's speech on diplomacy was nothing but a spewing of groundless arguments; the government and the people are in an uproar'.[54] Although Shidehara thought he had received the navy's support through discussions with Vice-Minister Yamanashi, Yamanashi was perplexed by Shidehara's speech. Even if only to some degree, there was a need for suitable comments to be directed at the nation. Beyond that, there was the problem of the Seiyūkai's policy. Although the Diet had no authority over ratification, their reaction posed a threat to the foundation of party politics; the authority for ratification rested with the Privy Council.[55] That said, while the manner in which the Seiyūkai and the navy reacted to the London Naval Treaty is typically viewed as problematic, that does not mean that they had the same stance. For example, as noted earlier, though it is true that Naval General Staff Director Katō presented a dissenting view in his 2 April report to the emperor, he did not actively seek to overturn the acceptance of the compromise agreement.

Even more so than Shidehara, it was Castle who had demonstrated the most caution when it came to the Diet and Japanese public opinion. Throughout the month of May, Castle went on a speaking tour of several Japanese cities, including Kyoto, Osaka, Kobe, Nagoya, Nara and Nikkō. For Castle's speech at Osaka, Shidehara gave him permission beforehand to mention some of the details of the London Naval Conference.[56] Castle, who handled the media shrewdly, later boasted that his speeches helped to hasten Japan's ratification of the London Naval Treaty. Shidehara himself acknowledged this fact. As Castle would later recall:

> The press was waiting, and the Navy was waiting for me to make the break of going over Shidehara to Hamaguchi or for me to make some public utterance that might be interpreted as bringing pressure to bear.[57]

For this reason, Castle was careful until the very end to always restrict himself to dealing with Shidehara and Yoshida.

It should be noted that, to begin with, it was on the occasion of the London Naval Conference that Castle was dispatched to Japan. Indeed, he had to return to the US after concluding his speeches in the various regions of Japan, even though this was still before Japan's final ratification of the London Naval Treaty. Along with the ratification of the treaty, there was one more matter that Castle was apprehensive about. Division of Far Eastern Affairs Chief Hornbeck had engaged in negotiations, albeit unofficial ones, with China's minister to the US, Wu Chaoshu, over the termination of extraterritorial rights in China. Shidehara, however, believed that Japan, the US and the UK ought to engage in coordinated negotiations with China, in Nanjing. Castle was sympathetic towards Shidehara's view and told Stimson he was concerned about Hornbeck overstepping on this matter.[58]

With Castle's scheduled return to the US drawing closer, Tani Masayuki, First Division director of the Asian Bureau at the Ministry of Foreign Affairs, assumed that Shidehara and Castle would have a final opportunity to meet. On 20 May, he drafted a proposal for Shidehara's use of topics to discuss in that final meeting. Tani wrote:

> As your ambassador was recently proclaiming, with respect to the policies towards China of Japan and the U.S., and the principle advocated by your ambassador of mutual prosperity through commerce, not only are [these policies] not opposed, they are actually entirely congruent.[59]

Upon receiving a copy of this draft, Asian Bureau Director-General Arita Hachirō made the following addition on the same day:

> Among officials and the people of some foreign nations, there are those who have misunderstandings regarding the problem of Japan's 'competitive lines' in Manchuria, believing that the South Manchuria Railway Company seeks to exclusively dominate all of Manchuria.[60]

Arita was attempting, through Shidehara, to gain Castle's understanding with respect to Japanese policy on the South Manchuria Railway. However, although Shidehara was aware of the Asian Bureau's opinion, he did not seek to emphasise this point during his meeting with Castle. It would seem that, when it came to Castle at least, Shidehara had judged him as already recognising Japan's initiative in matters of Chinese policy. We also know that Castle himself wanted to avoid directly touching upon Manchurian policy, given its controversial nature.[61]

On the occasion of Castle leaving his posting in Japan, the America–Japan Society hosted a dinner party on 23 May. Along with Shidehara and Yoshida, the dinner party was attended by Tokugawa Iesato, Chairman of the America–Japan Society and President of the House of Peers, and Hanihara Masanao, former ambassador to the US. In his address to the gathering, Castle spoke of the coming period following the conclusion of the London Naval Treaty. The US, he argued, needed to learn that 'Japan must be and will be the guardian of peace in the Pacific'.[62]

On the Japanese side, following Tokugawa, Hanihara began to read an address. He unexpectedly mentioned the Japanese Exclusion Act, arguing for the need of a 'renewal of friendship'.[63] This comment left Castle feeling ill at ease. Upon hearing of this incident, British Ambassador Tilley spoke with Yoshida, asking half-jokingly if Hanihara's speech had been suggested by the Ministry of Foreign Affairs. Yoshida replied that, during Hanihara's speech, both he and Shidehara were so uncomfortable that they did not even know where to look.[64]

Although the Japanese Exclusion Act Hanihara mentioned had been overshadowed by the proceedings of the disarmament conference, even in the US calls for its revision were growing stronger. Shidehara had been informed of this fact by ministry officials in the field. As one example, when president of Columbia University Nicholas Murray Butler invited Sawada Setsuzō, Japanese consul general in New York, to a luncheon, he responded positively to the idea of revising the immigration act. Similarly, MacMurray—who had resigned from his post as the US minister to China and taken up a position at Johns Hopkins University as the director of the Walter Hines Page School of International Relations—had discussed the Japanese Exclusion Act in a speech.[65]

The Japanese Exclusion Act Amendment Problem and Policy on China

In July 1930, following his return to the US, Castle was once more appointed assistant secretary of state.[66] William Cameron Forbes, Castle's replacement as the US ambassador to Japan, had previously served as governor-general of the Philippines. Shidehara was initially informed about Forbes through private correspondence from Castle, who mentioned that Forbes was a prominent Western expert on East Asia. As well as stating that he welcomed Forbes's appointment, Shidehara indicated that he appreciated the US government's position on reforming the Japanese Exclusion Act. It was best, he wrote, to avoid being overly hasty with such matters.[67]

In correspondence addressed to Forbes, Castle also wrote that Tokyo was a first-rate city, equal to London. He also took pains to offer advice to Forbes, who was then 60 years old and single, including on local living conditions. Following his return to the US, Castle did not neglect in his speeches to promote the importance of fostering goodwill between Japan and the US.[68] It may well have been that Castle's concerns over the US embassy in Japan were groundless. On this topic, further details can be found in the written recollections of Sir George Sansom, who resided long-term in Japan while serving as commercial counsellor at the British embassy. According to Sansom, 'the American embassy always had one or two very good counsellors like Edwin Neville'.[69] Sansom noted that Neville had developed friendships with many Japanese during his time in Japan and that Sansom's own close friend Dooman, the first secretary at the US embassy, was also talented. Finance Minister Inoue, who was an old acquaintance of Forbes's from his time as governor-general of the Philippines, also welcomed his posting as ambassador.

Another notable incident occurred on 10 June, when Naval General Staff Director Katō submitted his resignation to the emperor. Despite such protests, the London Naval Treaty was ratified on 2 October, following deliberation by the Privy Council. Shidehara had been waiting impatiently for this day, and it was to him that Castle immediately dispatched a letter once he learned of the result.[70] On the other hand, Debuchi, who was still serving as ambassador to the US, attempted to turn the ratification of the London Naval Treaty into an opportunity to reform the Japanese Exclusion Act. Secretary of State Stimson, who spoke with Debuchi on the topic on 30 October, agreed to the idea of Debuchi and Castle holding secret talks on the immigration act, an indication of his enthusiasm for the further improvement of Japanese–American relations.[71]

Shidehara and Castle acknowledged that resolving the issue of naval disarmament had helped improve relations between Japan and the US. At the same time, however, they believed that any sudden attempt to move forward with Japan's keenly desired reform of the Japanese Exclusion Act could backfire. For this reason, they viewed Debuchi's more insistent attempts at seeking a revision of the act as rash.[72]

Along with the matter of revising the Japanese Exclusion Act, an outstanding issue for Japan and the US was policy on China. Shidehara, as noted above, thought that the problem of extraterritorial rights in China should be handled through negotiations conducted in Nanjing, with Japan, the US and the UK jointly coordinating their efforts. Castle similarly argued in favour of cooperation between Japan and the US on this matter, bringing him into opposition with Hornbeck, chief of the State Department's Division of Far Eastern Affairs, who was more sympathetic toward China. Hornbeck frequently received private correspondence from Johnson, US minister to China. This placed him in the unique position of knowing what was going on inside China, including the movements of individuals such as British Minister Miles Lampson.[73] China hands such as Hornbeck and Johnson did not express interest in tying the success of the London Naval Conference to the matter of Japanese–American cooperation in China. While Stimson showed a degree of sympathy to Debuchi with respect to the immigration problem, when it came to policy on China, he was unable to overlook the advice and information from figures such as Hornbeck.[74]

As can be seen, Castle paid careful attention not only to how the press covered the London Naval Treaty but also to matters such as his successor, the immigration problem and policy on China. Thanks in part to Castle's efforts, the relationship between Japan and the US had begun to improve. Unfortunately, the situation soon worsened, and the cause was Shidehara himself. In November 1930, Prime Minister Hamaguchi was shot and badly wounded at Tokyo Station. This meant that Shidehara became acting prime minister. Then, in February 1931, he would misspeak during the 59th Diet, triggering an uproar.

The specific occasion was a meeting of the House of Representatives budget committee on 3 February. Nakajima Chikuhei of the Seiyūkai had asked some questions about naval disarmament. Because Navy Minister Abo Kiyokazu was absent due to sickness, initially these questions were answered by Yabuki Shōzō, parliamentary vice-minister for the navy. When Nakajima inquired about responsibility for 'causing our national defenses to be insufficient', Shidehara responded with the following ill-advised words: 'Given that it has now been ratified [by the emperor], it is clearly the case that the London Naval Treaty has not put our national defense into any danger'. The committee responded uproariously, with jeers to the effect of: 'What is the meaning of making it the emperor's responsibility?'[75] Further discussion was impossible. Even Committee Chief Takeuchi Sakuhei was unable to get the committee to reconvene the following day.

Shidehara meant to point out that the navy minister had also attended the military counsellor meeting and added his signature to the petition to the emperor requesting that the treaty be ratified. Therefore, it hardly made sense to speak of supreme command interference. And indeed, his response continued with the following justification:

> In saying that [the treaty] received ratification, [what I mean is that] it is entirely the government's responsibility. I do not seek to absolve myself of this responsibility in the slightest. At the same time, when the ratification petition to the emperor was sent.[76]

Yet Shidehara's voice was drowned out by the angry roar of the committee.

Judging from the committee minutes, it cannot be denied that Shidehara's response to Nakajima's line of questioning was careless. Reflecting upon this incident in later years, Shidehara suggested that the uproar was in fact orchestrated by Mori Tsutomu, secretary-general of the Seiyūkai. Castle must have surely been disturbed to learn of Shidehara's difficulties via sources such as the correspondence he received from Nitobe Inazō.[77]

The Limits of Japan–US Cooperation

So far in this chapter, I have provided an outline of both Shidehara's actions and Japanese–American relations during the period of the London Naval Conference. I will now expand upon this initial picture with some further details, while also considering the reality and the limits of Japan–US cooperation at this time. If asked to think of a party-based cabinet in modern Japan that attempted to carry out cooperative diplomacy between Japan and the US, most would probably name the cabinet of Hara Takashi. However, although the Hara cabinet was supposed to be the first fundamentally party-based cabinet, it was not highly regarded by the Wilson administration.[78] In fact, it was in the period of the London Naval Conference when party-cabinet-based cooperation with the US was at its most mature, as well as when there were those on the US side who sought to reach out as potential partners. At the centre of these efforts at cooperative diplomacy were Shidehara and Castle.

That said, from Castle's perspective, it was not the Minseitō that had taken the initiative of guiding cooperation between the two nations. Rather, it was Shidehara who Castle considered to be leading such efforts. His estimation of the man in this regard was close to overwhelming praise. In correspondence sent to President Hoover following the Hamaguchi cabinet's issuing of instructions to the Japanese delegation, the only Japanese individual Castle specifically named as deserving of merit was Shidehara, stating that he was the leader of those who sought closer cooperation with the US. Castle understood his own responsibility to be that of 'creating a friendly atmosphere' in a nation that he saw as of particular importance for the US. As he also wrote in a letter to Hoover: 'I cannot help feeling that London, Tokyo and Mexico are our three most critical posts'.[79]

As noted earlier, Shidehara and Castle saw eye to eye not only on the London Naval Treaty but also regarding policy on China, such as the matter of extraterritorial rights.[80] Castle was quick to discern that the 'China problem' was not unconnected to the issue of naval disarmament. Therefore, in seeking to have Japan's leadership recognised regarding the China problem, Castle was, at the same time, attempting to help guide the London Naval Conference to a successful conclusion. In reality, the Naval General Staff, beginning with Katō Hiroharu, had been arguing for some time that one of the reasons they could not compromise on naval disarmament was that they wanted to forestall US pressure on Japan's policies regarding China. A similar opinion was expressed by the Privy Council's London Naval Treaty Judging Committee. Committee member Kawai Misao, for example, was concerned about the US becoming emboldened in its regional diplomatic efforts. Pressing Hamaguchi on the topic, he once asserted that 'Japan has to militarily prepare with the China problem in mind'.[81]

It was Yoshida, meanwhile, who served as mediator between Shidehara and Castle so well. This is a bit surprising, given that Shidehara and Yoshida had differing views when it came to policy on China. In terms of personality as well, Yoshida found Tanaka, the previous foreign minister, to be easier to work for, due to his 'generous temperament'. By contrast, he was not fond of the 'stubbornly precise' Shidehara. According to Yoshida, Shidehara's obsession with the minutiae of ministry work was such that he could not stand to delegate tasks to the vice-minister as needed. Such behaviour, in his opinion, showed that Shidehara was not cut out to be the foreign minister. Given that Shidehara spent so much of his time holed up in the ministry, it often fell to Yoshida himself to take care of public relations. In doing so, he was able to make up for some of the shortcomings of Shidehara, the 'discreet worker'.[82] This dynamic was probably what inspired the running joke in the ministry that Shidehara was the vice-minister and Yoshida was the minister. Yoshida also took responsibility for sharing ministry information with certain key figures. For example, during one period he delivered summaries of discussions that were being held between Shidehara and China's minister to Japan, Wang Rongbao, to his father-in-law, the lord keeper of the privy seal, Makino Nobuaki.[83]

Castle's estimation of Makino was also extremely high. Indeed, Makino's shrewdness was one of the reasons he had long been trusted as the emperor's go-between. This kind of evaluation of Makino was not necessarily unreasonable, particularly given that Shidehara felt comfortable in providing him with top-secret documents from the navy and the Ministry of Foreign Affairs.[84] On the other hand, aside from concerning Hamaguchi's performance alongside Home Minister Adachi Kenzō in leading the Minseitō to electoral victory, Castle's opinion of Hamaguchi was not high.[85] Of course, the reason why Castle avoided directly negotiating with Hamaguchi was that he was wary of giving the impression that he was applying outside pressure on behalf of the US. Given that even in London the important negotiations between Japan and the US were unofficial, it was surely wise that Castle avoided negotiating with Hamaguchi. Shidehara had also been opposed to any direct discussions between Hamaguchi and Castle.

However, the more fundamental reason was that Castle had higher expectations of Foreign Ministry officials such as Shidehara and Yoshida than of the leaders of the ruling party. And indeed, Shidehara more than lived up to those expectations. From Castle's perspective, the role of the party politicians headed by Hamaguchi was not of primary importance. Hamaguchi's sheer determination to steer a meeting to a consensus, even at the risk of his own life,[86] was apparently a quality that the staff at the US embassy were not sufficiently aware of. In considering the nature of Japanese politics during the period in question, it is illuminating that the US ambassador held Makino in higher esteem than Hamaguchi. Further, Castle did not have contact with Nagai Ryūtarō, who supported Shidehara from within the Minseitō party, as parliamentary vice-minister for foreign affairs.[87] Evidently, as far as foreign affairs was concerned, the US embassy did not view Japanese party politics as mature.

When Castle sought to have his thinking communicated with the Japanese navy, a common path of transmission was from Shidehara to Navy Vice-Minister Yamanashi. Shidehara's English proficiency was invaluable in this regard. In fact, the closeness of Shidehara and Castle was such that it became a matter of concern for Naval General Staff Director Katō.[88] That Castle developed such a positive relationship with Shidehara following his dispatch to Japan for the period of the London Naval Conference was in itself quite significant. At that time, the US ambassador to Japan was generally thought to be of little importance, even compared to the minister to China.[89] It was rare for officials at the rank of undersecretary of state to have the experience of actually residing in Japan.

It was also during this period that officials more familiar with Japan, such as Secretary Dooman, began to work at the US embassy. This development would also have helped bring the two nations closer together.[90] Along with Dooman, another figure who was viewed as representative of a new generation of Japan was the State Department official Joseph W. Ballantine. Returning home after the London Naval Conference, Ballantine's choice for his next posting was not Japan but Guangdong, as consul general. Given that Ballantine had tended to be biased in favour of Japan at that point, this experience would have surely expanded his perspective.[91]

This is all to say that the relationship between Japan and the US in the modern period more or less reached its peak during the period of the London Naval Conference. On the Japanese side, there was Shidehara, a foreign minister who acted as a driving force for positive relations from the time of the conference. Then there was also Debuchi, Shidehara's subordinate and close confidant, who would go on to serve as ambassador to the US. In the US State Department, meanwhile, a pro-Japan clique was forming. Castle's appearance in the annals of US diplomacy can be

5. THE LONDON NAVAL CONFERENCE AND THE MANCHURIAN INCIDENT

seen as continuing down a path blazed by MacMurray, previous minister to China and chief of the State Department's Division of Far Eastern Affairs. After returning to the US, Castle initially served as assistant secretary of state from July 1930 to April 1931. He would subsequently become undersecretary of state, from April 1931 to March 1933.[92] While Japan–US relations were at their best in this era, this situation was not sustainable.

Certainly, the naval disarmament talks were not unconnected to the 'China problem' or to the immigration problem. Their successful conclusion, therefore, at the same time indicated that it was possible for a more secure regional order to arise in East Asia. Hence, we see, for example, figures such as Debuchi pushing quite strongly for a revision to the Japanese Exclusion Act, and Secretary of State Stimson showing his willingness to work on this issue. However, as they were familiar with the situation on the ground, Shidehara and Castle considered it overly hasty to tie the success of the London Naval Conference directly to the Japanese Exclusion Act reform. Instead, they were concerned about the possibility of a backlash. They did not think that the construction of a new order through Japan–US cooperation, including on immigration and China, could be realised so quickly. After all, while Castle was favourable to Japan, his perspective was not representative of US mainstream thought. The idea that China policy ought to be tied to the success of naval disarmament talks was a difficult sell to China hands such as Division of Far Eastern Affairs Chief Hornbeck, or Johnson, the US minister to China.

Stimson too, though sympathetic to the need to revise the Japanese Exclusion Act, could hardly ignore the wishes of the China hands in his department when it came to policy on China. This area may well have become a barrier to the development of a new international order, which was in turn essential to Japan–US relations. On this matter we have corroboration from Sansom, who was a commercial counsellor at the British Embassy in Japan. In his reminiscences on the period, he stated: 'The State Department and the American Government over-emphasised the importance and also the virtues of the Chinese'.[93] In his view, the State Department and the government ought to have paid greater heed to those officials who were more familiar with Japan.

The isolation of the pro-Japan faction in the State Department did not greatly improve in the subsequent period, when Joseph C. Grew served as ambassador to Japan. According to the recollections of Embassy First

Secretary Dooman, Hornbeck was eager to deny the wishes of Grew and Dooman. Understanding that it was hopeless, they apparently lost the motivation to even bother writing private correspondence to Hornbeck or his subordinates.[94] All this is to say that, given subsequent events, the London Naval Conference on Disarmament was undeniably not only a high point but also a turning point.[95] Matters deteriorated from then on. When looking at the problem of military disarmament, it is easy to pay too much attention to the ratios allotted to each nation that limited their naval forces. In reality, such ratios by no means guarantee that peace will prevail. Of far greater importance is the foundation of such disarmament treaties: the potential for the steady cultivation of a relationship of trust. Though it was over 90 years ago, Shidehara and Castle's friendship still provides this message to us today.

The Manchurian Incident

The Hamaguchi Shooting Incident: Assuming the Role of Acting Prime Minister

In December 1930, following the ratification of the London Naval Treaty, Shidehara replaced Yoshida Shigeru with Nagai Matsuzō as vice-minister for foreign affairs. Previously, when Shidehara served as vice-minister, Nagai was director of the Telegraph Division. Together, they would frequently work late into the night. Since that time, Nagai had progressed through the positions of International Trade Bureau director-general, minister to Sweden and ambassador to Belgium. During the London Naval Conference on Disarmament, he served as one of the plenipotentiary representatives in the Japanese delegation. It should be noted that his appointment as ambassador to Belgium in April 1928 was the wish of Vice-Minister Debuchi. Under the Meiji Constitution, ambassadors and vice-ministers were ranked as 'shinninkan' (officials appointed by the emperor) and 'chokuninkan' (imperial appointees), respectively. In other words, ambassadors actually ranked higher than vice-ministers. This meant that when Nagai became vice-minister after serving as ambassador to Belgium, he was technically being demoted. Nevertheless, Shidehara wanted his old acquaintance to take on the role.[96]

5. THE LONDON NAVAL CONFERENCE AND THE MANCHURIAN INCIDENT

Shortly before this staffing change, Shidehara had also requested that the ambassador to Italy, Matsuda Michikazu, serve as director-general of the Treaties and Conventions Bureau. Such personnel choices were certainly unusual. Yet, in this way, Shidehara was able to reinforce the ministry with the capable figures of Vice-Minister Nagai and Treaties and Conventions Bureau Director-General Matsuda. As a diplomat wrote:

> The army and the navy seemed quite displeased by these personnel changes ... What was the Ministry of Foreign Affairs planning by having three generals (shinninkan) at once? Were they seeking to gain leverage to push back against the San-Chokan [Three Chiefs] in the Army? There were people making jokes of this nature.[97]

The 'San-Chokan in the Army' referred to here were the war minister, the chief of army general staff and the inspector general of military training.

Shidehara was extremely busy during this period. As indicated earlier, this was because he was serving as the acting prime minister. According to Shidehara:

> I will never forget it. It was the fifth year of Shōwa [1930], November 14. That was the day that Prime Minister Hamaguchi was shot by an assassin at Tokyo Station.[98]

On the day in question, Shidehara had been standing on a platform at Tokyo Station. He had come to see off Hirota Kōki, who was departing to take his position as ambassador to the Soviet Union. Coincidentally, Prime Minister Hamaguchi appeared at the same time. He was headed for Okayama, where he intended to observe military exercises.

The next moment, Shidehara heard a gunshot. A right-wing youth had shot Hamaguchi. In shock, Shidehara pushed through the gathering crowd and found Hamaguchi bloodstained and gravely wounded. In a strained voice, Hamaguchi reportedly said: '*Danshi no Honkai da*'. Translated literally, this means 'a man's long-cherished desire'. What Hamaguchi meant was: 'I have served my country'. Struggling, Hamaguchi then added, with a groan: 'I dealt with the cabinet meeting for the budget draft yesterday, so this is good timing'. Shidehara replied, looking into Hamaguchi's face: 'If you keep talking, you'll only lose more blood, so be quiet now'.[99] The assailant's motive was opposition to the naval disarmament treaty. Apparently, the assassination plans had also included Shidehara as a target. As a result of the Hamaguchi Shooting Incident, Shidehara became acting prime minister.

Recommending Shidehara for the position of acting prime minister were the minister for railways, Egi Tasuku, and House of Peers member Izawa Takio. As Shidehara himself had no ambition for high political office, it was relatively easy to secure sufficient support for him to serve as acting prime minister. As he said: 'I merely took on the position temporarily'.[100] Yet, desired or not, Shidehara's appointment as acting prime minister was actually a disaster for his friend Hamaguchi. As mentioned above, in February 1931, Shidehara misspoke at a committee meeting during the Diet. Following this incident, in March, he was relieved of his position as acting prime minister. The problem was that there was no government mechanism allowing an acting prime minister to be replaced by another acting prime minister. The result was that Hamaguchi himself was forced to attend the House sessions as prime minister. As he began to attend the House sessions, Hamaguchi's condition soon deteriorated. At the time, Hamaguchi sought Shidehara's opinion on who should succeed him as president of the Minseitō. When Shidehara said that 'Wakatsuki would be a suitable choice', Hamaguchi replied: 'I agree entirely'.[101]

Thus, former prime minister Wakatsuki was chosen as the next Minseitō president. When the Hamaguchi cabinet resigned en masse in April 1931, the emperor instructed Wakatsuki to form his second cabinet. Naturally, Shidehara resumed his post as foreign minister. However, Hamaguchi's condition grew worse. He finally passed away on 26 August, aged 61. It was late summer, and a mere three weeks before the Manchurian Incident. If it were not for the shooting at Tokyo Station that Shidehara witnessed, the cabinet led by his old friend Hamaguchi might well have become the longest administration since the Hara cabinet. Further, if Hamaguchi, known as the 'lion prime minister', had still been in charge, the days following the Manchurian Incident might well have unfolded quite differently. For Shidehara, it was undoubtedly a heartbreaking loss.

As if this were not enough, Shidehara also had another problem on his hands at this time: the 'Black Chamber'. The Black Chamber was the name given to the US government's secret decoding room. There the diplomatic telegrams of various foreign nations were decoded in huge quantities. This included the diplomatic telegrams of Japan, which the US had been intercepting since before the Washington Naval Conference. The central figure in this effort was a man named Herbert O. Yardley.

Yardley's Black Chamber, however, was eventually abolished by Secretary of State Stimson. Displeased with this decision, Yardley would go on to publish a tell-all book on the decoding project, titled *The American Black Chamber*. Shidehara learned of this book in June 1931, through Ambassador Debuchi. The book apparently had many pages on Japan. The details of this project would subsequently become known throughout the world. The Japanese press, of course, was hardly likely to overlook such a story. The Osaka Mainichi Shimbun company quickly had it translated into Japanese and published it in August 1931 with the title *The Black Chamber: Beikoku wa Ikanishite Gaikō Hiden wo Nusundaka* (How did the US steal the secret diplomatic telegrams?). Although Shidehara worked out a plan for handling the Diet and issued warnings to Japan's overseas diplomatic establishments, the damage was done.[102]

The Manchurian Incident and Discussions with Stimson

Let us now turn to the matter of Japan's relationship with China. March 1930 saw the initial signing of the Sino-Japanese Tariff Agreement. With this agreement, Japan recognised China's tariff autonomy. At this time, the Hamaguchi cabinet also passed a resolution to change how China was formally referred to in official documents. Rather than simply 'China'—or, rather, the old equivalent, which was 'Shina' (支那) in Japanese—China would now be referred to as the 'Republic of China' (中華民国).[103] The Chinese government had criticised Japan's original designation of 'Shina', and the Hamaguchi cabinet decision was a response to that criticism.

With the matter of tariffs resolved, the focus of attention subsequently shifted to the termination of Japan's extraterritorial rights in China, and the refinancing of foreign loans. Concerning Japan's relationship with China, Shidehara gave a speech on national radio in which he argued: 'We are determined to do our utmost in working toward the goal of reciprocal benefit, that is to say, so-called prosperous co-existence'.[104] When it came to negotiations with China, however, Shidehara was hardly free to take the lead himself. Given the London Naval Conference on Disarmament and, later, his work as acting prime minister, Shidehara was buried in paperwork. He therefore delegated work in this area to Shigemitsu, the acting minister to China. Shigemitsu proceeded with the negotiations with an eye towards promoting greater cooperation between the two nations. He also went a step further and attempted to push Shidehara towards promoting Sino-Japanese partnership. Shidehara, however, did not acquiesce. As in the past, he continued to put far more emphasis on Japan's relationship with the US and the UK. He was also gradually moving beyond the economism that he once adhered to so strongly. Ironically, it was not until the Manchurian Incident that Shidehara's and Shigemitsu's positions began to converge.[105]

On the evening of 18 September 1931, the Kwantung Army (a division of the Japanese Imperial Army stationed in Kwantung) detonated a bomb that they set on a line of the South Manchuria Railway, near Liutiaohu on the outskirts of Shenyang. Blaming this explosion on the Chinese, the Kwantung Army then used the incident as a pretence for mobilisation. This conspiracy, which is also known as the Liutiaohu Incident, was the beginning of the Manchurian Incident. The core figures in this conspiracy were Ishiwara Kanji and Itagaki Seishirō of the Kwantung Army. Before the Liutiaohu Incident, Shidehara perceived signs of a plot by members of the Kwantung Army, thanks to telegrams from Hayashi Kyūjirō, consul general in Mukden.[106]

On 19 September, the day after the Liutiaohu Incident, numerous pieces of information gathered by the Ministry of Foreign Affairs were read aloud at a meeting of the Wakatsuki cabinet. This information included details such as how, before the explosion, the Fushun Independent Garrison had asked the South Manchuria Railway to prepare a train carriage for transport. Similarly, the General Headquarters of the Kwantung Army had also been preparing for mobilisation before the explosion. Thus, Shidehara was able to state that 'this incident almost appears as though it occurred as a result of planning by the military'.[107] For this reason, War Minister Minami Jirō was unable to secure a cabinet agreement that day to send reinforcements from the Japanese Korean Army. Instead, the Wakatsuki cabinet decided that the incident needed to be contained. The US likewise hoped that Shidehara would work to prevent any escalation.

The cabinet's wishes, however, were soon frustrated. On 21 September, the Kwantung Army moved into Jilin, and the Japanese Korean Army, led by Commander Hayashi Senjūro, crossed the border into Manchuria without orders. The following day, the cabinet voted to authorise the expense request sent by the Japanese Korean Army. On the Japanese Korean Army's unauthorised crossing of the border, Prime Minister Wakatsuki stated indifferently: 'Now that it has happened, I suppose it simply cannot be helped'.[108] On 8 October, the Kwantung Army bombed the city of Jinzhou, which was far away from the South Manchuria Railway line. The actions of the Japanese army were now expanding throughout the broader Manchuria region. When the Manchurian Incident erupted, Shidehara's basic thinking was that direct negotiations were necessary between Japan and China. He wished to avoid having any of the Western nations act as mediators.

On 9 October, the Wakatsuki cabinet agreed upon a new policy of withdrawing troops following the reaching of a general agreement with China on matters such as the prohibition of boycotting Japanese goods, and the signing of a Sino-Japanese railway agreement. While China had asserted that a troop withdrawal was a precondition for any negotiations, Japan decided it would withdraw only if its conditions were met through direct negotiation. The Nationalist government, however, appealed to the League of Nations over the Manchurian Incident, and resolved not to negotiate directly with Japan under the given circumstances. Chiang Kai-shek even sent a request to Zhang Xueliang, asking him not to begin any such negotiations.

At the end of November, V. K. Wellington Koo (Gu Weijun), who had taken the position of foreign minister for the Nationalist government, informed the UK, the US and France of a plan to establish a neutral zone around Jinzhou. Jinzhou, located in south-western Liaoning province, had become the base of operations for the government of Zhang Xueliang after he was ousted from Shenyang. Wellington Koo's proposal was for the Jinzhou region to be demilitarised and to be monitored by the other powers, so as to prevent any further conflict between Japanese and Chinese forces. At the same time, this plan can be seen as a signal for opening up negotiations with Japan. Wellington Koo had previously engaged Shidehara in debate at the Washington Naval Conference and had hopes that he would assist with his plan to prevent further conflict. This development increased the possibility of direct negotiations between Japan and China.

At the beginning of December, Shidehara also began to push Zhang Xueliang to accept the demilitarisation of Jinzhou. However, Shidehara sought not only to have the Chinese army withdraw but also to have the government of Zhang Xueliang withdraw west past Shanhaiguan. Chiang

Kai-shek and Zhang Xueliang would hardly accept such a request. Thus, it was not surprising that direct negotiations between Japan and China did not resolve the crisis.

Following this failure, Shidehara began to acquiesce to the idea of establishing a puppet government in north-eastern China led by the Japanese army. In mid-November, a fierce debate had broken out between War Minister Minami, who argued for an attack on Qiqihar city in Heilongjiang province, and Shidehara and Wakatsuki, who objected to such an idea. The agreement that was eventually reached was for a puppet government to be established in Qiqihar, with a subsequent withdrawal of Japanese troops. This was the moment when Shidehara compromised on the idea of a military-led puppet state. Thereafter, Shidehara gradually distanced himself from the ideal of the military being regulated by international cooperation. Increasingly, he acquiesced to the military having control over policy in China. With the style of Shidehara diplomacy in part disintegrating, in part metamorphosing, it can be said that the end of the Washington System of regional order in East Asia was instigated by the Japanese side.[109]

The Manchurian Incident would have serious implications for Japan's relationship with the US. Managing this relationship was a major problem, both for possible direct negotiations with China and for the plan for a puppet government. At the beginning of October, the Kwantung Army bombed Jinzhou, despite the fact that it was far away from the South Manchuria Railway. This event shocked Secretary of State Stimson, who urged President Hoover to impose economic sanctions on Japan. In his view, 'the militaristic elements in Japan could learn only through suffering and not by the sanctions of public opinion, which we in America are committed to and deem enough for ourselves'.[110] Hoover, however, was cautious about economic sanctions.

Of even more importance were some comments made by Secretary of State Stimson. Towards the end of November, Stimson received information that the Japanese army was being dispatched to Jinzhou. Fearful of this development, on 27 November, Stimson released to the US press corps a summary of a discussion that had taken place between Shidehara and Ambassador Forbes.[111] The details of Stimson's ill-considered press conference also reached Japan. According to the evening edition of the *Tokyo Asahi Shimbun* (29 November), Stimson claimed that Shidehara had declared Japan would not attack Jinzhou:

> On November 24, Foreign Minister Shidehara replied that Japan had no intention of pushing further in the direction of Jinzhou. Further, in that reply, Foreign Minister Shidehara has declared that the Japanese government had already announced the above fact to the commanders of the Japanese forces in Manchuria.[112]

Perhaps Stimson's aim with these comments was to try to restrain Japan. Shidehara, however, responded to Stimson's thoughtlessness with a mixture of grief and anger. This was because he had told Ambassador Forbes to keep the details of their discussion confidential.

These comments were also poorly timed. As the same newspaper pointed out, the Kwantung Army central command had already ordered its forces to cancel its attack on Jinzhou. This created the impression that Japan had simply bowed to US pressure. The result was that Stimson's comments damaged the authority not only of Shidehara but also of military central command. The League of Nations had been close to bringing about an agreement on the demilitarisation of Jinzhou. Shidehara responded by having Ambassador Debuchi begin an inquiry about Stimson's press conference.[113]

However, the situation went in the opposite direction of Shidehara's intention. On 28 November, Stimson held a second press conference in order to defend his previous comments. An extra edition of the *Tokyo Asahi Shimbun* (29 November) reported that Stimson made the following statement:

> On November 24, I received from Foreign Minister Shidehara, via Ambassador Forbes, the declaration that the foreign minister, the war minister, and the chief of army general staff had all reached the agreement that no military action would be taken against Jinzhou. Further, this decision had been relayed to the commander-in-chief on the ground. Given this fact, I struggle to understand the newspaper reports on the mobilization of Commander-in-Chief Honjō's forces.[114]

This second comment by Stimson only served to make a bad situation worse. This was because he had made public some details on the supreme command of Japan's forces. These details were also more explicit than in his first statement. The source of this information, of course, was Shidehara. Naturally, Shidehara responded by issuing a protest to

Ambassador Forbes. Upon receiving this protest, Forbes had no choice but to awkwardly apologise. Shidehara also found himself pressed by War Minister Minami during a cabinet meeting as to his own responsibility.[115]

Why did this situation occur in the first place? One interpretation is that the Ministry of Foreign Affairs ignored Japanese newspaper articles and instead read English-language sources such as the Associated Press. Thus they failed to grasp the essence of the problem: information relating to the supreme command had been made public by the US. For this reason, Debuchi's inquiry failed to touch upon matters such as the 'announcement' of orders to the Kwantung Army command. Therefore, when Stimson defended himself in a second press conference, he actually made matters worse by allowing further details relating to the supreme command of Japan's military to become public. This sequence of misunderstandings between Japan and the US has been pointed out by scholars and historical commentators for some time.[116] Yet this explanation leaves certain basic questions unanswered. In the first place, why did Shidehara leak to Forbes details relating to the supreme command? To answer this question, we need to go back in time a little, to when Shidehara and Forbes first met.

Shidehara and US Ambassador Forbes

According to Forbes's journal, he first met Shidehara in October 1926. At that time, Forbes was visiting Japan as part of a trip around the globe. On this occasion, he met not only Shidehara but also Debuchi, Hanihara and other ministry figures. They discussed topics such as the Philippines, Korea and Taiwan.[117]

Later, in September 1930, Forbes would return to Japan, this time as the US ambassador. His relationship with Shidehara was a good one. One example of their relations comes from a national holiday observed at that time celebrating the Meiji emperor's birthday on 3 November. On this day, not only were celebrations held at locations such as the Imperial Palace, military facilities and schools, but also the nation's citizens raised flags above their dwellings. In Japan today, this public holiday has survived, but it has been renamed 'Culture Day'. Shidehara and Forbes had been invited to the Imperial Palace by the Shōwa emperor, where they also met with Hamaguchi and other members of the government. On that occasion, Forbes remembered telling Shidehara that 'I had just heard from California that Senator Johnson was now friendly to a much desired modification of the immigration law'.[118] Another example of their strong relationship was from circumstances far less auspicious: they were quick to get in contact with each other after the shooting of Prime Minister Hamaguchi on 14 November.

In June 1931, Shidehara received an interesting proposal from Forbes: a suggestion to expand commercial relations between Taiwan and the Philippines. As Forbes had previously served as governor-general to the Philippines, he was far from indifferent about such matters. Shidehara responded by communicating the proposal to Ōta Masahiro, the governor-general of Taiwan, in order to get his opinion.[119] Even after the outbreak of the Manchurian Incident, Shidehara and Forbes's relationship remained strong. Shidehara met with Forbes in mid-November. When Shidehara stated that he was 'definite about the utter impossibility of Japan's immediate withdrawal of troops to the railway zone because the Chinese returning soldiers would drive out all Japanese and Korean residents of Manchuria', Forbes apparently responded that this was 'unquestionably true'.[120]

On 3 December, however, Forbes's opinion of Shidehara abruptly shifted. In his journal, he wrote: 'Baron Shidehara has been frank and conciliatory but it is evident that the army is hard to control'. Here Forbes was referring to the comments by Stimson, which had been published at the end of November. According to Forbes: 'Secretary Stimson gave out what seemed like a perfectly fair statement outlining perhaps in a little too much detail what Japan had represented to us of her plans'. Forbes noted that when he later met Shidehara to discuss the matter, he 'was almost tearing his hair over it'. It should be noted that Forbes was not indifferent to Shidehara's situation and felt he was partially responsible. In his diary, he remarks that he had 'failed to caution Washington about the delicacy of some of the situations' but also that he 'lost no sleep over it'. He added that 'Shidehara had given me this note with the statement that it was absolutely between ourselves'.[121] Following advice from counsellor Neville, Forbes decided to send a telegram to Stimson relaying Shidehara's wishes. Apparently, this message did not have a decisive impact on Stimson's thinking.

In fact, it was only after Shidehara pointed out Stimson's comments in a meeting that Forbes became aware of them. Upon returning to the embassy, Forbes confirmed the contents of the comments. Only minutes later, an Associated Press reporter burst into the room to speak with a dumbfounded Forbes. The reporter handed Forbes a copy of a statement by the Japanese Ministry of Foreign Affairs. In Forbes's words, the statement was 'a very bitter and intemperately worded attack on Secretary Stimson'. He noted that 'it didn't sound like Shidehara at all'. And indeed, its originator was in fact Shiratori Toshio, director-general of the Intelligence Department. Forbes relayed the details of their talks. Forbes then took the added step of apologising to Shidehara for Stimson's comments. This was when he learned that Shidehara had not written any statements of the kind that Shiratori had authored. Nevertheless, Shidehara expressed his concern that Stimson's comments 'might upset the plan of an accord between Japan and China then under negotiation'. As Forbes himself admitted, Stimson's comments 'did the opposite to Shidehara's plans'.[122]

As a result of this incident, criticism of Shidehara increased from the military and the Japanese public. Home Minister Adachi Kenzō, who had been pushing for a collaborative cabinet that incorporated members of the Seiyūkai party, chimed in: 'What Stimson said—that is going to become a serious political problem'.[123] Adachi was entirely correct. The political fallout from this incident gave the Wakatsuki cabinet no choice but to resign. On 11 December, Shidehara was once more pushed into opposition. According to rumours that reached Forbes sometime later, Shidehara's life had also been in danger on numerous occasions. As it happened, Shidehara would not have another opportunity to meet with Forbes before he left his posting as ambassador in March 1932.[124]

In November of the same year, Shidehara wrote to Forbes, who had by then returned to the US. In this letter, Shidehara objected to China's actions following the Manchurian Incident. In order 'to institute direct negotiations between the two Governments on the subject, the difficulties should have been adjusted long ago', he wrote. Yet China 'failed to appreciate the singleness of purpose shown in our overtures, and sought to fight out the case at Geneva'. Shidehara concluded by observing that 'the Sino-Japanese dispute should not be allowed to drift in such a way as to affect the friendly relations between America and Japan'.[125] To these comments Forbes responded sympathetically.

To summarise the above discussion, Stimson's comments must be understood in a broader context: Forbes failed to adequately warn Stimson that the details concerning Japanese supreme command had been given to him in the utmost confidence. There are also legitimate doubts as to whether either Forbes or Stimson had a correct understanding of the problem of supreme command, or of its seriousness for the

Japanese leadership.[126] Indeed, at the beginning, even Shidehara and Debuchi did not adequately grasp the essence of this problem and its political implications.

That said, an indirect cause of Stimson's comments was that Shidehara had placed too much trust in Forbes. Thus, he gave away too much information about matters relating to supreme command. These were details that normally would never have been revealed to outsiders. Shidehara had a friendly relationship with Forbes, and, as we have already seen, the building of relationships of trust was a fundamental tenet of Shidehara's 'honest diplomacy', which, in turn, constituted his guiding creed as a diplomat. On this occasion, however, Shidehara's 'honest diplomacy' led to unintended results. So, it came to pass that Shidehara ran into difficulties with the Japanese–American relationship, supposedly his field of expertise, and left the ministry to which he was so attached. Along the way, over 35 years had passed since he began as a consular assistant. It was early winter, and not long before his sixtieth birthday.

Endnotes

1   Itō and Hirose, *Makino Nobuaki Nikki*, 379; Ministry of Foreign Affairs Hundred-Year History Compilation Association, *Gaimushō no 100 Nen*, vol. 1, 928.

2   Kawashima Nobutarō to Ujita Naoyoshi, 1 July 1953, in 'Shidehara Heiwa Bunko', Reel 18.

3   'Eikoku Taishikan Sanjikan Saburi Sadao-kun no Enzetsu [A Speech by Mr. Saburi Sadao, Counsellor, Japanese Embassy in the U.K.], in Osaka Economic Association, ed., *Ōsaka Keizaikai Jōshūkai niokeru Enzetsu* [A Speech Given at the Regular Convention of the Osaka Economic Association] (Osaka: Osaka Economic Association, 1929), 2–5.

4   Shidehara, *Gaikō 50 Nen*, 102–103.

5   *Tokyo Asahi Shimbun*, 30 November, 1 December and 2 December 1929.

6   Shigemitsu Mamoru, 'Saburi Kōshi no Shi' [The death of Minister Saburi], *Chūgoku Kenkyū Geppō* 42, no. 11 (November 1988): 38–42.

7   Horinouchi, *Horinouchi Kensuke Kaikoroku*, 55–57.

8   Hattori, *Higashi Asia Kokusai Kankyō no Hendō to Nihon Gaikō, 1918–1931*, 264–65.

9   Shidehara, 'Washington Kaigi no Rimen-kan Sonota', 127–31; Hattori, *Higashi Asia Kokusai Kankyō no Hendō to Nihon Gaikō, 1918–1931*, 255–63.

10 See Akami Tomoko, *Internationalizing the Pacific: The United States, Japan and the Institute of Pacific Relations in War and Peace, 1919-1945* (London: Routledge, 2002).

11 Horiuchi to Shidehara, 16 September 1929, in 'Taiheiyō Mondai Chōsa-kai Kankei Ikken' [Institute of Pacific Relations], vol. 1, B.10.1.0.3, Diplomatic Archives of the Ministry of Foreign Affairs of Japan.

12 Interview with Baron Shidehara, 15 April 1926, in Ray Lyman Wilbur Papers, Box 42, Hoover Institution, Stanford University; Hattori Ryūji, 'Tanaka Jōsōbun to Nicchū Kankei' [The Tanaka memorial and the Sino-Japanese Relations], in *Minkoku Kōki Chūgoku Kokumin-tō Seiken no Kenkyū* [A study of the Chinese nationalist government in the late period of the Republic of China], ed. Chuo University Institute of Cultural Sciences (Hachiōji: Chūō University Press, 2005), 455–93;

Hattori Ryūji, 'Tanaka Jōsōbun wo Meguru Ronsō: Jitsuzon-setsu to Gizō-setsu no Aida' [The debate surrounding the 'Tanaka memorial to the emperor': Between theories of its authenticity and its fabrication], in *Kokkyō wo Koeru Rekishi Ninshiki: Nicchū Taiwa no Kokoromi* [Historical consciousness transcending national boundaries: An attempt at Sino-Japanese dialogue], ed. Liu Jie, Hiroshi Mitani, and Yang Daqing (University of Tokyo Press, 2006), 84–110.

13 Shidehara to Neville, US representative ambassador to Japan, 14 October 1929, in 'Bei Doku Chūsai Saiban narabini Wakai Jōyaku Kankei Ikken (Chōtei Jōyaku Shotei no Jōsetsu Iinkai wo Fukumu)' [Documents relating to the treaty on arbitration and amicable settlement between the US and Germany (including the permanent commission under the conciliation treaty)], B.5.0.0.G/U1, Diplomatic Archives of the Ministry of Foreign Affairs of Japan; Shidehara to Ernest Arthur Voreizsch, German ambassador to Japan, 14 October, ibid.; Shidehara, *Gaikō 50 Nen*, 157–58.

14 This section is based on my previous work: Hattori Ryūji, 'London Kaigun Gunshuku Kaigi to Nichi-Bei Kankei: Castle Chu-Nichi Beikoku Taishi no Manazashi' [The London Naval Conference on Disarmament and Japan–US relations: The gaze of Castle, US ambassador to Japan], *Shigaku Zasshi* 112, no. 7 (July 2003): 59–84.

15 For details on Japan's movements with respect to the London Conference, see Kobayashi Tatsuo, 'Kaigun Gunshuku Jōyaku' [The naval disarmament treaty], in *Taiheiyō Sensō eno Michi: Kaisen Gaikō-shi* [The road to the Pacific War: A diplomatic history of the commencement of the war], ed. Japanese International Politics Society Research Division for Causes of the Pacific War, vol. 1 (Tokyo: Asahi Shimbunsha, 1963), 1–160; Ikeda Kiyoshi, 'London Kaigun Jōyaku to Tōsuiken Mondai' [The London Naval Treaty and the problem of supreme command], *Ōsaka Shiritsu Daigaku Hōgaku Zasshi* 15, no. 2 (October 1968): 1–35; Itō Takashi, *Shōwa Shoki Seijishi Kenkyū: London Kaigun Gunshuku Mondai wo Meguru Sho-Seiji Shūdan no Taikō to Teikei* [A study of the political history of the early Shōwa period: Confrontation and partnership between various political organizations with respect to the London naval disarmament problem] (Tokyo: University of Tokyo Press, 1969); Shibata Shinichi, 'London Kaigun Gunshuku Kaigi nikansuru Ichi-Gokuhi-Den: Na wo Tsuraneta Hitobito to Yoshida Shigeru no Sono Go' [A top-secret telegram relating to the London Naval Conference on Disarmament: Participating individuals and what happened to Yoshida Shigeru afterwards], in., *Ningen, Yoshida Shigeru* [The person, Yoshida Shigeru], ed. Yoshida Shigeru Memorial Project Foundation (Tokyo: Chuōkōronsha, 1991), 249–66; Ikei Masaru and Hatano Masaru, 'London Kaigun Gunshuku Mondai to Hamaguchi Osachi' [The London naval disarmament problem and Hamaguchi Osachi], *Hōgaku Kenkyū* 63, no. 11 (November 1990): 1–34; Masuda Tomoko, *Tennōsei to Kokka: Kindai Nihon no Rikken Kunshusei* [The emperor system and the nation-state: Modern Japan's constitutional monarchy] (Tokyo: Aoki Shoten, 1999), 149–79; Kurono Taeru, *Teikoku Kokubō Hōshin no Kenkyū: Riku-Kai-Gun Kokubō Shisō no Tenkai to Tokuchō* [A study of the imperial defence policy: The development and characteristics of national defence theory in the army and navy] (Tokyo: Sōwasha, 2000), 275–95; Ōmae Shinya, 'London Kaigun Gunshuku Mondai niokeru Zaisei to Gunbi: Kaigun Hojū Mondai wo Meguru Seiji Katei' [The finance and armaments in the London naval disarmament problem: The political process surrounding the naval replenishment problem], *Suzuka Kokusai Daigaku Kiyō*, no. 7 (March 2000): 13–57; Banno Junji, *Nihon Seiji 'Shippai' no Kenkyū: Chūto Hanpa Gonomi no Kokumin no Yukue* [Research on the 'failure' of Japanese politics: Which way for a citizenry that favours half-measures] (Tokyo: Kōbōsha, 2001), 75–103; Katō Yōko, *Sensō no Ronri: Nichi-Ro Sensō kara Taiheiyō Sensō Made* [The logic of war: From the Russo-Japanese war to the Pacific War] (Tokyo: Keisō Shobō, 2005), 106–41; Itō Yukio, *Shōwa Tennō to Rikken Kunshusei no Hōkai* [The Shōwa emperor and the collapse of the system of constitutional monarchy] (Nagoya: Nagoya University Press, 2005), 139–224.

For previous research that assesses this topic from the perspective of Japanese–American relations, see Charles E. Neu, translated by Banno Junji, 'Higashi Asia niokeru America Gaikōkan' [American diplomats in East Asia], in *Washington Taisei to Nichi-Bei Kankei* [The Washington system and Japan–US relations], ed. Hosoya Chihiro and Saitō Makoto (Tokyo: University of Tokyo Press, 1978), 214–57; Kitaoka Shinichi, 'Washington Taisei to "Kokusai Kyōchō" no Seishin: MacMurray Memorandum (1935 Nen) niyosete' [The Washington system and the spirit of 'international cooperation': Examining the MacMurray memorandum (1935)], *Rikkyō Hōgaku*, no. 23 (December 1984): 68–113; Mitani Taiichirō, 'Senzen, Senchū-ki Nichi-Bei Kankei niokeru Beikoku Shinnichi-ha Gaikōkan no Yakuwari' [The role of US pro-Japan faction diplomats with respect to the Japan–US relationship during the prewar and wartime periods] (1) (2) (3) (4), *Gaikō Forum* 4, no. 9 (September 1991): 83–92, no. 10 (October 1991): 81–92, no. 11 (November 1991): 81–92, (December 1991): 67–80; Asada, *Ryō-Taisen-kan no Nichi-Bei Kankei*, 176–91; Hu, *Stanley K. Hornbeck and the Open Door Policy, 1919–1937*, 113–20; Alfred L. Castle, 'Ambassador Castle's Role in the Negotiations of the London Naval Conference' *Naval History*, (summer 1989): 16–21; Alfred L. Castle, *Diplomatic Realism: William R. Castle, Jr., and American Foreign Policy, 1919–1953* (Honolulu: University of Hawaii Press, 1998), 37–49; Iguchi Haruo, 'America no Kyokutō Seisaku: Herbert C. Hoover to Nichi-Bei Kankei' [The US's Far East policy: Herbert C. Hoover and Japan-US relations], in *Kan-Taiheiyō no Kokusai Chitsujo no Mosaku to Nihon: Daiichiji Sekai Taisen-go kara 55 Nen Taisei Seiritsu* [The search for an international order in the greater Pacific and Japan: From the aftermath of World War I to the establishment of the 1955 system], ed. Itō Yukio and Kawada Minoru (Tokyo: Yamakawa Shuppansha, 1999), 5–43.

16   Castle, who served as the US ambassador to Japan, recorded some of his own observations of the early stages of the London conference. See Castle to Cotton, 25 January 1930, Department of State, ed., *FRUS, 1930*, vol. 1 (Washington: Government Printing Office, 1945), 9–10.

17   His diary is held in Harvard University's Houghton Library. See William R. Castle, Jr., diary, Houghton Library, Harvard University; other Castle documents are found in the Herbert Hoover Presidential Library. See William R. Castle, Jr, Papers, Herbert Hoover Presidential Library.

18   Castle diary, vol. 16, 5 January 1930.

19   Castle diary, vol. 15, 11 December 1929.

20   Hattori, *Higashi Asia Kokusai Kankyō no Hendō to Nihon Gaikō, 1918–1931*, 255–63.

21   Ministry of Foreign Affairs, ed., *Nihon Gaikō Bunsho: 1930 Nen London Kaigun Kaigi* [Documents on Japanese foreign policy: The 1930 London Naval Conference], vol. 1 (Tokyo: Ministry of Foreign Affairs, 1983), 304–10.

22   Japanese delegation to Shidehara, 10 January 1930, ibid., 403–08.

23   Castle diary, vol. 16, 20 January 1930.

24   Castle diary, vol. 16, 24 January 1930.

25   Castle to Hoover, 27 January 1930, Herbert Hoover Papers, Box 995, Herbert Hoover Presidential Library.

26   Ibid.

27   Castle to Cotton, 14 February 1930, in Department of State, *FRUS, 1930*, vol. 1, 24–25.

28   Castle's diary, vol. 16, 15 February 1930. See also Shidehara to Japanese delegation, 15 February 1930, in Ministry of Foreign Affairs, ed., *Nihon Gaikō Bunsho: 1930 Nen London Kaigun Kaigi*, vol. 2 (Tokyo: Ministry of Foreign Affairs, 1984), 79–83.

29   Hirata Shinsaku, 'Beikoku Taishi Sai-Kaiken-ki' [Records of another meeting with the US ambassador], *Nihon oyobi Nihonjin*, no. 199 (March 1930): 73–76. The same manuscript was distributed in the form of a pamphlet. It is included in texts such as 'London Kaigun Kaigi Ikken: Yoron narabini Shimbun Ronchō (Honpō)' [London navy meeting: Public opinion and press comments (Japan)], vol. 2., B.12.0.0.1-4, Diplomatic Archives of the Ministry of Foreign Affairs of Japan; 'Saitō Makoto Kankei Bunsho' [Documents relating to Saitō Makoto], Document Department, Reel 249, Modern Japanese Political History Materials Room, National Diet Library.

For a monograph that outlines Hirata's thinking on disarmament, see Hirata Shinsaku, *Gunshuku no Fuan to Taiheiyō Sensō* [Concerns about disarmament and a Pacific War] (Tokyo: Tenjinsha, 1930). Pages 106–07, 125, and 213 contain criticism of Shidehara. On page 129 of the same text, Hirata stated that, when he subsequently met with Castle, Castle did his utmost to conceal that the US viewed Japan as a potential enemy. However, in Castle's own diary, there is no entry corresponding to Hirata's description of such a discussion.

For research on Hirata Shinsaku, see Sawada Jirō, *Kindai Nihonjin no America-kan: Nichi-Ro Sensō Igo wo Chūshin ni* [The modern Japanese perspective on the US: Focusing on the period following the Russo-Japanese War] (Tokyo: Keiō University Press, 1999), iv, 221–82; Louise Young, *Sōdōin Teikoku* [Japan's Total Empire], trans. Katō Yōko, Kawashima Shin, Takamitsu Yoshie, Chiba Isao and Furuichi Daisuke (Tokyo: Iwanami Shoten, 2001), 46.

30   Castle to Cotton, 24 February 1930, in Department of State, *FRUS, 1930,* vol. 1, 30; Shidehara–Castle talks, 25 February 1930, in Ministry of Foreign Affairs, *Nihon Gaikō Bunsho: 1930 Nen London Kaigun Kaigi*, vol. 2, 95–97; Castle diary, vol. 16, 26 February 1930.

31   Japanese delegation to Shidehara, 26 February 1930, in Ministry of Foreign Affairs, *Nihon Gaikō Bunsho: 1930 Nen London Kaigun Kaigi*, vol. 2, 97–99.

32   Castle to Cotton, 7 March 1930, in Department of State, *FRUS, 1930,* vol. 1, 49–51; Castle diary, vol. 16, 9 March 1930.

33   Ministry of Foreign Affairs, *Nihon Gaikō Nenpyō narabini Shuyō Bunsho*, vol. 1, 143–44; Shidehara to Japanese delegation, 15 March 1930, in Ministry of Foreign Affairs, *Nihon Gaikō Nenpyō narabini Shuyō Bunsho*, vol. 2, 133–34.

34   Ikei, Hatano and Kurosawa, *Hamaguchi Osachi Nikki, Zuikanroku*, 312–443; Yoshida to Makino, 26 January 1930, in Yoshida Shigeru Memorial Project Foundation, *Yoshida Shigeru Shokan*, 627–28; diary of Katō Hiroharu, 21–25 January 1930, in *Zoku Gendai-shi Shiryō, vol. 5: Kaigun—Katō Hiroharu Nikki* [Modern historical material, continued, 5: The navy—the diary of Katō Hiroharu], ed. Itō Takashi, Suzuki Jun, Koike Seiichi, Taura Masanori and Furukawa Takahisa (Tokyo: Misuzu Shobō, 1994), 90; diary of Okada Keisuke, 23 March – 2 April 1930, in *Okada Keisuke Kaikoroku* [The memoirs of Okada Keisuke], ed. Okada Sadahiro (Tokyo: Chūōkōronsha, 1987), 265–75.

35   Harada Kumao, *Saionji-kō to Seikyoku* [Lord Saionji and the political situation], vol. 1 (Tokyo: Iwanami Shoten, 1950), 28, 32–36; Suzuki Hajime, ed., *Suzuki Kantarō Jiden* [The autobiography of Suzuki Kantarō] (Tokyo: Jiji Tsūshinsha), 1968, 255–58; Takahashi Hiroshi, Awaya Kentarō and Otabe Yūji, eds, *Shōwa Shoki no Tennō to Kyūchū: Jijūjichō Kawai Yahachi Nikki* [The emperor and the imperial court in the early Shōwa period: The diary of Deputy Grand Chamberlain Kawai Yahachi], vol. 4 (Tokyo: Iwanami Shoten, 1994), 48–50, 56, 89; Shōyū Society Incorporated, *Okabe Nagakage Nikki*, 330; Castle diary, vol. 16, 16 March 1930. While the Makino Nobuaki diary entries for February to July 1930 are missing, there are still entries, such as that for 13 September, that reveal his support for the Hamaguchi cabinet. See Itō and Hirose, *Makino Nobuaki Nikki*, 408.

36   Castle to Cotton, 18 March 1930, in Department of State, *FRUS, 1930,* vol. 1, 66–67.

In his entry for 27 March 1930, Naval General Staff Director Katō wrote: 'Meeting with Prime Minister Hamaguchi at 3 o'clock this afternoon at the prime minister's residence. General Okada was also in attendance and stressed his objections'. See Itō et al., *Zoku Gendai-shi Shiryō*, vol. 5, 93. See also the discussion with Tōgō Heihachirō, on 16 March 1930, ibid., 469–70.

37   Ikei, Hatano and Kurosawa, *Hamaguchi Osachi Nikki, Zuikanroku*, 313–443; Shidehara to Japanese delegation, 18 March 1930, in Ministry of Foreign Affairs, *Nihon Gaikō Bunsho: 1930 Nen London Kaigun Kaigi*, vol. 2, 141–42.

According to Harada, *Saionji-kō to Seikyoku*, vol. 1, 25:

> Meanwhile, a statement of some form was suddenly issued from the Naval General Staff. The vice-chief handed it over to the Rengō Tsushin company. Basically, of the so-called three basic principles of the navy, the two principles of maintaining 70 per cent cruisers and 78,000 tons of submersibles would be adhered to, no matter what.

A related statement can be found in the Hamaguchi Osachi diary from 22 March 1930:

> We received a phone call from the foreign minister regarding a libelous document issued by the navy (this was now the second such inflammatory document, but it did not make it into the newspapers).

See Ikei, Hatano and Kurosawa, *Hamaguchi Osachi Nikki, Zuikanroku*, 315. A similar statement appears in ibid., 443–44.

According to a journal entry of the same date by Adjutant General Hori:

> Vice-Chief Suetsugu knew that newspaper reporters were aware of the distribution of 'prints' concerning the present problem and took action to prevent their disclosure. However, several smaller papers nevertheless proceeded to publish them.

See Kobayashi Tatsuo and Shimada Toshihiko, eds, *Gendai-shi Shiryo, vol. 7: Manshū Jihen* [Modern historical material, vol. 7: The Manchurian Incident] (Tokyo: Misuzu Shobō, 1964), 36. *Tokyo Nichi Shimbun* is the *Mainichi Shimbun* at present.

38   Ministry of Foreign Affairs Research Department, Section 4, ed., 'Wakatsuki Reijirō Dan Jutsu London Kaigun Gunshuku Kaigi [The London Naval Conference on Disarmament, described by Baron Wakatsuki Reijirō], 10 October 1939, in Hirose, *Kindai Gaikō Kaikoroku*, vol. 3, 248; Shidehara to Japanese delegation, 19 March 1930, in Ministry of Foreign Affairs, *Nihon Gaikō Bunsho: 1930 Nen London Kaigun Kaigi*, vol. 2, 144–46; Castle diary, vol. 16, 18 March 1930; Shidehara to Japanese delegation, 19 March 1930, in Ministry of Foreign Affairs, *Nihon Gaikō Bunsho: 1930 Nen London Kaigun Kaigi*, vol. 2, 147–49. Wakatsuki also stated that there were those among the delegation who argued in favour of cooperation between Japan and France, yet he did not specify who those individuals were. See Wakatsuki Reijirō, *Meiji, Taishō, Shōwa Seikai Hishi: Kofū-an Kaikoroku* [A secret history of the political world of the Meiji, Taishō and Shōwa eras: Memoirs of an old-fashioned man] (Tokyo: Kōdansha, 1983), 311.

39   Shidehara to Saitō Makoto, 21 March 1930, in 'Saitō Makoto Kankei Bunsho', Document Department, Reel 34; Henry Lewis Stimson diary, 19 March 1930, Henry Lewis Stimson Papers, Reel 2, Yale University Library.

40   Castle diary, vol. 16, 21 March 1930.

41   Castle candidly presented this opinion to President Hoover in correspondence, writing:

> I have not seen and do not expect to see the Prime Minister. He is a silent man who speaks only Japanese and is not known by any of the Diplomatic Corps. If I asked for an interview it would probably be given but it would create a sensation in the press which would have a very bad effect.

Conversely, Castle spoke highly of Finance Minister Inoue and Foreign Minister Shidehara. Another important point in Castle's correspondence with Hoover was his noting that he was using Makino, the lord keeper of the Privy Seal, as a mediator for communicating with the Shōwa emperor. To put it simply, the scenario presented by Castle was that Shidehara would summarise the cabinet's diplomatic instructions and Makino would convince the emperor. In any respect, Castle's position was that 'I must work within the recognized channels'. See Castle to Hoover, 25 March 1930, Hoover Papers, Box 995. See also Castle to Cotton, 21 March 1930, in Department of State, *FRUS, 1930*, vol. 1, 70.

42   Castle's diary, vol. 16, 24 March 1930; Stimson to Cotton, 2 March 1930, in Department of State, *FRUS, 1930*, vol. 1, 75; Stimson to Cotton, 28 March, ibid., 91; Shidehara to Japanese delegation, 19 March 1930, in Ministry of Foreign Affairs, *Nihon Gaikō Bunsho: 1930 Nen London Kaigun Kaigi*, vol. 2, 149–51; Shidehara to Japanese delegation, March 24, ibid., 165–66.

43   Shidehara to Japanese delegation, 24 March 1930, in Ministry of Foreign Affairs, *Nihon Gaikō Bunsho: 1930 Nen London Kaigun Kaigi*, vol. 2, 164–65; Shidehara to Japanese delegation, 24 March 1930, ibid., 165–66. After Castle returned home, he checked with Ballantine concerning the circumstances of the message sent to Hamaguchi. See Ballantine memoirs, Joseph W. Ballantine Papers, Box 1, Hoover Institution, Stanford University.

44   Ministry of Foreign Affairs, *Nihon Gaikō Nenpyō narabini Shuyō Bunsho*, vol. 2, 147–57; Ikei, Hatano and Kurosawa, *Hamaguchi Osachi Nikki, Zuikanroku*, 320, 445–47; Kawada Minoru, ed., *Hamaguchi Osachi Shū: Ronjūtsu, Koen Hen* [The Hamaguchi Osachi collection: Statements, lectures section] (Tokyo: Miraisha, 2000), 253–56; Castle's diary, vol. 16, 3 April 1930; from Stimson to Cotton, 1 April 1930, in Department of State, *FRUS, 1930*, vol. 1, 99–100.

45   Diary of Nara Takeji, 1 April 1930, in *Jijū Bukanchō Nara Takeji Nikki, Kaikoroku* [The diary and memoirs of Nara Takeji, chief aide-de-camp to the emperor of Japan], ed. Hatano Sumio, Kurosawa Fumitaka, Hatano Masaru, Sakurai Ryōju and Kobayashi Kazuyuki, vol. 3 (Tokyo: Kashiwa Shobō, 2000), 217.

46   Inaba Masao, Kobayashi Tatsuo, Shimada Toshihiko and Tsunoda Jun, eds, *Taiheiyō Sensō eno Michi: Kaisen Gaikō-shi* [The road to the Pacific War: A diplomatic history of the commencement of the war], extra vol.: Resources (Tokyo: Asahi Shimbunsha, 1963), 48. See also Itō et al., *Zoku Gendai-shi Shiryō*, vol. 5, 94.

47   Diary of Nara Takeji, 2 April 1930, in Hatano et al., *Jijū Bukanchō Nara Takeji Nikki, Kaikoroku*, vol. 3, 217.

48   In fact, as indicated by the aforementioned Kato Jōsōbun (report to the throne), the point of emphasis was: 'it will bring about a serious change in our plan of operations based upon the policy of national defense'.

The report 'London Kaigun Jōyaku Teiketsu Keii' [The circumstances of the signing of the London Naval Reduction Treaty], arranged at the end of 1930 by Adjutant General Hori Teikichi, having also quoted this section, states:

> The public have even mistakenly viewed this report to the throne as constituting an objection to the diplomatic instructions issued by the government … whereas it in fact corresponded with the unanimous agreement reached by the House of Councilors' meeting on military affairs, held at a later date.

See Inaba et al., *Taiheiyō Sensō eno Michi*, extra vol.: Resources, 48; Kobayashi and Shimada, *Gendai-shi Shiryo*, vol. 7, 92; 'Hōtōbun' [Reply to the throne] is included in Inaba et al., *Taiheiyō Sensō eno Michi*, extra vol.: Resources, 55–56; Kobayashi and Shimada, *Gendai-shi Shiryo*, vol. 7, 96.

Further, just after the report to the throne, Katō made the following statement to the press:

> While I cannot agree to the number of troops proposed by the United States … with respect to the current instructions, the navy will be sure to not act rashly, adjusting to the circumstances as they unfold and taking the appropriate steps.

See *Tokyo Asahi Shimbun*, evening edition, April 3, 1930.

49   Consequently, at the House of Peers society meeting (5 April), Suetsugu presented figures for the Japan–US compromise proposal, asserting: 'light cruisers are at 70%, however, large cruisers are at 60%, in line with the initial U.S. request, and submersibles are to be reduced to one-third of the current number'. He added: 'As [vice-chief of] the Naval General Staff, I presented my own position to the emperor in a report the following day [2 April]'. Suetsugu further argued: 'If Japan simply gives in to the proposal of the U.S., we will be unable to have a single large cruiser or a single submersible', and he concluded with the assertion that, 'the establishment of such an agreement would naturally lead to critical shortcomings in national defense'. See Hatano Masaru, 'Hamaguchi-ke Shozō no "Hamaguchi Osachi Bunsho"' ['Hamaguchi Osachi documents' held by the Hamaguchi family], *Hōgaku Kenkyū* 67, no. 7 (July 1994): 103–05.

50   Meeting between the Shōwa emperor and John Tilley, ambassador for the UK, 13 April 1930, in 'London Kaigun Kaigi Ikken' [London Navy Meeting], vol. 2, B.12.0.0.1-4, Diplomatic Archives of the Ministry of Foreign Affairs of Japan.

51   Shidehara to Japanese delegation, 15 April, in 'London Kaigun Kaigi Ikken', vol. 2; Sawada, *Gaisenmon Hiroba*, 114–16; Shibata, 'London Kaigun Gunshuku Kaigi nikansuru Ichi-Gokuhi-Den', 249–66; Hatano, *Hirohito Kōtaishi Europe Gaiyū-ki*, 206.

52   Department of State, *FRUS, 1930*, vol. 1, 107–25; Ministry of Foreign Affairs, *Nihon Gaikō Nenpyō narabini Shuyō Bunsho*, vol. 2, 159–61.

53   *Teikoku Gikai Shūgiin Giji Sokkiroku* [Shorthand record of the proceedings of the Imperial Diet House of Representatives], vol. 54 (Tokyo: University of Tokyo Press, 1983), 13, 16, 26.

54   Itō et al., *Zoku Gendai-shi Shiryō*, vol. 5, 96; diary of Okada Keisuke, 2 and 11 May 1930, in Okada, *Okada Keisuke Kaikoroku*, 281–82, 286–87. Katō's displeasure with Shidehara is outlined in Harada, *Saionji-kō to Seikyoku*, vol. 1, 47. Katō's views on the violation of supreme command authority (*tōsuiken kanpan*) are evident in his correspondence to Saitō Makoto, 6 May 1930, in 'Saitō Makoto Kankei Bunsho', Document Department, Reel 164.

55   The Seiyūkai asserted, quite bombastically, that Grand Chamberlain Suzuki Kantarō had colluded with the cabinet to prevent the '*Kato Jōsō*' (Katō's report to the throne) before the diplomatic instructions were sent. Reflecting on this period, Suzuki Kantarō wrote:

5. THE LONDON NAVAL CONFERENCE AND THE MANCHURIAN INCIDENT

At the time, I felt annoyed that the chief of the Naval General Staff did not have a suitably clear understanding of the responsibilities of his own position, and that this led to a lot of pointless confusion. Reflecting upon that problem now from a broader perspective, I think that one way of interpreting the situation was that the chief of the Naval General Staff was played with by some conspirators within the Seiyūkai.

See Harada, *Saionji-kō to Seikyoku*, vol. 1, 48; Suzuki, *Suzuki Kantarō Jiden*, 258. It should also be noted that in 'London Gunshuku Kaigi-ron' [My view on the London Naval Conference on Disarmament], November 1933, Kobayashi Seizō argued that the opposition party was in 'collusion' with the Naval General Staff. See Itō Takashi and Nomura Minoru, eds, *Kaigun Taishō Kobayashi Seizō Oboegaki* [The memorandum of Admiral Kobayashi Seizō] (Tokyo: Yamakawa Shuppansha, 1981), 60.

56   Castle diary, vol. 16, 8 May 1930.

57   Castle diary, vol. 16, 31 May 1930.

58   Castle to Stimson, 26 April 1930, Nelson T. Johnson Papers, vol. 13, Manuscript Division, Library of Congress.

59   'Teikoku no Tai-Shi Gaikō Seisaku Kankei Ikken' [Diplomatic policy of Japan towards China], vol. 2, A.1.1.0.10, Diplomatic Archives of the Ministry of Foreign Affairs of Japan. See also Koike, *Manshū Jihen to Tai-Chūgoku Seisaku*, 32; Nishida Toshihiro, 'Washington Taisei no Henyō to Shidehara Gaikō: 1929–1931 Nen' [Shifts in the Washington system and Shidehara diplomacy: 1929–1931] (1), *Hōgaku Ronsō* 149, no. 3 (June 2001): 89.

60   Teikoku no Tai-Shi Gaikō Seisaku Kankei Ikken', vol. 2.

61   Castle diary, vol. 16, 23, 28, 29, 31 May 1930.

62   Address by Castle at dinner hosted by the America–Japan Society at the Peers' Club, 23 May 1930, Castle Papers, Box 27. See also address by Tokugawa, 23 May 1930, in 'Nichi-Bei Kyōkai Shiryō' [Historical documents of the America–Japan Society], A5–05, America–Japan Society; *Tokyo Asahi Shimbun*, 24 May 1930; *Trans-Pacific*, 29 May 1930, in Castle Papers, Box 27; Hirobe, *Japanese Pride, American Prejudice*, 135.

63   Address by Hanihara, 23 May 1930, *America–Japan Society Special Bulletin*, no. 11 (1931): 14–16, in 'Nichi-Bei Kyōkai Shiryō', C3–11.

64   John Tilley, *London to Tokyo* (London: Hutchinson, 1942), 204.

65   Sawada Setsuzō, consul general in New York, to Shidehara, 13 February 1930, in 'Makino Nobuaki Kankei Bunsho', Document Department, Reel 35; Debuchi Katsuji, ambassador to the US, to Shidehara, 26 February, ibid.

66   Castle remained the ambassador to Japan from the evening after returning home until the end of June. On 30 June, Castle wrote a letter to Matsudaira, Japan's ambassador to the UK, expressing some regret that his service as ambassador was due to end just a few hours later. In this letter, Castle praised the results of the Matsudaira–Reed negotiations and then remarked on how to approach the disarmament treaty:

> It is true that the best treaty is one which will be gladly accepted by all parties concerned, but I doubt whether this is ever possible in a treaty which has broad political angles. The next best treaty, therefore, is one which causes irritation in all the countries concerned because then one can well believe that all have made wise compromises for the sake of a happy result.

Castle to Matsudaira, 30 June 1930, Castle Papers, Box 9.

67   Castle to Shidehara, 25 June 1930, Castle Papers, Box 9; Shidehara to Castle, 27 July 1930, Castle Papers, Box 9.

68   Castle to Forbes, 27 June 1930, Castle Papers, Box 9; Kimura Atsushi, consul in Chicago, to Shidehara, 12 July 1930, in 'London Kaigun Kaigi Ikken: Yoron narabini Shimbun Ronchō (Beikoku)' [London navy meeting: Public opinion and press comments (the U.S.)], B.12.0.0.1-4, Diplomatic Archives of the Ministry of Foreign Affairs of Japan; *Chugai Shōgyō Shinpō*, 29 August

1930. Forbes was also residing in the Imperial Hotel, which was not exactly a pleasant place to stay. See Forbes to Castle, 18 September 1930, Castle Papers, Box 9. The completion of the US ambassador's residence would have to wait until 1931.

69   Reminiscences of Sansom; Inoue Junnosuke Essay Collection Editing Association, ed., *Inoue Junnosuke: Ronsō* [Inoue Junnosuke: Essay Collection], vol. 4 (Tokyo: Hara Shobō, 1982), 557–60.

70   Castle to Shidehara, 3 October 1930, Castle Papers, Box 9. Drafts of letters from Shidehara to Castle in September 1930 that outline the attitudes of the Privy Council can be found in 'Makino Nobuaki Kankei Bunsho', Document Department, Reel 18.

Katō's successor was Admiral Taniguchi Naomi. According to the Bureau of Naval Affairs Chief Hori Teikichi (in the aforementioned 'London Kaigun Jōyaku Teiketsu Keii'):

> Even though the change of naval general staff director happened on that very day, the minister had arranged it. This was done, of course, not because Chief of the Naval General Staff Katō's report to the throne was delivered.

See also Kobayashi and Shimada, *Gendai-shi Shiryo*, vol. 7, 94.

Further, in his diary entry for 10 June, Nara Takeji stated that the emperor also went through Nara to secure Tōgō Heihachirō's approval to have Taniguchi installed in this position. At the time, Tōgō responded:

> To the effect that he felt it extremely regrettable that the treaty details were improper, and that diplomatic instructions have been issued without first receiving the approval of the Naval General Staff.

Tōgō also 'expressed dissatisfaction with the actions of plenipotentiary Takarabe'. See Hatano et al., *Jijū Bukanchō Nara Takeji Nikki, Kaikoroku*, vol. 3, 235–36. Banno, *Nihon Seiji 'Shippai' no Kenkyū*, 93, looks at the diary entry from that same day in Takarabe Takeshi's diary, asserting that the emperor did not respond directly to Katō's resignation; instead, he entrusted Navy Minister Takarabe to consider the matter. Takarabe issued a report to the effect that Taniguchi supported the London Treaty. It was only after receiving this confirmation that the emperor gave his own approval. See 'Takarabe Takeshi Kankei Bunsho' [Documents relating to Takarabe Takeshi], vol. 41, Modern Japanese Political History Materials Room, National Diet Library.

On that same day, 10 June, both Navy Vice-Minister Yamanashi and Suetsugu, vice chief of the Naval General Staff, were transferred from their roles. According to the Bureau of Naval Affairs Chief Hori Teikichi, in 'London Kaigun Jōyaku Teiketsu Keii', the former was transferred due to illness, while the latter was transferred due to voicing his personal views in a newspaper on 17 March. See Kobayashi and Shimada, *Gendai-shi Shiryo*, vol. 7, 95. Their replacements were Vice Admiral Kobayashi Seizō and Vice Admiral Nagano Osami, respectively.

71   Debuchi Katsuji, 'Beikoku Hai-Nichi Imin-hō Shūsei Mondai' [The US Japanese Exclusion Act revision problem], October 1939, in Hirose, *Kindai Gaikō Kaikoroku*, vol. 4, 225–75; memorandum by Stimson, 30 October 1930, in Department of State, *FRUS, 1930*, vol. 3 (Washington: Government Printing Office, 1945), 315. See also Takahashi Katsuhiro, '"Beikoku Hai-Nichi Imin-hō Shūsei Mondai" to Chu-Bei Taishi Debuchi Katsuji' ['The US Japanese Exclusion Act revision problem' and Ambassador to the US Debuchi Katsuji], *Nihon Rekishi*, no. 523 (December 1991): 59–75.

72   In other words, according to Castle, 'Debuchi realizes that he will not remain very much longer as Ambassador in Washington and that, for the sake of his own reputation, he wants to clear up this situation'. The aforementioned correspondence with Shidehara implies that Castle thought Shidehara was prudent about the immigration problem and, conversely, he saw Debuchi's attitude as rash. According to Castle's understanding, Debuchi was also in a hurry to resolve the immigration problem, because he wanted Japan to stay within the framework of the naval treaty.

However, Castle thought that the naval issue and the immigration problem should not be directly linked. On this matter, Castle received confirmation from senators Reed and Robinson and Secretary of State Stimson and sent a private message to Forbes. These details also indicate that Castle had more trust in Shidehara than in Debuchi. See Castle to Forbes, 4 December 1930, Castle Papers, Box 9.

73   Castle to Dooman, 10 October 1930, Castle Papers, Box 9; Johnson to Hornbeck, 31 October 1930, Johnson Papers, vol. 14.

5. THE LONDON NAVAL CONFERENCE AND THE MANCHURIAN INCIDENT

74   As one example, on the matter of what measures to take with respect to the Sino-Soviet conflict that broke out in the fall of 1929, G. C. Hanson, US consul in Harbin, created a lengthy memorandum together with members of the State Department's Division of Far Eastern Affairs. However, what was handed over to Stimson from Hornbeck was only the concluding section. The section stated that Stimson's approach to China led to the restoration of the Chinese Eastern Railway. The conservative of Chinese north-eastern political power was also viewed as having a close relationship with Japan. See Hornbeck to Stimson, 4 November 1930, Stimson Papers, Reel 80.

75   *Teikoku Gikai Shūgiin Iinkaigiroku* [Record of the Imperial Diet House of Representatives Committee], Reel 6 (Tokyo: Rinsen Shoten, 1989), 196–202.

76   Ibid., 199.

77   Shidehara, *Gaikō 50 Nen*, 137–39; Nitobe to Castle, 7 March 1931, Castle Papers, Box 9.

78   For further details on this point, see Hattori, *Higashi Asia Kokusai Kankyō no Hendō to Nihon Gaikō, 1918–1931*, Chapter 1.

79   Castle to Hoover, 7 April 1930, Hoover Papers, Box 995.

80   Castle diary, vol. 16, 27 April 1930.

81   Imperial Japanese Naval General Staff, 'Washington Kaigi-go niokeru Beikoku no Senbi' [US military preparedness following the Washington Conference], 14 December 1929, in 'Saitō Makoto Kankei Bunsho', Document Department, Reel 164; Katō Hiroharu, 'Gunshuku Shoken' [Opinion on disarmament], January 1930, ibid.; Seventh London Naval Treaty Investigation Committee, 5 September 1930, in *Nihon Gaikō Bunsho: Kaigun Gunbi Seigen Jōyaku Sūmitsuin Shinsa Kiroku* [Documents on Japanese foreign policy: Naval Armament Limitation Treaty Privy Council investigation records], ed. Ministry of Foreign Affairs (Tokyo: Ministry of Foreign Affairs, 1984), 234–35.

82   Yoshida Shigeru, *Kaisō 10 Nen* [Reflections on a decade], vol. 4 (Tokyo: Shinchōsha, 1958), 102, 148–49.

83   Yoshida to Makino, around the end of February 1930, in 'Makino Nobuaki Kankei Bunsho', Document Department, Reel 77. According to Kase Toshikazu, Yoshida's view was:

> Tanaka was somebody who understood politics, but Shidehara was hopeless. The cabinet meeting would end. And even if the ministers were all going to have a meal together, he would simply say 'OK then, goodbye' and return to the Ministry of Foreign Affairs. We had a senior official dining saloon, and we would all pass a little time eating something like curry rice and chatting about inconsequential matters. You can't deal with politics acting like that. I would usually be the one making up for this deficiency [on Shidehara's behalf].

See Kase Toshikazu, 'Yoshida Shigeru wo Kataru' [On Yoshida Shigeru], *Kasumigaseki-kai Kaihō*, no. 280 (January 1969): 16–17.

84   It was already a different age from that of the Paris Peace Conference when Williams, the former chief of the US State Department's Division of Far Eastern Affairs, had heaped praise on Wellington Koo, plenipotentiary representative for China. Conversely, Williams was scornful of plenipotentiary Makino, who stubbornly persisted in fighting for Japan's interests in Shandong. See Castle's diary, vol. 16, 5, 6, 11 February, 16, 29 March, 12, 17 April, and 17, 21, 28, 31 May 1930. See also Shidehara to Makino, 7 June 1930, in 'Makino Nobuaki Kankei Bunsho', Document Department, Reel 37; Williams (Paris) to Breckinridge Long (Washington, DC, third assistant secretary of state), 21 February 1919, Williams Papers, Box 1; Higuchi, *Nihon Kaigun kara Mita Nicchu Kankei-shi Kenkyū*, 121.

85   Castle to Stimson, 10 March 1930, *Records of the U.S. Department of State Relating to the Internal Affairs of Japan, 1930–1939*, Reel 1.

86   Hori Teikichi journal, 25 March 1930, in Kobayashi and Shimada, *Gendai-shi Shiryo*, vol. 7, 37.

87   Nagai Ryūtarō, 'Shidehara Gaikō to Tai-Shi Bōeki no Kōten' [Shidehara diplomacy and the improvement of trade with China], *Minsei* 3, no. 11 (November 1929): 28–29; Nagai Ryūtarō, 'Shidehara Gaikō no Konpon Hōshin to London Jōyaku' [The fundamental orientation of Shidehara diplomacy and the London treaty], *Minsei* 4, no. 9 (September 1930): 26–31. For more recent

research on Nagai Ryūtarō, see Sakamoto Kenzō, 'Nagai Ryūtarō no Nicchū Teikei-ron: Daiichiji Taisen-ki wo Chūshin ni' [Nagai Ryūtarō's argument for Sino-Japanese Partnership: Focusing on the era of World War I], *Hōgaku Kenkyū* 73, no. 9 (September 2000): 33–73.

88   Extraordinary meeting of the supreme council of the Navy, 15 March 1930, in Inaba et al., *Taiheiyō Sensō eno Michi*, extra vol.: Resources, 13; Katō's diary entry for 18 February includes the following: 'Spoke with Shidehara on the topic of "Castle" and the U.S. Navy planning for a potential Tokyo air raid'. See Itō et al., *Zoku Gendai-shi Shiryō*, vol. 5, 92.

89   This situation improved after the war, as the role of US ambassador to Japan became important. Figures who took this position included former Harvard University Professor Edwin O. Reischauer, future undersecretary of state U. Alexis Johnson, Labor Secretary James D. Hodgson, Democratic Party Senate Floor Leader Michael Mansfield, former vice president Walter F. Mondale and former house speaker Thomas S. Foley. For general information on US ambassadors to Japan in the postwar period, see Ikei Masaru, *Chu-Nichi America Taishi* [US ambassadors to Japan] (Tokyo: Bungei Shunjū, 2001).

90   As Minohara Toshihiro pointed out, according to what Dooman told Castle, the phrasing 'grave consequences' contained within the Hanihara letter, which was an important moment in passing the Japanese Exclusion Act, was written by MacMurray, the chief of the State Department's Division of Far Eastern Affairs. Dooman learned of this from Taketomi Toshihiko, chief of the International Trade Bureau at the Ministry of Foreign Affairs. Castle trusted Dooman and wrote in his diary, 'Dooman I like immensely. His knowledge of things Japanese is endless'. See Castle's diary, vol. 16, 11, 25 February 1930; Minohara, *Hai-Nichi Imin-hō to Nichi-Bei Kankei*, 197.

It should be noted that Dooman himself publicly reflected upon the link between the Japanese Exclusion Act and the 'grave consequences' phrasing. In a May 1962 interview, Dooman recalled the address of Sakatani Yoshirō, member of the House of Peers, who stated that, if the Japanese Exclusion Act were passed, 'it would prejudice the willingness of the Japanese people to continue in the collaboration which was the ultimate object of the nine-power treaty'. He then began to speak on the circumstances surrounding the Hanihara letter. According to Dooman, when Secretary of State Hughes requested that Hanihara Masanao, Japan's ambassador to the US, write a letter addressed to Hughes, Hanihara wrote the letter draft while consulting Sakatani's address to the House of Peers.

According to Dooman, although Sakatani saw the passage of the Japanese Exclusion Act as entailing 'grave consequences', what Sakatani meant by those 'grave consequences' was not war or something similar but Japan's abandoning cooperation with the other Great Powers on China policy. Dooman stated that this was the actual context within which Hanihara used the expression 'grave consequences'. Hughes and MacMurray, who confidentially received a copy of the draft from Hanihara, proposed several revisions. They did not, at this stage, object to the language of 'grave consequences', giving it their implicit consent. Yet this expression would then be singled out by individuals such as Senate Diplomatic Affairs Committee Chief Henry Cabot Lodge, who criticised it as representing a threat. As a result, according to Dooman, the Japanese Exclusion Act was passed. See reminiscences of Dooman.

There are no surviving ministry records that provide evidence of a causal relationship between the Sakatani address and Hanihara letter. That said, at the very least, with respect to his remarks on the Sakatani address, Dooman's recollections are basically correct. In his address to the House of Peers on 23 January 1924, Sakatani began by remarking that he had 'a deep affection' for the US. Yet, he expressed concerns about the efforts of individuals such as Albert Johnson and John E. Raker in the US Congress. For Sakatani, if the Japanese Exclusion Act were to pass, it would 'lead to an extremely loathsome result for Japan–U.S. relations'. Sakatani forcefully argued that, even if it did not lead to war, such a decision would be 'completely inconsistent with the spirit of the naval limitation treaty that was agreed upon at the famous Washington Naval Conference, as well as with the spirit of other such treaties'. As Dooman also noted, Sakatani, who had served as honorary vice-president of the America–Japan Society, had no reason to risk a possible war between the two nations.

On Sakatani's address, see *Teikoku Gikai Kizokuin Giji Sokkiroku, vol. 44: Dai 48, 49-kai Gikai, Taishō 12 Nen* [Shorthand record of the proceedings of the Imperial Diet House of Peers, vol. 44: Diet Nos 48, 49, Taisho 12] (Tokyo: University of Tokyo Press, 1982), 47–49. Also see Viscount Sakatani

Memorial Project Foundation, ed., *Sakatani Yoshirō Den* [The biography of Sakatani Yoshirō] (Tokyo: Viscount Sakatani Memorial Project Foundation, 1951), 706. Texts that shed light on Sakatani's perspective on the US include Sakatani Sōkō [Sakatani Manuscript], 6 June 1921, in 'Sakatani Yoshirō Kankei Bunsho', Document Department, no. 812; address given to the directors of the Japan Peace Society by Sakatani, 13 May 1921, in *Japan Advertiser*, 24 June 1921, in 'Sakatani Yoshirō Kankei Bunsho', Document Department, no. 814.

At that time, Sakatani debated the Japanese Exclusion Act with a number of individuals, including Foreign Minister Matsui Keishirō; Saburi Sadao, who, after returning to Japan, became the acting director of the International Trade Bureau at the Ministry of Foreign Affairs; Akamatsu Sukeyuki, director of the Immigration Division at the International Trade Bureau; Sawada Setsuzō, director of both the correspondence section and the translation section; Hanihara Masanao, Japan's previous ambassador to the US; and Cyrus E. Woods, the US ambassador to Japan. For further details on these discussions, see Sakatani Yoshirō's diary, 16, 24 March, 25 April, 24, 25, 27, 28 May and 2, 5 June 1924, in 'Sakatani Yoshirō Kankei Bunsho', Document Department, no. 698; Sakatani's notebook, 2, 7, February and 1 November 1924, in 'Sakatani Yoshirō Kankei Bunsho', Document Department, no. 751.

For further details on the manner in which Sakatani, as chairman of the Carnegie Endowment for International Peace Economic Research Association, cooperated with matters such as the Manchurian Inquiry, see 'Sakatani Yoshirō Bunsho' [Sakatani Yoshirō documents], nos 60, 81–84, Institute of Social Science Library, the University of Tokyo.

91 Ballantine was also the first to recognise that the 'Tanaka Jōsōbun' [Tanaka memorial]—which was disseminated just before the London conference and handed over to him by Hornbeck—was a fake. See reminiscences of Joseph W. Ballantine, 1961, Oral History Research Office, Columbia University.

92 On the non-governmental side, it was soon time for the fourth Lincoln Essay Contest, an event held for Japanese students and hosted by the America–Japan Society. The awards ceremony, held in March 1930, was attended by the society chairman, Lord Speaker of the House of Peers Tokugawa Iesato, Castle and Dooman. See: *America–Japan Society Special Bulletin*, no. 10 (1930): 3–9, in 'Nichi-Bei Kyōkai Shiryō', C3–10.

93 Reminiscences of Sansom.

94 Reminiscences of Dooman.

95 On 24 January 1930, just after his visit to Japan, Castle wrote: 'Congress would never go to war over the open door, nor over Japanese annexation of Manchuria—and Japan has no intention of annexing Manchuria'. See Castle diary, vol. 16, 24 January 1930.

However, only the first half of the above statement was actually correct. It must have been a matter of great sorrow for Castle when, during his time as undersecretary, the relations between Japan and the US deteriorated as a result of the Manchurian Incident. Japan's foreign minister at that time was Shidehara. Thus, many Americans were growing increasingly concerned about Japan's foreign policy, while at the same time were irritated at its inability to take more resolute steps.

96 Nagai, 'Shidehara Danshaku no Omoide'.

97 Kuwabara Tsuru, 'Shidehara Danshaku no Omoide' [Memories of Baron Shidehara], *Kasumigaseki-kai Kaihō*, no. 234 (August 1965): 2–3.

98 Shidehara, *Gaikō 50 Nen*, 133.

99 *Asahi Shimbun*, 15 November (evening edition) and 16 November (evening edition) 1930; Shidehara, *Gaikō 50 Nen*, 133–44.

100 Itō and Hirose, *Makino Nobuaki Nikki*, 420–21; Izawa Takio Biography Compilation Committee, *Izawa Takio*, 197–198; Ōnishi Hiroshi, 'Izawa Takio to Ugaki Kazushige: Ugaki Yōritsu Kōsaku wo Chūshin ni' [Izawa Takio and Ugaki Kazushige: Focusing on the campaign to support Ugaki], in *Ugaki Kazushige to Sono Jidai: Taishō, Shōwa-ki no Gunbu, Seitō, Kanryō* [Ugaki Kazushige and his era: The military, political parties, and bureaucracy in the Taishō and Shōwa eras], ed. Hori Makiyo (Tokyo: Shinhyōron, 1999), 248.

101 Itō and Hirose, *Makino Nobuaki Nikki*, 441.

102 Debuchi to Shidehara, 5 June 1931, in 'Yardley-cho, *American Black Chamber* Mondai Ikken' [The problem of Yardley's *The American Black Chamber*], N.2.2.0.9, Diplomatic Archives of the Ministry of Foreign Affairs of Japan; Herbert O. Yardley, *The American Black Chamber* (New York: Blue Ribbon Books, 1931); Ministry of Foreign Affairs Hundred-Year History Compilation Association, *Gaimushō no 100 Nen*, vol. 2, 1329–38; John Prados, *Combined Fleet Decoded: The Secret History of American Intelligence and the Japanese Navy in World War II* (Annapolis: Naval Institute Press, 1995), 12–13, 69.

103 Ministry of Foreign Affairs, *Nihon Gaikō Bunsho*, Shōwa Era I, part 1, vol. 4, 1041–1045; Kawashima Shin, '"Shina" "Shina-koku" "Shina Kyōwakoku": Nihon Gaimushō no Tai-Chu Koshō Seisaku' ['Shina', 'Nation of Shina', 'The Republic of Shina': The Japanese Ministry of Foreign Affairs' China-naming policy], *Chūgoku Kenkyū Geppō* 49, no. 9 (September 1995): 1–15; Yu Hong, 'Dainiji Shidehara Gaikō-ki niokeru Chugoku no Kokugō Koshō Mondai: "Shina Kyōwakoku" kara "Chūka Minkoku" e' [The problem of the naming of China during the second period of Shidehara diplomacy: From the 'Chinese Republic' to the 'Republic of China'], *Ochanomizu Shigaku*, no. 46 (2002): 79–108.

104 Shidehara Kijūrō, 'Kokusai Heiwa to Sekai no Taisei' [International peace and the global situation], (originally a radio lecture given on 11 November 1929), *Gaikō Jihō*, no. 601 (December 1929): 162.

105 Hattori, *Higashi Asia Kokusai Kankyō no Hendō to Nihon Gaikō, 1918–1931*, 263–78.

106 Kobayashi and Shimada, *Gendai-shi Shiryo*, vol. 7, 184; Kobayashi Tatsuo, Shimada Toshihiko and Inaba Masao, eds, *Gendai-shi Shiryo, vol. 11: Zoku Manshū Jihen* [Modern historical material, vol. 11: Continued, the Manchurian Incident] (Tokyo: Misuzu Shobō, 1965), 313.

See also Morishima Morito, *Inbō, Ansatsu, Guntō* [Conspiracy, assassination, military swords] (Tokyo: Iwanami Shoten, 1950), 49; Seki Hiroharu, 'Manshū Jihen Zenshi' [The prehistory of the Manchurian Incident], in Japanese International Politics Society Research Division for Causes of the Pacific War, *Taiheiyō Sensō eno Michi*, vol. 1, 412, 419, 433; Shimada Toshihiko, 'Manshū Jihen no Tenkai' [The unfolding of the Manchurian Incident], in *Taiheiyō Sensō eno Michi*, ed. Japanese International Politics Society Research Division for Causes of the Pacific War, vol. 2 (Tokyo: Asahi Shimbun, 1962), 12–13; Ogata Sadako, *Manshū Jihen to Seisaku no Keisei Katei* [The Manchurian Incident and the policy formation process] (Tokyo: Hara Shobō, 1966), 104; Hayashi Kyūjirō, *Manshū Jihen to Hōten Sōryōji: Hayashi Kyūjirō Ikō* [The Manchurian Incident and the Japanese consul general in Mukden: The posthumous manuscript of Hayashi Kyūjirō] (Tokyo: Harashobō, 1978), 114–15.

107 Inaba et al., *Taiheiyō Sensō eno Michi*, extra vol.: Resources, 114–15.

108 Ibid., 123.

109 I have previously written on the above circumstances and on response to the Lytton Commission. See Hattori, *Higashi Asia Kokusai Kankyō no Hendō to Nihon Gaikō, 1918–1931*, 278–88; Hattori, *Manshū Jihen to Shigemitsu Chūka Kōshi Hōkokusho*.

110 Stimson diary, 27 November 1931, Stimson Papers, Reel 4.

111 Forbes to Stimson, 24 November 1931, in *FRUS, Japan: 1931–1941*, ed. Department of State, vol. 1 (Washington: Government Printing Office, 1945), 50.

112 *Tokyo Asahi Shimbun*, evening edition, 29 November 1931.

113 Stimson diary, 22, 24, 26, 27, 28 November 1931, Stimson Papers, Reel 4; Shidehara to Debuchi, 28 November 1931, in *Nihon Gaikō Bunsho: Manshū Jihen* [Documents on Japanese foreign policy: The Manchurian Incident], Ministry of Foreign Affairs, vol. 1, no. 3 (Tokyo: Ministry of Foreign Affairs, 1978), 113–14; Takahashi Katsuhiro, ed., '"Debuchi Katsuji Nikki" (3): Shōwa 6 Nen–8 Nen' [The diary of Debuchi Katsuji (3): Shōwa 6–8], *Kokugakuin Daigaku Nihon Bunka Kenkyū-jo Kiyo*, no. 86 (September 2000): 120–21.

114 *Tokyo Asahi Shimbun*, extra edition, 29 November 1931.

115 Shidehara to Debuchi, 29 November 1931, in Ministry of Foreign Affairs, *Nihon Gaikō Bunsho: Manshū Jihen*, vol. 1, no. 3, 117–19; Harada, *Saionji-kō to Seikyoku*, vol. 2 (Tokyo: Iwanami Shoten, 1951), 147; *Tokyo Asahi Shimbun*, 30 November 1931.

116 Banno Junji, *Kindai Nihon no Gaikō to Seiji* [Modern Japanese diplomacy and politics] (Tokyo: Kenbun Shuppan, 1985), 185–211.

117 Journal of W. Cameron Forbes, William Cameron Forbes Papers, second series, vol. 2, Houghton Library, Harvard University. For further details on Forbes, see Gary Ross, 'W. Cameron Forbes: The Diplomacy of a Darwinist', in *Diplomats in Crisis: United States-Chinese-Japanese Relations, 1919–1941*, ed. Richard Dean Burns and Edward M. Bennett (Santa Barbara: ABC-Clio, 1974), 49–64.

118 Journal of Forbes, 27, 29 September, 8, 15, 18 October, 3, 14 November and 30 December 1930, and 12 April, 7 May, 2, 21, August and 14 September 1931, Forbes Papers, second series, vol. 3.

119 Shidehara to Ōta Masahiro, governor-general of Taiwan, 24 June 1931, in 'Shidehara Heiwa Bunko', Reel 17. I received advice on this topic from Asano Toyomi.

120 Journal of Forbes, 24 September and 17 November 1931, Forbes Papers, second series, vol. 3.

121 Journal of Forbes, 3 December 1931, Forbes Papers, second series, vol. 3. See also Forbes to Stimson, 28 November 1931, in Stanley K. Hornbeck Papers, Box 167, Hoover Institution, Stanford University. For further details on Shiratori in this period, see Tobe Ryōichi, 'Shiratori Toshio to Manshū Jihen' [Shiratori Toshio and the Manchurian Incident], *Bōei Daigakkō Kiyō*, no. 39 (September 1979): 77–130.

122 Journal of Forbes, 3 December 1931.

123 Harada, *Saionji-kō to Seikyoku*, vol. 2, 149–50.

124 Forbes to Stimson, 2 December 1931, in Journal of Forbes, Forbes Papers, second series, vol. 4; Forbes to Joseph C. Grew, 14 March 1932, in Journal of Forbes, Forbes Papers, second series, vol. 4.

125 Shidehara to Forbes, 24 November 1932, in Journal of Forbes, Forbes Papers, second series, vol. 4; Forbes to Shidehara, 22 December 1932, in Journal of Forbes, Forbes Papers, second series, vol. 4. Shidehara's correspondence was also passed from Forbes to Hornbeck. See Forbes to Hornbeck, 22 December 1932, Hornbeck Papers, Box 167.

126 Forbes to Stimson, 29 November 1931, in *FRUS, 1931*, ed. Department of State, vol. 3 (Washington: Government Printing Office, 1945), 587–88; Stimson to Forbes, 30 November, ibid., 595–96.

6

From the Second Sino-Japanese War to the Pacific War

Following the May 15 Incident

National Unity Governments

In December 1931, the Wakatsuki cabinet resigned en masse. The direct cause was disunity in the cabinet surrounding the plan for a coalition that included members of the Seiyūkai party.[1] As a result of the cabinet's dissolution, administrative power shifted from the Minseitō to the Seiyūkai, with the Seiyūkai president Inukai Tsuyoshi forming a new cabinet. For the position of foreign minister, the Inukai cabinet called upon Yoshizawa Kenkichi, former ambassador to France. When Shidehara left the Ministry of Foreign Affairs, he had spent a cumulative total of five years and three months as foreign minister.[2] Now in political opposition, he was merely a House of Peers member.

As it happened, still more shocking events would occur the following year, in 1932. First, on 9 February, Inoue Junnosuke, who had just left his post as finance minister, was shot and killed by Onuma Shō, a member of the right-wing organisation, Ketsumeidan (League of Blood). Inoue was assassinated in Komagome, close to Shidehara's temporary residence.[3] This, however, was only a foreshadowing of what was to come. On 15 May Prime Minister Inukai was assassinated by young naval officers. This became known as the May 15 Incident.

Following the May 15 Incident and the death of Prime Minister Inukai, a new cabinet was formed, led by Saitō Makoto. Saitō was originally from the Imperial Japanese Navy and had no party affiliation. The formation of his government, therefore, was at the same time an end to the period of party-based cabinets, which had continued for eight years until that point. It should be noted that members of the Saitō cabinet were appointed from both the Seiyūkai and the Minseitō. For this reason, the Saitō cabinet, as well as the subsequent Okada cabinet, was referred to as a national unity government. On 27 May, Shidehara wrote to Saitō expressing his 'utmost delight' at the smooth formation of the cabinet.[4] At the time of the London Naval Treaty on Disarmament, Shidehara had been working with Saitō, who had temporarily returned to Japan while serving as the governor-general of Korea. Given their past relationship, it can be presumed that Shidehara was not necessarily discouraged by the birth of the Saitō cabinet.

Shidehara even wrote a letter expressing the 'utmost delight in my heart' to House of Peers Member Izawa Takio, who had assisted in the formation of the Saitō cabinet.[5] Later, in May 1934, Shidehara asked Prime Minister Saitō to select Suzuki Fujiya as a member of the House of Peers. Suzuki had been the chief cabinet secretary for the Hamaguchi cabinet. What made Shidehara most anxious was the direction of Japan's policies on China. With the formation of the Saitō cabinet, Uchida Yasuya returned as foreign minister after a nine-year break. Under Foreign Minister Uchida, Japan recognised Manchukuo as a state in September 1932, and, in March 1933, it notified the League of Nations of its withdrawal in opposition to the adoption of the report of the Lytton Commission and the non-recognition of Manchukuo.

Ashida Hitoshi, who became a member of the House of Representatives after an initial career as a diplomat, would reflect upon this in the postwar years:

> Soon after I gained a seat in the House of Representatives, in January, the eighth year of Shōwa [1933], I gave a speech criticising the military's continental policy. When this led to me being attacked by the right-wingers, I received an invitation from Mr. Shidehara for a chat. He said to me, 'At the very least, you're brave enough to say things that will make you unpopular, aren't you?' To this day, I still strongly remember those words of consolation.[6]

Of these continental policies, the 'Rehe Strategy' was of particular concern for Shidehara. In February 1933, the Kwantung Army had launched an assault on China's Rehe province. This development prompted Shidehara to pay a visit to Saionji Kinmochi at his home in Okitsu. Yoshida Shigeru, who was then waiting for a new posting, had given Shidehara an idea. Like Shidehara, Yoshida was anxious about the situation in China. His proposal was to call a meeting of the Imperial Council to try to resolve the situation, and he wanted Shidehara to try to convince Saionji of this approach. However, despite Yoshida's best efforts, he did not succeed in convening the Imperial Council. It should be noted that Shidehara was much more indifferent to this plan than Yoshida was.[7]

Nevertheless, Shidehara did subsequently support Yoshida in other matters, such as requesting that he be dispatched to Europe. The Shōwa emperor also deeply trusted Shidehara.[8]

Table 3: Prime ministers and foreign ministers, 1931–45

Prime Minister	Foreign Minister
Inukai Tsuyoshi (1931–32)	Yoshizawa Kenkichi
Saitō Makoto (1932–34)	Uchida Yasuya Hirota Kōki
Okada Keisuke (1934–36)	Hirota Kōki
Hirota Kōki (1936–37)	Arita Hachirō
Hayashi Senjūrō (1937)	Satō Naotake
Konoe Fumimaro (1937–39)	Hirota Kōki Ugaki Kazushige Arita Hachirō
Hiranuma Kiichirō (1939)	Arita Hachirō
Abe Nobuyuki (1939–40)	Nomura Kichisaburō
Yonai Mitsumasa (1940)	Arita Hachirō
Konoe Fumimaro (1940–41)	Matsuoka Yōsuke Toyoda Teijirō
Tōjō Hideki (1941–44)	Tōgō Shigenori Tani Masayuki Shigemitsu Mamoru
Koiso Kuniaki (1944–45)	Shigemitsu Mamoru
Suzuki Kantarō (1945)	Tōgō Shigenori
Higashikuni Naruhiko (1945)	Shigemitsu Mamoru Yoshida Shigeru
Shidehara Kijūrō (1945–46)	Yoshida Shigeru

Note: Acting foreign ministers are not listed here.

A 20-Year Memorial Anniversary for Denison

It was 3 July 1933. As the sun set upon Aoyama Cemetery, Shidehara lingered in front of the tombstone of former ministry adviser Denison. It had been exactly 20 years since Denison's death from illness in Tokyo. Also in attendance was Foreign Minister Uchida Yasuya. It was Uchida who hosted the gathering marking the anniversary of Denison's passing.

Other diplomatic and political figures who came to pay their respects included Lord Keeper of the Privy Seal Makino Nobuaki; Imperial Household Ministry Lord Chamberlain Hayashi Gonsuke; Matsui Keishirō, who had already retired from the Ministry of Foreign Affairs; House of Peers Member Yoshizawa Kenkichi; and Yoshida Shigeru, who was still waiting to be assigned to a new position. These individuals were also joined by Arita Hachirō, who had just given up the post of foreign affairs vice-minister to Shigemitsu Mamoru; American and European Bureau Director-General Tōgō Shigenori; and Intelligence Department Director-General Amō Eiji. Of those gathered, however, it was Shidehara who had by far been the closest to Denison.

Before long, the attendees departed the cemetery and went to the foreign minister's residence for a dinner in honour of Denison. Following the dinner, the group were loath to part and return home, so instead they started a discussion in the drawing room. It was there that Uchida asked Shidehara to say a few words, since he and Denison had had a 'special relationship'. Shidehara related an anecdote that he had prepared for such an occasion.

Once, Denison had informed Shidehara that the Nile River was so fertile because of the confluence of the Blue Nile and the White Nile further inland. Denison had said: 'The [First] Sino-Japanese War is just like that meeting of the Blue Nile and the White Nile. Reactionary ideas and Europeanism were harmonized, fostering Japan's advancement'. With the Russo-Japanese War, meanwhile, Japan 'did not seek to rush forward, but at the right timing tightened the reins and then dealt with the Treaty of Portsmouth'.[9] Denison had expressed the hope that, if the nation ever faced an existential crisis in the future, a similar attitude would help to open up a way forward.

With this anecdote, Shidehara may have sought subtly to prompt some self-reflection in Uchida, who tended to be dogmatically nationalist. Shidehara also mentioned how Denison, towards the end of his life, had wished to quit the Ministry of Foreign Affairs and retire to Hayama. This wish was, unfortunately, left unfulfilled. A portrait of Denison watched over a subsequent discussion between Shidehara and Uchida. It was after 10 pm when the gathering finally dispersed.

In September that year, Uchida resigned as foreign minister. His successor was Hirota Kōki. Foreign Minister Hirota would remain in his position during the subsequent Okada cabinet, which formed in July 1934. Shidehara also expressed his admiration for Denison in a diplomacy roundtable discussion, the content of which was published in the *Asahi Shimbun*. This discussion took place at the Imperial Hotel on 19 February 1934. Along with Shidehara, other attendees included Makino Nobuaki, Akizuki Satsuo, Hayashi Gonsuke, Matsui Keishirō, Ishii Kikujirō and Yoshizawa Kenkichi. Kurino Shinichirō would have attended but was absent due to illness.

Beginning with treaty revision, the roundtable participants discussed a wide range of topics, including the First Sino-Japanese War, the Yihetuan Movement, the Anglo-Japanese Alliance, the Russo-Japanese War and the era following World War I. This occasion similarly presented Shidehara with the opportunity to reminisce on Denison's achievements and virtuousness to Japan's most eminent diplomats. The discussion began at 3 pm and lasted until 11 pm.[10]

Foreign Threats

In January 1933, Adolf Hitler took power in Germany. Japan, which left the League of Nations in March that year, gradually came to seek an anti-communist partnership with the Nazi Party. Shidehara received information on developments in Germany from Ambassador Nagai Matsuzō. That he was critical of the Nazis is a matter of public record.[11]

When 1934 began, Shidehara's attention turned to the upcoming Second London Naval Conference on Disarmament, to be held as early as the following year. In April, he visited Lord Keeper of the Privy Seal Makino and expressed his opinion. 'The current authorities', Shidehara argued, 'are not capable of properly dealing with the situation'. Shidehara further suggested that Navy Minister Ōsumi Mineo be replaced. 'The top priority is to secure somebody far more capable for the role.'¹² Makino had no objections on this front. Shidehara also conversed with Makino on the topic of Soviet policy.

In May 1934, Shidehara exchanged views with Konoe Fumimaro, the lord speaker of the House of Peers, concerning the Second London Naval Conference. Shidehara predicted that problems of the Far East, a number of issues regarding territory in China—and Manchuria, in particular— would not be covered during the conference. Konoe relayed Shidehara's view to Kido Kōchi, lord keeper chief private secretary. Foreign Minister Hirota, on the other hand, believed that Far East problems could be up for deliberation.¹³ Shidehara turned out to be correct: problems of the Far East were not discussed at the Second London Naval Conference of 1935.

Regardless, Japan pulled out of the London Conference in January 1936. Then a group of military officers attempted to carry out a coup, in what became known as the 'February 26 Incident'. Although Prime Minister Okada narrowly avoided harm, Lord Keeper of the Privy Seal Saitō Makoto and Finance Minister Takahashi Korekiyo were killed. Shidehara, who was staying at his Rikugien residence at that time, fled to Kamakura upon the instructions of police.¹⁴

After the February 26 Incident, Foreign Minister Hirota replaced Okada as prime minister. The foreign minister of the new Hirota cabinet was Arita Hachirō. This government would later approve the November 1936 signing of the Anti-Comintern Pact with Germany. The Soviet Union was naturally displeased, indicating that it was now unwilling to revise the Japan–Soviet Fisheries Treaty. It was then that Shidehara, who was still in political opposition, received a visitor: Konstantin K. Yurenev, the Soviet ambassador to Japan. Ambassador Yurenev alluded to the possibility of the Soviet Union refusing to sign the fisheries treaty. Shidehara strongly protested, arguing that a refusal would not only worsen the situation but also could 'lead to us witnessing the tragedy of a Russo-Japanese War by April or May of next year'.¹⁵ He proposed that the two powers provisionally agree to extend the current treaty before it expired at the end of 1936.

Shidehara's proposal was accepted. On 28 December, an interim agreement was signed in Moscow. A public proclamation of the agreement's signing that same day would have helped ease tension between the two powers. In later years, Shigemitsu, Japan's ambassador to the Soviet Union, was displeased to learn of Shidehara's unofficial diplomatic activities. According to Shigemitsu, the Soviet side:

Knew that the signing of an interim agreement had originally been suggested by Mr. Shidehara. This, unfortunately, revealed to them that the Japanese side had already given up on reaching an accord on a new treaty and would be satisfied with a mere interim agreement.[16]

February 1937 saw the formation of a new cabinet under the leadership of Hayashi Senjūrō. The foreign minister was Satō Naotake.

US Ambassador Grew: The Semblance of Shidehara Diplomacy

Although Shidehara was a member of the House of Peers, he had no official post in government. Thus, he had almost no involvement in diplomatic negotiations during this period. The aforementioned Japan–Soviet Fisheries Interim Agreement was an exception. Nevertheless, that is not to say that Shidehara was left entirely without influence. Following the inauguration of Franklin D. Roosevelt as president of the US in March 1933, preliminary negotiations commenced for a world economic conference. It was rumoured that both Shidehara and Ishii Kikujirō were strong contenders for the role of Japan's plenipotentiary representative. In the end, Ishii was selected.[17]

Deserving of closer attention here is the relationship between Shidehara and US Ambassador Grew. Grew was posted to Japan for close to 10 years, from 1932 until the war between Japan and the US began. Nevertheless, Grew was unable to correctly assess the political situation in Japan. His major sources of information were from moderates such as Makino Nobuaki, Kabayama Aisuke, Yoshida Shigeru and Shidehara. Grew first met Shidehara on 24 October 1932 and was deeply impressed. As he wrote in his diary: 'I could talk with absolute frankness without the slightest fear of being misunderstood, and he has a fine sense of humor'.[18]

Through his communication with Shidehara, Grew arrived at two conclusions. First, Japanese diplomacy would swing back like a 'pendulum' and, before long, return to a more normal state. Grew particularly hoped for a return to the kind of diplomacy that had been practised by Shidehara. Grew also saw a semblance of 'Shidehara diplomacy' in the approaches of Foreign Minister Hirota Kōki and Foreign Minister Satō Naotake. Although Shidehara and Grew were not in frequent contact, Grew came to see Shidehara as a pole by which to orient himself in interpreting

Japanese diplomacy. Second, Grew saw that the Shōwa emperor was a pacifist. Upon returning to the US in December 1941 after hostilities between the two nations had begun, he began to push for the preservation of the emperor system. His efforts were not unconnected to the present-day system of the emperor as symbol.

Grew's faint hope of a return to the model of Shidehara diplomacy was to be cruelly betrayed by Japan's attack on Pearl Harbor. Nevertheless, during the war years, Grew attempted to inform Americans of the moderate politicians and officials in Japan. In 1944, Grew published a collection of diary entries and official papers under the title *Ten Years in Japan*. In this book, Shidehara was frequently mentioned as a member of the Japanese moderates. Many Americans presumably first learned of Shidehara by reading *Ten Years in Japan*.[19]

While Grew saw a semblance of 'Shidehara diplomacy' in Hirota's actions, such an interpretation does not appear in the recollections of Craigie, the British ambassador to Japan. According to Craigie, the Japanese army had been more sympathetic towards Foreign Minister Hirota of the Konoe cabinet than it had been towards former foreign minister Satō. This was because, for the army, Satō's policy of appeasement towards China was 'so unpleasantly associated with the name of Baron Shidehara'.[20] It should be noted that, during this period, Shidehara continued to correspond with former ambassador Forbes.

The Second Sino-Japanese War and World War II

The Ministry of Foreign Affairs Research Department

Amid these troubles both at home and abroad, in October 1936 Shidehara had the opportunity to give the directors of the Honolulu Museum of Art a tour of the Rikugien. The trip was organised through the America–Japan Society in the hope that it would help improve relations with the US.[21]

However, these hopes were not to be realised. The outbreak of the Second Sino-Japanese War in July 1937 would further damage Japan's foreign relations. At that time, the governing Konoe cabinet decided to restore

Hirota Kōki as foreign minister. Peace initiatives attempted under Foreign Minister Hirota include the Trautmann Initiative and the Wang Jingwei Initiative. These initiatives received their names from two key figures: respectively, Oskar Paul Trautmann, German ambassador to China, and Wang Jingwei, a powerful figure in the Chinese Nationalist Party. According to *A Shōwa Emperor Monologue*, the Shōwa emperor once stated that:

> After the fall of Nanjing, a peace initiative was carried out through the mediation of the German ambassador. However, according to Shidehara [Kijūrō, former foreign minister], Japan's proposal at that time was apparently torn up by Soong Mei-ling [Madame Chiang Kai-shek] and never reached Chiang Kai-shek himself.[22]

Another peace initiative undertaken during the Second Sino-Japanese War was the Ugaki Initiative. In May 1938, former war minister Ugaki Kazushige replaced Hirota as foreign minister in the Konoe cabinet. At that time, Ugaki made peace negotiations with China a condition for his joining the cabinet. While in agreement with this new Ugaki Initiative, Shidehara undertook his own manoeuvrings from the outside. Kido Kōichi, minister of health and welfare, wrote in his diary: 'I have information that Mr. Shidehara is being very active outside of the cabinet'.[23] Shidehara also made contact with his ex-subordinate, Asian Bureau Director-General Ishii Itarō. Ishii had been working to try and prevent the Second Sino-Japanese War from expanding.

However, the Konoe cabinet was unsuccessful in resolving the conflict, leading to resignation en masse. A new cabinet was subsequently formed under Hiranuma Kiichirō in January 1939. Before his nomination as prime minister, Hiranuma was serving as the chairman of the Privy Council. During the Hiranuma cabinet, Shidehara met with Ugaki Kazushige and critically examined the proposal for an alliance between Japan and Germany.[24]

At this time, the Ministry of Foreign Affairs' Research Department was editing a compilation of ministry records and diplomatic officer memoirs. The Research Department had been established in December 1933. In June 1936, the Research Department published the first volume of *Dai Nihon Gaikō Bunsho* (Documents on Japanese foreign policy) from the Japan International Association.[25] This important inaugural volume was a systematic collection of diplomatic documents from the early Meiji period relating to unequal treaty reform. To this day it constitutes a foundational resource for scholars seeking to understand Japan's modern diplomatic history. By 1940, a total of nine volumes were published in this series. However, work ceased at that point due to the Pacific War. In fact, Shidehara himself assisted the Research Department with this project. Fonder of the ministry than anyone, meticulous Shidehara could hardly be indifferent to such an undertaking relating to ministry records and diplomatic history.[26]

Having been away from the ministry for so long by this point, Shidehara had no objection to writing his own contributions to the history of Japanese diplomacy. In February 1939, Shidehara wrote a draft for ministry officials, titled 'Washington Kaigi no Rimen-kan Sonota' (Behind the scenes of the Washington Naval Conference and others). In this text, Shidehara made reference to the 'equality of opportunity' and 'open door' provisions of the Nine-Power Treaty. He described how 'in recent years I have heard speculation that these provisions were initially proposed by the U.K. and the U.S., so that these powers could restrict Japan's economic activities in China'. However, he responded that the pursuit of:

> Equality of opportunity and open-door [ideals] in China was originally promoted by our nation since the time of the Anglo-Japanese Alliance, as an important principle for regulating China's relationships with outside nations.[27]

In a roundabout way, Shidehara was criticising contemporary Japanese diplomacy with respect to the Second Sino-Japanese War.

Next, in April of the same year, Shidehara wrote a paper detailing the circumstances surrounding the Japan–Soviet Fisheries Interim Agreement, again for practical use by ministry officials as a reference. It was titled: 'Shōwa 11-nen 12-gatsu Nisso Gyogyō Zantei Kyōtei Seiritsu nikansuru Keii no Ichikyokumen' (A perspective on the circumstances relating to the establishment of the Japan–Soviet Fisheries Interim Agreement in December, Shōwa 11 [1936]). Then, in April 1940, Shidehara composed another paper, titled 'Gaikō Bunsho no Buntai, Kisōsha no Kokoroe narabini Shoshu no Keishiki' (Writing style for diplomatic documents, important knowledge for drafters, different types of forms). In this text, Shidehara drew upon such sources as the teachings he once received from Denison on topics such as the diplomacy surrounding the commencement of the Russo-Japanese War, and the style rules to follow when writing diplomatic documents.[28]

World War II

In August 1939 Nazi Germany and the Soviet Union signed the German–Soviet Nonaggression Pact. The following month, Germany invaded Poland, triggering World War II. Shown to be at the mercy of developments in Europe, the Hiranuma cabinet resigned. The subsequent cabinets of Abe Nobuyuki and Yonai Mitsumasa were similarly short-lived.

In June 1940, Shidehara wrote an essay in English expressing his thoughts on the situation. In this English essay, titled 'Outlook of the European War', Shidehara considered the influence that World War II would have upon the Second Sino-Japanese War, while at the same time attempting to take a clear view of the events in Europe. He sent a five-page draft of this essay to Makino Nobuaki. However, he later asked Nobuaki to burn this draft, because it was based on inaccurate information.[29]

In 'Outlook of the European War', Shidehara asserted that, in order to gain an upper hand in the war, Germany could take one of three paths. First, Germany could try to pressure the UK and France to surrender on the condition that they disarm themselves and dismantle their empires. Yet, Shidehara noted, this approach was unlikely to proceed smoothly. It was hard to believe that the UK or France would tolerate foreign domination. The British Commonwealth, in particular, was not under the influence of the German military. Second, Germany could seek a compromise, offering a peace deal that would spare the UK and France from complete defeat. Shidehara regarded this option as more feasible than the first. In this case, the UK and France would gradually recover their strength with the help of the US. Third, Germany could pursue the war to the very end. In this scenario, the UK and France would be supported by their colonies' resources and would probably be more able than Germany to maintain the strength necessary for victory.

From Shidehara's perspective, therefore, the general outlook for Germany was grim. Its flagrantly illegal actions were unlikely to be forgiven, and 'the memory of the tragedy will long stand in the way of a lasting peace in Europe'.[30] At the end of the essay, Shidehara quoted A. L. Kennedy's work *Old Diplomacy and New, 1876–1922, from Salisbury to Lloyd-George*, concerning Germany and the UK during World War I. Kennedy wrote: 'Germany had no scruples; we had some—too few for honor, too many for success'.[31] Shidehara concluded 'Outlook of the European War' with the well-known observation: 'History often repeats itself'.[32] Shidehara wrote this manuscript on 14 June 1940—the very day the German army occupied Paris. Hitler's advance continued unimpeded. Given this situation, Shidehara's prediction that Germany would ultimately not prevail was quite insightful. It was the kind of assessment to be expected from a man such as Shidehara, whose ideals had been inspired by British-style diplomacy.

The Pacific War

Outbreak of War between Japan and the US

The second Konoe cabinet was formed in July 1940. This time, the post of foreign minister went to Matsuoka Yōsuke. Under his guidance, Japan signed the Tripartite Pact with Germany and Italy in September that year. As the above discussion makes clear, Shidehara was critical of Matsuoka's diplomatic efforts and his siding with Germany.

October saw the inauguration of a new organisation of a government-made national movement known as the Taisei Yokusankai (Imperial Rule Assistance Association). While Shidehara was a member of the House of Peers, he did not participate. Shidehara was absolutely opposed to the idea of Japan going to war with the US.[33] Nevertheless, this is not to say that he personally did all that he could to prevent the situation from heading in that direction. Towards the end of July 1941, the Japanese army advanced into the southern part of French Indochina. In response, the Roosevelt administration banned all oil exports to Japan. It was then that Shidehara had a meeting with Prime Minister Konoe. Shidehara has left behind some testimony as to what was discussed during the meeting. According to Shidehara:

> I did my best to warn Duke Konoe that his diplomatic policy was mistaken. Duke Konoe was extremely regretful that Japan had already taken such steps as signing the Anti-Comintern Pact and the Tripartite Pact.[34]

In other words, Shidehara had urged Konoe to reflect seriously on how he had contributed to the current crisis.

Following this meeting, Konoe began to mull over a plan: to visit the US himself and meet directly with Roosevelt. Such a decisive stance was quite rare for Konoe. At the beginning of August, Konoe secretly dispatched

Itō Nobufumi, director-general of the Intelligence Department, to Shidehara's residence in Sendagaya. The intention was to seek out the opinion of a third party concerning this plan. However, Shidehara:

> Would not easily offer a constructive opinion, simply repeating modestly that he had been away from the political world for so long that he could not really say what ought to be done.[35]

In the end, the cabinet collapsed without Konoe ever meeting Roosevelt. October 1941 saw the formation of the Tōjō Hideki cabinet, with Tōgō Shigenori as foreign minister. Before the outbreak of the Pacific War, there was a final attempt at negotiations with the US. The proposal was that Japan would offer to withdraw its army from southern French Indochina on the condition that the embargo on oil exports would be dropped. It was Shidehara who initially suggested this approach. He had suggested it to Yoshida Shigeru, who then passed it on to Foreign Minister Tōgō, who in turn made his own additions. Even at the last minute, Shidehara responded to Yoshida's request in offering advice to Konoe and Kido.[36] In the end, however, negotiations with the US were abandoned, and Japan ultimately launched an attack on Pearl Harbor on 7 December.

Kiyosawa Kiyoshi

Even as the Pacific War loomed ever closer, Shidehara did not lose his interest in diplomatic history. In fact, through cooperation with diplomatic commentator Kiyosawa Kiyoshi, Shidehara began to involve himself in diplomatic history research. In June 1941, Kiyosawa published a historical overview titled *Gaikō-shi* (Diplomatic history).[37] Kiyosawa presented a copy of his book to Shidehara. Shidehara's letter of thanks is fascinating. He wrote:

> There are many, even among our own citizens, who need to properly grasp the true nature of our government's politics and actions … Your book is extremely valuable for its potential to help improve our present situation.[38]

In other words, it was difficult for insiders and outsiders alike to fully appreciate the realities of Japanese diplomacy. Shidehara hoped that Kiyosawa's work could make a significant contribution in this respect and thus even assist in addressing the then-unfolding crisis. Shidehara lamented the extent to which Japan's citizens were ignorant of how diplomacy actually worked.

Even after war broke out between Japan and the US in December 1941, Shidehara continued to support Kiyosawa's production of a chronology of Japanese diplomacy. Indeed, if anything, Shidehara was more of a scholar than Kiyosawa; he was very strict in noting erroneous entries or the omission of important documents. When given a copy of *Tōan Kou Seiwa* (A dialogue by Tōan-kō [Saionji Kinmochi]) by the editor Harada Kumao, Shidehara even pointed out a mistake with regard to the Chinese name that appeared in the work.[39] 'Tōan' was a moniker of Saionji Kinmochi. Harada had worked as Saionji's secretary for many years, but the elder statesman passed away in November 1940.

Shidehara met with Kiyosawa again at the end of February 1943 to relay details on proceedings in the House of Peers. According to Shidehara, several members had inquired as to the 'postwar plan', but Foreign Minister Tani Masayuki of the Tōjō cabinet had simply replied that it was under consideration. Aoki Kazuo, the minister for Greater East Asia, had reacted furiously, demanding: 'How can you ask about postwar plans when the war is still going on?'[40]

On 20 November 1944, Kiyosawa visited Shidehara at his home. Shidehara brought Kiyosawa up to the second floor, where he had an impressive study of over 36 square metres. Shidehara's study was filled with books, including recent publications. Kiyosawa had come to ask Shidehara to give an address on the occasion of the inauguration of the Japanese Diplomatic History Research Institute. Shidehara willingly accepted and even promised to join the institute in an advisory role.

The new institute was inaugurated on 5 December that year. Along with Shidehara himself, attendees included such figures as Itō Masanori, Ishibashi Tanzan, Tamura Kōsaku, Uehara Etsujirō, Matsumoto Jōji, Ashida Hitoshi, Baba Tsunego and Shinobu Junpei. Following welcomes by Kiyosawa and Ashida, it was time for Shidehara's address. Shidehara used the opportunity to share some little-known anecdotes regarding the Russo-Japanese War and the Washington Naval Conference. Later, he would attend regular meetings of the institute, giving him the opportunity to go into more detail about his memories of various Japanese diplomatic events.

Kiyosawa wrote in his diary that Shidehara 'was certainly an extremely capable diplomat'. Kiyosawa also transcribed the contents of these discussions, which he sent to Shidehara. While Kiyosawa also visited other diplomatic figures such as Matsui Keishirō, Ishii Kikujirō and

Makino Nobuaki, he thought that when it came to powers of recollection, 'Shidehara was outstanding'.[41] Shidehara gave another address to Kiyosawa's institute on 18 January 1945. However, he was apparently dissatisfied with Kiyosawa's shorthand notetaking. He wanted every word and phrase captured, down to the smallest detail. His solution was to write the draft for his talk himself and give it to Kiyosawa. According to Kiyosawa, Shidehara was:

> Very sensitive about [the importance of] accurate wording, both as a diplomat and as a man of law. If I shared a draft with him, he would make so many changes that the original text would become entirely obliterated.[42]

Shidehara also published some anecdotes about Denison in a diplomatic journal, *Gaikō Jihō*.[43]

Arguments for an Early Peace

During this time, around 1943, the war situation began to deteriorate. Though now a former diplomat, Yoshida Shigeru made great efforts to secure a peaceful resolution to the conflict. Along with Wakatsuki Reijirō, Yoshida began to lay a plan to gain Masaki Jinzaburō's cooperation in forming a new cabinet, headed by Kobayashi Seizō. His hope was to install Shidehara as foreign minister and 'entrust him with conducting peace talks'.[44] Though perhaps not to the extent that Yoshida did, Shidehara also contributed to this plan. He spoke with figures such as Konoe, Kido, Prince Takamatsu and Prince Higashikuni in an attempt to bring them around. The idea was to sue for peace with the UK and the US under favourable conditions, while the war situation was still sufficiently advantageous. Shidehara held to the idea of suing for an early peace until at least August 1943.[45]

In reality, by this time, there was no real hope for establishing a peace agreement. In June 1944, Japan lost the Battle of the Philippine Sea, and, the following month, the island of Saipan fell to the Allied forces. By this stage, it was undeniable that Japan was losing. At around this time, Shidehara was able to keep up with events via sources such as House of Representatives Member Tsurumi Yūsuke. Shidehara also attended, on a near-monthly basis, the regular meetings of the Diplomatic Research Institute hosted by the Gaikō Jihōsha (Diplomatic Review Company). There, he would listen to explanations provided by the Ministry of Foreign Affairs and by military officials.[46]

In July 1944, a new cabinet was formed under Koiso Kuniaki. On the Allied side, meanwhile, October that year saw the issuance of the Dumbarton Oaks Proposal. This proposal concerned the founding of a new international organisation that could replace the League of Nations after the war. In response to this development, Vice-Minister for Foreign Affairs Sawada Renzō invited Shidehara to his residence in December. Also in attendance on that day was temporary ministry employee Takayanagi Kenzō, professor at the University of Tokyo. The topic for discussion was how to respond to the Dumbarton Oaks Proposal. We do not know for sure what kind of comments Shidehara made.[47] However, we do know that Shidehara was sceptical not only of the League of Nations but also of its successor, the United Nations. Presumably, had Japan still been at war, he would not have supported the proposal.

At this time, Shidehara began to argue to Kiyosawa that 'attempts at reaching a peace deal are completely hopeless and only harmful'. If Japan wants peace, he thought, 'we should create a situation where the other side is forced to seek it'.[48] As the war situation became increasingly grim, Shidehara apparently began to embrace the view that Japan should resist to the bitter end. Kiyosawa was unable to comprehend Shidehara's thinking in this regard. Kiyosawa could not foresee how an opportunity for peace could ever arise out of stubborn resistance.

Shidehara was also resistant to the plan to end the war put forth by former member of the House of Representatives Uehara Etsujirō. Uehara had met with figures such as Shidehara, Wakatsuki Reijirō, and Okada Keisuke. Okada himself had already given up on the Koiso cabinet. According to Uehara, however, Shidehara 'simply thought that [Japan] ought to resist to the very end; [Shidehara] was not thinking about domestic political matters at all'.[49] Uehara therefore decided to seek out Kiyosawa's assistance in convincing Shidehara.

Another plan to end the war was formulated by seven professors from the University of Tokyo Law Department, including Nanbara Shigeru, Takagi Yasaka and Tanaka Kōtarō. They had received word of the moderate peace policy advanced by Undersecretary of State Grew and other members of the State Department. Nanbara and Takagi argued that 'we should take appropriate steps with regard to the war situation, while emphasizing the need to protect the national polity'.[50] However, Shidehara was similarly nonplussed at this idea. Shidehara conversely told Nanbara and his associates that a scorched-earth policy was the only option; the citizens of

Japan needed to fight until the bitter end. The professors were extremely surprised and disappointed by this stance. Responding in such a fashion, Shidehara must have seemed particularly lacking in enthusiasm for peace, even when compared with Ugaki Kazushige, whom Nanbara and Takaki had also spoken with.

In the Great Tokyo Air Raid of 10 March 1945, Shidehara's one-time matchmaker, Ishii Kikujirō, went missing. Shidehara's residence in Sendagaya also burned down. Concerning what was left of the book collection bequeathed to him by Denison, Shidehara noted that:

> It was destroyed in Shōwa 20 [1945] when my home in Sendagaya was hit by bombing. Not a single volume remains. Reflecting back upon the past, I am truly filled with deep emotion.[51]

In April, yet another cabinet was formed. This time the leader was Suzuki Kantarō. In the bombing of 26 May, even the headquarters of the Ministry of Foreign Affairs was destroyed, forcing the staff to move to the fourth floor of the Ministry of Education.[52] In July, Prime Minister Suzuki and Foreign Minister Tōgō Shigenori began to seek a peace accord via Soviet mediation. Konoe Fumimaro's name arose for the role of special envoy to the Soviets. The plan was for Konoe to visit the Soviet Union with a special letter from the Shōwa emperor. Shidehara was deeply mistrustful of this proposal. A letter from the emperor would have no hope of changing the course of events. If anything, it would simply bring trouble to the imperial household. Naturally, the response from the Soviet Union was frosty, and the proposal was abandoned.[53]

Ministry of Foreign Affairs records that have been made public in recent years show that Shidehara's premonition about the plan was correct. According to these records, in mid-July a message was sent from Tokyo to Moscow. It 'effectively' expressed, 'in accordance with the will of the emperor of Japan, the desire to end the war'.[54] The main meaning of the emperor's letter that Konoe was supposed to bring with him had apparently reached the Soviet Union regardless. Premier Stalin relayed the details of the emperor's message to the UK and the US during the Potsdam Conference. However, thanks to their interception of Japan's radio communication, US president Harry S. Truman and Secretary of State James F. Byrnes were already well aware of Japan's efforts to seek peace through mediation with the Soviet Union.

At the beginning of August, US forces dropped atomic bombs on Hiroshima and Nagasaki, and the Soviet Union also entered the war against Japan, advancing into Manchuria and Sakhalin. Japan now had no choice but to accept the Potsdam Declaration, through the Shōwa emperor's 'imperial decision' or *seidan* in Japanese.

From Defeat to Recovery

This chapter has traced Japan's path from the collapse of the Wakatsuki cabinet to wartime defeat. Now in political opposition, Shidehara had already been effectively forgotten. Probably his only direct participation in diplomatic affairs was with the negotiations for the Japan–Soviet Fisheries Interim Agreement. That said, his mind remained sharp. This was demonstrated by his participation in various roundtable discussions, while at the same time assisting the Ministry of Foreign Affairs Research Department with their efforts to compile historical documents. Even with respect to his relationship with Kiyosawa Kiyoshi, Shidehara remained, if anything, too exact when it came to accounts of events in Japanese diplomatic history. Shidehara also displayed some insight when formulating his assessment of how World War II was likely to unfold.

However, when it came to the formulation of peace plans, Shidehara did not demonstrate the kind of resolute action displayed by Yoshida Shigeru. Although he proposed suing for early peace after the Pacific War began, the hard realities of the time did not permit such a strategy. What is particularly enigmatic is how Shidehara became a proponent of fighting to the bitter end once the Pacific War reached its final stages. He had lost his ability to understand the situation. There is an undeniable inconsistency between this position and his previous call for suing for an early peace.

There are two possible ways of understanding Shidehara's thinking in this regard. The first interpretation is that Shidehara was poor at handling a crisis. This interpretation fits with how he reacted to the Manchurian Incident as foreign minister. The second interpretation was that Shidehara foresaw Japan's total defeat. Although this theory cannot be proven on the basis of historical documents, it is not altogether unlikely. It may be that Shidehara anticipated that Japan would be utterly defeated and yet held onto the hope that it would subsequently recover.

Endnotes

1   This chapter is based on my previous work: Hattori Ryūji, 'Nicchū Sensō-ki no Shidehara Kijūrō' [Shidehara Kijūrō during the period of the Second Sino-Japanese War], *Chūō Daigaku Seisaku Bunka Sōgō Kenkyū-jo Nenpō*, no. 7 (June 2004): 3–15.

2   Broadly speaking, there are two views on Shidehara's career regarding the period beginning here and stretching until the outbreak of the Pacific War. According to the first interpretation, Shidehara was a pacifist who was tirelessly concerned with the fate of Japan. A classic example of this view is presented in Shidehara Peace Foundation, *Shidehara Kijūrō*, 492–551, which focuses on Shidehara's correspondence with his close friend, Ōdaira Komatsuchi, to emphasise that 'Shidehara was a noble-minded human being, patriotically concerned for the welfare of his country'. It is in this context that the text emphasises incidents such as Shidehara's objection to Japan forming the Tripartite Pact with Germany and Italy.

The second interpretation sees Shidehara as an apologist for invasion, which is evident in Kunugi Toshihiro, 'Shidehara Kijūrō: "Heiwa Gaikō" no Honne to Tatemae' [Shidehara Kijūrō: The underlying motives and the official stance of the 'diplomacy of peace'], in *Haisen Zengo* [Before and after the defeat], ed. Hiroshi Yoshida et al. (Tokyo: Aoki Shoten, 1995), 85–131. According to Kunugi, Shidehara was an 'international apologist for the Kwantung Army' during the period of the Manchurian Incident, and even as defeat inevitably approached in the Pacific War, he argued that Japan had to resist to the bitter end.

Thus, we have been presented with two different interpretations of Shidehara's actions in this period. In the following discussion, I clarify the matter through historical documents that have become public in recent years, including Itō and Hirose, *Makino Nobuaki Nikki*; Yoshida Shigeru Memorial Project Foundation, *Yoshida Shigeru Shokan*; Prince Takamatsu Nobuhito, *Takamatsu-no-miya Nikki* [The diary of Takamatsu-no-miya], vols 4–7 (Tokyo: Chuōkōronsha, 1996–1997); Izawa Takio Document Research Association, *Izawa Takio Kankei Bunsho*. Through these historical documents, Shidehara's stance will be contrasted with that of Yoshida Shigeru.

3   Inoue Junnosuke Essay Collection Editing Association, ed., *Inoue Junnosuke Den* [The biography of Inoue Junnosuke] (Tokyo: Inoue Junnosuke Essay Collection Editing Association, 1935), 868–70; Shidehara, *Gaikō 50 Nen*, 193. I have also referred to the following, in the same volume: Sasaki Takashi, 'Kaisetsu [Commentary], in Kijūrō Shidehara, *Gaikō 50 Nen* [Fifty years of diplomacy] (Tokyo: Chuōkōronsha, 1987), 331–37.

4   Shidehara to Saitō, 27 May 1932, in 'Saitō Makoto Kankei Bunsho', Correspondence Department, Reel 34.

5   Shidehara to Izawa, 1 June 1932, in Izawa Takio Document Research Association, *Izawa Takio Kankei Bunsho*, 266; Shidehara to Saitō, 14 May 1934, 'Saitō Makoto Kankei Bunsho', Correspondence Department, Reel 34.

For further information on Izawa during this period, see Kurokawa Norio, 'Chūkan Naikaku-ki no Izawa Takio' [Izawa Takio during the period of the interim cabinet], in *Izawa Takio to Kindai Nihon* [Izawa Takio and modern Japan], ed. Ōnishi Hiroshi (Tokyo: Fuyō Shobō Shuppan, 2003), 141–65.

6   *Asahi Shimbun*, 11 March 1951.

7   Itō and Hirose, *Makino Nobuaki Nikki*, 544–46; Harada, *Saionji-kō to Seikyoku*, vol. 3 (Tokyo: Iwanami Shoten, 1951), 20–25; Shibata, *Shōwa-ki no Kōshitsu to Seiji Gaikō*, 197; Chadani Seiichi, 'Kokusai Renmei Dattai no Seiji Katei: Hohitsu Taisei Saihen no Shikaku kara' [The political process of withdrawal from the League of Nations: From the perspective of the restructuring of the advisor system], *Nihon-shi Kenkyū*, no. 457 (September 2000): 10.

8   Itō and Hirose, *Makino Nobuaki Nikki*, 495, 588, 611.

9   Kishi Kuramatsu, 'Ko-Gaimusho Hōritsu Komon Denison-shi 20 Nenki Tsuioku-kai-ki' [Records of the 20-year anniversary memorial for the late Mr Denison, legal advisor to the Ministry of Foreign Affairs], September 1933, in 'Gaimushō Gaikokujin Yatoiire Ikken (Fu-Keiyakusho) Bessatsu "Denison"-shi Kankei'. There is also a document titled 'Denison Tsuioku-kai deno Makino Nobuaki Danwa (1 Tsuzuri)' [A discussion on Makino Nobuaki at the Denison anniversary memorial (a writing pad)],

in 'Makino Nobuaki Kankei Bunsho', Document Department, Reel 19. See also Shidehara, *Gaikō 50 Nen*, 246–48; Takeuchi Haruhisa, 'Denison-zō to Meiji no Omokage' [The remnants of the Meiji era and a portrait of Denison], *Gaikō Forum*, no. 171 (October 2002): 76–81.

10   Tonedachi, *Nihon Gaikō Hiroku*, 18–20, 70, 74–75, 94–95, 122–23; Itō and Hirose, *Makino Nobuaki Nikki*, 564.

11   Nagai, 'Shidehara Danshaku no Omoide'.

12   Itō and Hirose, *Makino Nobuaki Nikki*, 559–71.

13   Kido Diary Research Association, ed., *Kido Kōichi Nikki* [The diary of Kido Kōichi], vol. 1 (Tokyo: University of Tokyo Press, 1966), 328.

14   Shidehara, *Gaikō 50 Nen*, 194–97; Shidehara Peace Foundation, *Shidehara Kijūrō*, 498.

15   Shidehara Kijūrō, 'Shōwa 11-nen 12-gatsu Nisso Gyogyō Zantei Kyōtei Seiritsu nikansuru Keii no Ichiyokumen' [A perspective on the circumstances relating to the establishment of the Japan–Soviet Fisheries Interim Agreement in December, Shōwa 11 (1936)], April 1939, in Hirose, *Kindai Gaikō Kaikoroku*, vol. 4., 154–60.

16   Shigemitsu Mamoru, 'Unmei no Chōkohō Jiken Zengo: Moscow eno Tabi' [Around the time of the fated battle of Lake Khasan: The journey to Moscow], *Nihon Shūhō*, no. 193 (December 1951): 30–36. See also Ministry of Foreign Affairs, ed., *Gaimushō Kōhyō-shū* [Ministry of Foreign Affairs publications collection], vol. 15 (Tokyo: Ministry of Foreign Affairs, 1937), 136–41; Ministry of Foreign Affairs European and Oceanic Affairs Bureau First Section, eds, *Nichi 'So' Kōshō-shi* [A history of Japan–Soviet negotiations] (Tokyo: Gannandō, 1942), 448.

17   Kubota Kanichirō, ed., 'Ishii Shishaku Nikki: Shōwa 7 Nen 12 Gatsu 14 Nichi–Shōwa 8 Nen 4 Gatsu 11 Nichi' [Diary of Viscount Ishii: 14 December, 7th Year of Shōwa – 11 April, 8th Year of Shōwa], *Kokusai Mondai*, no. 71 (February 1966): 83; *Tokyo Asahi Shimbun*, evening edition, 11 April 1933.

18   Grew diary, 24 October and 1 November 1932, in Joseph Clark Grew Papers, Letters, vol. 58, Houghton Library, Harvard University.

19   Grew diary, 14 February 1933, Grew Papers, Letters, vol. 65; Grew diary, 23 February 1934, Grew Papers, Letters, vol. 71; Grew to Shidehara, 15 May 1935, Grew Papers, Letters, vol. 77; Grew diary, 19–31 March 1937, Grew Papers, Letters, vol. 85; Grew diary, December 1937, Grew Papers, Letters, vol. 94; Grew to Cordell Hull, 27 December 1934, in Department of State, ed., *FRUS, 1935*, vol. 3 (Washington: Government Printing Office, 1953), 821–29. Joseph C. Grew, *Ten Years in Japan: A Contemporary Record Drawn from the Diaries and Private and Official Papers of Joseph C. Grew* (1944; reprint, New York: Arno Press, 1972), 68, 122, 206, 305, 471; Waldo H. Heinrichs, Jr., *American Ambassador: Joseph C. Grew and the Development of the United States Diplomatic Tradition* (Oxford: Oxford University Press, 1986), 180–81, 184, 199, 205–06, 237, 367; J. W. Dower, *Empire and Aftermath: Yoshida Shigeru and the Japanese Experience, 1878–1954* (Cambridge: Harvard University Press, 1988), 108–09.

The expectations that Grew had for Shidehara were not realistic for Japan at that time. Baba Tsunego suggested that, even if Shidehara diplomacy were to revive, the situation would not have significantly changed. See Baba Tsunego, 'Shidehara Gaikō wa Doko e Yuku' [Which way for Shidehara diplomacy], *Bungei Shunjū 11*, no. 6 (June 1933): 206–10. For details on Grew's expectations with Foreign Minister Hirota, see Maxwell McGaughey Hamilton diary, 29 September 1933, Maxwell McGaughey Hamilton Papers, Box 1, Hoover Institution, Stanford University.

For further discussion of Grew, see Iokibe Makoto, *Beikoku no Nihon Senryō Seisaku: Sengo Nihon no Sekkei-zu* [The US's Japanese occupation policy: A blueprint for postwar Japan], vols 1–2 (Tokyo: Chuōkōronsha, 1985); Nakamura Masanori, *Shōchō Tennō-sei eno Michi: Beikoku Taishi Grew to sono Shūhen* [The road to the symbolic emperor system: US ambassador Grew and his periphery] (Tokyo: Iwanami Shoten, 1989).

20   Robert Craigie, *Behind the Japanese Mask* (London: Hutchinson & Co. Ltd., 1945), 36; Forbes to Shidehara, 3 January 1935, in Journal of Forbes, Forbes Papers, second series, vol. 5. See also Hosoya Chihiro, *Nihon Gaikō no Zahyō* [The coordinates of Japanese diplomacy] (Tokyo: Chuōkōronsha, 1979), 145.

21 America–Japan Society to Shidehara, 20 October 1936, in 'Nichi-Bei Kyōkai Shiryō', A2-04.

22 Terasaki Hidenari and Mariko Terasaki Miller, eds, *Shōwa Tennō Dokuhaku-roku: Terasaki Hidenari, Goyōgakari Nikki* [A Shōwa emperor monologue: The diary of Terasaki Hidenari, imperial household official] (Tokyo: Bungei Shunjū, 1991), 37–38. See also Matsuura Masataka, 'Nicchū Sensō wa Naze Nanka-shita noka' [Why did the Second Sino-Japanese War move southwards?] (1), *Hokudai Hōgaku Ronshū* 57, no. 1 (May 2006): 31.

23 Kido Diary Research Association, *Kido Kōichi Nikki*, vol. 2, 657; Itō Takashi and Liu Jie, eds, *Ishii Itarō Nikki* [The diary of Ishii Itarō] (Tokyo: Chuōkōronsha, 1993), 248, 272, 521, 522.

For further details on Ugaki's manoeuvring at this time, see Tobe Ryōichi, *Peace Feeler: Shina Jihen Wahei Kōsaku no Gunzō* [The peace feelers: A group portrait of peace initiatives in the Second Sino–Japanese War] (Tokyo: Ronsōsha, 1991), 201–77; Tobe Ryōichi, 'Nicchū Sensō Wahei Kōsaku Kenkyū no Dōkō to Genjō' [Trends and the present state of research into peace initiatives during the Second Sino-Japanese War], *Gaikō Shiryo Kanpō*, no. 15 (June 2001): 1–26; Liu Jie, *Nicchū Sensō-ka no Gaikō* [Diplomacy during the Second Sino-Japanese War] (Tokyo: Yoshikawa Kōbunkan, 1995), 181–245. See also Shidehara, *Gaikō 50 Nen*, 165–70; Shidehara Peace Foundation, *Shidehara Kijūrō*, 505–11.

24 Shidehara, *Gaikō 50 Nen*, 191–92. It must be noted that there are no corresponding entries in Ugaki's diary. The correspondence with Shidehara observed in *Documents Relating to Ugaki Kazushige* is also unrelated. See Ugaki Kazushige Document Research Association, eds, *Ugaki Kazushige Kankei Bunsho* [Documents relating to Ugaki Kazushige] (Tokyo: Fuyō Shobō Shuppan, 1995), 225–26.

25 Ministry of Foreign Affairs Research Department, Section 1, 'Gaikō Shiryō Hensan Jigyō nitsuite', 46–56. For details on the Research Department, see Takahashi, 'Gaimushō Kakushin-ha no Shisō to Kōdō', 42–46.

26 Outline of a dialogue with Shidehara (Komagome Residence), 24 October 1933, in 'Shoshushi Kankei Zakken', vol. 1.

27 Shidehara, 'Washington Kaigi no Rimen-kan Sonota', 116.

28 Shidehara, 'Shōwa 11-nen 12-gatsu Nisso Gyogyō Zantei Kyōtei Seiritsu nikansuru Keii no Ichikyokumen', 154–60; Shidehara, 'Gaikō Bunsho no Buntai, Kisōsha no Kokoroe narabini Shoshu no Keishiki', 83–94. With respect to the aforementioned 'Shōwa 11-nen 12-gatsu Nisso Gyogyō Zantei Kyōtei Seiritsu nikansuru Keii no Ichikyokumen', Minister to the Netherlands Ishii Itarō made reference to it. See Itō and Liu, *Ishii Itarō Nikki*, 317.

29 Shidehara to Makino, 28 July 1940, in 'Makino Nobuaki Kankei Bunsho', Correspondence Department, vol. 28.

30 Shidehara Kijūrō, 'Outlook of the European War', 14 June 1940, in 'Makino Nobuaki Kankei Bunsho', Correspondence Department, vol. 28.

31 A. L. Kennedy, with an introduction by Sir Valentine Chirol, *Old Diplomacy and New, 1876–1922, from Salisbury to Lloyd-George* (London: John Murray, 1922), 253, doi.org/10.2307/3014470.

32 Shidehara, 'Outlook of the European War'.

33 Shidehara, *Gaikō 50 Nen*, 202–06; Watanabe Tetsuzō, *Jimetsu no Tatakai* [A suicidal war] (Tokyo: Chūōkōronsha, 1988), 322–29. See also Itō Takashi, *Zoku Shōwa-ki no Seiji* [The politics of the Shōwa era, continued] (Tokyo: Yamakawa Shuppansha, 1993), 211.

34 Shidehara Kijūrō, 'Nakajima Yadanji-shi no Nihon Sensō Kaihi narabini Sōki Teisen Kowa Sokushin Undo nikansuru Shōgen' [Testimony relating to Mr Nakajima Yadanji's work to promote the avoidance of war and an early peace], 8 May 1949, in 'Shidehara Heiwa Bunko', Reel 7; Shidehara, *Gaikō 50 Nen*, 207–09.

35 Itō Nobufumi, 'Nihon no Shin-Gaikō to Shidehara-san' [Mr Shidehara and Japan's new diplomacy], date unknown, in 'Shidehara Heiwa Bunko', Reel 13.

36 Tōgō Shigenori, *Jidai no Ichimen: Taisen Gaikō no Shuki* [An aspect of the age: Memoirs of wartime diplomacy] (Tokyo: Chūōkōronsha, 1989), 317–18. See also Yoshida to Makino, 14 November and 1 December 1941, in Yoshida Shigeru Memorial Project Foundation, *Yoshida Shigeru Shokan*, 663–64,

664–65; Awaya Kentarō, Adachi Hiroaki and Kobayashi Motohiro, eds, *Tōkyō Saiban Shiryō: Tanaka Ryūkichi Jinmon Chōsho* [The Tokyo Trial documents: Record of the questioning of Tanaka Ryūkichi], trans. Ryōnosuke Okada (Tokyo: Ōtsuki Shoten, 1994), 156.

37 Kiyosawa Kiyoshi, *Gaikō-shi* [Diplomatic history] (Tokyo: Tōyō Keizai Shimpōsha, 1941).

38 Kitaoka Shinichi, *Seitō Seiji no Saisei: Sengo Seiji no Keisei to Hōkai* [The rebirth of party politics: The formation and collapse of postwar politics] (Tokyo: Chuōkōronsha, 1994), 188–89.

39 Kiyosawa, *Ankoku Nikki*, 43; Shidehara to Harada, 23 August 1943, in 'Harada Kumao Kankei Bunsho' [Documents relating to Harada Kumao], Document Department, no. 45, Modern Japanese Political History Materials Room, National Diet Library; Harada Kumao, ed, *Tōan-kō Seiwa* [A dialogue by Tōan-kō (Saionji Kinmochi)] (Tokyo: Iwanami Shoten, 1943); Kitaoka, *Seitō Seiji no Saisei*, 188–92.

40 Kiyosawa, *Ankoku Nikki*, 51. For Tani and Aoki's understanding of the situation, see *Kanpō*, extra edition, 29, 30 January, 4 February and 3 March 1943; *Teikoku Gikai Kizokuin Iinkai Sokkiroku, Shōwa Hen* [Shorthand record of the Imperial Diet House of Peers Committee, Shōwa Section], vol. 103 (Tokyo: University of Tokyo Press, 1998), 71–72, 265–66, 275–86.

41 Kiyosawa, *Ankoku Nikki*, 478, 490, 499–500, 502, 504, 524, 541; Kitaoka Shinichi, *Zōhoban Kiyosawa Kiyoshi* [Kiyosawa Kiyoshi], 2nd ed. (Tokyo: Chuō Kōron Shinsha, 2004), 189. Some dictation remains, including Shidehara Kijūrō (speaking), Kiyosawa Kiyoshi (transcribing), 'Washington Kaigi no Hanashi' [On the Washington conference], date unknown, in 'Shidehara Heiwa Bunko', Reel 18.

42 Kiyosawa Kiyoshi, 'Shidehara-dan Kaiko-dan nitaisuru Shokan' [Impressions on Baron Shidehara's reminiscences], 11 February 1945, in 'Shidehara Heiwa Bunko', Reel 13.

43 Shidehara Kijūrō, 'Gaijin nimo Kono Hito Ari' [Even among foreigners there are men such as this], *Gaikō Jihō*, no. 948 (August 1944): 24–28.

44 Yoshida to Wakatsuki, 21 March 1944, in Yoshida Shigeru Memorial Project Foundation, *Yoshida Shigeru Shokan*, 667–69. See also Itō and Nomura, *Kaigun Taishō Kobayashi Seizō Oboegaki*, 129–211; Itō Takashi, *Shōwa-ki no Seiji* [The politics of the Shōwa era] (Tokyo: Yamakawa Shuppansha, 1983), 129–216.

45 'Higashikuni-no-miya Nisshi' [The journal of Higashikuni-no-miya], 4, 17 August and 2 September 1943, in Chūō/Sensō Shidō Jūyō Kokusaku Bunsho/1298, Military Archives, Center for Military History, the National Institute for Defense Studies; Hosokawa Morisada, *Hosokawa Nikki* [The diary of Hosokawa], vol. 1 (Tokyo: Chūōkōronsha, 1979), 153, 203; Etō Jun, Kurihara Ken, and Hatano Sumio, eds, *Shūsen Kōsaku no Kiroku* [A record of end-of-war manoeuvring], vol. 1 (Tokyo: Kōdansha. 1986), 56–63; Yoshida to Makino, March 1942, 3 April 1942, 11 August 1943 and 21 March 1944, in Yoshida Shigeru Memorial Project Foundation, *Yoshida Shigeru Shokan*, 665–69; Prince Takamatsu Nobuhito, *Takamatsu-no-miya Nikki*, vol. 4, 269, vol. 6, 544, 558, 559, vol. 7, 374.

It should also be noted that Higashikuni Naruhiko, *Higashikuni Naruhiko Nikki: Nihon Gekidō-ki no Hiroku* [The diary of Higashikuni Naruhiko: Confidential papers on Japan's era of tumult] (Tokyo: Tokuma Shoten, 1968), 121–23, is not a correct reprinting of 'Higashikuni-no-miya Nisshi'.

46 Shidehara to Tsurumi Yūsuke, 29 July 1944, in 'Tsurumi Yūsuke Kankei Bunsho' [Documents relating to Tsurumi Yūsuke], Document Department, no. 325, Modern Japanese Political History Materials Room, National Diet Library; 'Gaikō Kenkyūkai' [Diplomatic research association], *Gaikō Jihō*, no. 953 (January 1945): 40.

47 The full details of this matter remain unclear, even within works such as Sawada, *Gaisenmon Hiroba*; Sawada, *Zuikan, Zuihitsu*.

48 Kiyosawa Kiyoshi, 'Shidehara-dan to Dai-Tōa Sensō Wahei-kan' [Baron Shidehara and his perspective on war and peace in Greater East Asia], 11 February 1945, in 'Shidehara Heiwa Bunko', Reel 18; Kiyosawa, *Ankoku Nikki*, 492; Hatano Sumio, *Taiheiyō Sensō to Asia Gaikō* [The Pacific War and Asian diplomacy] (Tokyo: University of Tokyo Press, 1996), 200–05; Nishimura Shigeo, 'Nihon Gaimusho Shiryo ni Miru Dumbarton Oaks Teian (1994 Nen 10 Gatsu) eno "Shūsei Iken"' ['Argument for amendment' of the Dumbarton Oaks Proposal (October 1944) as found in Japanese

Ministry of Foreign Affairs records], in *Chūgoku Gaikō to Kokuren no Seiritsu* [Chinese Diplomacy and the Establishment of the United Nations], ed. Nishimura Shigeo (Kyoto: Hōritsu Bunkasha, 2004), 147–57.

49   Kiyosawa Kiyoshi also depicted Shidehara as indifferent to attempts to bring the war to an end. See Kiyosawa, *Ankoku Nikki*, 563–64; Watanabe Tetsuzō, *Tenno no Aru Kuni no Kenpo* [The constitution of a nation with an emperor] (Tokyo: Jiyū Asia-sha, 1964), 166.

50   Itō Takashi, ed., *Takagi Sōkichi Nikki to Jōhō* [Takagi Sōkichi diary and information], vol. 2 (Tokyo: Misuzu Shobō, 2000), 886; Shinohara Hajime and Mitani Taichirō, eds, *Oka Yoshitake, London Nikki: 1936–1937* [Oka Yoshitake, London diary: 1936–1937] (Tokyo: Iwanami Shoten, 1997), 310–11, 355–56; Tsunoda Jun, ed., *Ugaki Kazushige Nikki* [The diary of Ugaki Kazushige], vol. 3 (Tokyo: Misuzu Shobō, 1971), 1638.

For details on the political manoeuvring of Nanbara and others, see Itō Takashi, *Shōwa 10 Nen-dai-shi Danshō* [Fragments of the second decade of the Shōwa era] (Tokyo: University of Tokyo Press, 1981), 283–88; Maruyama Masao and Fukuda Kanichi, eds, *Kikigaki: Nanbara Shigeru Kaikoroku* [Dictation: The memoirs of Nanbara Shigeru] (Tokyo: University of Tokyo Press, 1989), 268–77. Further, according to the Shidehara to Nanbara (17 December 1944), Shidehara listened to the condolences given by Nanbara at the funeral of Onozuka Kiheiji. See Fukuda Kanichi, ed., *Nanbara Shigeru Shokanshū* [The correspondence of Nanbara Shigeru] (Tokyo: Iwanami Shoten, 1987), 649.

51   Shidehara, *Gaikō 50 Nen*, 248.

52   'Gaimushō Shōsoku' [Ministry of Foreign Affairs news], *Kasumigaseki-kai Kaihō*, no. 12 (December 1945): 1.

53   Kido Diary Research Association, *Kido Kōichi Nikki*, vol. 2, 1216–17; Shidehara, *Gaikō 50 Nen*, 211–12; Ministry of Foreign Affairs, ed., *Shūsen-shi-roku* [Historical records of the end of the war] (Tokyo: End of the War Historical Records Publishing Association, 1986), 424–64; Itō, *Takagi Sōkichi Nikki to Jōhō*, vol. 2, 909–22; Satō Motoei and Kurosawa Fumitaka, eds, *GHQ Rekishi-ka Chinjutsu-roku: Shūsen-shi Shiryō* [GHQ historical section's statement records: Material on the history of the war's end], vol. 1 (Tokyo: Harashobō, 2002), 302–07, 330–32.

54   Ministry of Foreign Affairs Research Bureau, Third Section, 'Soren no Tai-Nichi Seisaku Shiryo' [Material on Soviet Union policy vis-à-vis Japan], March 1948, in 'Nisso Gaikō Kankei Zakken: Soren Kankei Shitsumu Hōkoku' [Miscellaneous issues relating to Japan–Soviet diplomacy: Work reports relating to the Soviet Union], A'.1.3.3.2-1, CD-R A'-428, Diplomatic Archives of the Ministry of Foreign Affairs of Japan; Iokibe, *Beikoku no Nihon Senryō Seisaku*, vol. 2, 227–30.

Part III.
Recovery: The Postwar Period

7

Prime Minister of an Occupied Nation: The Emperor System and the New Constitution

The Formation of the Shidehara Cabinet

Accepting Defeat

At noon on 15 August 1945, the Shōwa emperor's voice was directly broadcast to the nation via radio for the very first time.[1] Known as the Jewel Voice Broadcast, this broadcast informed the citizens of Japan that the war had been lost. Today, this broadcast is seen as synonymous with the official end of the war. However, it should be remembered, first, that the formal, indirect language of the Jewel Voice Broadcast made it extremely difficult for ordinary Japanese people to understand what the emperor was saying. Many citizens only learned that the war was lost from the subsequent explanations in newspaper reports and on the radio. Second, the imperial edict was actually promulgated on 14 August, and the emperor's reading of it was also recorded on that day. Thus, the Jewel Voice Broadcast on 15 August was merely the occasion when that reading was broadcast to the public.

Preceding the Jewel Voice Broadcast was the 'imperial decision' of the Shōwa emperor. This imperial decision was handed down on two occasions. The first occasion was 10 August. It led to the Suzuki Kantarō cabinet contacting the Allies with word of their acceptance of the Potsdam Declaration (i.e. that Japan was offering its unconditional surrender). However, this offer was made based on the understanding that there would be no changes to Japan's sovereignty and the supreme authority of the emperor. Secretary of State Byrnes responded in a somewhat elusive manner to this request. The second imperial decision was handed down on 14 August. This confirmed the acceptance of the Potsdam Declaration. On that same day, the official imperial edict declaring an end to the war was promulgated. The command to cease hostilities was given on 16 August. On the following day, the Suzuki cabinet was replaced by a new cabinet headed by Prince Higashikuni.

On 2 September, on the deck of the USS *Missouri*, Foreign Minister Shigemitsu Mamoru and Chief of Army General Staff Umezu Yoshijirō signed the terms of surrender. It is said that the ministers of the Higashikuni cabinet 'had extremely pained expressions' when learning that the word 'surrender' appeared in the document.[2] As noted above, the foreign minister in Prince Higashikuni's cabinet was Shigemitsu Mamoru. He would later be replaced with Yoshida Shigeru. As it happened, the Higashikuni cabinet was extremely short-lived. Its members resigned at the beginning of October. Such a cabinet, led by a member of the imperial household, was formed in order to suppress any resistance to surrender from the military. It could not remain in office because the General Headquarters of the Supreme Commander for the Allied Powers (GHQ) demanded far more political democratisation than was expected.

The following cabinet was the Shidehara cabinet. Shidehara asked Yoshida Shigeru to continue as foreign minister. In the immediate aftermath of the war, Shidehara, Yoshida and the other leaders of the nation faced four urgent political tasks. First, there was the issue of how to deal with the defeat itself. This was basically the problem of who was responsible for the war. Second, there was the issue of what would happen to the Shōwa emperor. Although the emperor was understood to have brought about peace by issuing an 'imperial decision', the very issuing of an 'imperial decision' connected him to the problem of who was responsible for the war in the first place. Third, there was the matter of reforming the constitution. Finally, there was the reconstruction of party politics.

Shidehara was deeply involved in each of these tasks. Although he had once helped lay the foundations for an age with his work as foreign minister, he had been practically forgotten during the war years.

Now, in the unprecedented circumstances of an occupied Japan, he would once again be pushed into political life. Following the resignation of the Higashikuni cabinet, Shidehara became the prime minister of Japan in the early period of occupation. How did Shidehara deal with questions that arose in the aftermath of Japan's defeat? Further, what role did he have to play in the construction of the postwar political system?

In this chapter I shall seek to shed light on these topics. Beginning with the formation of the Shidehara cabinet, I will proceed to examine Shidehara's involvement in the Investigation Committee for the Greater East Asia War, his relationship with the Shōwa emperor, his contribution to the creation of a new constitution and his participation in party politics.[3]

Forming the Cabinet

On the morning of 15 August 1945, Shidehara departed for a social gathering at the Japan Club. It was there that he would hear the Jewel Voice Broadcast. 'The unconditional surrender of the imperial army was of the greatest regret. Upon hearing the emperor's voice announcing the imperial rescript on the radio, my tears flowed quite involuntarily.' Shidehara found he could hardly remain at the club following such momentous news. Instead, under the blazing sun, he hurried home, and there he stayed. Shidehara wrote a letter to his close friend Ōdaira Komatsuchi, former vice-president of the South Manchuria Railway Company. With 'the whole country banding firmly together', Shidehara wrote, 'I believe that within a short time, we may enhance the glory of the nation to a point beyond that of the prewar era'.[4]

For Shidehara, Japan's defeat did not necessarily mean a complete loss of confidence. He saw that it could actually be an opportunity for rebirth. Indeed, this was certainly the case for Shidehara personally. Japan's prime minister during the period of occupation could not be somebody who was at risk of being accused of complicity in the war. As he had once been so active on the world stage, Shidehara quickly rose to the top of the potential candidates for the role. In truth, had the Pacific War not broken out, he would have been forgotten as simply a diplomat who had been unpopular with the citizenry. Yet the war, and Japan's eventual defeat, would instead offer him an abrupt reversal of fortunes.

Directly after the end of the war, Shidehara wrote a paper titled 'Shūsen Zengosaku' (Postwar remedial measures). In it, Shidehara recommended that Japan work to build relationships of trust with the Allied nations. It would need to remember its defeat yet look towards the future. With effort, Japan could secure an advantageous position in the international order. To this end, it was also important that the government properly investigate the causes of the defeat and make its findings public. Shidehara proceeded to offer four reasons for why Japan had lost the war: the conflation of state affairs and supreme command, insufficient research in the natural sciences, the termination of military production due to air raids and the destructive force of the atomic bombs. Shidehara would provide a copy of 'Shūsen Zengosaku' to Foreign Minister Yoshida in the Higashikuni cabinet in October 1945.[5]

It might be asked, however, why Shidehara prepared this paper. In fact, we know that by the end of the Pacific War, government figures such as former home affairs officials Tsugita Daisaburō and Nagaoka Ryūichirō had already asked Shidehara to put himself forward as a candidate for prime minister. Shidehara's writing of 'Shūsen Zengosaku' was not unrelated to his possible return to politics.[6] Shidehara knew it was possible that he might become the next leader of Japan.

Lord Keeper of the Privy Seal Kido Kōichi had raised the possibility of Foreign Minister Yoshida succeeding Prince Higashikuni as prime minister. However, Yoshida thought Shidehara was more appropriate for the job. To discuss the matter further, Kido met with Prince Higashikuni, Konoe Fumimaro and Chairman of the Privy Council Hiranuma Kiichirō. They concluded that Shidehara was the top candidate, followed by Yoshida. Their criteria were that the candidate needed to be 'somebody without ill feelings towards the US, who was free of any doubt as to their responsibility for the war, and who was well versed in matters of diplomacy'.[7] When Yoshida thereafter obtained the informal agreement of Douglas MacArthur, the Supreme Commander for the Allied Powers, Yoshida asked Shidehara to be appointed as prime minister. However, Shidehara himself was not easily persuaded to accept this responsibility.

On 6 October, Shidehara had an audience with the Shōwa emperor. When the emperor sought to draw Shidehara out on the topic of becoming prime minister, he refused to accept the implicit offer, saying, 'I do not believe I am capable'.[8] Shidehara was already 73 years old and had spent

7. PRIME MINISTER OF AN OCCUPIED NATION

10 years in political opposition. Further, even when serving as a diplomat, he had sought to keep his distance from domestic politics. Yet, Shidehara recollects, he then:

> Observed just how much [this answer] pained [the emperor]. Things had already gotten to this stage, so [I] could hardly bear to cause the emperor further worry. I therefore swore to myself that I would do whatever I could, even at the cost of my own life. Then I responded: '[I] am lacking in confidence that I can handle this important responsibility. However, let me do everything in my power to honor your will.' I then withdrew from his presence.[9]

Although Shidehara may not have been filled with confidence, it should be remembered that only less than two months had gone by since the war ended in ruinous defeat. Surely there was not a soul who could have confidently assumed responsibility for the nation in such circumstances. The emperor also understood this. After all, even Yoshida, who was known for his daring, hesitated to agree to become prime minister during such unprecedented difficulties. Shidehara fortified his will and eventually issued his reply to the throne: 'I will devote all of my strength to do what is necessary'.[10] Ultimately, Kido's cooperation with the emperor ensured that Shidehara was unable to decline the offer. Kido himself believed that 'there was nobody else we could turn to … it is best if we have the emperor himself thoroughly bring him around'.[11] The key cabinet ministers were thus selected: Shidehara, Yoshida and Tsugita. Yoshida remained foreign minister, while Tsugita became the chief cabinet secretary.

On 9 October, the Shidehara cabinet was at last officially sworn in. As newspaper reporters surrounded Shidehara, one blurted out: 'So, Mr. Shidehara, it turns out you were still alive, huh?'[12] It is also worth pointing out that to this day, Shidehara and Suzuki Kantarō remain the only prime ministers of Japan who were originally from Osaka.

Given Shidehara's background, it would not have been unnatural for the positions in his cabinet to be filled with individuals affiliated with the old Minseitō party. And, indeed, there were Minseitō-affiliated ministers in the cabinet beyond Tsugita. For example, there was the agriculture minister, Matsumura Kenzō; the transport minister, Tanaka Takeo; and the minister for commerce and industry, Ogasawara Sankurō. However, Ashida Hitoshi, the health and welfare minister, was originally a member of the old Seiyūkai party. Yoshida Shigeru, who continued as foreign minister under Shidehara, had also once served as vice-minister for foreign affairs in the Seiyūkai party cabinet of Tanaka Giichi. From Shidehara's perspective, Yoshida was more of a collateral than a mainstream member of the Ministry of Foreign Affairs. Nevertheless, during his time in political opposition, Shidehara had strengthened his relationship with Yoshida.

While Home Minister Horikiri Zenjirō was once an official at the Ministry of Home Affairs, he did not have strong party affiliations. With Shidehara's permission, he proceeded to work on revising the electoral laws, a task that included the incorporation of women's suffrage. Meanwhile, the chief of the Cabinet Legislation Bureau, Narahashi Wataru, was an international lawyer who had studied in France. Minister of State Matsumoto Jōji was a scholar of commercial law but had previously served as the minister of commerce and industry in the Saitō Makoto cabinet. Finance Minister Shibusawa Keizō had been the governor of the Bank of Japan. Justice Minister Iwata Chūzō and Education Minister Maeda Tamon remained in their positions from the earlier Higashikuni cabinet.[13] Meanwhile, War Minister Shimomura Sadamu and Navy Minister Yonai Mitsumasa remained in their posts at the request of the emperor.

In a letter to Makino, Yoshida wrote that 'the staffing of the cabinet has generally been going smoothly'.[14] Certainly, this was a cabinet staffed primarily on the basis of ability. Former Ministry of Home Affairs official Izawa Takio also used his behind the scenes influence to assist with the selection of cabinet personnel. As mentioned earlier, Shidehara and Izawa had been classmates at the Osaka Third Higher Middle School. However, Tsugita, Matsumura, Tanaka, Horikiri and Maeda were eventually forced out of the cabinet when they were purged from public office.

Meeting with MacArthur: 'Japanese-Style Democracy'

As soon as Shidehara became prime minister, the GHQ commissioned a report on him for their own purposes. The beginning of this report features a quote from former ambassador Grew's published diary, *Ten Years in Japan*. There were also references to a book by Moore, a former Ministry of Foreign Affairs adviser, titled *With Japan's Leaders*. The GHQ report referred to Shidehara as 'one of the old school of Japanese diplomats, a man of integrity as well as caution'. The report also contains some details from an interrogation of Tokuda Kyūichi, the leader of Japan's Communist Party. Tokuda had stated: 'Because of his weak nature, SHIDEHARA has the tendency to yield to any strong demand of the *zaibatsu* or even the military clique'.[15]

Viewed from another perspective, there was little information here that was of significance for the occupying army. Even MacArthur, upon hearing that Shidehara had been informally picked for prime minister, reportedly remarked to Foreign Minister Yoshida: 'Damn, he's old … Can he speak English?' Yoshida, who had himself put Shidehara forward as a candidate, lamented this sorry state of affairs: 'Here is Mr. Shidehara, a master of English, as anybody who knows him would attest, and yet the general thinks it necessary to even ask, "Can he speak English?"'[16] In Washington, President Truman was also struggling to size up Shidehara. He had to turn to former ambassador Forbes to get a sense of this man. Forbes told Truman that he regarded Shidehara to be 'a close personal friend of mine' and that he 'had the highest opinion of him'. Truman responded by saying that he was 'extremely glad to know that'.[17] Although Forbes's relationship with Shidehara had been strained by the Manchurian Incident, Forbes had not forgotten him.

As the new prime minister of Japan, Shidehara faced the vital task of building a relationship with MacArthur. Just after the new cabinet was formed on 11 October, Shidehara visited the general. MacArthur had no time for pleasantries and sought to get down to business immediately. He asked Shidehara to carry out five reforms, now known in Japanese as the Five Great Reforms: women's suffrage, the encouragement of labour unions, liberal-style education, the abolition of secret trials and the democratisation of the economic system.

To these requests for democratisation, Shidehara responded without hesitation. He noted that the cabinet had already begun work on matters such as women's suffrage and that, as Japan already had 'democratic trends' before the war, it would not be difficult to move in that direction once again. Shidehara asserted that what Japan required was not US-style democracy but rather 'the development of a Japanese-style "democracy"' more suitable to the nation's own circumstances. 'Quite so', responded MacArthur.[18] This suggests that Shidehara had a positive impression of MacArthur, believing that he would be easy to deal with. From Shidehara's perspective, meanwhile, MacArthur's requests were already incorporated into the policy planning of his cabinet. There was, however, a pitfall to this way of thinking: Shidehara lacked sufficient awareness of GHQ's request for constitutional revision. In other words, MacArthur saw a new constitution as a prerequisite for his desired reforms. On the other hand, Shidehara had not acknowledged that a radical revision of the constitution was essential.

Although the Shidehara cabinet met on 12 October and discussed MacArthur's requested Five Great Reforms, Shidehara still did not seriously consider constitutional revision.[19] Of course, it is worth pointing out that these were the early days of Japan's occupation, and innumerable tasks faced the country.

What, then, was the basic policy direction pursued by the Shidehara cabinet? Shidehara gave a speech on his administrative policy before the House of Representatives on 28 November. In this speech, Shidehara listed a number of specific policies to be pursued. Beginning with the revision of the electoral law, these policies addressed issues such as educational reform, freedom of expression, stability of the lives of the citizens, farmland reform, support for demobilised soldiers, restoration of regions damaged by war, improvement of land and sea transportation, and an investigation into the causes of the defeat.[20] Of these, the investigation of the defeat would link directly to questions of who was responsible for the war to begin with. It also had the potential to touch upon the emperor system itself. Thus, this task required both prudence and speed.

The Survey Association of Greater East Asia War

At this time, the Ministry of Foreign Affairs was discreetly establishing a board for researching problems relating to the peace conditions. The aim was to conduct preliminary research on the implications of the signing of the peace treaty. The chief secretary of the board was Sugihara Arata, director-general of the Treaties and Conventions Bureau, while secretaries were selected from among the director-ranked staff of the various bureaus.[21]

That said, the finalisation of the peace process was still a long way off. The first challenge that the Shidehara cabinet faced was what lessons to take away from the defeat, and what changes would need to be made in the way the nation was run. One particularly difficult topic was that of responsibility for the war. On 30 October 1945, the Shidehara cabinet decided to create a new survey association specifically for the purpose of investigating the causes of the defeat. Towards the end of November, the government proclaimed the establishment of the Dai Tōa Sensō Chōsa-kai (Survey Association of Greater East Asia War).[22]

Aoki Tokuzō was selected as the secretary-general of the association. Chief Cabinet Secretary Tsugita had sounded out Aoki on assuming this position. Previously, Aoki had served as a Ministry of Finance official affiliated with the old Minseitō party. The more difficult problem was who to appoint as president. Through Yoshida, Shidehara asked Makino Nobuaki if he would accept the responsibility. However, Makino firmly declined. Shidehara then sought out former prime minister Wakatsuki Reijirō. However, Wakatsuki also refused. In January 1946, the Dai Tōa Sensō Chōsa-kai was renamed the Sensō Chōsa-kai (War Research Institute). Even by this time, no one willing to act as president had been found. In the end, Shidehara had to take on the role himself. The institute's first general meeting was held on 27 March.

To start the meeting, Shidehara gave an address in his role as committee president, stating: 'The purpose of this institute is to clarify the causes behind, and facts relating to, the defeat in the war'. He added: 'Our mission is not that of investigating war criminals and holding them to account'.[23] Shidehara also emphasised the significance of Article 9 contained in the draft for the new constitution. Aoki, who had written the original outline for Shidehara's address, noted that 'Mr. Shidehara had completely reworded what I had written'.[24] There were 20 members of the Sensō Chōsa-kai, including the president of the Yomiuri Newspaper Company, Baba Tsunego. There were a further 18 provisional members of vice-ministerial level from the various government ministries. The Sensō Chōsa-kai consisted of a total of five subcommittees. The first of these was tasked with inquiring into political and diplomatic matters. The other four subcommittees were charged with considering the respective topics of military affairs, finance and economy, ideology, and science and technology.

The committee's second general meeting was held on 4 April 1946. Shidehara served as the chairman. On this occasion, Shidehara also stated that the 'problem of wartime responsibility' was not 'the main object of this institute'. On the contrary, Shidehara hoped that an inquiry into the facts and their relations, and the relaying of these details to the broader public, could 'help bring about an end to the fantasies that some individuals held about wars of this nature'.[25]

However, at this point, unexpected interference emerged. In a July meeting of the Allied Council for Japan, the Soviet Union criticised the Sensō Chōsa-kai for its inclusion of former military personnel. The Allied Council for Japan was an advisory body to the Supreme Commander for the Allied Powers, which had been established in Tokyo. The need for such an advisory body had been agreed upon in November of the previous year, during a foreign ministers' conference in Moscow. Although Shidehara objected to the Soviets' denunciation, the institute was abolished at the end of September 1946.[26]

These developments have been criticised for trivialising the pursuit of wartime responsibility.[27] Certainly, the investigation of who had responsibility for the war may well have been insufficient. Nevertheless, Shidehara had an uncommonly strong will, as demonstrated in the following correspondence that Shidehara had sent to Makino:

> The work of the Dai Tōa Sensō Chōsa-kai will serve to provide lessons of the greatest importance for ages to come, to ensure that the citizens of our nation do not repeat the mistakes of the past. This is why, as a matter of the greatest importance, I have disturbed you in particular with respect to the role of president of this committee, and why I earnestly await your instruction as to the general policies the committee should adopt.[28]

In other words, Shidehara, through Yoshida, had urged Makino to reconsider his refusal to accept the position of president. Shidehara also did not simply look on as the Sensō Chōsa-kai was abolished. Even after Shidehara left the office of prime minister on 22 April, he continued to show passion for preparing Japan for the future by thoroughly assessing the events of the past. Later, on 30 May, during the Yoshida cabinet, Shidehara met with Ashida and asked that he take on the role of vice-president of the Sensō Chōsa-kai before it was abolished. Ashida accepted this offer on 7 June.[29]

Once it was decided to disband the Sensō Chōsa-kai, Shidehara drafted a revised 'plan for a civil research organization' and requested that the provisional committee members 'continue to cooperate'.[30] Shidehara's plan was for the work of the original committee to continue through the creation of an incorporated foundation. However, the GHQ would not allow it. At this point, Shidehara personally entrusted the matter to Aoki Tokuzō.

Aoki proceeded to write a meticulous outline of the sequence of events leading up to the commencement of war with the US, taking the London Naval Conference on Disarmament as the starting point. Of course, Aoki made use of the historical documents that had thus far been collected by the Sensō Chōsa-kai. This was how Aoki came to write the six-volume series *Taiheiyō Sensō Zenshi* (The prehistory of the Pacific War). This work omitted all subjective evaluation. It resembles a collection of historical material, just as Shidehara would presumably have intended for such an endeavour. In fact, Shidehara provided the foreword for this series, including the following line: 'I believe [this work] is sufficient for [the purposes of] convincing future generations of citizens, and for calling upon them to reflect'.[31]

It should be noted, however, that Shidehara's activity of determining the causes of the war was very much official in nature. Thus, these actions do not reveal what Shidehara thought as an individual about the issue of wartime responsibility. As it happens, Shidehara expressed his personal thinking on the subject after an unexpected event: the suicide of Konoe on 16 December 1945. Following Konoe's death, there were moves towards having his biography written. Shidehara was asked to formally initiate such an undertaking. However, he was unwilling to comply. His reasoning was that 'responsibility for causing the Pacific War lay above all with individuals like Duke Konoe and Lord Kido'.[32]

How would Shidehara have dealt with the military? Let us go back in time a few months to mention one more matter from this initial period of the Shidehara cabinet. At the end of November 1945, the cabinet decided to abolish the War Ministry and the Navy Ministry. To replace them in overseeing the ongoing demobilisation, on 1 December, the cabinet further established the Daiichi Fukuin-sho (First Demobilization Ministry) and the Daini Fukuin-sho (Second Demobilization Ministry).[33] Shidehara himself took the responsibility of heading both of these ministries.

Shidehara observed that many of the survivors of the conflict 'had tasted the sorrow of disillusionment' upon returning to see their war-torn homeland. To this end, rather than merely discussing how to help the returnees with the Ministry of Health and Welfare or the Ministry of Justice, Shidehara made a plea on the radio for 'heartfelt solidarity between those returning and those who remained'.[34]

The Shōwa Emperor

Amid Criticisms of the Emperor System

When the Shidehara cabinet was formed at the beginning of October 1945, the GHQ ordered the Japanese government to release its political prisoners. This meant that the Japanese Communist Party was able to publicly resume its activities. Tokuda Kyūichi and other leaders of the Communist Party were particularly critical of the emperor system. The cabinet minister who reacted most strongly to the communists' criticisms of the emperor system was Narahashi Wataru, chief of the Cabinet Legislation Bureau. In a cabinet meeting, Narahashi proposed responding to the communists. Although Yoshida voiced his disagreement, Shidehara consented to the idea. Narahashi thereafter personally criticised the Communist Party on NHK Radio and argued for the continuation of the emperor system.[35]

Of course, it was not only the Japanese Communist Party that criticised the emperor system. In China and the US, much of the public regarded the Shōwa emperor himself as a war criminal. It was in this context that the US State-War-Navy Coordinating Committee reached out to MacArthur to seek his opinion on the matter. MacArthur responded that if the emperor were accused, it would lead to a chaotic situation for the occupation, and a million soldiers would be needed to maintain order. In other words, MacArthur responded to Washington by paradoxically stressing the usefulness of the emperor.[36]

Shidehara himself also worked to help preserve the emperor system. He began such efforts even before becoming prime minister. Shidehara anticipated that the emperor would eventually have the opportunity to speak with reporters from the *New York Times* on the matter. Therefore, towards the end of September 1945, he set about writing a draft in English for the emperor to utilise on such an occasion. In this draft, Shidehara noted that the imperial edict issued by the Tōjō cabinet announcing the war included the statement that specifics of wartime strategy 'should be left to the decision of the commander-in-chief of these forces'.[37] In other words, Shidehara was careful that the emperor not mention Tōjō specifically.

Taking this draft of answers into consideration, the emperor met with US reporters on 25 September. The press conference with the emperor proceeded much as Shidehara had anticipated. Nevertheless, the manner in which the *New York Times* reported on the emperor's response made it sound as though he was attempting to shift blame on to Tōjō. On this topic, a standard interpretation is that the summary of the meeting drafted by the newspaper was incorrect.[38]

However, the documentary records from the emperor's meeting with Frank Kluckhohn, reporter for the *New York Times*, state: 'His Majesty had no intention to have the war rescript used as General Tōjō used it'.[39] If we take into account the contents of Kido's diary, we can infer another possibility: that the emperor himself told the reporter that it had been 'heartbreaking' to issue to Tōjō the imperial rescript for commencing the war. If that were the case, then it would mean that the emperor's statement went further than what Shidehara prepared for him. This is what the *New York Times* had suggested. Further, the article also appeared on the 29 September front page of the *Asahi Shimbun*. Upon seeing this, Shidehara could not help but be 'pained' at the 'audaciousness of the questioning'.[40]

The first meeting between the emperor and MacArthur was held on 27 September. Almost all of what was said is known, as the historical records were recently made public. According to those meeting records, the emperor told MacArthur: 'With respect to the war, I myself wished to the fullest extent to avoid it. When I saw that the war would nevertheless take place, I felt the greatest regret'.[41] Although the emperor did not mention Tōjō, his use of the expression 'regret' could be tied to theories of his responsibility for the war.

Exactly how Shidehara learned of the specifics of this first meeting is unclear. However, he was the type to go into the smallest details. Of the 11 meetings that eventually took place between the emperor and MacArthur, Shidehara received fairly accurate reports on at least some of them. Presumably, he received much of this information from contacts in the Ministry of Foreign Affairs. In the case of this first meeting, the emperor's statement that he felt 'regret' must have been cause for great concern for Shidehara, who viewed the wording as 'imprudent'.[42]

At around this time, the Treaties and Conventions Bureau at the Ministry of Foreign Affairs had begun to examine questions of the emperor's responsibility for the war from the perspective of the Meiji Constitution. According to the bureau, responsibility for beginning the war 'should be borne by the government, which was responsible for advising the emperor, and not by the emperor himself'.[43] On 5 November 1945, the Shidehara cabinet reached a decision on the problem of war responsibility. This cabinet decision stressed that the emperor was exempt from responsibility. More specifically, it stated that the emperor 'sought a peaceful settlement when it came to negotiations with the U.S.'. However, 'with respect to matters such as the decision to go to war and the carrying out of war strategy, he had no choice but to follow certain conventions established within the constitution'.[44]

On the surface, this may appear to be an example of the typical justification given by the Japanese side. In reality, the wishes of the GHQ were surely also at play here to some degree. After all, MacArthur had a positive attitude towards the emperor and fretted over the condemnation of him from the US public and the Soviets. Further, reports on MacArthur's disposition were relayed from Brigadier General Bonner F. Fellers, who was a close adviser to MacArthur, to Chief Cabinet Secretary Tsugita via former army lieutenant general Haraguchi Hatsutarō.[45]

Declaration of Humanity

On New Year's Day 1946, an imperial rescript was promulgated that denied the Shōwa emperor's divinity. This was known as the 'Declaration of Humanity'. However, aside from the imperial oath consisting of five articles at the beginning, the Declaration of Humanity was not conceived by the emperor himself. Here, too, Prime Minister Shidehara played a role. However, the primary leader of this undertaking is understood to have been Lieutenant Colonel H. G. Henderson, adviser to the GHQ Civil Information and Educational Section. There are also those who emphasise the guidance of Yamanashi Katsunoshin. Previously an admiral in the navy, Yamanashi had become president of Gakushūin.[46]

The Yamanashi Katsunoshin documents held at Gakushūin include an English-language draft of the Declaration of Humanity. In the margins of the draft, the following names are written: 'Dyke, Henderson, Blyth, Yamanashi'. The draft was written on 15–20 December 1945. Here, the names 'Dyke' and 'Blyth' refer to Ken R. Dyke, chief of the

Civil Information and Educational Section, and R. H. Blyth, a teacher at Gakushūin. Notes written on the Yamanashi document also state the following:

> A (written by Blyth) → minister of the imperial household → emperor → minister of the imperial household → vice-minister, Asano → (Foreign Minister Yoshida → prime minister → Foreign Minister Yoshida) → vice-minister → Asano → Mr. B → Henderson + Dyke → M'Arth.
>
> Approval of M'Arth → Mr. B → Asano → minister of the imperial household, vice-minister → emperor → prime minister → Cabinet council etc. → Proclamation.[47]

To clarify, what it states is that the English-language draft was given to the Japanese side by Blyth. It then passed through the hands of individuals such as Minister of the Imperial Household Ishiwata Sōtarō, Vice-Minister of the Imperial Household Ōgane Masujirō and Gakushūin administrative official Asano Nagamitsu, before eventually reaching Prime Minister Shidehara. The Yamanashi document notes also feature the statement: 'This draft has been shown beforehand to Dyke-M'ck, in order to receive their input'.[48] Of course, the names 'M'Arth' and 'M'ck' in these notes refer to MacArthur. In summary, although the proposal for the Declaration of Humanity originated on the GHQ side, its actual contents were a joint effort between the Japanese and US sides. Naturally, this joint effort included Shidehara.

On 25 December, as hunger and bitter cold swept over the ruins of Tokyo, Shidehara continued to work on the English-language draft of the Declaration of Humanity at the Prime Minister's Office. For this task he had the consent of the GHQ, as well as the approval of the emperor, received via Maeda, the minister for education. As it happens, Kinoshita Michio, the deputy grand chamberlain, was critical of Shidehara's draft. Specifically, he was resistant to a document such as this that denied the emperor's divinity. Yet, Shidehara fought this opposition. 'To change the meaning of the text now that it has been shown to MacArthur', Shidehara stated, 'would trespass against the faith [he has put in us]'.[49] Shidehara collapsed the following morning with acute pneumonia, due to his exhausting workload. He was eventually confined to bed to recover. Upon learning about Shidehara's illness, MacArthur personally ensured that he received a special delivery of penicillin.

Thus, on New Year's Day 1946, the morning editions of the nation's newspapers published the imperial rescript, which began: 'We are together with thee, the citizens'. It would later become known as the Declaration of Humanity. These morning editions also displayed unprecedented pictures of the emperor wearing a regular suit. The public had never seen him shown in such a manner before. At this time, Shidehara issued his own comment as prime minister: 'Carrying out the will of our lord's imperial command, we will build a new nation that is permeated with the ideals of democracy, pacifism, and rationalism'.[50] Of course, what Shidehara meant by 'democracy' was something different from the Western-style concept. For Shidehara, Japanese democracy was to be developed on the basis the emperor's five-article imperial oath.

Some at the time were aware of Shidehara's involvement in the emperor's Declaration of Humanity.[51] The Shōwa emperor himself acknowledged this in the late 1970s, when he made the following public statement:

> The first goal of that declaration was the imperial oath. The matter of divinity [its rejection] was actually a secondary matter … I think it was very necessary at that time to point out that democracy was not an import from outside … I also spoke with Prime Minister Shidehara Kijūrō. When the prime minister showed [the draft] to Supreme Commander MacArthur of the GHQ, he responded very positively, praising it for 'being excellent beyond expectations,' and was strongly in favor of the whole text being published. Hence it was decided to release the entire text.[52]

Although the emperor claimed that the rejection of his divinity was 'a secondary matter', this interpretation differs from Shidehara's intention. I note that Shidehara had also suggested to the emperor that he consider conducting an imperial tour of the nation and bestow funds from the imperial household finances to the people.[53]

There are other details that help to paint a picture of Shidehara's perception of the imperial household. At that time Japan was suffering from food shortages. Shidehara told Finance Minister Shibusawa: 'Japan has run out of food. If we do not ask the U.S. for food aid, then Japanese people will starve to death'. Casting about for ideas, Shibusawa even urged Shidehara: 'Please send the crown prince to study in the U.S.'. Shibusawa worried that the US might not send enough food unless Japan signalled its obedience by sending its crown prince there as a hostage, so to speak. This gives us some idea of just how concerned he was about the situation.

Shidehara declined Shibusawa's request on the spot: 'I cannot present such a discourteous request to His Majesty'.⁵⁴ At a loss as to what should be done, Shibusawa could only weep.

Establishing the New Constitution

The Constitutional Problems Investigation Committee

Another ordeal awaited the Shidehara cabinet after the Declaration of Humanity. This was the mass purging of individuals from public office on 4 January 1946. Five ministers from the Shidehara cabinet were among those purged that day. Furious, Shidehara summoned Chief Cabinet Secretary Tsugita to his sickbed and began to fiercely criticise MacArthur:

> That bastard Mac, to give such a ridiculous order … I simply cannot agree to this. I cannot execute such orders. I am unable to force out my cabinet ministers who have worked with me up until today, so I am determined instead to trigger a mass resignation of the cabinet. Please tell the ministers of my decision and gather all their letters of resignation.⁵⁵

In sum, Shidehara informed Tsugita that he had decided that the cabinet should resign en masse. However, he tearfully retracted this decision after strenuous persuasion by Matsumura, the minister for agriculture.

Hence the Shidehara cabinet was instead reshuffled. Along with Chief Cabinet Secretary Tsugita and Agriculture Minister Matsumura, the five ministers forced to resign included Home Minister Horikiri, Education Minister Maeda and Transport Minister Tanaka. Their respective positions were filled by Narahashi Wataru, Soejima Senpachi, Micchi Chūzō, Abe Yoshishige and Murakami Yoshikazu. As Narahashi took on the role of chief cabinet secretary, the now-vacated chief of the Cabinet Legislation Bureau was in turn filled by Ishiguro Takeshige. The GHQ Government Section was critical of this reshuffle.⁵⁶

The most serious point of contention during the cabinet reshuffle was that of constitutional reform. In truth, Shidehara was not enthusiastic about the proposition. When Shidehara originally formed his cabinet at the beginning of October 1945, he had expressed the opinion that constitutional reform ought to be carried out 'extremely passively, with changes made [only] as specific needs arose'.⁵⁷ Nevertheless, he also felt that if the US demanded constitutional reform, it would be difficult to resist. On 13 October of that same year, the cabinet decided to establish the Constitutional Problems Investigation Committee. The committee chairman was State Minister Matsumoto Jōji. The committee members included scholars such as Miyazawa Toshiyoshi, Chief of the Cabinet Legislation Bureau Narahashi, Cabinet Legislation Bureau First Department Director Irie Toshio and Second Department Director Satō Tatsuo.⁵⁸

That said, Shidehara's intention was to examine whether constitutional reform was even required. His establishment of this committee did not mean he had committed to a course of reform. Although the Constitutional Problems Investigation Committee convened at the meeting room of the prime minister's official residence, there is practically no evidence that Shidehara actually offered the committee any guidance. Indeed, the committee itself was entirely unofficial. Moreover, Shidehara was at a loss when it came to dealing with Konoe Fumimaro, who pushed for constitutional reform from outside of the cabinet.⁵⁹

Another occasion when Shidehara revealed his perspective on constitutional matters was his address to the House of Representatives on 28 November 1945. To a question from Saitō Takao, Shidehara responded that it was still premature to speak of reforming the constitution. As he stated: 'The articles of the imperial constitution are highly flexible and do not obstruct the development of democracy'. At the same time, Shidehara noted that while the Meiji Constitution could operate in a flexible manner, it might also need some revisions to 'put an end to long-running concerns over its abuse'.⁶⁰ Shidehara's thinking on the matter was two-tiered, as it were. Therefore, while the kind of constitutional reform Shidehara had in mind was not comprehensive, he did not think to stand by idly. From the outside, he may have appeared to be merely indecisive. George Sansom, an old acquaintance who was visiting Japan at this time, wrote that Shidehara:

> Is old and tired … [He] had no experience in domestic politics … [and] was interested more in the past than the future … [He was] a melancholy figure certainly unfit to lead his country in a desperate crisis.⁶¹

Sansom was then serving as the British representative to the Far Eastern Advisory Commission.

The Origin of Article 9

One of the problems that arises when considering the history of this period is the origin of Article 9 of the Japanese constitution. This is the famous article that prevents Japan from participating in wars. Although some have theorised that MacArthur proposed Article 9, MacArthur himself stated that the article was based upon a proposal from Prime Minister Shidehara. It has been said that MacArthur and Shidehara had a debate over this article during a meeting between the two on 24 January 1946. Shidehara had returned to his duties following his recovery only three days earlier. According to his close friend Ōdaira Komatsuchi, Shidehara had initially visited MacArthur to thank him for the penicillin he had received. However, recalls Ōdaira, Shidehara also used the opportunity to 'tell MacArthur that he wanted to maintain the emperor system, no matter what, and wanted to know if he would receive MacArthur's cooperation in that respect'. MacArthur responded by 'promising that he wanted to cooperate as much as possible, which was a great relief for Shidehara'.[62]

Shidehara also reportedly:

> Began to talk about how, for some time, he had thought that in order for the world to give up on military force, in order for that ideal to be realized, and for the world as a whole to stop engaging in war, the only way would be [for nations] to renounce the right to wage war. As it happened, MacArthur suddenly stood up and grasped Shidehara's hand with both of his hands and expressed his heartfelt agreement with tears in his eyes, such that Shidehara was quite surprised for a moment.[63]

For the most part, both Shidehara and MacArthur placed the highest importance upon the continuation of the emperor system. 'Clearly announcing to the world' that Japan renounced the waging of war has hence been understood by commentators as a method for achieving this end. In other words, it was necessary to renounce war in order to placate international opinion, which had thus far been critical of the emperor system. It must be added that, at this point, the Japanese side had just begun to prepare a draft of the revised constitution. They had no way of foreseeing that the GHQ would produce its own draft. Further, Shidehara's talk of renouncing war had, at that stage, been only an expression of ideals. It is hard to imagine Shidehara proposing that such an article be included in the constitution. Yet, this is just what MacArthur would soon work towards having incorporated into the draft.

At any rate, it is important to clarify the context within which Shidehara mentioned the renunciation of war. Fortunately, some details on this matter appear in the unearthed correspondence of Shiratori Toshio. The former diplomat Shiratori had been arrested and detained in Sugamo Prison as a suspected A-class war criminal. On 10 December 1945, Shiratori composed a letter in English to Foreign Minister Yoshida, stating that it was necessary to carry out 'a totally new departure in constitutional legislation … binding up that [peace] clause indissolubly with the provisions concerning the Emperor'.[64] In other words, Shiratori proposed including a renunciation of war in the constitution in order to protect the emperor system. Shiratori asked Yoshida to make a copy of his letter and provide it to Shidehara. However, the letter was held by GHQ censors until 20 January 1946.

Later, at the Tokyo Trial, former diplomat Hirota Yōji acted as Shiratori's assistant counsel. According to the affidavit of Yoshida Shigeru, as prepared by Hirota, Shiratori had met with Yoshida just before his detention. On that occasion, he told Yoshida that he wished to speak with Shidehara on matters that included a proposal for a new constitution. Upon hearing this, Yoshida requested that he put the details of this request in writing, which Shiratori then did. This is why Yoshida would later hand a copy of Shiratori's letter to Shidehara. Shidehara is believed to have received Shiratori's letter directly after its release by the GHQ censors, around 20 January 1946. If that was the case, it means that Shidehara would have had the chance to look at Shiratori's letter just before the 24 January meeting with MacArthur. Therefore, Shidehara's mentioning of the renunciation of war during that meeting may well have occurred as a result of his coming into contact with that letter.[65]

Did Shidehara's talk of renunciation of war bring about the inclusion of Article 9 in the new constitution? Drawing upon comments by Shidehara's secretary, Kishi Kuramatsu, Hirota Yōji says the following about the 24 January meeting between Shidehara and MacArthur:

> It is true that Prime Minister Shidehara had spoken of the idea, or the ideal of renouncing war, and that General MacArthur completely agreed with him on the matter. However, they did not at all discuss the inclusion of any such provision in the Japanese constitution. That is why, when the U.S. draft of the Japanese constitution was shown to the Japanese side on February 19 [sic.], even the prime minister appeared somewhat surprised. Even the Matsumoto draft that the Japanese side created contained nothing

remotely like the renunciation of the right to wage war. This is because Mr. Shidehara never thought to use the constitution to prescribe such a thing.[66]

In other words, while Shidehara and MacArthur had seen eye to eye on the topic of renouncing war, this was simply at the level of an ideal, and not as an article in the constitution. Further, when Hirota visited Shidehara and Yoshida:

> The two of them said that they had read Shiratori's letter. However, they would not tell me anything at all about how they would respond to his war renunciation proposal, or the other contents of the letter.[67]

We can surmise that what Shiratori had in mind when he composed his letter was something like the Kellogg–Briand Pact of some 20 years prior. This pact was named for the US secretary of state and the French foreign minister who spearheaded its formulation. The Kellogg–Briand Pact included the renunciation of warfare as an instrument of national policy, prescribing that arguments between nations were to be resolved peacefully. It was signed in Paris in August 1928. When plenipotentiary representative Uchida Yasuya signed the pact in Paris, Shiratori had been present as his attendant. For this reason, Shiratori was well acquainted with the details of the pact.

Thus, it is possible that the spirit of the Kellogg–Briand Pact had a real impact on MacArthur, via the mediation of Shidehara's comments following his reading of Shiratori's letter. However, it should be noted that, through its censors, the GHQ would have known of Shiratori's war renunciation proposal before Shidehara did. Further, although Shidehara spoke of the renunciation of war after seeing Shiratori's letter, his comments were, as noted above, only at the level of ideals. He did not propose incorporating a war renunciation article into the constitution. It is also worth pointing out that Shiratori hoped to use this letter at the Tokyo Trial as proof of his own pacifism.[68]

At a cabinet meeting held on 30 January 1946, Matsumoto reported on the progress of the Constitutional Problems Investigation Committee. The cabinet subsequently deliberated upon topics such as Matsumoto's own proposal for constitutional reform. In this proposal, Shidehara stated that the article on the emperor left the relationship between 'His Majesty' and 'inviolable' unclear. Shidehara further argued emphatically that the military provisions needed to be removed from the constitution draft:

> If we leave military provisions in the constitution, then the Allies will definitely come and complain about it. I am concerned that it may be a problem if, at the present time, we place a provision in the constitution with the premise that we would be able to have a military in the future. Won't we end up spending one, two months in negotiations with headquarters [GHQ] for the sake of this provision? ... Thinking [of the matter] from the perspective of the general world situation, our nation may well be able to have an army again one day. However, I think it would be too provocative to put this provision in here today.[69]

What Shidehara had in mind with this statement was the planned submission to the GHQ of the Japanese constitutional draft. The Japanese proposal did not strongly reflect Shidehara's own intentions. On top of that, it was rejected by the GHQ. This makes it unlikely that Shidehara was the one who originally proposed Article 9.

A record of an interview conducted at this time has been preserved in a collection of Shidehara's personal documents. According to these records, Shidehara asserted that 'a liberal democratic system with the Emperor as constitutional monarch is the only regime that will prove stable and beneficial for Japan'. He added:

> The constitution of Japan should not be an exact reproduction of the British or any other monarchical system ... it must be adapted to the Japanese character and traditions.[70]

Here, too, Shidehara was thinking mainly of the emperor system.

The Emperor System and Renouncing the Right to Wage War

A significant turning point came on 1 February 1946. Nishiyama Takichi, a journalist for the *Mainichi Shimbun*, published a scoop on the conservative draft plan of the Constitutional Problems Investigation Committee. The *Mainichi Shimbun* editorial launched the following criticism:

> When it comes to what may be regarded as the core of the constitution, the sovereignty of the emperor, this new plan is based on exactly the same principles as the current constitution.[71]

Surprised by the conservative plan for constitutional reform that the Japanese side had devised, the GHQ began work on its own proposal for a new constitution. However, if Nishiyama had not succeeded in securing the above scoop, the GHQ's draft might well have arrived much later, and, as a result, led to further chaos.

The above circumstances show that the only way that Shidehara could have been responsible for introducing Article 9 into the new constitution is if the prime minister had buried the conservative Japanese draft and instead endorsed the GHQ draft. Information could potentially have been purposely leaked to the press to such ends. Indeed, from the outside, the *Mainichi Shimbun* scoop does look as though it might have been the result of such a political manoeuvre. However, Shidehara was not the source of Nishiyama's information. We know this because Nishiyama himself has spoken out on the matter, stating that Shidehara 'absolutely did not allow reporters to approach him' and that, in any case, Shidehara 'hated newspaper reporters'.[72] It is therefore difficult to imagine that Shidehara would leak the Japanese draft. Nishiyama has also said of Shidehara:

> The symbolic emperor system uniting the citizens and the emperor constitutes the underlying framework of postwar Japan, and it was Shidehara (Kijūrō) who created it. He was a great figure. Mr. Yoshida (Shigeru) is lionized these days; however, I want the young people of today to know about Mr. Shidehara.[73]

On 3 February, MacArthur's three basic principles on constitutional reform were shown to Courtney Whitney, chief of the GHQ Government Section. These three basic principles were the emperor system, the renunciation of war, and the abolition of feudalistic systems. Here, the retention of the emperor system was combined with the renunciation of war. In other words, MacArthur was concerned about the Far Eastern Commission, which was critical of the emperor system.[74] The Far Eastern Commission was a policymaking body focused on Japan that the Allied nations had set up in Washington. Its establishment had been decided upon at a foreign ministers' conference in Moscow in December 1945.

On 8 February 1946, the Japanese side submitted a general outline of its proposal for constitutional reform to the GHQ. This outline was not reflective of the views that Shidehara had earlier expressed at the cabinet meeting on 30 January.[75] Moreover, not only did the GHQ have a poor impression of the reform outline, but also they viewed it as effectively preserving the Meiji Constitution.

As a result, the initiative for reforming the constitution shifted entirely to the GHQ. As early as 13 February, Whitney and Colonel Charles L. Kades handed over a copy of their own draft, known as the 'MacArthur Draft', to Matsumoto and Yoshida. Matsumoto and Yoshida had only expected to hear GHQ's opinion of the revisions proposed by the Japanese side. When they were suddenly shown this 'MacArthur Draft', they were shocked, especially once they saw its contents. With Shidehara's assistance, Matsumoto submitted a supplementary explanation on the Japanese proposal to GHQ. However, Whitney not only replied that there was no leeway for reconsideration but also warned him that if they did not receive a response by 20 February, they would publicly announce the GHQ proposal.[76]

Left with little choice, Shidehara slipped out of the Prime Minister's Office on 21 February and paid a visit to MacArthur. Their discussion lasted a full three hours. MacArthur argued that, although he very much wished to keep the emperor's position secure, the Far Eastern Commission was taking a hard line. It was therefore necessary for GHQ to create a proposal that would prescribe both the symbolic emperor system and the renunciation of war. MacArthur further stated that he thought 'Japan should take moral leadership [on this matter] by declaring it will renounce its right to wage war'. In response, Shidehara replied: 'It might be called leadership, but I doubt that there will be any followers'. MacArthur immediately countered: 'Even if there are no followers, Japan has nothing to lose'.[77] On the following day, 22 February, after a visit to the Imperial Palace, Shidehara reported to the cabinet on his meeting with MacArthur. Matsumoto responded in a raised voice:

> As can be clearly seen from precedents such as Germany and South America, constitutions that are pressed upon a nation from the outside are, in the end, not deserving of observance.[78]

Yet Shidehara believed there was 'some room for compromise' regarding the GHQ proposal.[79] What finally convinced Shidehara was MacArthur's argument that if Japan did not accept the US proposal, he would be unable to guarantee the survival of the emperor system. To put it another way, the emperor system could be protected by codifying Japan's renunciation of war. This may well have been why Shidehara returned from his meeting with MacArthur 'in a slightly cheerful mood'.[80]

Shidehara took the further step of revising Article 1 of the Japanese proposal. It now stated that the emperor was a symbol that was based upon 'the supreme collective will of the Japanese people'.[81] Shidehara also changed the prescriptions on constitutional reform, allowing them to take place via special national referendums, and not merely at the time of general elections. Following further consultation with GHQ, on 6 March, the cabinet was able to announce a summary of its constitutional reform proposal. When giving his statement, Shidehara emphasised Japan's renunciation of the right to wage war.

There was a suitable reason for expediting the process. On 27 February, the *Yomiuri Hōchi* had reported that 'the emperor wished to abdicate'.[82] The source of this report was Prince Higashikuni. So, the cabinet finally agreed to accept the GHQ proposal on 5 March, following a visit to the Imperial Palace by Shidehara and Matsumoto to gain the emperor's approval. This was the moment in which the basic political framework for postwar Japan was decided. The cabinet meeting held that day stretched late into the night, and more than a few of the cabinet ministers had tears in their eyes. Before his assembled ministers, including Yoshida and Matsumoto, Shidehara concluded the cabinet meeting with the following words:

> It is an extremely serious responsibility to accept such a constitutional draft. In all likelihood, it is a responsibility that will have an impact upon our descendants. If we announce this plan, there shall be some who will praise it. There shall also be those who will remain silent, yet their hearts will surely be filled with a deep indignation at our attitude. However, when we take a broad view of the situation, we can see that today there is no other path that we can take.[83]

Shortly afterwards, on 20 March, Shidehara attended a plenary session of the Privy Council. There Shidehara sought to convince those present that the renunciation of war was important to protect the emperor system. Shidehara told them frankly that, due to the involvement of the Far Eastern Commission, MacArthur had been able to 'suddenly rush the announcement of the constitution draft in order to create a situation where everything had already been effectively decided'.[84]

On 22 April, Shidehara gave an even more detailed explanation to the First Privy Council Investigative Committee for Proposed Revisions to the Imperial Constitution. Shidehara also frequently spoke with Suzuki Kantarō, who was then serving as the chairman of the Privy Council.[85]

Meanwhile, although the Constitutional Problems Investigation Committee would never again convene, it was not actually abolished. This was due to Shidehara's concern for Committee Chairman Matsumoto. What gave Shidehara the most reason for anxiety was the 'rumour' that Article 9 had been forced upon Japan by the US. He responded by making sure that all officials had their story straight: it was a proposal from the Japanese side.[86]

Shidehara's reshuffled cabinet paved the way for constitutional reform. When Shidehara said to Kanamori Tokujirō that 'we absolutely must push for a peace constitution that renounces war', his intention was to protect the emperor system. He understood that it was possible for a clause renouncing war to one day be changed. Yet if the emperor system were abolished, the loss would be irreversible. In a meeting with the emperor, MacArthur also made the following meaningful statement: 'Thanks to His Majesty's assistance, the constitution is now ready. [Smiling] If we did not have His Majesty, we would not have this constitution'.[87]

Resignations of the Shidehara Cabinet

Inauguration as President of the Progressive Party

Along with the problem of the constitution, Shidehara's reshuffled cabinet was also tasked with the challenge of improving the lives of the citizenry. The opposition party had been severely denouncing Shidehara over the tightening of supply restrictions and the rationing system. In a letter to Izawa, he expressed the feeling of being 'surrounded by enemies on all sides'.[88]

From the outset, the Shidehara cabinet had been regarded as a 'stopgap cabinet'. Its most important mission was to carry out electoral reform and an election for the House of Representatives. That is to say, the calling of a general election was seen as the cabinet's primary purpose. It was expected, as it were, 'to serve as a midwife for the establishment of democratic politics'.[89] Once the Shidehara cabinet had revised the electoral law in December 1945, the next general election was scheduled for April 1946. It was the first postwar election, as well as the first election in Japan where women received suffrage. In a radio broadcast, Shidehara appealed to the significance of 'this election as the departure point for democratic politics in our nation'.[90] Yet he made no comment as to what course of action ought to be pursued following the election.

When the election was held on 10 April 1946, the leading party was Hatoyama Ichirō's Liberal Party (Jiyūtō). The runner-up was the Japan Progressive Party (Nihon Shinpotō), followed by the Japan Socialist Party (Nihon Shakaitō). However, the Shidehara cabinet would not readily step down. This was because, even though the Liberal Party took first place, it had secured less than a third of the seats in the house. The work of establishing the new constitution was also yet to be completed. Mitsuchi, Narahashi and Ishiguro were particularly eager to see the cabinet continue. For this reason, Shidehara—who had once served as foreign minister in the so-called Goken Sanpa coalition cabinet—was now the target of public criticism for his 'turncoat scheming'. In the end, the Shidehara cabinet resigned on 22 April. On 23 April, Shidehara agreed to serve as president of the Progressive Party. For the first time, Shidehara joined a political party, probably because he wished to ensure that constitutional reform was carried out correctly.[91]

The Progressive Party that Shidehara now presided over had been formed in November 1945. Despite its name, it was actually a conservative political party, and the only party in power that had previously lent its support to the Shidehara cabinet. Initially, the party found it difficult to select a president. Eventually the role was filled by Machida Chūji, but he was soon caught up in the aforementioned purge of public officials. The Progressive Party suffered a major defeat in the general election of April 1946, ceding the position of leading conservative party to the Liberal Party. As for its alignment, the party understood itself to be 'to the right of the Socialist Party and to the left of the Liberal Party'.[92]

Following the resignation of his cabinet, Shidehara intended to formally petition the emperor to have the Liberal Party president Hatoyama Ichirō become the next prime minster. On 4 May he sought informal consent for this move from MacArthur, via Yoshida's mediation. Just after sending this request, however, even Hatoyama fell victim to the purge of officials. He would be replaced by Yoshida. Shidehara thereafter sought to have Yoshida installed as prime minister. On 15 May, he had Yoshida himself make this request to MacArthur, who granted his approval.[93]

From the Democratic Party to the Liberal Party

On 16 May 1946, Shidehara formally recommended Yoshida Shigeru to the imperial throne as the next prime minister of Japan. The Yoshida cabinet was formed on 22 May as a coalition cabinet containing ministers from both the Liberal Party and the Progressive Party. As president of the Progressive Party, Shidehara entered the cabinet as minister of state.[94] As a minister without a portfolio of his own, Shidehara was assigned to deal with constitutional reform and also sought to work on policy relating to the Diet.

On the Progressive Party side, the cabinet included figures such as Saitō Takao, who served as an adviser, and Inukai Takeru, who was the chairperson of the general affairs committee.[95] However, alongside such allies, Shidehara also had to endure working with Ashida Hitoshi from the Liberal Party. Although Ashida had previously served as health and welfare minister in the Shidehara cabinet, they did not see eye to eye. When Shidehara sought to have the two parties coordinate their efforts, Ashida instead argued for a three-party coalition that included the Socialist Party. This disagreement had deepened the divide between the two.

In correspondence sent to Shidehara when he was prime minister, Ashida wrote:

> Regrettably, it seems that one or two ministers have sought to create a ruling party that supports the cabinet by shifting their political alignments. I believe that at this present crucial moment, such actions may push the political world in a more chaotic direction and give rise to anxiety among the citizenry.[96]

Discontented with these developments, on 19 April 1946, Ashida submitted to Prime Minister Shidehara his resignation as minister of health and welfare 'due to personal circumstances'.[97] Just after this, however, the Shidehara cabinet resigned en masse.

Before long, the Yoshida cabinet also began to run into difficulties. It was at this time that Ashida decided to visit Shidehara. The day was New Year's Eve 1946. Ashida asked Shidehara if he would consider becoming prime minister once more, this time of a three-party coalition cabinet that would include the Socialist Party. Yet Shidehara replied that he instead 'wanted to find a way of pushing ahead with some reshuffling'.[98] Meanwhile, there were disquieting movements in the Progressive Party. Hori Shigeru of the Progressive Party approached Ashida and informed him that 'there are those [in the party] who would be comfortable with pushing Mr. Shidehara out'.[99] Progressive Party reformists became bolder and began rallying around younger figures such as Inukai Takeru. This inner discord would lead to the dissolution of the party on 31 March 1947, and the subsequent founding of a new party known as the Democratic Party (Minshutō). The Democratic Party also gathered members from the National Cooperative Party (Kokumin Kyōdōtō). At this time, Shidehara was focused on the coming general election and wanted Yoshida's Liberal Party to merge with the remnants of the Progressive Party. However, the Liberal Party was not amenable to this idea. Left with no other choice, Shidehara participated in the creation of the Democratic Party, out of the core of the old Progressive Party.

Although Shidehara was successful in the April 1947 election, he had lost the favour of the general public. The Democratic Party did not get around to selecting its very first leader until after the election. The position would go to Ashida, who had previously left the Liberal Party. Having lost out to Ashida, Shidehara was instead elected honorary president of the party. Although the Democratic Party had the most House seats at the time of its formation, in the fourth general election it slipped to third place. In fact, it was the Socialist Party that took first place in the election, with Yoshida's Liberal Party pushed into opposition in second place.

Katayama Tetsu, chairman of the Socialist Party, formed a new cabinet towards the end of May. Democratic Party President Ashida formed a coalition with the Katayama cabinet, taking the role of foreign minister for himself. In other words, the Katayama cabinet was a coalition cabinet consisting of ministers from the leading Socialist Party, as well as from the Democratic Party, which had come in third. Shidehara was particularly displeased with the Democratic Party for this decision. He had wished to merge the party with the Liberal Party but was ultimately unable to. Although he did not go so far as to leave the party, at the end of May he submitted his resignation as honorary president, arguing for the 'level-headed development of the party'.[100] In the Democratic Party were some 30 individuals who were viewed as belonging to the Shidehara clique, including Hitomatsu Sadayoshi, minister of health and welfare.

Significantly, it appears that GHQ's Government Section played some role in Ashida's rise to the position of Democratic Party president. While Shidehara promoted a 'conservative coalition' between the Democratic Party and the Liberal Party, there is a theory that the Government Section was against this idea. It seems likely that Shidehara was not sufficiently aware of this fact. At any rate, Shidehara was not at all comfortable with Ashida's rise to party president. As for these movements, there were also dark rumours in the air relating to money. A supremely proud individual, Shidehara felt humiliated. His ill feelings towards Ashida never disappeared.[101] Ashida, meanwhile, focused on creating a gathering of political moderates.

At the end of November 1947, Shidehara left the Democratic Party altogether. The direct cause was his voting against the Katayama cabinet's proposed Coal Mining Nation Management Law. Twenty-two members of the Shidehara clique left the Democratic Party with him, and together they created a new party called the Dōshi Club. This meant that Shidehara was once again in political opposition.

Shidehara disclosed his intentions in a letter he wrote on New Year's Day 1948, addressed to Ishibashi Tanzan, who was still barred from public office:

> Happy New Year
>
> It has been some time since I had the pleasure of seeing you. When I reminisce about those happier days when I had the honor of speaking with you regularly, I am filled with a vague sense of loneliness.
>
> As you are aware, I find myself deploring the current state of events in the political world and have resolutely decided to end my ties with the Democratic Party. It has become necessary for me to push forward on the basis of my own convictions.
>
> From the beginning, I have tried not to dwell upon such matters as the collapse of the current cabinet or the future of the administration. Rather, I have only hoped that affairs of state might be carried out smoothly, and that we might keep the political situation stable.
>
> I am aware that it would be absurd for this failure of an old man to continue in such farcical performances. And so, I have set sail on this voyage. Until I arrive at my port of destination, I beg you to take into consideration the real state of affairs.
>
> These days it grows ever colder, and I pray that you will take all the more care of your health.
>
> Respectfully yours,
> New Year's Day
> Kijūrō
> Ishibashi Kendai Jisō[102]

Upon receiving this letter, Ishibashi noted that he 'felt a special affection for Mr. Shidehara'.[103]

Before long, the Katayama cabinet entered a deadlock with the Socialist Party over a budget proposal. On 10 March 1948, it was replaced by the Ashida cabinet. The Ashida cabinet was a coalition, containing ministers from the Socialist Party, the Democratic Party and the National Cooperative Party.

Following this event, Shidehara formed a political party known as the Democracy Club with 36 other individuals, including Saitō Takao, who had also left the Democratic Party at that time. Only a few days later, on 15 March, it merged with Yoshida's Liberal Party. This was the birth of the Democratic Liberal Party (Minshu Jiyūtō). Apart from Yoshida, who served as president, leaders of the Democratic Liberal Party included such figures as Shidehara, who was appointed 'supreme adviser', and Yamazaki Takeshi, who was secretary-general. At its founding, the Democratic Liberal Party was the strongest party in Japan, boasting 152 members in the House of Representatives. Among those politicians who had followed Shidehara out of the Democratic Party and into the Democratic Liberal Party, there was a young lawmaker by the name of Tanaka Kakuei; he would become prime minister one day. When the second Yoshida cabinet was inaugurated in October that year, Tanaka would become the parliamentary vice-minister of justice on the basis of a recommendation from Shidehara.[104]

'Those I Will Never Forget'

I would like to conclude this chapter by probing the relationship between elections and political parties in Japan at this time. Shidehara had faced the election of April 1946 as prime minister. Yet he remained a member of the House of Peers without having to run as a candidate. The House of Peers would later be abolished on 3 May 1947, as a result of the new constitution coming into effect. By then over 20 years had passed since Shidehara became a member in 1926. Following the enactment of constitutional reform, fresh elections were held for the House of Representatives and the new House of Councillors (the upper house) in April of the same year. Shidehara would run as a candidate for the House of Representatives and subsequently won election to the Diet for the first time.

Shidehara was voted into office a total of two times in his life: the first in the aforementioned election of April 1947, and the second in an election held in January 1949. While Shidehara ran as a representative for the Third Ward of Osaka prefecture, he continued to live in Tokyo; his formal residence was in Sendagaya, and his actual residence was in Setagaya. Already over 70 years old when he first joined a political party and became president of the Progressive Party, Shidehara would have understood that he was not the type of politician who could count on popular support. He nevertheless sought to lead a political party late in life because he believed it necessary to stabilise Japan's political situation with a conservative coalition. From Shidehara's perspective, a bulwark was needed to shield the nation from the chaos that could arise in the wake of such challenges as the ongoing purging of public officials. However, as shown above, it was due to this same 'conservative coalition theory' that Shidehara lost his chance to lead the Democratic Party. Shidehara was not adept at the kind of manoeuvring necessary for a party politician.

Yet, after entering the world of party politics, Shidehara devoted a great deal of attention to both domestic affairs and diplomatic matters. There had long been an unwritten law among Foreign Ministry officials that they did not become involved in domestic affairs. This attitude was practically an article of faith for Shidehara in the prewar era. He also saw it as the price that needed to be paid for the centralisation of diplomacy under bureaucratic control. Hence, although implored by Hamaguchi, Shidehara had been entirely unwilling to accept the position of party vice-president. In his memoirs, he wrote:

> I took the ideological position that the foreign minister must not
> be connected to a political party. At that time, I had no interest at
> all in getting involved in politics.[105]

However, under the conditions of postwar democracy, the Ministry of Foreign Affairs was no longer in a position to fully control diplomatic efforts. In due course, political parties would begin to involve themselves in diplomacy. Thus, it became necessary to rethink the connection between domestic affairs and diplomacy. Shidehara's position therefore gradually underwent a metamorphosis. Towards the very end of his life, upon becoming speaker of the House of Representatives, Shidehara soon became engaged in nonpartisan diplomacy. I will discuss this topic in the following chapter.

There is also the question of Shidehara's reaction to the postwar era. In fact, by no means did he have a higher regard for it. In a 1951 essay, he wrote:

> These days I do not even have any interests … My greatest pleasure would simply be to have an interesting book to read. But even if I go and visit Maruzen [a major Japanese bookstore], I am unable to freely order foreign books like I used to. Things have become altogether inconvenient.

Shidehara went on to say:

> I think politicians of the prewar era were also most serious … Nowadays it has become common to say that people of the previous generation were entirely feudalistic in their thinking and so on. I have the impression that people who say such things are actually merely shallow. For example, whether it is freedom of thought, or whether it is democracy, I think there are more than a few people who do not look at such matters from the perspective of obligations or responsibilities; they simply believe that freedom and democracy mean being free to do as they please. This tendency is really worrisome, in my opinion. However, it may be that I am simply incapable of holding forth on postwar matters.

Shidehara reserved his highest praise for prewar politicians such as Itō Hirobumi and Saionji Kinmochi. In the case of foreigners, those he 'could never forget' included names such as Denison, Hughes, Bryce and Morris. Although the country had paid a great price to get to the postwar era, Shidehara found it disconcerting. His preference was for people who selflessly 'strived for the sake of the nation'. In this respect, he was very much of the prewar world.[106]

Endnotes

1   This chapter is based on my previous work: Hattori Ryūji, 'Shidehara Kijūrō to Sengo Seiji' [Shidehara Kijūrō and the postwar politics], *Jinbunken Kiyō*, no. 55 (October 2005): 1–37.

2   *Asahi Shimbun*, 15 August 1945; Matsumura Kenzō, *Sandai Kaikoroku* [A three-generation memoir] (Tokyo: Tōyō Keizai Shimpōsha, 1964), 245; 'Higashikuni-no-miya Nisshi', 23 August and 2 September 1945, Chūō/Sensō Shidō Jūyō Kokusaku Bunsho/1307; Satō Takumi, 'Kōfuku Kinenbi kara Shūsen Kinenbi e: Kioku no Media Event' [From the anniversary of surrender to the anniversary of the end of the war: Memory as a media event], in *Sengo Nihon no Media Event: 1945–1960 Nen* [Postwar Japan's media events: 1945–1960], ed. Tsuganesawa Toshihiro (Tokyo: Sekai Shisōsha, 2002), 71–93. It should also be noted that Higashikuni, *Higashikuni Naruhiko Nikki*, 221–28, is not the correct reprinting of 'Higashikuni-no-miya Nisshi'.

3   Studies of Shidehara of this period, which relate to this chapter as a whole, include Kunugi, 'Shidehara Kijūrō', 85–131; Iokibe Makoto, *Senryō-ki: Shushō-tachi no Shin-Nihon* [The age of occupation: The prime ministers' new Japan], (Tokyo: Yomiuri Shimbun, 1997), 106–226. These two works present sharply different interpretations. While the latter takes a favourable view of Shidehara, the former levels harsh criticism, stating:

The apologetic, passive policy for wartime responsibility adopted by the Shidehara cabinet eventually led to the failure of Shidehara's desire to rehabilitate the empire, with GHQ demanding the purging of public officials and the fundamental revision of the Japanese constitution (p. 115).

As both these texts are written for the larger public, they do not contain a detailed analysis that goes beyond Shidehara's public statements to reflect the significance that Shidehara privately attached to the Survey Association of Greater East Asia War, and how he viewed the matter of war responsibility. Along these lines, in this chapter I will also examine disagreements between Shidehara and the Shōwa emperor, and his relationship with party politics.

On the topic of constitutional reform, while the focus has traditionally been on whether Shidehara was the initial proposer of Article 9, in this chapter I will draw on material such as interview records and historical documents related to the Constitution Research Council to trace the contours of Shidehara's own views on the constitution. I note that Shidehara was in favour of conducting constitutional reform, not only through the process of a general election but also through a national referendum. I also investigate his radio broadcasts.

4   Shidehara to Ōdaira, 25 August 1945, in 'Shidehara Heiwa Bunko', Reel 17. See also Shidehara Peace Foundation, *Shidehara Kijūrō*, 546–48; Shidehara, *Gaikō 50 Nen*, 216–18.

Ōdaira was the former vice-president of the Manchurian Railway Company and became a member of the House of Peers in November 1945. On 19 March 1946, he became a privy councillor at the recommendation of Shidehara. See 'Nin Sūmitsu Komonkan Ōdaira Komatsuchi' [Appointing Ōdaira Komatsuchi to privy councillor], 19 March 1946, 1-2A-001-00-Betsu-00230-100, National Archives of Japan. For a brief history of Ōdaira's life, see Hamuro Michiko, ed., *Hinmin Kyūgo Jigyō Shitashirabe* [Investigation into projects to assist the needy] (Tokyo: Seitoku Memorial Welfare Office, 1989), 107. For details on Shidehara's selection as the chairman of the Japan Club in June 1946, see Japan Club, *Nihon Club 100 Nen-shi* [A hundred-year history of the Japan club] (Tokyo: Japan Club, 1999), 55.

5   'Shidehara Heiwa Bunko', Reels 7 and 17; Shidehara Peace Foundation, *Shidehara Kijūrō*, 548–51, 560.

6   Ōta et al., *Tsugita Daisaburō Nikki*, 34, 50–51, 193.

7   Kido Diary Research Association, *Kido Kōichi Nikki*, vol. 2, 1240–41; Hosokawa, *Hosokawa Nikki*, vol. 2, 167–68; Kinoshita Michio, *Sokkin Nisshi* [Journal of an advisor] (Tokyo: Bungei Shunjū, 1990), 103–04.

8   Ōta et al., *Tsugita Daisaburō Nikki*, 35, 48. See also 'Higashikuni-no-miya Nisshi' 7 October 1945; Higashikuni, *Higashikuni Naruhiko Nikki*, 247; Kojima Kazuo, *Ichi Rō-Seijika no Kaisō* [The memories of an old politician] (Tokyo: Chūōkōronsha, 1975), 263–66; Itō Takashi and Watanabe Yukio, eds, *Zoku Shigemitsu Mamoru Shuki* [The notes of Shigemitsu Mamoru, continued] (Tokyo: Chuōkōronsha, 1988), 270; Asahi Shimbun, ed., *Irie Sukemasa Nikki* [The diary of Irie Sukemasa], vol. 2 (Tokyo: Asahi Shimbun, 1990), 13.

9   Shidehara, *Gaikō 50 Nen*, 214.

10 Ōta et al., *Tsugita Daisaburō Nikki*, 49.

11 'Kido Kōichi Seiji Danwa Rokuon Sokkiroku' [Shorthand record of a recording of a conversation with Kido Kōichi], vols 1–2, Modern Japanese Political History Materials Room, National Diet Library.

12 Shidehara Peace Foundation, *Shidehara Kijūrō*, 559–63.

13 Shindō Eiichi and Shimokōbe Motoharu, eds, *Ashida Hitoshi Nikki* [The diary of Ashida Hitoshi], vol. 1 (Tokyo: Iwanami Shoten, 1986), 50; Domestic Political History Research Association, ed., *Horikiri Zenjirō-shi Danwa Dai 1 Kai Sokkiroku* [First shorthand record of discussion with Mr Horikiri Zenjirō] (Tokyo: Domestic Political History Research Association, 1963), 29; Domestic Political History Research Association, ed., *Horikiri Zenjirō-shi Danwa Dai 3 Kai Sokkiroku* [Third shorthand record of discussion with Mr Horikiri Zenjirō] (Tokyo: Domestic Political History Research Association, 1964), 14–18; Taika Society History of the Ministry of Home Affairs Compilation Committee, ed., *Naimu-shō-shi* [History of the Ministry of Home Affairs], vol. 4 (Tokyo: Taika Society, 1971), 210–11; Narahashi Wataru, *Gekiryū ni Saosashite* [Punting through the rapids] (Tokyo: Tsubasa Soin, 1968), 43–45, 54–55; Shibusawa Keizō, *Shibusawa Keizō Chosaku-shū* [Selected works of Shibusawa Keizō], vol. 5 (Tokyo: Heibonsha, 1993), 405.

14 Yoshida Shigeru Memorial Project Foundation, *Yoshida Shigeru Shokan*, 670; Izawa Takio Document Research Association, *Izawa Takio Kankei Bunsho*, 56; Ōnishi Hiroshi, 'Senchū Sengo no Izawa Takio: Naimu Kanryō Shihai no Shūen' [Izawa Takio during and after the war: The end of the dominance of the home affairs bureaucrats], in *Izawa Takio to Kindai Nihon* [Izawa Takio and modern Japan], ed. Ōnishi Hiroshi (Tokyo: Fuyō Shobō Shuppan, 2003), 210–15.

15 Office of the Chief of Counter Intelligence, GHQ, 'Biographical Notes on the Members of the Shidehara Cabinet', 23 October 1945, Record Group 331, Box 2044, National Archives.

16 Yoshida, *Kaisō 10 Nen*, vol. 1, 128.

17 Journal of Forbes, Forbes Papers, second series, vol. 5.

18 '10 Gatsu 11 Nichi Shidehara Shushō nitaishi Hyōmei-seru "MacArthur" Iken' [11 October, the declaration of the MacArthur opinion with regard to Prime Minister Shidehara], date unknown, in 'Rengō-gun no Hondo Shinchū narabini Gunsei Kankei Ikken: Rengō-gun-gawa to Nihon-gawa tono Renraku Kankei, Rengō-koku Saikō Shikan oyobi Bakuryō to Honpō Shushō narabini Kakushō Yōjin tono Kaidan Yoroku narabini Ōfuku Shokan Kankei' [Matter concerning the occupation of the homeland by allied forces and the establishment of a military government: Relating to communication between the allied forces and the Japanese side, abridged records of dialogue as well as correspondence between the supreme commander for the allied powers and staff officers, and the prime minister of Japan and leading figures of respective ministries], A'.1.0.0.2-3-4, reel A'-0055, Diplomatic Archives of the Ministry of Foreign Affairs of Japan; 'Sōri 'MacArthur' Kaidan Yōshi' [Summary of discussion between the prime minister and MacArthur], 13 October 1945, ibid.

See also '10 Gatsu 11 Nichi Sōri "MacArthur" Kaidan-go niokeru Rengō-gun Shirei-bu Shimbun Happyō (Kayaku)' [Newspaper announcement by the allied forces headquarters following the 11 October talks between the prime minister and MacArthur (provisional translation)], in 'Satō Tatsuo Kankei Bunsho' [Documents relating to Satō Tatsuo], Constitution Department, Reel 1, Modern Japanese Political History Materials Room, National Diet Library; Government Section, Supreme Commander for the Allied Powers, *Political Reorientation of Japan, September 1945 to September 1948*, vol. 2 (Westport: Greenwood Press, 1970), 741; Etō Jun, ed., *Senryō Shiroku* [Historical Records of the Occupation], comp. Hatano Sumio, vol. 2 (Tokyo: Kōdansha, 1995), 111–20; Ōta et al., *Tsugita Daisaburō Nikki*, 78–79; Shindō and Shimokōbe, *Ashida Hitoshi Nikki*, vol. 1, 52.

19 Ōta et al., *Tsugita Daisaburō Nikki*, 36, 81–83.

20 *Kanpō*, extra edition, 29 November 1945. The draft was by Tsugita. See Ōta et al., *Tsugita Daisaburō Nikki*, 137.

21 'Heiwa Jōyaku Mondai Kenkyū Kanji-kai no Ken' [Matter of the research board for the peace treaty problem], 21 November 1945, in 'Tai-Nichi Heiwa Jōyaku Kankei: Junbi Kenkyū Kankei' [Relating to the peace treaty with Japan: Relating to preparatory research], vol. 1, B'.4.0.0.1, Reel B'-0008, Diplomatic Archives of the Ministry of Foreign Affairs of Japan. Also see Nishimura Kumao, 'San Francisco Heiwa Jōyaku nitsuite' [Regarding the San Francisco peace treaty], *Kasumigaseki-kai Kaihō*, no. 400 (May 1979): 24.

22 Shidehara cabinet meeting decision, 'Haisen no Genin oyobi Jissō Chōsa no Ken' [The matter of the investigation of the cause and true nature of the defeat], 30 October 1945, 1-2A-029-04-Shō 57 Sō -00128-100, National Archives of Japan; Shidehara cabinet meeting decision, 'Dai Tōa Sensō Chōsa-kai Kansei' [Governmental regulation on the survey association of Greater East Asia War], 29 November 1945, ibid.

23 Sensō Chōsa-kai Jimukyoku [The War Research Institute secretariat], 'Sensō Chōsa-kai Dai 1 Kai Sōkai niokeru Shidehara Sōsai no Aisatsu' [President Shidehara's opening remarks for the War Research Institute's first general meeting], 27 March 1946, 1-2A-040-00-Shi-00306-100.

24 Aoki Tokuzō's comments within the subcommittee on the establishment of the new constitution, 10 July 1958, in *Kenpō Seitei no Keika nikansuru Shouiinkai Dai 8 Kai Gijiroku* [Proceedings of the eighth subcommittee meeting, relating to the establishment of the new constitution], ed. Constitution Research Council (Tokyo: Constitution Research Council, 1958), 2.

25 'Sensō Chōsa-kai Shiryō Tsuzuri' [The War Research Institute resource file], Bunko/Miyazaki Shūichi /95, Military Archives, Center for Military History, the National Institute for Defense Studies.

26 'Kensei Shiryō-shitsu Shūshū Bunsho' [Collected documentation of the Constitutional Resource Center], no. 1244, Modern Japanese Political History Materials Room, National Diet Library; Aoki Tokuzō, 'Sensō Chōsa-kai no Hossoku kara Haishi made' [The War Research Institute, from its inception to its termination], date unknown, in 'Shidehara Heiwa Bunko', Reel 12; Domestic Political History Research Association, ed., *Aoki Tokuzō-shi Danwa Sokkiroku* [Shorthand record of a discussion with Mr Aoki Tokuzō] (Tokyo: Domestic Political History Research Association, 1964), 1–4, 10, 15, 24–25, 81–82; Ōta et al., *Tsugita Daisaburō Nikki*, 135.

27 Yoshida Yutaka, *Nihonjin no Sensōkan* [The Japanese view on war] (Tokyo: Iwanami Shoten, 1995), 29.

28 Shidehara to Makino, 8 December 1945, in 'Makino Nobuaki Kankei Bunsho', Correspondence Department, vol. 28, 476–76.

29 Shindō and Shimokōbe, *Ashida Hitoshi Nikki*, vol. 1, 115–16, 262, 263, 265.

30 Journal of Miyazaki Shuichi, 17 August 1946, in 'Miyazaki Shūichi Chūjō Nisshi: Fukuin Jidai Nisshi, Ni' [The Journal of Lieutenant General Miyazaki Shūichi: Writings on the era of demobilization, 2], Chūō/Sakusen Shidō Nisshi/564, Military Archives, Center for Military History, the National Institute for Defense Studies; Aoki Tokuzō's comments within the subcommittee on the establishment of the new constitution, 10 July 1958, in Constitution Research Council, *Kenpō Seitei no Keika nikansuru Shouiinkai Dai 8 Kai Gijiroku*, 3.

31 Shidehara Kijūrō, 'Jo' [Introduction], in Aoki Tokuzō, *Taiheiyō Sensō Zenshi* [The prehistory of the Pacific War], vol. 1 (Tokyo: World Peace Construction Society, 1951), 1–5.

32 Kishi Kuramatsu, 'Shidehara-san to Konoe Kō Den' [Mr Shidehara and the biography of Lord Konoe], date unknown, in 'Shidehara Heiwa Bunko', Reel 13.

33 Shidehara cabinet meeting decision, 'Rikukaigun-shō no Haishi nikansuru Ken' [Abolishing the Ministry of War and Ministry of Navy], 26 October 1945, 1-2A-029-04-Shō 57 Sō-00128-100, National Archives of Japan.

34 Contents of Prime Minister Shidehara's broadcast, 'Fukuin Gunjin nitsuite' [regarding demobilised soldiers], 7 February 1946, 1-2A-040-00-shi-00306-100, National Archives of Japan. See also 'Shidehara Heiwa Bunko', Reel 12.

35 Narahashi Wataru's discourse, date unknown, in 'Shidehara Heiwa Bunko', Reel 13; Narahashi's discourse, 22 October 1954, in 'Nihon-koku Kenpō Seitei nikansuru Danwa Rokuon' [Recording of conversations regarding the establishment of Japan's constitution], no. 1, Modern Japanese Political History Materials Room, National Diet Library. Narahashi, *Gekiryū ni Saosashite*, 55–64; Japanese Communist Party Central Committee, *Zōhōban Nihon Kyōsantō no 50 Nen* [Fifty years of the Japanese Communist Party], 2nd ed. (Tokyo: Japanese Communist Party Central Committee Press, 1977), 101–04; Biography of Narahashi Wataru Editing Committee, *Narahashi Wataru Den* [Biography of Narahashi Wataru] (Tokyo: Biography of Narahashi Wataru Publishing Association, 1982), 110–15.

36 Yamagiwa Akira and Nakamura Masanori, eds, *Shiryō Nihon Senryō, vol. 1: Tennōsei* [Documents on Japan's occupation, vol. 1: The emperor system], trans. Ryōnosuke Okada (Tokyo: Ōtsuki Shoten, 1990), 404, 411–13, 414–16, 454–55, 463–64. See also Masumi Junnosuke, *Shōwa Tennō to Sono Jidai* [The Shōwa emperor and his era] (Tokyo: Yamakawa Shuppansha, 1998), 45–48, 63–64.

37 Kido Diary Research Association, ed. *Kido Kōichi Kankei Bunsho* [Documents relating to Kido Kōichi] (Tokyo: University of Tokyo Press, 1966), 512–14. Toyoshita Narahiko, 'Tennō ha Nani wo Katattaka: "Tennō, MacArthur Kaiken" no Rekishi-teki Ichi' [What did the emperor say? The historical significance of the emperor–MacArthur meeting] (1), *Sekai*, no. 537 (February 1990): 234–36; Shibata Shinichi, 'Dai 1 Kai Shōwa Tennō–MacArthur Kaiken to Yoshida Shigeru' [The first Shōwa emperor–MacArthur meeting and Yoshida Shigeru], *Kokugakuin Daigaku Nihon Bunka Kenkyū-jo Kiyo*, no. 82 (September 1998): 98–106.

38 *New York Times*, 25 September 1945; Matsuo Takayoshi, *Sengo Nihon eno Shuppatsu* [Embarking on postwar Japan] (Tokyo: Iwanami Shoten, 2002), 101.

39 'Shikibushoku: Ekken-roku' [Board of the ceremonies: Record of audience with the emperor], 1945, Imperial Household Archives.

40   Kido Diary Research Association, *Kido Kōichi Nikki*, vol. 2, 1237; Shidehara to Ōdaira, 29 September 1945, in 'Shidehara Heiwa Bunko', Reel 17; Asahi Shimbun, *Irie Sukemasa Nikki*, vol. 2, 10–11; *Asahi Shimbun*, 27 July 2006.

41   Okumura Katsuzō, '"MacArthur" Gensui tono Go-Kaiken-roku' [Record of a meeting with General MacArthur], 27 September 1945, in 'Shōwa Tennō to Rengō-koku Saikō Shireikan MacArthur Gensui no Kaidan-roku (1945 Nen 9 Gatsu 27 Nichi)' [Record of meeting between the Shōwa emperor and General MacArthur, supreme commander of the allied powers (27 September 1945)], 01-385, Diplomatic Archives of the Ministry of Foreign Affairs of Japan. The same meeting record also appears in 'Gaikō Zatsuroku: Shikibushoku' [Miscellaneous diplomatic records: Board of the ceremonies], 1945, Imperial Household Archives. Also see *Asahi Shimbun*, evening edition, 17, 24 October 2002.

Further, according to MacArthur's own memoirs, the emperor stated, 'I take full responsibility'. See Douglas MacArthur, *Reminiscences* (New York: McGraw-Hill Book Company, 1964), 288. There is no entry of this nature in the reference: Okumura Katsuzō, '"MacArthur" Gensui tono Go-Kaiken-roku'. However, according to Matsui Akira's documents, with respect to the statement 'by the Emperor that he took full responsibility for the war', Okumura 'deleted this from the record out of consideration of its enormous importance'. For this reason, it seems highly possible that the relevant entry was removed. See *Asahi Shimbun*, 5 August 2002; Toyoshita Narahiko, 'Shōwa Tennō–MacArthur Kaiken wo Kenshō Suru: "Matsui Bunsho" wo Yomitoku' [Examining the meeting between the Shōwa emperor and MacArthur: Close reading and analysis of the 'Matsui documents'] (1), *Ronza*, no. 90 (November 2002): 60–61.

42   Terasaki Hidenari, '"MacArthur Gensui" tono Go-Kaiken-roku' [Record of a meeting with General MacArthur], 16 October 1946, in 'Shidehara Heiwa Bunko', Reel 3. This is a record of the third meeting between the Emperor and MacArthur, and it was written using the ruled paper of the Ministry of the Imperial Household. This meeting is discussed in Naganuma Setsuo, 'Hatsu-Kōkai Sareta "Tennō–MacArthur" Dai 3 Kai Kaiken no Zenyō' [The full story of the third 'emperor–MacArthur' meeting, now public for the first time], *Asahi Journal* 31, no. 10 (March 1989): 26–30.

Considering the historical material of the above reference, over time, in his meetings with MacArthur, the emperor became more pronounced in making political statements, such as criticising the strikes at the time or speaking about the threat of communism. Such behavior exceeded the purely ceremonial role of the emperor by the newly established constitution. MacArthur also sought to draw out the emperor's opinions. This sheds light on MacArthur's own attitude with respect to the new constitution.

43   Ministry of Foreign Affairs Treaties and Conventions Bureau, 'Kaisen no Sekinin to Kokunai-hō-jō niokeru Tennō no Go Chii' [Responsibility for the commencement of the war, and the position of the emperor with respect to domestic law], date unknown, in 'Honpō Sensō Hanzainin Kankei Zakken: Chosa Shiryo Kankei (Shimbun, Kirinuki wo Fukumu)' [Miscellaneous cases concerning Japanese war criminals: Relating to investigation documents (including newspaper cuttings)], vol. 1, D'.1.3.0.1-13, Diplomatic Archives of the Ministry of Foreign Affairs of Japan.

44   Awaya Kentarō, ed., *Shiryo, Nihon Gendai-shi* [Resources, modern Japanese history], vol. 2 (Tokyo: Ōtsuki Shoten, 1980), 341–43. See also Awaya Kentarō, *Tōkyō Saiban-ron* [Discourse on the Tokyo trial] (Tokyo: Ōtsuki Shoten, 1989), 69; Awaya Kentar., *Gendai-shi Hakkutsu* [Excavating modern history] (Tokyo: Ōtsuki Shoten, 1996), 152–53. However, according to Higurashi Yoshinobu, it was not decided by the cabinet but indeterminate. See Higurashi Yoshinobu, *Toyko Saiban no Kokusai Kankei: Kokusai Seiji niokeru Kenryoku to Kihan* [The Tokyo trial's international relations: Power and standards in international politics] (Tokyo: Bokutakusha, 2002), 310.

I also note that in the document 'Sensō Sekinin nikansuru Ken' [Matter concerning responsibility for the war], date unknown, which was written on lined paper that was standard for the Japanese army, there are statements concerning the emperor:

> With respect to the decision to begin the war, and matters such as the carrying out of strategy planning, etc., what the supreme command staff and the government decided upon had to conform to the working precedence of the constitution; these decisions were not rejected.

See 'Fukuin-sho Kaneki Shiryo' [Documents relating to the Ministry for Demobilization], 12-5, Modern Japanese Political History Materials Room, National Diet Library.

45 Ōta et al., *Tsugita Daisaburō Nikki*, 118–19. Fellers saw the emperor as the 'living symbol of the race'. See Fellers to the Commander-in-Chief, 2 October 1945, Bonner F. Fellers Papers, Box 3, Hoover Institution, Stanford University. For further information on Fellers, see Iguchi Haruo, 'Sengo Nihon no Kunshu-sei to America' [Postwar Japan's monarchy and the US], in *20 Seiki Nihon no Tenno to Kunshusei: Kokusai Hikaku no Shiten kara, 1867–1947* [20th-century Japan's emperor system and monarchy: From the perspective of an international comparison, 1867–1947], ed. Itō Yukio and Kawada Minoru (Tokyo: Yoshikawa Kōbunkan, 2004), 129–55.

46 Conversation with Narahashi Wataru, 22 October 1954, in 'Nihon-koku Kenpō Seitei nikansuru Danwa Rokuon', no. 1; Ishiwata Sōtarō Biography Compilation Society, ed., *Ishiwata Sōtarō* [Ishiwata Sōtarō] (Tokyo: Ishiwata Sōtarō Biography Compilation Society, 1954), 485; Yamanashi Katsunoshin Memorial Publishing Committee, ed., *Yamanashi Katsunoshin Sensei Ihō-roku* [In remembrance of Mr Yamanashi Katsunoshin] (Tokyo: Yamanashi Katsunoshin Memorial Publishing Committee, 1968), 315–17; William P. Woodard, *The Allied Occupation of Japan 1945–1952 and Japanese Religions* (Leiden: E. J. Brill, 1972), 252–68; Togashi Junji, *Tennō totomoni Gojū-nen* [Fifty years with the emperor] (Tokyo: Asahi Shimbun, 1977), 98–112; Shishikui Seiichi, ed., *Shin Jo Sui: Ishiwata-san wo Shinobu* [A heart like water: Remembering Ishiwata-san] (Tokyo: Tokyo Post, 1982), 267–74; Kawashima Yasuyoshi, ed., *Kaisō no Blyth* [Our memories of Blyth] (Tokyo: Memories of Blyth Publishing Association Office, 1984), 161–66; Takahashi Hiroshi and Suzuki Kunihiko, *Tenno-ke no Misshi-tachi: Senryō to Kōshitsu* [The confidential agents of the imperial household: The occupation and the imperial family] (Tokyo: Bungei Shunjū, 1989), 72–92; Hirakawa Sukehiro, *Heiwa no Umi to Tatakai no Umi* [Sea of peace, sea of war] (Tokyo: Kōdansha, 1993), 240–91; Adrian Pinnington, 'R. H. Blyth, 1898–1964', in *Britain and Japan: Biographical Portraits*, ed. Ian Nish (London: Routledge Curzon, 1994), 259–60; Masumi, *Shōwa Tennō to Sono Jidai*, 56–59.

47 Declaration of Humanity, English Draft, 15–20 December 1945, in 'Yamanashi Katsunoshin Bunsho' [Documents of Yamanashi Katsunoshin], A 1 Appendix, Gakushūin University Historical Document Room; 'Shōsho no Anbun Sakusei, Kanpatsu made no Tejun oyobi Ryūiten-to nikansuru Kyōgi Memo' [Conference notes relating to the procedure and points for consideration, etc., relating to the drafting and promulgation of the imperial rescript], date unknown, in 'Yamanashi Katsunoshin Bunsho', A4 Appendix. However, the author of the notes in the 'Yamanashi Katsunoshin Documents' is not stated. See also Kinoshita, *Sokkin Nisshi*, 336–40; *Asahi Shimbun*, 1, 4 January 2006.

48 Declaration of Humanity, English Draft, 15–20 December 1945; 'Shōsho no Anbun Sakusei, Kanpatsu made no Tejun oyobi Ryūiten-to nikansuru Kyōgi Memo'.

49 Maeda Tamon, 'Ningen Sengen no Uchisoto' [The public and private aspects of the 'Declaration of Humanity'], *Bungei Shunjū* 40, no. 3 (March 1962), 84–90; Kinoshita, *Sokkin Nisshi*, 84, 86, 89–96. According to this Kinoshita journal, Yoshida Shigeru was also involved in formulating the Declaration of Humanity. According to Sodei Rinjirō, Yoshida sent the translated version of the declaration to MacArthur. See Sodei Rinjirō, ed., *Yoshida–MacArthur Ōfuku Shokanshū, 1945–1951* [Yoshida–MacArthur correspondence collection, 1945–1951] (Tokyo: Hōsei University Press, 2000), 119–20.

However, for some reason, Yoshida stated in a discussion that he was not a party to the circumstances of the Declaration of Humanity. See conversation with Yoshida Shigeru, 5 October 1955, in 'Nihon-koku Kenpō Seitei nikansuru Danwa Rokuon', no. 8.

50 *Asahi Shimbun*, 1 January 1946.

51 Togashi Junji, *Heika no 'Ningen' Sengen* [The Declaration of Humanity of his highness] (Tokyo: Dōwa Shobō, 1946), 6–7.

In Prince Takamatsu, *Takamatsu-no-miya Nikki*, vol. 8, 287, an entry states:

> The promulgation of the Imperial Rescript was extremely well executed. However, I wished that we could have used an alternative to the three-character word 'Akitsumikami' [現御神, living God], replacing it with simply the character for 'Kami' [God, 神] instead. Prime Minister Shidehara showed the English-language manuscript to 'Mac,' and then this was turned back into Japanese. So, while the Board of Chamberlains made some revisions, it ended up being put out in a form that was fairly different from the original.

52 *Asahi Shimbun*, 24 August 1977.

7. PRIME MINISTER OF AN OCCUPIED NATION

53   Fujita Hisanori, *Jijūchō no Kaiso* [Recollections of the grand chamberlain of the emperor] (Tokyo: Chūōkōronsha, 1987), 217; Kinoshita, *Sokkin Nisshi*, 54–126. See also 'Kansai Gyōkō nikansuru Shidehara Naikaku Sōri Daijin Kinwa' [Prime Minister Shidehara's respectful comments relating to the emperor's visit to the Kansai region], 21 November 1945, 1-2A-040-00-shi-00306-100, National Archives of Japan.

54   Ministry of Foreign Affairs Public Information and Cultural Affairs Bureau, eds, *Korekara no Nihon no Gaikō: Ōhira Gaimu Daijin ni Kiku* [Japanese diplomacy going forward: Listening to Foreign Minister Ōhira] (Tokyo: Ministry of Foreign Affairs, 1973), 13.

55   Matsumura, *Sandai Kaikoroku*, 271–75.

56   Shindō and Shimokōbe, *Ashida Hitoshi Nikki*, vol. 1, 63–66, 237; Fukunaga Fumio, *Senryōka Chūdō Seiken no Keisei to Hōkai* [The formation and disintegration of the centrist government under the occupation] (Tokyo: Iwanami Shoten, 1997), 52.

57   Kido Diary Research Association, *Kido Kōichi Nikki*, vol. 2, 1241; 'Kido Kōichi Seiji Danwa Rokuon Sokkiroku', vol. 2. Also see Shigemitsu Mamoru, *Sugamo Nikki* [Sugamo diary] (Tokyo: Bungei Shunjū Shinsha, 1953), 374; Itō Takashi and Watanabe Yukio, eds, *Shigemitsu Mamoru Shuki* [The notes of Shigemitsu Mamoru] (Tokyo: Chuōkōronsha, 1986), 575; Itō and Watanabe, *Zoku Shigemitsu Mamoru Shuki*, 271. For more recent research on the history of the establishment of Japan's constitution, see Nishi Osamu, *Nihon-koku Kenpō Seiritsu Katei no Kenkyū* [A study of the establishment of the Japanese constitution] (Tokyo: Seibundō, 2004).

58   Etō, *Senryō Shiroku*, 123–27.

59   The first general meeting of the Constitutional Problems Investigation Committee, 27 October 1945, in 'Satō Tatsuo Kankei Bunsho', Constitution Department, Reel 1. For the minutes of the Constitutional Problems Investigation Committee, see Ashibe Nobuyoshi, Takahashi Kazuyuki, Takami Katsutoshi and Hibino Tsutomu, eds, *Nihon Kenpō Seitei Shiryō Zenshū I: Kenpō Mondai Chōsa Iinkai Kankeki Shiryō-tō* [A complete collection of documents relating to the establishment of the Japanese constitution—I: Documents, etc., relating to the Constitutional Problems Investigation Committee] (Tokyo: Shinzansha, 1997), 319–400.

Also see Satō Tatsuo, *Nihon-koku Kenpō Seiritsu-shi* [A history of the establishment of the Japanese constitution], vol. 1 (Tokyo: Yūhikaku, 1962), 252; Ōta et al., *Tsugita Daisaburō Nikki*, 87–88; Yoshida Shigeru Memorial Project Foundation, *Yoshida Shigeru Shokan*, 671; Itō, *Takagi Sōkichi Nikki to Jōhō*, vol. 2, 963.

60   *Kanpō*, extra edition, 29 November 1945.

61   George Sansom diary, 22 January 1946, F 3595/2/23, FO 371/54086, National Archives. See also Katharine Sansom, *Sir George Sansom and Japan: A Memoir* (Tallahassee: Diplomatic Press, 1972), 151.

62   Kenpō Chōsa-kai Jimukyoku [Office of the Constitution Research Council], 'Sensō Hōki Jōkō to Tennō-sei Iji tono Kanren nitsuite: Ōdaira Komatsuchi-shi no Sokujo no Memo' [On the relation of the war waiver clause and the retention of the emperor system: Notes by the daughter of Mr Ōdaira Komatsuchi], February 1959, 1-2A-038-08-ken-00115-105, National Archives of Japan. The same historical material is also available in 'Satō Tatsuo Kankei Bunsho', Constitution Department, Reel 60; 'Kenpō Chōsa-kai Shiryō' [Constitution Research Council material], Reel 20, Modern Japanese Political History Materials Room, National Diet Library. There is also a section included in Ōtake Hideo, ed., *Sengo Nihon Bōei Mondai Shiryōshū* [Postwar Japan defence issues sourcebook], vol. 1 (Tokyo: Sanichi Shobō, 1991), 66–67; Government Periodical Contents Publication Association, *Kenpō Chōsa-kai Shiryō Mokuji Sōran* [Contents overview of resources relating to the Constitution Research Council], vol. 3 (Tokyo: Bunka Tosho, 2002), 304.

Also see conversation with Narahashi Wataru, 22 October 1954, in 'Nihon-koku Kenpō Seitei nikansuru Danwa Rokuon', no. 1; conversation with Yoshida Shigeru, 5 October 1955, ibid., no. 8; Yoshida, *Kaisō 10 Nen*, vol. 4, 178; Office of the Constitution Research Council, ed., *Kenpō Seitei no Keika nikansuru Shōiinkai Hōkokusho* [Subcommittee report on the process of establishing the constitution] (Tokyo: Ministry of Finance Printing Bureau, 1961), 323–38; Hata Ikuhito, *Shiroku: Nihon Saigunbi* [Historical records: The rearmament of Japan] (Tokyo: Bungei Shunjū, 1976), 58–67; Tanaka Hideo,

Kenpō Seitei Katei Oboegaki [Memorandum on the process of establishing the constitution] (Tokyo: Yūhikaku, 1979), 90–100; Aoki Kazuo, *Waga 90 Nen no Shōgai wo Kaerimite* [Looking back on my 90 years] (Tokyo: Kōdansha, 1981), 281–92; Satō Tatsuo, *Nihon-koku Kenpō Tanjō-ki* [Record of the birth of the Japanese constitution] (Tokyo: Chūō Kōron Shinsha, 1999), 78, 92–93.

63   Kenpō Chōsa-kai Jimukyoku, 'Sensō Hōki Jōkō to Tennō-sei Iji tono Kanren nitsuite'.

64   Shiratori to Yoshida (English), 10 December 1945, in 'Kyokutō Kokusai Gunji Saiban Shiryō' [Documents on the International Military Tribunal for the Far East], D2919, Box 192, Modern Japanese Political History Materials Room, National Diet Library. For the Japanese-language text, see D2919, Box 57. See also *Asahi Shimbun*, 14 October 2005.

65   Affidavit of Yoshida Shigeru (English), 4 December 1947, in 'Kyokutō Kokusai Gunji Saiban Shiryō', D2920, Box 192, Modern Japanese Political History Materials Room, National Diet Library. For the Japanese-language version, see D2920, Box 17.

According to Kanamori Tokujirō:

> Shiratori apparently submitted a petition to MacArthur and Shidehara to the effect that war had to be renounced. I think this is probably true ... Actually, Mr. Kishi [Shidehara's secretary, Kishi Kuramatsu] himself also said that he saw the petition being submitted to Shidehara.

See conversation with Kanamori Tokujirō, 16 December 1957, in 'Nihon-koku Kenpō Seitei nikansuru Danwa Rokuon', vol. 9. Kanamori was a member of the House of Peers and served as the minister of state in the first Yoshida cabinet.

66   Hirota Yōji, '"Senpan" Shiratori Toshio to Kenpō Dai Kyū-jō' ['War criminal' Shiratori Toshio and Article 9 of the constitution], *Nihon Shūhō*, no. 374 (July 1956): 43–47. The same manuscript is also included in Hirota Yōji, 'Kenpō Dai-Kyū-jō wa Dare ga Tsukutta ka' [Who created Article 9 of the constitution?], *Nihon Shūhō*, no. 525 (December 1960): 78–83.

67   Hirota, '"Senpan" Shiratori Toshio to Kenpō Dai Kyū-jō', 43–47.

68   Shigemitsu, *Sugamo Nikki*, 109; Tobe Ryōichi, 'Shiratori Toshio to Manshū Jihen' [Shiratori Toshio and the Manchurian Incident], *Bōei Daigakkō Kiyō*, no. 39 (September 1979): 83; Higurashi, *Tokyo Saiban no Kokusai Kankei*, 375.

69   Satō Tatsuo, *Nihon-koku Kenpō Seiritsu-shi*, vol. 2 (Tokyo: Yūhikaku, 1964), 631–34. Irie Toshio, *Kenpō Seiritsu no Keii to Kenpō-jō no Sho-Mondai: Irie Toshio Ronshū* [The circumstances surrounding the establishment of the constitution, and the various constitutional problems: Irie Toshio essay collection] (Tokyo: Irie Toshio Essay Collection Publishing Committee, 1976), 69–81, 96–107, 201–03.

70   Interview of Shidehara by the National Catholic Welfare Conference News Service (Father Patrick O'Connor, correspondent), 31 January 1946, in 'Shidehara Heiwa Bunko', Reel 17.

71   *Mainichi Shimbun*, 1 February 1946. Also see Tanaka, *Kenpō Seitei Katei Oboegaki*, 39–49.

72   *Mainichi Shimbun*, 3 May 1997. See also Hosokawa, *Hosokawa Nikki*, vol. 2, 173–74; Iokibe, *Senryō-ki*, 205–08.

73   Mainichi Shimbun, 3 May 1997.

74   Charles L. Kades oral history, 12 December 1961, Oral History Research Office, Columbia University; Takayanagi Kenzō, Ōtomo Ichirō and Tanaka Hideo, eds, *Nihon-koku Kenpō Seitei no Katei, 1, Genbun to Honyaku: Rengō-koku So-Shireibu-gawa no Kiroku niyoru* [The process of the establishment of the constitution of Japan, 1, the original and the translation: According to the records of the general headquarters of the allied powers] (Tokyo: Yūhikaku, 1972), 98–107.

75   Satō, *Nihon-koku Kenpō Seiritsu-shi*, vol. 2, 689–91.

76   Etō, *Senryō Shiroku*, vol. 2, 185–91; Takayanagi, Ōtomo and Tanaka, *Nihon-koku Kenpō Seitei no Katei, 1, Genbun to Honyaku*, 352–71; Satō Tatsuo, *Nihon-koku Kenpō Seiritsu-shi*, rev. Satō Isao, vol. 3 (Tokyo: Yūhikaku, 1994), 47–58.

77   Shindō and Shimokōbe, *Ashida Hitoshi Nikki*, vol. 1, 75–79. See also Kinoshita, *Sokkin Nisshi*, 155–56; Matsumura, *Sandai Kaikoroku*, 289–90.

78   Shindō and Shimokōbe, *Ashida Hitoshi Nikki*, vol. 1, 79–80.

7. PRIME MINISTER OF AN OCCUPIED NATION

79   Ibid., 80.

80   Comment by Ashida Hitoshi at the Constitution Research Council general meeting, 5 December 1957, in *Kenpō Chōsa-kai Dai 7 Sōkai Gijiroku* [Minutes of the seventh general meeting of the Constitution Research Council], ed. Constitution Research Council (Tokyo: Constitution Research Council, 1957), 76; Takayanagi Kenzō, Ōtomo Ichirō and Tanaka Hideo, eds, *Nihon-koku Kenpō Seitei no Katei, 2, Kaisetsu: Rengō-koku So-Shireibu-gawa no Kiroku niyoru* [The process of the establishment of the constitution of Japan, 2, commentary: according to the records of the general headquarters of the allied powers] (Tokyo: Yūhikaku, 1972), 84.

81   Respectful comment draft by Shidehara, 6 March 1946, in 'Shidehara Heiwa Bunko', Reel 2. Also see respectful comment by Shidehara, 6 March, in 'Irie Toshio Kankei Bunsho' [Documents relating to Irie Toshio], Reel 7, Modern Japanese Political History Materials Room, National Diet Library; conversation with Satō Tatsuo, 28 February and 20 April 1955, in 'Nihon-koku Kenpō Seitei nikansuru Danwa Rokuon', no. 5; *Asahi Shimbun*, 7 March 1946; Satō, *Nihon-koku Kenpō Seiritsu-shi*, vol. 3, 74–75, 93, 111, 164, 177, 189, 200; Matsumura, *Sandai Kaikoroku*, 288, 291. The word *shikō* (superiority) was removed during the creation of the new constitution.

82   *Yomiuri Hōchi*, 27 February 1946.

83   Shindō and Shimokōbe, *Ashida Hitoshi Nikki*, vol. 1, 87–91; Kinoshita, *Sokkin Nisshi*, 163–65; Masumi, *Shōwa Tennō to Sono Jidai*, 67–70.

84   '21 Nen 3 Gatsu 20 Nichi Sūmitsuin niokeru Shidehara Sōridaijin no Kenpō Sōan nikansuru Setsumei Yoshi' [Summary of the explanation of the constitution draft as given by Prime Minister Shidehara at the Privy Council on 20 March of the 21st (Shōwa) year], in 'Shidehara Heiwa Bunko', Reel 3; Murakawa Ichirō, ed., *Teikoku Kenpo Kaisei-an Gijiroku* [Minutes of a meeting to draft a revised imperial constitution] (Tokyo: Kokusho Kankō-kai, 1986), 13–40.

85   'Teikoku Kenpō Kaisei nitsuki, Naikaku Sōri Daijin Setsumei Yōshi' [Outline of prime minister's explanation regarding the revision of the imperial constitution], 22 April 1946, in 'Suzuki Kantarō Kankei Bunsho' [Documents relating to Suzuki Kantarō], no. 13, Modern Japanese Political History Materials Room, National Diet Library; Sakurai Ryōjū, 'Suzuki Kantarō Nikki (Shōwa 21 Nen) nitsuite' [Regarding the diary of Suzuki Kantarō (Shōwa 21)], *Noda-shi-shi Kenkyū*, no. 16 (March 2005): 16, 24, 25.

86   Irie Toshio, *Kenpō Seiritsu no Keii to Kenpō-jō no Sho-Mondai*, 21; comment by Aoki Tokuzō at the subcommittee on the process of the establishment of a new constitution, 10 July 1958, in Constitution Research Council, *Kenpō Seitei no Keika nikansuru Shouiinkai Dai 8 Kai Gijiroku*, 3–4.

87   Conversation with Kanamori Tokujirō, 16 December 1957, in 'Nihon-koku Kenpō Seitei nikansuru Danwa Rokuon', no. 9; Terasaki, '"MacArthur Gensui" tono Go-Kaiken-roku'. Kanamori served positions such as the minister of state in the first Yoshida cabinet.

88   Mark Gayn, *Japan Diary* (New York: William Sloane Associates, 1948), 164–71; Izawa Takio Document Research Association, *Izawa Takio Kankei Bunsho*, 270.

89   Society for the Study of Parliamentary Government, *Seitō Nenkan: Shōwa 22 Nen* [Political party yearbook: Shōwa 22] (Tokyo: News Co., 1947), 37.

90   Shidehara Kijūrō, 'Konkai no Sōsenkyo nitsuite' [On this general election]', broadcast 9 April 1946, 1-2A-040-00-shi-00306-100, National Archives of Japan. See also 'Shidehara Heiwa Bunko', Reel 11.

91   Society for the Study of Parliamentary Government, *Seitō Nenkan*, 37–41; Kojima, *Ichi Rō-Seijika no Kaisō*, 266–269; Saitō Takao, *Kaiko 70 Nen* [Reflecting on 70 years] (Tokyo: Chūōkōronsha, 1987), 206–07.

See also Fukunaga, *Senryōka Chūdō Seiken no Keisei to Hōkai*, 70–74; Nakakita Kōji, *Keizai Fukkō to Sengo Seiji: Nihon Shakaitō, 1945–1951 Nen* [The economic recovery and postwar politics: The Socialist Party of Japan, 1945–1951] (Tokyo: University of Tokyo Press, 1998), 13–16.

92   Itō Takashi and Watanabe Yukio, eds, 'Saitō Takao Nikki (Shō)' [The diary of Saitō Takao (extract)], *Chūōkōron* 106, no. 1 (January 1991): 147–63. See also Narahashi, *Gekiryū ni Saosashite*, 135; Itō, *Shōwa-ki no Seiji*, 219–29, 273–74; Itō, *Zoku Shōwa-ki no Seiji*, 121.

93 Sodei, *Yoshida–MacArthur Ōfuku Shokanshū, 1945–1951*, 4–5, 121–23; Yoshida Shigeru Memorial Project Foundation, *Yoshida Shigeru Shokan*, 672; Hosokawa, *Hosokawa Nikki*, vol. 2, 197, 199; Itō Takashi and Suetake Yoshiya, eds, *Hatoyama Ichirō, Kaoru Nikki* [The diaries of Hatoyama Ichirō and Kaoru], vol. 1 (Tokyo: Chūō Kōron Shinsha, 1999), 437–40, 443.

94 Asahi Shimbun, *Irie Sukemasa Nikki*, vol. 2, 58; Ishibashi Tanzan, *Ishibashi Tanzan Nikki: Shōwa 20–31 Nen* [The diary of Tanzan Ishibashi: Shōwa 20–31], ed. Itō Takashi, vol. 1 (Tokyo: Misuzu Shobō, 2001), 115.

95 Society for the Study of Parliamentary Government, *Seitō Nenkan*, 40–42, 145–56.

For records of deliberations on revising the constitution, see Office of the Constitution Research Council, ed., *Teikoku Kenpō Kaisei Shingi-roku* [Records on deliberation concerning the revision of the imperial constitution], vol. 3 (Tokyo: Office of the Constitution Research Council, 1959), 16–17; ibid., vol. 4, 72–74, 189–190, 385; ibid., vol. 5, 287–89, 320–22, 394–95, 452–53, 459–62. See also Shimizu Shin, ed., *Chikujō Nihon-koku Kenpō Shingi-roku* [Records on article-by-article deliberation on the Japanese constitution], vol. 1 (Tokyo: Yūhikaku, 1962), 508–09, 519–20; ibid., vol. 2, 21–22; Maruyama and Fukuda, *Kikigaki*, 333.

96 Ashida to Shidehara, 19 April, 'Ashida Hitoshi Kankei Bunsho' [Documents relating to Ashida Hitoshi], Document Department, no. 165-2, Modern Japanese Political History Materials Room, National Diet Library.

97 Ashida to Shidehara, 'Jishokunegai' [Letter of resignation], 19 April 1946, in 'Ashida Hitoshi Kankei Bunsho', Document Department, no. 165-1.

98 Shindō and Shimokōbe, *Ashida Hitoshi Nikki*, vol. 1, 98–101, 138–40.

99 Ibid., 148.

100 Shidehara to Izawa, 2 June 1947, in Izawa Takio Document Research Association, *Izawa Takio Kankei Bunsho*, 271–72. See also Shindō and Shimokōbe, *Ashida Hitoshi Nikki*, vol. 1, 149, 152, 158, 161–62, 165, 167, 173, 181, 183, 184, 189, 193, 194, 197, 198, 199, 200, 324, 325, 326; Sugawara Tsūsai, 'Ashida Minshutō Sōsai no Kettei Made' [Until the selection of Ashida as president of the Democratic Party of Japan], 14 September, year unknown, in 'Shidehara Heiwa Bunko', Reel 13; Ishibashi, *Ishibashi Tanzan Nikki*, vol 1., 164, 191; Asahi Shimbun Political Party Press Corp, *Seitō Nenkan: Shōwa 23 Nen* [The political party yearbook: Shōwa 23] (Tokyo: News Co., 1948), 30–53, 79–90, 206–23.

101 A conversation with Ashida Hitoshi, 7 September, year unknown, in 'Shidehara Heiwa Bunko', Reel 4; Shindō and Shimokōbe, *Ashida Hitoshi Nikki*, vol. 2, 10–11.

102 Shidehara to Ishibashi Tanzan, 1 January 1948, in 'Ishibashi Tanzan Kankei Bunsho' [Documents relating to Ishibashi Tanzan], no. 292, Modern Japanese Political History Materials Room, National Diet Library.

103 Ishibashi Tanzan, 'Shidehara-san no Omoide' [Memories of Mr Shidehara], 1, *Tōyō Keizai Shinpō*, no. 2465 (March 1951): 21.

104 *Asahi Shimbun*, 16, 29 November 1947 and 16 March 1948; Asahi Shimbun Political Party Press Corp, *Seitō Nenkan: Shōwa 24 Nen* [The political party yearbook: Shōwa 24] (Tokyo: News Co., 1949), 130–46; National Graduate Institute for Policy Studies, ed., *Oral History Matsuno Raizō* [Oral history Matsuno Raizō], vol. 1 (Tokyo: National Graduate Institute for Policy Studies, 2003), 50–51. For details on the movements of the Shidehara clique, see Fukunaga, *Senryōka Chūdō Seiken no Keisei to Hōkai*, 190, 198–200, 216, 245, 270, 272.

105 Shidehara, *Gaikō 50 Nen*, 148–49.

106 Shidehara, 'Wasureenu Hitobito', 54–61.

8

War Responsibility and Nonpartisan Diplomacy for Peace

The Tokyo Trial

Shidehara and the Tokyo Trial

When the Yoshida cabinet was inaugurated in May 1946, Shidehara was given the position of minister of state. In the previous chapter, I outlined some details of Shidehara's engagement with party politics. In this chapter, I wish to focus on how an ageing Shidehara viewed Japan's foreign relations and his perspective on history.[1] For this purpose, the Tokyo Trial is particularly important. In fact, Shidehara himself appeared in court during the trials, and his testimony can provide us with some insight into his understanding of history.

The Tokyo Trial was a series of international war crimes trials that were carried out on the basis of the tenth article of the Potsdam Declaration. The target of these trials was Japan's wartime leaders. Eleven foreign nations participated in all: the US, the UK, the Soviet Union, China, France, the Netherlands, Canada, Australia, New Zealand, the Philippines and India. The official name for the trial was the International Military Tribunal for the Far East. A total of 28 people stood accused as suspected A-class war criminals. The trials commenced in May 1946 in Ichigaya. The chief justice was William Flood Webb of Australia, while the chief prosecutor was Joseph Berry Keenan of the US. In the November 1948 judgement, seven defendants were sentenced to death by hanging: Tōjō Hideki, Dohihara Kenji, Itagaki Seishirō, Kimura Heitarō, Mutō Akira, Matsui Iwane and Hirota Kōki. A further 16 people were sentenced to life imprisonment, including Araki Sadao, Hata Shunroku, Hiranuma Kiichirō, Kido Kōichi, Koiso Kuniaki, Minami Jirō, Shiratori Toshio and Umezu Yoshijirō.

Few topics are as controversial as the Tokyo Trial. One frequent point of contention regards the application of the ex post facto charges of 'crimes against peace' and 'crimes against humanity'. Needless to say, there was no questioning as to whether Allied actions such as the dropping of atomic bombs were themselves instances of such crimes.

For such reasons, the Tokyo Trial has been referred to as an example of 'victors' justice'. In the debates surrounding the trial, the term 'the Tokyo Trial view of history' appears. Although there is no precise definition of 'the Tokyo Trial view of history', it is used to criticise an interpretation that seeks to reject Japanese modern history. I suggest that it is more or less synonymous with the expression 'a masochistic view of history'.[2] It must be added that 'the Tokyo Trial view of history' has a somewhat unusual ring to it to begin with. Certainly, the Tokyo Trial may have been a case of 'victor's justice'. However, while the trial operated with the premise that a conspiracy had taken place, they did not in fact reject modern Japanese history totally. Moreover, the Shōwa emperor was not prosecuted. This was an outcome that the various participants—from the Japanese government and Tōjō Hideki to MacArthur and Chief Prosecutor Keenan—had been most concerned to avoid.

If the Tokyo Trial view of history is not a rejection of modern Japan per se, then what exactly is it? One basic theme of the trial was the US's perspective on Japan at that time, which was founded upon a good-versus-evil dualism. According to this schema, moderates in Japan were confronted and overpowered by the militarists. Naturally, for the purposes of the occupation, the Shōwa emperor was classified as a moderate. If there was an understanding of history that comprehensively rejected modern Japan, then that would be the official historical view of the Soviet Union. Although the Japanese *zaibatsu* (financial conglomerates) were not brought to account at the Tokyo Trial, the Soviet Union regarded them as having considerable responsibility for the war. It also believed that the 'Tanaka Memorial', which set out Japan's invasion plans, was a real document. In China, meanwhile, there was a tendency to distinguish between the Japanese people and the militarists. This can be considered a different kind of dualism than the US's model.[3]

If we were to adopt an American-style dualistic model, then we would certainly have to categorise Shidehara as a representative of the moderate faction. Indeed, US Ambassador Grew had previously viewed Shidehara in such a manner. Shidehara was not the only Japanese official called to the witness stand who was viewed as a moderate. Figures such as Wakatsuki Reijirō, Okada Keisuke and Ugaki Kazushige were also viewed sympathetically. In fact, Keenan actually invited Wakatsuki, Okada, Ugaki and Yonai Mitsumasa to a cocktail party at his residence, where he cheerfully told them that 'you four gentlemen are the true lovers of peace in Japan'.[4] Reading such accounts may naturally generate doubts as to whether the US could truly distinguish between the so-called moderates and militarists. Yonai, after all, was navy minister during the Second Sino-Japanese War and one of the officials responsible for expanding that conflict.[5]

With these details in mind, I would now like to outline Shidehara's final years. Shidehara was serving as minister of state in the Yoshida cabinet when he first appeared as a witness at the Tokyo Trial.[6] He also testified on topics such as the Manchurian Incident when questioned by the international prosecution. Shidehara also helped in the reformation of the Ministry of Foreign Affairs. The following discussion addresses two important questions: How did Shidehara evaluate the prewar years and the lead-up to the collapse of the empire? And how did he view the international status of Japan in the postwar era?

As a Witness for the Prosecution

The Tokyo Trial began on 3 May 1946. The Ministry of Foreign Affairs established a satellite office in Ichigaya in order to maintain necessary lines of communication.[7] The Shidehara cabinet had recently resigned, on 22 April. Shidehara was now a minister of state in its successor, the Yoshida cabinet. The Yoshida cabinet was a coalition cabinet, containing ministers from Yoshida's own Liberal Party, as well as Shidehara's Progressive Party. On 18 June, the chief prosecutor, Keenan—who was visiting the US at the time—made some noteworthy comments on the Shōwa emperor. At a press conference in Washington, Keenan had stated that the emperor would not be prosecuted. News of this statement quickly reached Japan.[8]

With a feeling of relief, Shidehara headed towards Ichigaya on 25 June. He was to appear as a witness for the prosecution. Taking the witness stand with a tense expression, Shidehara was flanked on his right side by 10 court judges. In front of him, the prosecutors and the chief defence counsel faced each other, while to his left he was met with the stares of the assembled defendants. Sitting among the accused were some of Shidehara's former subordinates: Hirota Kōki, Shigemitsu Mamoru, Tōgō Shigenori and Shiratori Toshio. However, Matsuoka Yōsuke and Ōkawa Shūmei were not present. On the edges of the courtroom were sections for the press corps and members of the public as well as booths for interpreters. At the beginning of the trial, the prosecutor read Shidehara's affidavit out loud. The defence counsel for Ōshima Hiroshi then objected to the admission of Shidehara's affidavit. However, the objection was overruled by Chief Justice Webb. Ōshima previously served as Japan's ambassador to Germany, despite being from the army. Together with Shiratori Toshio— who was then the ambassador to Italy—he had advocated a Tripartite Pact between Japan, Germany and Italy.

The focus of Shidehara's affidavit was the Manchurian Incident. He stated that, just before the Liutiaohu Incident, he had received a 'secret report' stating that the Kwantung Army had assembled and had taken explosive materials with them. Therefore, Shidehara wrote, he had anticipated that the army intended to take 'some kind of action'.[9] Further, he claimed that although the Wakatsuki cabinet had worked to prevent further escalation following the incident, they were eventually left with no choice but to resign. In response, the defence counsel for Minami Jirō carried out a cross-examination (questioning conducted by the opposing party). As Shidehara had come to court to act as a witness for the prosecution, the defence counsel's questioning of him constituted cross-examination.

Minami Jirō's defence counsel carried out cross-examination concerning the source of Shidehara's so-called secret report. While struggling with his words, Shidehara admitted that the source was actually no more than a 'rumour' heard from Japanese residents of Manchuria who were visiting Tokyo, and that he 'did not mean to say he had received an official report'. Shidehara further testified that, at that time, War Minister Minami had 'cooperated to the extent that he could' and that, while Minami had sought to have the Kwantung Army restrained through cooperation from the War Ministry, the Ministry of Foreign Affairs was unable to directly investigate the cause of the incident.[10] Although he did not seek to sacrifice Minami, Shidehara emphasised that the Ministry of Foreign Affairs was not at fault.

The defence counsel for Matsui Iwane would also not remain quiet. As a member of the military, Matsui had served as an army commander in the Central China Area Army during the Second Sino-Japanese War and had been charged with assisting in the attack on Nanjing. Matsui's defence counsel cited a number of incidents that occurred during Shidehara's time as foreign minister. These were the Nanjing Incident of 1927, the Wanpaoshan Incident and the Nakamura Incident. The Nanjing Incident of 1927 was discussed in Chapter 3. The Wanpaoshan Incident refers to a clash between Chinese peasants and Korean peasants that took place in Wanpaoshan, on the outskirts of the north-eastern Chinese city of Changchun. Finally, the Nakamura Incident refers to the murder of Captain Nakamura Shintarō of the Office of Army General Staff, who had been conducting a military geographical intelligence survey near Taonan in north-eastern China. Both the Wanpaoshan Incident and the Nakamura Incident took place in the summer of 1931 and were understood to have helped cause the Manchurian Incident.

With the defence counsel now attempting to assert Japan's own victimhood concerning the events of the period, Shidehara was able to regain his composure. His response regarding the Nanjing Incident of 1927 is particularly noteworthy:

> Japanese residents [of the city] certainly suffered from looting, and some individuals were even wounded. However, I believe that there were no deaths … I think the impact on the U.K. and the U.S. in particular was actually more horrendous.[11]

There was also cross-examination from the defence counsel for Shiratori Toshio. Shiratori was director-general of the Intelligence Department during Shidehara's second term as foreign minister and had also been a central figure among the reformist clique at the Ministry of Foreign Affairs. Yet surprisingly, Shidehara showed a more favourable attitude towards Shiratori. He asserted that Shiratori had 'followed the peace policy line' of the Wakatsuki cabinet.[12] Here, Shidehara took a milder tone. In fact, he had absolutely no criticisms to make of former diplomatic officials, including Shiratori. This friendliness angered the prosecution, who argued that the cross-examination had turned into a direct examination (in other words, questioning by the side that called the witness).

Further strengthening this tendency was the cross-examination by Shigemitsu's defence counsel. Here Shidehara's testimony practically amounted to a defence of Shigemitsu. According to Shidehara, Shigemitsu became Japan's minister to China on his recommendation, and he was 'completely satisfied' with Shigemitsu's performance in that role.[13] However, Shidehara acknowledged that he did not receive any early information from Shigemitsu on the plotting by the Kwangtung Army. Shidehara also noted that after the Liutiaohu Incident, Shigemitsu proposed a meeting with Song Ziwen (Soong Tzu-wen).

Shigemitsu's defence counsel continued his cross-examination of Shidehara on 26 June. Reflecting upon the Manchurian Incident, Shidehara stated emphatically that 'at that time, Minister Shigemitsu faithfully' cooperated. Shidehara also stated that, given the supreme command authority of the emperor:

> It was hardly possible for the cabinet to issue official reprimands to all of the army, not just the Manchurian army. This was not within the official authority of the government.[14]

From Shidehara's perspective, it was not Minami who was ultimately responsible for the Manchurian Incident. Rather, the root issues of the incident could be traced to the army officials in the field, together with flaws in the system relating to chain of command.

Shidehara's testimony clearly included some distortions; though a witness for the prosecution, he repeatedly made statements that benefitted Shiratori and Shigemitsu. Although Shidehara was ideologically opposed to these two individuals, he sought to protect them. His true motivation here may well have been less the protection of the individuals and more the protection of the Ministry of Foreign Affairs as an organisation. One passage in Shigemitsu's diary states: 'When he appeared in court as a witness, Shidehara's testimony was beneficial to me'.[15] It would seem that, standing before Minami and Shigemitsu, Shidehara acted as a witness for both the defence and the prosecution at the same time.

So it was that Shidehara offered his now quite distant memories as a form of testimony in the trials. As the accused, both Minami and Araki listened tensely to his answers. The manner of the proceedings would inform headlines in the *Asahi Shimbun*, such as 'Unable to "Restrain" the Kwantung Army, the Manchurian Incident Expanded: Minister of State Shidehara Takes the Stand' and 'Responsibility for the Manchurian

Incident is with Army Minister Minami, Minister of State Shidehara Clearly Testifies'.[16] Yet as noted above, Shidehara's true intention was not necessarily to criticise Minami. According to other newspapers, such as the *Yomiuri Shimbun*, Shidehara 'did not so much as smile, as though he had bitten into a bitter-tasting bug'. Here, too, the headline read, 'Responsibility for the Manchurian Incident with the Army Minister'.[17]

Let us now move forward roughly one year in time, to 24 June 1947. On that day, Shidehara was questioned by the international prosecution at the National Diet Building. Here, too, the focus of the questioning was the Manchurian Incident. The international prosecution wanted to know how much Shidehara had guessed about the scheming of the Kwantung Army on the basis of information received before the incident from Hayashi Kyūjirō, former consul general in Fengtian (Mukden). They also wanted Shidehara to tell them more about the respective positions of War Minister Minami Jirō, Fengtian Special Service Agency Chief Dohihara Kenji and Kwantung Army Commander-in-Chief Honjō Shigeru.[18] They were particularly persistent with their questions on Minami.

Concerning what the Liutiaohu Incident foreshadowed, Shidehara responded that the information he received came not from Hayashi but from Japanese merchants who had temporarily returned to Tokyo. When he then called for Minami after hearing this information, the war minister informed him that, while he was to respond to the situation, he also 'could not carry out strict punishments in order to maintain discipline, due to his concerns about potential disorder'.[19] When questioned about Honjō and Dohihara, Shidehara replied he was not the only one insufficiently aware of the scheming taking place in the field; Minami, he said, was also relatively in the dark. In this case, however, Shidehara criticised Minami for being weak-willed. The international prosecutors were sceptical of Shidehara's testimony that day, particularly with regard to the claim that he did not receive sufficient information from Consul General Hayashi. Yet it was not Shidehara who was a defendant at the Tokyo Trial but Minami and Dohihara. It seemed as if the international prosecutors and Shidehara had reached an unspoken agreement to collaborate in laying most of the responsibility for the Manchurian Incident and its aftermath at the feet of the army.

Nevertheless, Shidehara's criticisms of Minami were not unusual. For example, Hirota Kōki, though he did not take the witness stand in court, indicated during questioning that he thought Minami had a great deal to answer for regarding the Manchurian Incident.[20] It must be admitted that aspects of Shidehara's testimony were not much more than excuses. We know that Consul General Hayashi was actually aware of the Kwantung Army's plans before the Manchurian Incident, due to a warning from Kimura Eiichi, the director of the South Manchuria Railway. Further, Hayashi had passed this information on to the central authorities. Immediately after the incident, he also informed Shidehara that it was highly likely to have been a false-flag attack. As I discussed in Chapter 5 (Section 3), during a cabinet meeting held the day after the Liutiaohu Incident, Shidehara revealed that he had received a telegram from Hayashi. This was the reason that War Minister Minami did not receive the go-ahead to send the Japanese Korean Army as reinforcements.[21]

As a Witness for the Defence

In February 1947, the defence counsel began to present its counterevidence. On this occasion Shidehara was again called to testify, only this time as a witness for the accused. In July that year, Shidehara prepared the affidavit required for his appearance in court as a defence witness. Compared to the affidavit prepared in July the previous year, this affidavit went into more detail on Shidehara's relationship with Minami at the time of the Manchurian Incident. Shidehara claimed that he and Minami had cooperated to try to prevent the Manchurian Incident from expanding, and described the claim that they were at odds over the incident as no more than an 'empty rumor'.[22] This statement appears to have been aimed at rebutting testimony from prosecution witness Tanaka Ryūkichi, who had claimed that Shidehara and Minami were at odds with each other.

As the day of the court hearing drew closer, however, Shidehara began to experience difficulty walking. Unable even to rise from bed due to extreme pain, he was taken to St Luke's International Hospital, where he was diagnosed with psoas muscle pain. The hospital medical report stated that, 'for the time being, he should remain warm and rest in bed, and receive ongoing medical care'.[23] He was now almost 77 years of age, and years of fatigue had finally caught up with him. With Shidehara in no condition to appear in court, the defence counsel was forced to visit his residence to question him.

Shidehara's residence was in Okamoto, in the Setagaya ward of Tokyo. In the early afternoon of 11 November 1947, a judge, three prosecutors and three members of the defence counsel arrived at the residence.

The head prosecutor was the Britain Arthur S. Comyns-Carr, who was accompanied by two other individuals. The defence counsels were those responsible for defending Koiso Kuniaki, Shigemitsu Mamoru and Minami Jirō, respectively. Of course, a stenographer and a member of the secretariat were also in attendance. Apart from one member of the defence counsel, practically the entire group were foreigners. Receiving the go-ahead from the prosecutors and the defence counsel, Shidehara began to give his testimony in fluent English.

According to Shidehara, before the Liutiaohu Incident, several Japanese residents of Manchuria visited the Ministry of Foreign Affairs to report that 'something unusual was happening'. Upon hearing this, Shidehara summoned War Minister Minami and asked him to enforce military discipline. Minami replied that he would take the necessary steps to deal with the situation. After the outbreak of the Manchurian Incident, Shidehara continued to disclose to Minami copies of all telegrams received from the area. That said, Shidehara did not assert that Minami alone was responsible. He noted that Minami had attempted to carry out the decisions of the Wakatsuki cabinet; however, his instructions were not carried out by subordinates in the field. He also did not press for the sending of reinforcements from the Japanese Korean Army. Shidehara added that, when Minami attempted to prevent further expansion of the incident by restricting military funding, 'it appeared that members of the military might carry out a coup', and so 'Minami was forced to approach the problem in a more practical manner'.[24] As can be seen, Shidehara also sought to defend Minami in certain respects.

The report on Shidehara's testimony would be considered in court on 19 November 1947. In response, the defence counsel for Dohihara raised an objection. Even though Shidehara's testimony was of real significance for Dohihara, his defence was not warned beforehand that it would be considered that day. On the following day, 20 November, Dohihara's defence counsel made the same objection. Nevertheless, prosecutor Comyns-Carr somehow managed to have the cross-examination read out to the court. The court was also shown nine telegrams sent from Hayashi to Shidehara after the Liutiaohu Incident. These telegrams informed Shidehara of Dohihara's manoeuvring with respect to Puyi, last emperor of the Qing dynasty and future ruler of the puppet state of Manchukuo. The contents of the telegrams thus constituted a blow for Dohihara rather than for Minami.[25]

Yet from the perspective of the court, the discussions surrounding the report on Shidehara's testimony had a negative impact on both Minami and Dohihara. In a diary entry dated to that time, Shigemitsu wrote:

> The report on Shidehara's testimony continues—after arguing his position, Prosecutor Carr was permitted to read out aloud the document that the witness has approved of. There were exchanges of telegrams between the consul general in Mukden and the foreign minister, and [this information] has been disadvantageous for both Minami and Dohihara.[26]

The *Yomiuri Shimbun* reported on the developments under the headline 'Minami without Power to Control the Kwantung Army, Report on Shidehara's Testimony'.[27] That said, the defence counsel was certainly not going to overlook the potential utility of Shidehara's testimony for their own ends. The defence counsel referenced Shidehara's testimony in the closing statement that they gave on Minami. According to this statement, Shidehara and Minami had remained close friends up until the present-day. Further, Minami had not proposed in cabinet meetings that Japan leave the League of Nations. Minami had also been cooperative during the Manchurian Incident. Finally, the information relating to the schemes of the Kwantung Army before the incident was unofficial.[28]

The Tokyo Trial concluded with a ruling in November 1948. The ruling itself consisted of an extremely long text that only Chief Justice Webb was permitted to read aloud. For this reason, the reading of the judgement alone took an entire week. Minami and Dohihara were sentenced to life imprisonment and execution by hanging, respectively. Were these rulings just? There is reason to doubt that they were. Even if we look only at a specific part of the ruling, namely Section 1, Chapter 5, Part B, which is titled 'Invasion and Occupation of Manchuria', there are some conspicuous contradictions. The entry titled 'Foreign Minister Shidehara Continued Efforts at Mediation' states that, although Shidehara heard rumours before the Liutiaohu Incident that the Kwangtung Army was plotting something, he did not have any conclusive evidence. The entry emphasises that Shidehara thus pressed Minami for answers directly after the incident. This information, however, conflicts with that presented in another entry. The entry titled 'The Manchurian Incident Was Planned' states that Hayashi sent Shidehara information prior to the incident. When Shidehara protested to Minami, Minami responded by dispatching Tatekawa Yoshitsugu to Manchuria in order to prevent the plot.[29]

As noted earlier, a basic theme of the trial was the US view of Japan. More specifically, I mean the schemata by which the Americans divided the Japanese leadership into the moderates (which included the Shōwa emperor) and the militarists. Following these schemata, when individuals such as Shidehara, Ugaki Kazushige, Wakatsuki Reijirō or Okada Keisuke took the witness stand, there was a tendency to interpret their testimony as that of 'moderate' figures accusing the 'militarists'.[30] Certainly, there is some degree of truth to this interpretation. However, in Shidehara's case at the very least, there was no desire to denounce the military. Indeed, the defence actually deployed Shidehara's testimony in its closing statement because it helped to give a favourable impression. The criticism that Shidehara sought to shift blame to military figures is not necessarily accurate. This fact demonstrates just how ambiguous Shidehara's position was regarding who was responsible for the war. As his testimony suggests, Shidehara disliked the rashness of Konoe Fumimaro far more than he did the military.[31] In any case, what was crucially important for Shidehara was that the Ministry of Foreign Affairs be protected.

The Foreign Service Training Institute

Shidehara's enduring commitment to the Ministry of Foreign Affairs was on display in contexts outside the Ichigaya courtroom as well. Among these, we cannot overlook the establishment of the Foreign Service Training Institute. This institute had a predecessor. As early as 1941, the Ministry of Foreign Affairs had set up a centre to train its new hires. This training centre was maintained until the period immediately following the end of the war. However, the lack of a proper organisational basis hindered its operation. The Ministry of Foreign Affairs organisation reform in February 1946 led to the formal establishment of the Foreign Service Training Institute. For a site to run the institute, the ministry borrowed a building from Tōhō Bunka Gakuin, located in Ōtsuka, which is in Tokyo's Bunkyō ward.

Along with Yoshida, Shidehara was instrumental in pushing for the opening of this institute. The first director was Vice-Minister Matsushima Shikao. At an opening ceremony held on 1 March, Shidehara had attended in his role as prime minister. Foreign Minister Yoshida was also in attendance. Upon rising to give his welcoming address, Director Matsushima 'pointed out that the establishment of the institution was entirely thanks to the efforts of Prime Minister Shidehara'. Shidehara then gave his own congratulatory speech, in which he 'touched upon the indispensability of cultivating one's character and improving one's foreign language capabilities. Overflowing with genuine feeling, it deeply moved the assembled juniors'.[32] The institute library contained some 17,000 volumes, including the collections of Ishii Kikujirō and Yamakawa Tadao. Naturally, there were foreign language classes available, but there were also classes on typing. The training period for new hires was set at six months.

The director who eventually succeeded Matsushima, Terasaki Tarō, was also vice-minister for foreign affairs. Although it was not unusual for the directorship to be handled by vice-ministers, having somebody work as director in name only did limit the training that new hires would receive. Hence it was recognised that the best possible outcome would be for a full-time director who could focus entirely upon the job. Shidehara and Yoshida both had the same person in mind for this role: Satō Naotake. At that time, Satō was still serving as Japan's ambassador to the Soviet Union. He would finally return in May 1946. As noted above, this was the time when the Shidehara cabinet resigned. Asked if he would be interested in directing the institute, Satō responded cautiously. Only after he had confirmed with GHQ that he was not a potential target for the purges from public office did he finally accept. Hence, in August of that same year, Satō became the third director of the institute. He was the institute's first full-time director, and, in a sense, he was also the first real director. Indeed, Satō also viewed himself in this manner.[33]

Now a minister of state, Shidehara gave a speech at the ceremony for Satō's inauguration. With Satō sitting before him, Shidehara recalled the days of his friendship with ministry adviser Denison and told the assembled institute trainees: 'In my opinion, honesty is truly the best possible diplomatic policy'.[34] Prime Minister Yoshida, who at that time was also serving as foreign minister, was also in attendance. Elder ministry figures such as Obata Yūkichi and Matsudaira Tsuneo were also hired to help as advisers to the institute. From Shidehara's perspective, Yoshida and the others were all once his subordinates. A famous specialist in diplomatic history would also come to give some lectures as a form of special training.

Why did Shidehara and Yoshida seek to establish the Foreign Service Training Institute at this time? After all, the occupation by the Allied forces had only just started, and even neutral countries had more or less cut off their diplomatic relations with Japan.[35] The prospects for regaining sovereignty in the near term were hardly bright. Under the occupation, the Ministry of Foreign Affairs was relegated to handling communication and negotiation between the Japanese government and the occupying force. For this reason, it had established an external bureau called the Central Liaison Office. Numerous ministry staff were sent to work in this bureau at the time.

Japan's overseas diplomatic establishments also remained closed, with a continuous stream of ministry officials withdrawing from the field and returning home. The ministry was also forced to make severe personnel cuts, causing a great deal of concern about the loss of talented staff. Numerous ministry officials began to seek out alternative employment as interpreters or lawyers. That said, Shidehara and Yoshida well understood that the day would come when Japan would regain its sovereignty and resume diplomatic relations with other countries. In preparation for the restoration of these relations, it was essential that the ministry retained a core of properly trained staff. Once, during his time as prime minister, Shidehara made the following remarks:

> With a country such as ours that has many of its own peculiarities, the training of diplomatic officials necessarily differs from how it is carried out in, for example, the Western nations. It is extremely arduous and time-consuming. It is not something that can be done overnight. In order to be prepared for the future, therefore, it is necessary to devote ceaseless effort to cultivating and training [our future diplomats].[36]

This is all to say that Shidehara understood that diplomats could not be properly trained in a short time. I note that the political power of those supporting the ministry was also essential for halting the loss of talented officials. Shidehara and Yoshida established the training institute for this very reason—to ensure that the ministry would have adequate numbers of able staff in the future. Yoshida also enjoyed looking out for young and upcoming staff, and, once a year, he would give instructional lectures at the institute. For Shidehara and Yoshida, therefore, the institute was no mere training facility.[37]

It should be noted that the Demobilization Agency was also established under the Yoshida cabinet, in June 1946. Shidehara, who at that time was serving in the cabinet as a minister of state, was chosen as director of the agency. Shidehara also became the chairman of the Kasumigaseki Association, an informal social organisation for people associated with the Ministry of Foreign Affairs.[38]

The UK and China

A high-priority task during the occupation was the restoration of the Japanese–American relationship. At that time, anyone in a position of responsibility was well aware of the overwhelming importance of the US. Upon forming a new cabinet as prime minister, Shidehara had once said to Prince Higashikuni:

> Going forward, I aim to ensure that Japan–U.S. diplomacy proceeds in a measured manner. We will focus on coordinating with the U.S. to the best of our ability, with an eye towards the eventual revival of Japan's position.[39]

To this end, Shidehara would frequently write correspondence not only to MacArthur but also to former US ambassadors to Japan such as Castle, Grew and Forbes.[40]

Of course, Shidehara was not merely a pro-American politician. While his actions were very friendly toward the US, it had long been British-style diplomacy that had furnished him with his ideals. This did not change under the occupation. A particularly illuminating event in this respect was the December 1949 roundtable discussion between Shidehara, Yoshida Shigeru and Satō Naotake. While Yoshida was famous for his pro-British tendencies, Shidehara and Satō were hardly to be beaten in this regard. When Shidehara would praise Bryce or Grey during their talk, Satō would respond by citing British foreign ministers such as John Allsebrook Simon or Anthony Eden. The recollections shared by the three elder statesmen on this occasion invariably centred on the UK. In fact, the US did not come up at all.[41]

It should be noted that Shidehara did not have a rosy view of Japan's relationship with the UK. Once, in January 1946, when Shidehara was serving as prime minister, he met with his old acquaintance Sansom. Sansom, as noted in the previous chapter, was visiting Japan at that time in the role of the British representative to the Far Eastern Advisory Commission. At their meeting, Sansom informed Shidehara that in the UK, 'opinion was still very bitter by reason of Japanese atrocities, and that the Japanese Army had perhaps done more damage to Japan by their cruelties than by losing the war'.[42] Shidehara must have been shocked by these words, for he subsequently relayed them to the Shōwa emperor and arranged for him to meet with Sansom. However, this meeting never took place. As it happened, Sansom himself declined the offer of an audience with the emperor, citing his ongoing role as a member of an international delegation.

While Shidehara considered Japan's relationship with the UK and the US highly valuable, he did not ignore Asia. In March 1946, while serving as prime minister, Shidehara gave a lecture titled 'Watashi no Shina-kan' (My perspective on China). The audience was the Sino-Japanese Friendship Society of the Industry Club of Japan. In this lecture, Shidehara noted that:

> From the time I arrived at Kasumigaseki [the district in central Tokyo where most of the major government ministries are located] … I firmly believed that when it came to relations between China and Japan, what was needed was goodwill, cooperation, and understanding.[43]

Yet, he added, the Chinese government and domestic (Japanese) public opinion remained unsympathetic. As for the present moment, Shidehara expressed his admiration for Chiang Kai-shek, who had said that China ought to 'turn bitterness into benevolence'. He added, 'I am extremely pleased to see how Mr. Chiang Kai-shek is dealing with the situation'.[44]

However, Shidehara noted, if Japan were to urgently seek amicable relations with China at the current time, with the war only recently ended, it could place the Chinese government in an awkward position. Any immediate restoration of good relations would therefore be difficult. Nevertheless, Shidehara commented:

> I am truly thankful, from the bottom of my heart, that Mr. Chiang Kai-shek has provided as much protection as possible to those Japanese citizens who remain residents in China. I believe that it is with just such actions that the foundation for future Sino-Japanese relations can be secured.[45]

It would seem that, in the long-term at least, Shidehara was optimistic about Sino-Japanese relations.

In any case, the situation in China and Korea remained too fluid to make predictions. So, at this point, Shidehara did not prioritise plans for improving relations with Asia. Instead, he sought to assist with the more modest undertaking of academic research—specifically the rebuilding of Tōyō Bunko (the Oriental Library).

Tōyō Bunko was an Asian research institution known around the world. Shidehara had long been connected to this institution, from as far back as the period following the Great Kantō Earthquake. As mentioned earlier, Shidehara lost his home in one of the fires that broke out in the aftermath of the earthquake. It was at this point that the Iwasaki family gifted him the residence at Rikugien to serve as his new home. When Shidehara began to live at Rikugien, which is located in Komagome, Tōyō Bunko was just finishing the construction of its new building. In fact, it was directly opposite Shidehara's Rikugien residence. This was no coincidence. Tōyō Bunko was established by Iwasaki Hisaya, who was Iwasaki Yatarō's eldest son and the founder of the Mitsubishi *zaibatsu*. The Iwasaki family, which had turned part of the Rikugien gardens into grounds for their villa, had also allotted a south-eastern part of the original land area to Tōyō Bunko.[46] The chief director of Tōyō Bunko at the time was Inoue Junnosuke, who would later become minister of finance in the Hamaguchi cabinet.

In 1932, Shidehara's old acquaintance Hayashi Gonsuke became chief director of Tōyō Bunko. Then, in November 1935, Shidehara himself became councillor of Tōyō Bunko. Shidehara would be promoted to director in December 1939, after Chief Director Hayashi passed away in June that year. Later, in February 1941, Shidehara had his brother Shidehara Taira donate his collection of books to Tōyō Bunko.[47]

Shidehara became chief director of Tōyō Bunko in October 1947. This directorship was more than an honorary post for Shidehara. As mentioned in Chapter 2, Shidehara had always been particularly fond of books. Unfortunately, the destruction wrought by the war had effectively led to the Tōyō Bunko shutting its doors for several years. Shidehara had also just become a member of the House of Representatives at this time. The president of the House of Councillors was Matsudaira Tsuneo, who was later followed by Satō Naotake. From Shidehara's perspective, both were still the equivalent of his juniors from their days at the Ministry of Foreign Affairs. Making use of his status, Shidehara poured his energy into negotiations with the National Diet Library and succeeded in having Tōyō Bunko re-opened as a branch of the National Diet Library. As chief director of Tōyō Bunko, Shidehara himself would sign the eventual agreement with the National Diet Library in August 1948.[48]

Further, in the same year, Shidehara also became the chairman of the newly established Tōhō Kenkyū-kai (the Oriental Research Association). The purpose of this association was to sponsor informal gatherings to discuss matters relating to China. It was attended by former diplomatic officials such as Ishii Itarō and Hayashide Kenjirō. Tōhō Kenkyū-kai is also known for publishing *Gendai Tōa-Jin Meikan* (Directory of contemporary East Asians). In the foreword that he supplied for this book in his capacity as chairman, Shidehara wrote: 'Today, understanding the various nations of East Asia must be our urgent undertaking. Tōhō Kenkyū-kai was formed just after the war as a result of this very realization'.[49] In fact, the editing of the directory was effectively undertaken by the First Division of the Ministry of Foreign Affairs Research Bureau.

Nonpartisan Diplomacy and National Security

Nonpartisan Diplomacy

During this period, the executive branch of the Japanese government also underwent a series of transitions—from the first Yoshida cabinet to the Katayama cabinet and, subsequently, to the Ashida cabinet. Then, in October 1948, the Ashida cabinet also resigned en masse. The cause for this resignation was a corruption scandal relating to financing for Shōwa Denkō, a large chemical firm. The result was the formation of the second Yoshida cabinet. This cabinet would last for a long time, until the end of 1954. Meanwhile, Shidehara was re-elected in the general election of January 1949 and, in February, became the speaker of the House of Representatives. That is to say, rather than being made a minister of state again in the Yoshida cabinet, he was kicked upstairs to an honorary position.

At this time, in preparation for the conclusion of the peace-making process, Shidehara tasked himself with the development of a new diplomacy that would transcend party lines. I am speaking here of nonpartisan diplomacy. Of course, Shidehara had argued for many years that diplomacy and domestic politics ought to be separated. Yet his efforts to establish a new nonpartisan diplomacy were directly triggered by the June 1950 visit to Japan of John Foster Dulles, the special peace envoy. President Truman had entrusted Dulles with the handling of peace negotiations with Japan.

It should be noted that this was not Dulles's first time in Japan. He had visited Japan and China in February and March 1938. In preparation for his upcoming visit to Japan, which would last 10 days, Dulles had asked Ambassador to the US Saitō Hiroshi to write him numerous introductory letters. In Tokyo, he would meet with moderates such as Vice-Minister for Foreign Affairs Horinouchi Kensuke, Yoshizawa Kenkichi, Makino Nobuaki, Kabayama Aisuke and Shidehara himself. Dulles had formed a positive opinion of these moderate-faction politicians at the time. It should be noted that because Shidehara met with Dulles only briefly, Dulles did not come away with a particularly strong impression of Shidehara.[50] It was US Ambassador Grew who had strongly recommended to Shidehara that he meet with Dulles. In his letter to Shidehara, Grew said that Dulles, 'an old friend of mine', was investigating the Far East and wanted very much to meet with Shidehara.[51] There is reason to question whether Dulles was really as eager to meet Shidehara as Grew stated. It may instead have been that Grew himself thought Shidehara was the kind of person whom Dulles ought to meet. In any case, Grew's enthusiasm for Shidehara did not infect Dulles in 1938.

Yet, as it turned out, Grew's efforts would bear fruit over 20 years later. When Dulles visited Japan in June 1950, Shidehara had earned a reputation as a liberal politician. This was when Shidehara began to push for the development of nonpartisan diplomacy, and it seems that he received some prompting from Dulles. It should be noted that Dulles had been involved with foreign policy as far back as before the war, when he was working as a Republican Party–affiliated lawyer.[52]

Shidehara's first step was to reach out to figures such as Tomabechi Gizō, the Democratic Party of Japan's supreme committee chairman, and Asanuma Inejirō, the Socialist Party of Japan's chief secretary, to sound them out on the idea of nonpartisan diplomacy. While Tomabechi was receptive to the idea, the Socialist Party declined Shidehara's proposal. In June 1950 Asanuma had already told Dulles, who was then in Japan, that 'the Socialist Party is unable to accept the nonpartisan diplomacy of the Liberal Party'.[53] It may have been that Shidehara's ties to the Socialist Party leaders were not strong enough to win them over to such plans. Nevertheless, Shidehara was so enthused about the prospects of nonpartisan diplomacy that it seemed rash to Prime Minister Yoshida and Ashida of the Democratic Party.

If that was the case, what exactly did Shidehara's nonpartisan diplomacy consist of? In fact, there was nothing special about it. It was simply about not allowing diplomacy to be used as a political football. More details on this point can be found in a speech Shidehara gave in November 1950. According to this speech, Shidehara had been motivated by a 'bitter experience' that he underwent during his time in the Ministry of Foreign Affairs. 'Diplomatic problems were frequently turned into fodder for political disputes', he noted. 'Caught between the political parties, our ministry, which was tasked with actually raising diplomatic problems [with the politicians], often ended up being worked half to death.' Having once undergone such experiences firsthand in the days before he become a politician, Shidehara took a certain pride in believing he was the right person to promote nonpartisan diplomacy. Shidehara's model for this new form of diplomacy was the UK. He argued that 'in the U.K. they speak of the continuity of prior diplomacy … I [therefore] received the impression that the U.K.'s diplomacy was the most trustworthy'. Conversely, in the US even the Treaty of Versailles was rejected in Congress. Only in recent years had the US begun to recognise the importance of nonpartisan diplomatic efforts. It was for this reason that Shidehara 'argued for the need to remove diplomatic problems from the sphere for party conflicts'.[54]

Hence Shidehara sought to promote the continuity of diplomatic policy within the party politics system. Certainly, Shidehara's convictions about nonpartisan diplomacy were right. It could even be said that he demonstrated considerable discernment in this regard. It is also clear why he saw the UK as a model for such diplomacy. However, the kind of nonpartisan diplomacy that Shidehara envisaged presumed a certain maturity among opposition politicians, the general public and the mass media. It is highly doubtful that such a style of diplomacy could have been promptly applied in Japan at that time. In the end, Shidehara's proposed nonpartisan diplomacy was ignored not only by the political opposition but also by Prime Minister Yoshida and the secretary-general of the Liberal Party, Satō Eisaku. The possibility that the Socialist Party would agree to support nonpartisan diplomacy was also slim.[55]

National Security

Nevertheless, during this period Shidehara's diplomatic stance continued to evolve. Before the war, he saw the initiative of the Ministry of Foreign Affairs as only natural. After the war he came to recognise that the governing party had a role to play and even busied himself with attempts at bringing the opposition on board. Given this new stance, what kind of foreign policy issues was Shidehara seeking to have addressed?

Major issues of contention included Japan's rearmament and the stationing of US forces. From the beginning, Shidehara did not have any clear plans regarding Japan's national security in the postwar era. In a meeting with Yoshida Shigeru, Satō Naotake and Matsudaira Tsuneo, Shidehara recognised that Japan was defenceless against possible invasion but still trusted in a vaguely defined 'world public opinion'. At the same time, Shidehara also asserted that he was 'absolutely opposed to joining the United Nations'.[56] In his view, such an international body could not be relied upon for national defence and should not be permitted to erode Japan's ability to undertake its own independent diplomatic efforts. Shidehara's perspective here appears to have hardly changed from the days when he was angered by the intervention of the League of Nations in East Asia. During a different roundtable discussion, when questioned about permanent neutrality, Shidehara disdainfully replied: 'What benefit would doing something like that have?'[57]

Nevertheless, with the outbreak of the Korean War in June 1950, Shidehara began to think more seriously about national security. It should be noted that, in those days, the biggest concern was domestic political stability. A July 1950 report by Dulles is quite informative in this regard. According to Dulles, who had just concluded his visit to Japan, Shidehara was far franker than the ambiguous Prime Minister Yoshida. Shidehara had told Dulles that, because 'any rearmament would be far too expensive', he very much wanted the US to continue to station its soldiers in Japan. Dulles said Shidehara had told him that 'the Communists had been allowed too much liberty and that if American forces were withdrawn at once, the Japanese would not be able to contain possible Communist activity'. Shidehara had further told Dulles that 'there was strong sentiment against Russia among the Japanese'. Therefore, even if Japan were one day occupied by the Soviet Union, they would never cooperate with the Soviets in the way that they currently cooperated with the Americans. Hence, he argued, 'in the end their military victory would prove a failure'. According to Dulles, 'Baron Shidehara was the only one with whom we talked who expressed this rather extreme view'.[58]

As this report shows, Shidehara was even more enthusiastic than Yoshida about the potential of keeping Japan only lightly armed and focusing on economic development. Shidehara's thinking on the Soviet Union also seems to have changed somewhat from the prewar years. After all, before the war, Shidehara had been relatively uncommitted to the fight against communism. It may be that as the Cold War progressed, he revised his opinions on the matter.

As the turmoil of the Korean War deepened, Shidehara became the chairman of a joint council for considering problems of national defence. Members of the council included figures such as Satō Naotake, president of the House of Councillors; Uehara Etsujirō, chairperson of the Liberal Party's House of Representatives Diplomacy Committee; Tomabechi Gizō, chairperson of the Democrat Party's Supreme Committee; and Baba Tsunego, president of the Yomiuri Shimbun Company. Shidehara had apparently come to recognise the necessity of rearming Japan, despite the dilemmas presented by Article 9 of the constitution. On the other hand, Shidehara also informed Matsumura Kenzō—still purged from public office—that 'the U.S. will not force us to rearm'.[59] Such statements indicate the extent to which Shidehara valued the US army forces garrisoned in Japan.

Last Writings

Fifty Years of Diplomacy

In the summer of 1950, Shidehara began to feel that Japan–US relations were improving—not only in politics and economics, but also in cultural matters. Shidehara noted:

> Americans are particularly enthusiastic about Japan studies. They are also interested in traditional arts such as *ikebana* flower arrangement, tea ceremonies, and haiku and tanka poetry. I am exceedingly pleased to see that people are beginning to see Japan with fresh eyes.[60]

To Shidehara, it felt like the dawn of a new era. It was at this time that the US army invited him to Yokosuka. He also attended a play with members of the occupation forces: *Madame Butterfly*, a tragic love story about the relationship between a Nagasaki geisha and an US naval officer. However, viewers from the occupation forces hated the play. One officer sitting alongside Shidehara grumbled: 'I do not think any American would be as heartless as the man in this play'. Shidehara noted that the experience 'caused me to engage in some reflection' about his own perceptions.[61]

Shidehara also criticised another play being produced at the time, titled *Tōjin Okichi*. This play was based on a fictionalised account of an actual person from Shimoda named Okichi, who had served as a waiting maid for US Consul General Townsend Harris near the end of the Tokugawa shogunate. Upon seeing the play, Shidehara could not help but voice his displeasure. In his words, *Tōjin Okichi* mixed 'Japanese-style sentimentalism with a hefty amount of sexual allure', with the result that the play 'slighted Harris's integrity and caused the Americans to take offense'. In Shidehara's view, the real-life Harris had 'devoted himself to the opening up of Japan and to its culture'. Shidehara decided to express his criticisms in a piece for the New Year's issue of *Kaizō* magazine. Quoting Harris's biography, which had been published in New York, he pointed out that it painted a picture of a man who lived a 'virtuous life, in complete opposition to the problems [shown] in *Tōjin Okichi*'. Shidehara concluded by noting that, given that the peace conference was now drawing near, 'it may be necessary to reconsider, once more, the achievements of Harris, who had contributed so much to the opening up of Japan'.[62] In fact, Shidehara wrote these words just a few months before his sudden passing.

The year 1950 was the last one that Shidehara would live out in full. Shidehara responded to a request from the *Yomiuri Shimbun* for a serialised dictation, which began in the autumn of 1950. He dictated a series of pieces that were then edited and appeared in the newspaper under the title 'Gaikō 50 Nen' (Fifty years of diplomacy). Sixty-one instalments were published in all, with the Manchurian Incident covered from parts 39 to 46. 'Gaikō Gojūnen' would later be published by the Yomiuri Shimbun Company as a standalone book, also titled *Gaikō Gojūnen*. Shidehara composed the foreword for this collection on 2 March 1951. In this foreword, he wrote:

> The historical facts raised in this work have not been adulterated with imaginary hypothesis or dramatization. Rather, I have relied upon my memories of the events and have resolved to be as accurate as possible.[63]

To edit the work, Shidehara received assistance from former diplomatic officials Mushanokōji Kintomo and Ishii Itarō.

He also devoted part of this final year to the task of writing an essay in English. His aim was to make a contribution to the journal *Foreign Affairs*. This was not the first time that Shidehara had written a piece for a US magazine. As noted above, he took a similar step during the Washington Naval Conference.[64] That said, it was certainly rare. On this occasion, Shidehara had begun to write at the direct request of John Gunther. In 1950, this well-known US journalist was covering MacArthur and other head staffs at GHQ. It was Gunther's first time in Japan since 1938. After meeting with Shidehara, Gunther strongly recommended that he consider submitting an essay to *Foreign Affairs*. Gunther viewed Shidehara as an old liberal who had resisted Japanese proponents of war. He was also well disposed towards Shidehara's secretary, Kishi Kuramatsu.[65]

With Gunther having been kind enough to offer this advice, Shidehara decided to follow through. He began work on an essay in English titled 'Genesis of the Manchurian Incident of 1931'. The recollections that it contained stretched back to before World War I. At that time Japan was a debtor nation. With the coming of World War I, it managed to become a creditor nation, to only then endure the disaster of the Great Kantō Earthquake. Another distinguishing feature of the 1920s was that it was a time of disarmament—so much so, in fact, that military men became disgruntled. As Shidehara pointed out, the Japanese military was desperate to recover some of the glory of the past. On the diplomatic side, Japan's relationship with China had also been put under strain. In Shidehara's view, this was because 'the Chinese did not seem ready to grasp the hand of friendship which I, as Foreign Minister, was constantly holding out for them'.[66] On the contrary, the Nationalist government had rejected Japan's request for formal approval of the appointment of Obata Yūkichi as minister. There was also the Nakamura Incident and the Wanpaoshan Incident.

From here, Shidehara's draft of the 'Genesis of the Manchurian Incident' reached its main conclusions. Shidehara noted that:

> Whispers among our civilian population in Manchuria, hinting that some secret warlike manoeuvres were in the course of preparation by a clique of Japanese junior officers reached my ears towards the beginning of September, 1931.[67]

Upon hearing this, Shidehara warned War Minister Minami. Yet, although Minami signalled that he would deal with the situation, the following weeks saw only further escalation. Upon learning of the Liutiaohu

Incident from the morning edition of a newspaper on 19 September, Shidehara rushed to call the Ministry of Foreign Affairs. He was informed that the ministry had received a telegram from Consul General Hayashi with the same information. Shidehara depicted Minami at the time of the Manchurian Incident as somebody who was, for the most part, cooperative. Shidehara also noted that Japan's then minister to China, Shigemitsu Mamoru, attempted to negotiate directly with Song Ziwen. However, the Chinese government instead appealed to the League of Nations. Shidehara concluded his draft by arguing that China should have prioritised direct negotiations over such an appeal. In his view, the result of China's course of action was that an early resolution to the Manchurian Incident was frustrated, and 'the specter of an extensive and intensive war was fast approaching'.[68]

As can be seen from the above outline, Shidehara's draft of the 'Genesis of the Manchurian Incident' for *Foreign Affairs* was hardly full of novel ideas. For the most part, it was a rehash of the testimony that he had given at the Tokyo Trial. Shidehara presumably wrote 'Genesis of the Manchurian Incident' with 'Gaikō Gojūnen' by his side for reference. The contents of 'Genesis of the Manchurian Incident' were extremely similar to 'Gaikō Gojūnen'. One thing the above details reveal is that the 'Genesis of the Manchurian Incident' was not merely a collection of reminiscences. This work can also be seen as including Shidehara's attempts at self-justification. It was necessary for Shidehara to present himself as the 'old liberal' that Gunther saw him as. The appearance of the essay in *Foreign Affairs* appeared to be just a matter of time.

Sadly, however, 'Genesis of the Manchurian Incident' would be Shidehara's last work. On 10 March 1951, Shidehara suddenly passed away. Only eight days had gone by since he wrote the foreword for *Gaikō Gojūnen*. As a result, 'Genesis' never appeared in *Foreign Affairs*. However, the draft did catch the attention of the editors of *Chūō Kōron*. After receiving permission from Shidehara's family, the literary magazine prepared the manuscript for publication. For this task they also received assistance from Shidehara's former secretary, Kishi Kuramatsu. The work was published in the May 1951 edition of *Chūō Kōron* under the revised title 'The Ghosts of War: Origins of the Manchurian Incident'. During this same period, *Foreign Affairs* published an essay by Yoshida Shigeru. While Yoshida did not use this opportunity to advocate the kind of nonpartisan diplomacy that Shidehara desired, it did show the extent to which both he and Dulles were now beginning to look ahead to the era that would follow the peace settlement.[69]

What Did Shidehara Leave Unfinished?

In this chapter we have looked at Shidehara's final years. As mentioned in the previous chapter, Shidehara had struggled to deal with party politics. While he participated in the formation of the Democratic Party as president of the Progressive Party, he soon fell out with the Ashida clique and, in the end, led his own faction to merge with Yoshida's Liberal Party. According to Nagai Matsuzō, who had served as vice-minister for foreign affairs during Shidehara's second term as foreign minister, Shidehara ought to have withdrawn from politics following the dissolution of his cabinet, without coming into conflict with Ashida.[70]

There were some matters that Shidehara had left unfinished. The dissemination of the new constitution that he himself had worked on was one obvious example. Yet his largest concern was the future of Japan's foreign relations. His diplomatic activities in his final years can be placed into four major categories. First, Shidehara was concerned about the fate of the Ministry of Foreign Affairs under the occupation and endeavoured to ensure it was revamped. Second, with an eye to the future conclusion of a peace settlement and Japan's regaining of sovereignty, he advocated the development of nonpartisan diplomacy. Although Shidehara's promotion of nonpartisan diplomacy was directly triggered by Dulles's visit to Japan, its intellectual precursors can be found in the UK. Third, Shidehara was even more enthusiastic than Yoshida in hoping that the US forces would remain garrisoned in Japan. Fourth, as can be seen with his criticism of *Tōjin Okichi*, or his efforts to rebuild Tōyō Bunko, Shidehara also understood the importance of culture for foreign relations.

In particular, Shidehara's feelings for the Ministry of Foreign Affairs concealed a fondness for the glories of the past. Although he had attended the Tokyo Trial as a witness for the prosecution, in truth, he sought to protect figures such as Shigemitsu and Shiratori, whom he considered as collateral family. Shidehara had also attended court as a witness for the defence. Indeed, his comments were referenced by Minami's defence counsel in his closing statement, as they benefitted the client. This basic tone did not change in Shidehara's final work, written for *Foreign Affairs*. Hence a degree of ambiguity remains in Shidehara's thinking on wartime responsibility. Of course, Shidehara was hardly unusual in this regard. In any case, as can be seen from his work in establishing the training institute, Shidehara saw his highest priority as the preservation of the Ministry of Foreign Affairs.

The above points are also interesting when considered with respect to their continuity (or discontinuity) between the prewar and postwar eras. From Shidehara's perspective, if we exclude Tanaka diplomacy and the Twenty-One Demands issued to China, Japanese domestic and foreign policy developed smoothly until the early 1930s. Starting with the Manchurian Incident, however, that policy went off the rails. Shidehara therefore considered it important that he use his own experience to benefit postwar Japan. In his view, what this experience showed was that two things needed to occur: first, economic-centred diplomacy needed to be established; second, a new order had to be created in East Asia that would be based upon cooperation with the US and the UK. Essential for these purposes was the restoration of trust in Japan's foreign relations, and this in turn required the promotion of nonpartisan diplomacy.

Unfortunately, Shidehara had neither the authority nor the remaining years needed to fully achieve these goals. With Japan yet to recover its sovereignty, he would pass away in March 1951. In this sense, both the continuities and the discontinuities of Japanese diplomacy were encapsulated in Shidehara's short postwar experience. And that is not all. Shidehara also had a secret wish that ultimately went unfulfilled. From the very beginning, Shidehara had had a fastidious and scholarly nature. He spent his final years surrounded by books, both foreign and domestic, and dreamed of writing his life's work in English—a history of Japanese diplomacy. In practice, however, he spent the last of his years as a politician, an occupation for which he was ill suited. It might have been far better if he had devoted himself to writing. We may wonder whether, at the time of his death, Shidehara spared a moment to regret that he had to leave with this diplomatic history still unwritten.[71]

Endnotes

1   This chapter is based on my previous work: Hattori Ryūji, 'Shidehara Kijūrō no Senzen to Sengo: Tokyo Saiban wo Koete' [Shidehara Kijūrō before and after the war: Beyond the Tokyo Trial], *Chūō Daigaku Ronshū*, no. 26 (March 2005): 1–15.

Important studies with respect to this chapter are Shidehara Peace Foundation, *Shidehara Kijūrō*; Kunugi, 'Shidehara Kijūrō', 87–131. The former is a hagiographic biography written by a close associate of Shidehara. Although much can be learned from the latter, it emphasises how Shidehara

8. WAR RESPONSIBILITY AND NONPARTISAN DIPLOMACY FOR PEACE

sought to transfer responsibility of the Manchurian Incident to Minami Jirō at the Tokyo Trial, and it requires some re-examination. Further, it does not mention that Shidehara attended the Tokyo Trial as a defence witness, and there are areas where a comparison with Ministry of Foreign Affairs records reveals that the research was insufficient.

2   Texts that discuss 'the Tokyo Trial view of history' include Yoshida Yutaka, *Nihonjin no Sensōkan*, 206–08; Nakamura Masanori, *Gendai-shi wo Manabu: Sengo Kaikaku to Gendai Nihon* [Learning modern history: Postwar reform and modern Japan] (Tokyo: Yoshikawa Kōbunkan, 1997), 93–120.

3   L. N. Smirnov and E. B. Zaytsev, *Sud v Tokio* (Moscow: Voennoe izdatel'stvo Ministerstva oborony SSSR, 1978), 8–11, 34–47; L. N. Smirnov and E. B. Zaytsev, *Tokyo Saiban* [The Tokyo Trial], trans. Kawakami Takeshi and Naono Atsushi, comm. Awaya Kentarō (Tokyo: Ōtsuki Shoten, 1980), 8–11, 31–42, 500–01, 510, 517; Anatolii Andreevich Gromyko and Boris Nikolaevich Ponomarev, eds, *Istoriya vneshnei politiki SSSR, 1917–1985*, vol. 1 (Moscow: Nauka, 1986), 264.

For details on the Soviet's actions, see Awaya, *Tōkyō Saiban-ron*, 209–26; Awaya Kentarō and NHK News Crew, *Tōkyō Saiban eno Michi* [The road to the Tokyo Trial] (Tokyo: Japan Broadcast Publishing Co., 1994), 144–62, 205–07. For more recent research on the Tokyo Trial, see Higurashi, *Tokyo Saiban no Kokusai Kankei*. However, this text rarely mentions Shidehara.

It should also be noted that Keenan visited China and reported to MacArthur on the situation there. See interview with Madame Chiang Kai-shek, Shanghai, 28 March 1946, Joseph Berry Keenan Papers, Box 2, Harvard Law School Library, Harvard University; Keenan to MacArthur, 8 April 1946, Keenan Papers, Box 2.

4   Wakatsuki, *Meiji, Taishō, Shōwa Seikai Hishi*, 406.

5   Aizawa Kiyoshi, *Kaigun no Sentaku: Saikō—Shinjuwan eno Michi* [The choice of the navy: Reconsidered—the road to Pearl Harbour] (Tokyo: Chūō Kōron Shinsha, 2002), 85–86, 101–12, 135–40, 171, 202–04.

6   As minister of state, Shidehara was once invited by the Shōwa emperor to a tea party at the imperial court. Upon arrival, he was seated next to Prime Minister Yoshida. See diary of Wada Hirō, 14 August 1946, in 'Wada Hirō Kankei Bunsho' [Documents relating to Wada Hirō], no. 477, Modern Japanese Political History Materials Room, National Diet Library.

7   The Tokyo Trial was not the only war crime trials to be held. For a more detailed examination of the general situation of war crime trials at that time, see Minister of Foreign Affairs Liaison Office, Investigation Section, 'Senpan Saiban no Kihon Shiryō' [Basic resources on war crimes trials], November 1950, in 'Honpō Sensō Hanzainin Kankei Zakken', vol. 1.

For court stenographic transcripts of the Tokyo Trial, as prepared by the Ministry of Foreign Affairs Liaison Office, see Ministry of Foreign Affairs Liaison Office, ed., *Kyokutō Kokusai Gunji Saiban Hanketsu Sokki-roku* [Stenographic records of rulings at the International Military Tribunal for the Far East] (Tokyo: Ministry of Foreign Affairs Liaison Office, 1948).

8   *Asahi Shimbun*, 20 June 1946.

9   'Kyokutō Kokusai Gunji Saiban Sokki-roku' [Stenographic records of the International Military Tribunal for the Far East], no. 18, 25 June 1946, in *Kyokutō Kokusai Gunji Saiban Sokki-roku* [Stenographic records of the International Military Tribunal for the Far East], ed. Nitta Mitsuo, vol. 1 (Tokyo: Yūshōdō, 1968), 178.

10   Ibid., 180–81.

11   Ibid., 183.

12   Ibid., 184.

13   Ibid., 185.

14   'Kyokutō Kokusai Gunji Saiban Sokki-roku', no. 19, June 26, 1946, in Nitta, *Kyokutō Kokusai Gunji Saiban Sokki-roku*, vol. 1, 188–92.

15   Shigemitsu, *Sugamo Nikki*, 22. Essentially the same point is made in Itō and Watanabe, *Shigemitsu Mamoru Shuki*, 660.

16   *Asahi Shimbun*, 26, 27 June 1946.

17 *Yomiuri Shimbun*, 26, 27 June 1946.

18 Former Kwantung Army Commander-in-Chief Honjō committed suicide in November 1945.

19 Awaya Kentarō and Yoshida Yutaka, eds, *Kokusai Kensatsu-kyoku (IPS) Jinmon Chōsho* [Interrogation records of the International Prosecution Section], vol. 48 (Tokyo: Nihon Tosho Center, 1993), 1–14.

Shidehara's telegrams from Hayashi from August to September 1931 were submitted by order of GHQ. A copy can be found in 'Manshū Jihen: Zai Hōten Hayashi Sōryōji Hatsu Shidehara Gaishō Ate Denpō Tsuzuri (Fuku)' [The Manchurian Incident: File on telegraphs from Mukden Consul General Hayashi to Foreign Minister Shidehara (duplicates)], vol. 2, A.1.1.0.21, Diplomatic Archives of the Ministry of Foreign Affairs of Japan. On the cover it states, 'August and September, Shōwa 6: File on Telegraphs from Mukden Consul General Hayashi to Foreign Minister Shidehara—file of all document copies submitted on June 10, Shōwa 21, under GHQ order 16894-1B'. These telegrams addressed to Shidehara are also included in *Archives in the Japanese Ministry of Foreign Affairs, Tokyo, Japan, 1868–1945: Documents of the International Military Tribunal*, Reels 55, 56 (Washington: Library of Congress, 1949–1951).

20 Awaya and Yoshida, *Kokusai Kensatsu-kyoku (IPS) Jinmon Chōsho*, vol. 28, 385. See also Awaya Kentarō, *Miketsu no Sensō Sekinin* [The undetermined responsibility for the war] (Tokyo: Kashiwa Shobō, 1994), 108.

21 Inaba et al., *Taiheiyō Sensō eno Michi*, extra vol.: Resources, 114–15; Kobayashi and Shimada, *Gendai-shi Shiryo*, vol. 7, 184; Kobayashi, Shimada and Inaba, *Gendai-shi Shiryo*, vol. 11, 313; Hayashi to Shidehara, 19 September 1931, in Ministry of Foreign Affairs, *Nihon Gaikō Bunsho: Manshū Jihen*, vol. 1, no. 3, 3; Hayashi to Shidehara, 19 September, ibid., 6.

See also Morishima, *Inbō, Ansatsu, Guntō*, 419; Seki, 'Manshū Jihen Zenshi', 412, 419, 433; Shimada Toshihiko, 'Manshū Jihen no Tenkai', 12–13; Ogata, *Manshū Jihen to Seisaku no Keisei Katei*, 104; Hayashi, *Manshū Jihen to Hōten Sōryōji*, 114–15.

22 Affidavit by Shidehara Kijūrō, 28 July 1947, in 'Kyokutō Kokusai Gunji Saiban Shiryō' [Documents on the International Military Tribunal for the Far East], vol. 288, Special Documents Room, Kokushikan University Library. For the copy, see 'Shidehara Kijūrō Sensei Kyōjutsusho' [Affidavit of Shidehara Kijūrō], 28 July 1947, 1-4E-013-00-Shō 49 Kunai-04859-100, National Archives of Japan.

For information on Tanaka's testimony, see 'Kyokutō Kokusai Gunji Saiban Sokki-roku', no. 26, 6 July 1946, in Nitta Mitsuo, *Kyokutō Kokusai Gunji Saiban Sokki-roku*, vol. 1, 290; Awaya, Adachi and Kobayashi, *Tōkyō Saiban Shiryō*, 3, 138, 217.

23 Shidehara Kijūrō's medical certificate, as issued by St Luke's International Hospital, 7 November 1947, in 'Kyokutō Kokusai Gunji Saiban Shiryō', vol. 287, Special Documents Room, Kokushikan University Library.

24 Court testimony no. 3479, in 'Kyokutō Kokusai Gunji Saiban Shiryō', vol. 288, Special Documents Room, Kokushikan University Library.

25 'Kyokutō Kokusai Gunji Saiban Sokki-roku', no. 317, 19 November 1947, in Nitta, *Kyokutō Kokusai Gunji Saiban Sokki-roku*, vol. 7, 560–562; 'Kyokutō Kokusai Gunji Saiban Sokki-roku', no. 318, 20 November 1947, *ibid.*, 563–583; Asahi Shimbun Court Press Corp, *Tōkyō Saiban* [The Tokyo Trial], vol. 2 (Tokyo: Tokyo Trial Publication Society, 1962), 616–18.

26 Shigemitsu, *Sugamo Nikki*, 300.

27 *Yomiuri Shimbun*, 21 November 1947.

28 'Kyokutō Kokusai Gunji Saiban Shiryō', vol. 44, Special Documents Room, Kokushikan University Library.

29 Ministry of Foreign Affairs Liaison Office, *Kyokutō Kokusai Gunji Saiban Hanketsu Sokki-roku*, 99–101; Mainichi Shimbunsha, ed., *Tōkyō Saiban Hanketsu: Kyokutō Gunji Saiban-sho Hanketsu-bun* [Tokyo Trial ruling: The judgement of the International Military Tribunal for the Far East] (Tokyo: Mainichi Shimbun, 1949), 141–44.

8. WAR RESPONSIBILITY AND NONPARTISAN DIPLOMACY FOR PEACE

30   Arai Shinichi, *Dainiji Sekai Taisen* [World War II] (Tokyo: University of Tokyo Press, 1973), 5–6; Yoshida Yutaka, *Shōwa Tennō no Shūsen-shi* [A history of the Shōwa emperor at the end of the war] (Tokyo: Iwanami Shoten, 1992), 196.

31   Shidehara, *Gaikō 50 Nen*, 207–12.

32   *Kasumigaseki-kai Kaihō*, no. 14 (February 1946): 5–6; Foreign Service Training Institute, *Gaimu Kanri Kenshūjo Gaikan* [Overview of the Foreign Service Training Institute] (Tokyo: Foreign Service Training Institute, 1948), 1–7, 15; Ministry of Foreign Affairs Hundred-Year History Compilation Association, *Gaimushō no 100 Nen*, vol. 2, 1354–69; Matsunaga Nobuo, *Aru Gaikō-kan no Kaiso* [Recollections of a diplomat] (Tokyo: Nihon Keizai Shimbunsha, 2002), 29.

33   Satō, *Kaiko 80 Nen*, 517. Satō would also serve as the privy councillor at the same time, from November 1946. See Satō to Suzuki Tadakatsu, 11 December 1946, in 'Suzuki Tadakatsu Kankei Bunsho' [Documents relating to Suzuki Tadakatsu], no. 15, Modern Japanese Political History Materials Room, National Diet Library.

34   *Kasumigaseki-kai Kaihō*, no. 19 (July 1946): 1–3; Shidehara Peace Foundation, *Shidehara Kijūrō*, 56–60.

One such lecture was given by Irie Keishirō, who spoke on topics such as the Xinhai Revolution, Swiss permanent neutrality and the Locarno security arrangements. See Irie Keishirō, *Kindai Gaikō-shi Shō* [Excerpts of modern diplomatic history] (Tokyo: Foreign Service Training Institute, 1960).

35   Foreign Minister Yoshida to Kase Shunichi, minister to Switzerland, Morishima Morito, minister to Portugal, and Shichida Motoharu, minister to Afghanistan, 20 November 1945, in 'Taiheiyō Sensō Shūketsu niyoru Honpō Gaikōken no Teishi oyobi Kaifuku niitaru Keii' [The loss of Japan's diplomatic rights as a result of the conclusion of the Pacific War, and the circumstances surrounding their recovery], A'.1.0.0.13, Reel A'-0090, Diplomatic Archives of the Ministry of Foreign Affairs of Japan.

36   'Shidehara Naikaku Sōridaijin Shachūdan' [Talk given on a train by Prime Minister Shidehara], printed in every newspaper on 8 November 1945, 1-2A-040-00-shi-00306-100, National Archives of Japan.

37   Okazaki Katsuo, 'Sengo 20 Nen no Henreki' [Wandering through 20 years of the postwar era] (4), *Kasumigaseki-kai Kaihō*, no. 244 (June 1966): 16; Miyake, 'Yoshida-san wo Shinobite Omou Kotodomo (11)', *Kasumigaseki-kai Kaihō*, no. 294 (August 1970): 10–12; Foreign Service Training Institute, *Gaimushō Kenshūjo 10 Nenshi* [A 10-year history of the Foreign Service Training Institute] (Tokyo: Foreign Service Training Institute, 1956), 1–17, 59; Kajima Peace Research Center, ed., *Keizai Gaikō no Genjō wo Kataru: Ichi Gaikō Jitsumu-ka no Me* [Speaking on the realities of economic diplomacy: From the perspective of a practitioner of diplomacy] (Tokyo: Bensei Shuppan, 2003), 5.

38   *Kasumigaseki-kai Kaihō*, no. 39 (February 1948): 7. Shidehara also became the chairman of the Japan Club in June 1946. See Japan Club, *Nihon Club 100 Nen-shi*, 55.

39   Higashikuni, *Higashikuni Naruhiko Nikki*, 247. However, in the relevant entry of 'Higashikuni-no-miya Nisshi', 7 October 1945, there are no statements of this nature.

40   'Shidehara Heiwa Bunko', Reel 17.

41   Yoshida, Shidehara and Sato, 'Gaikō Jūō-dan'.

42   Sansom to Sterndale Bennett, 22 February 1946, F 3512/556/23, FO 371/54286, National Archives. See also Yamagiwa and Nakamura, *Shiryō Nihon Senryō*, vol. 1, 537–38, 557–59; Kosuge Nobuko, *Sengo Wakai* [The postwar reconciliation] (Tokyo: Chūō Kōron Shinsha, 2005), 121.

43   Shidehara Kijūrō, 'Watashi no Shina-kan' [My perspective on China], 25 March 1946, in 'Shidehara Heiwa Bunko', Reel 18.

44   Ibid.

45   Ibid.

46   Iwasaki Family Bibliographical Publishing Association, ed., *Iwasaki Hisaya Den* [A biography of Iwasaki Hisaya] (Tokyo: University of Tokyo Press, 1979), 270–80, 299–304.

47   Tōyō Bunko, *Tōyōbunko 15 Nen-shi* [A 15-year history of Tōyō Bunko] (Tokyo: Tōyō Bunko, 1939), 35; Tōyō Bunko, *Zaidan Hōjin Tōyōbunko Ryaku-shi* [A brief history of Tōyō Bunko Foundation] (Tokyo: Tōyō Bunko, 1957), 10–15.

48   Tōyō Bunko, *Shōwa 30 Nendo: Tōyōbunko Nenpō* [The 30th year of Shōwa: Tōyō Bunko annual report] (Tokyo: Tōyō Bunko, 1957), 2–5, 9. For details on the circumstances leading up to the appointment of both individuals to the office of president of the House of Councillors, see Yamamoto Yūzō, 'Satō-san to Ryokufūkai' [Mr Satō and the Ryokufūkai], *Kasumigaseki-kai Kaihō*, no. 301 (March 1971): 14–15.

49   Shidehara to Wakayama Press Co., 30 March 1948, Record Group 331, Box 22750, National Archives; *Kasumigaseki-kai Kaihō*, no. 37 (January 1948): 5; Ministry of Foreign Affairs Research Bureau, *Gendai Tōa-Jin Meikan* [Directory of contemporary East Asians] (Tokyo: Tōhō Kenkyū-kai, 1950). See also Shidehara to Cai Mengjian, 23 January 1951, in *Zhuanji Wenxue* 42, no. 2 (February 1983), 72, Chengting T. Wang Papers, Box 2, Sterling Memorial Library, Yale University.

50   Schedule of Dulles, 16 February 1938, John Foster Dulles Papers, Reel 3, Princeton University Library; Dulles to Saito Hiroshi, 25 March 1938, Reel 3, Dulles Papers. I also referred to Iguchi Haruo, 'John Foster Dulles no Gaikō Shisō: Senzen, Sengo no Renzokusei' [The diplomatic thought of John Foster Dulles: The continuity of the prewar and postwar eras], *Dōshisha America Kenkyū*, no. 34 (March 1998): 43, 45.

51   Grew to Shidehara, 11 February 1938, Grew Papers, Letters, vol. 92. See also Shidehara, *Gaikō 50 Nen*, 285.

52   Summary Report by J. F. Dulles, 7 July 1950, 794.00/7–750, Decimal File 1950–54, Box 4229, Record Group 59, National Archives; tribute by Dulles, *New York Times*, 11 March 1951. A similar entry is in Department of State, ed., *FRUS, 1950*, vol. 6 (Washington: Government Printing Office, 1976), 1230–37.

For further details on nonpartisan diplomacy and the argument for peace advanced by the opposition party, see Igarashi Takeshi, *Tai-Nichi Kowa to Reisen* [Peace with Japan and the Cold War] (Tokyo: University of Tokyo Press, 1986), 209–30; Nakakita, *Keizai Fukkō to Sengo Seiji*, 287–309; Hattori Ryūji, 'Shidehara Kijūrō and the Supra-Party Diplomacy, 1950', *Chūō Daigaku Seisaku Bunka Sōgō Kenkyū-jo Nenpō*, no. 8 (June 2005): 171–87.

53   Policy Research and Information Departments of the Social Democratic Party of Japan, 'Jōhō Tsushin' [Information communication], no. 11, July 1, 1950, in 'Asanuma Inejirō Kankei Bunsho' [Documents relating to Asanuma Inejirō], Reel 29, Modern Japanese Political History Materials Room, National Diet Library; Policy Research Association of the National Democratic Party, ed., 'Kokumin Minshutō Kowa Jōyaku eno Shuchō' [National Democratic Party's arguments for a peace treaty], May 1951, in 'Tomabechi Gizō Kankei Bunsho' [Documents relating to Tomabechi Gizō], Reel 6, Center for Modern Japanese Legal and Political Documents, the Faculty of Law, the University of Tokyo; Shindō and Shimokōbe, *Ashida Hitoshi Nikki*, vol. 3, 298–307, 317, 370, 382–83, 393, 395–97; Ishibashi, *Ishibashi Tanzan Nikki*, vol 1., 328, 335.

54   Magō Club, ed., 'Shidehara Shūgiin Gichō Kōen' [Address by Shidehara, speaker of the House of Representatives], 17 November 1950, in 'Shidehara Heiwa Bunko', Reel 18. See also Murai Ryōta, 'Dai Ichiji Taisen-go Sekai to Kenseikai no Fukkō: Seiken-tō eno Seichō to Seitō Naikaku-sei, 1918–25 Nen' [The world after World War I and the rise of the Kenseikai: The trend towards becoming a governing party and the party cabinet system, 1918–25], *Kōbe Hōgaku Nenpō*, no. 17 (March 2001): 213–15.

55   W. J. Sebald to Department of State, 2 December 1950, 794.00/12–250, Decimal File 1950–54, Box 4229, Record Group 59, National Archives.

56   Memo by Chief of the Treaties and Conventions Bureau of the Ministry of Foreign Affairs, Hagiwara Tōru, 3 September 1947, in 'Tai-Nichi Heiwa Jōyaku Kankei', vol. 3. I have been guided by Kusunoki Ayako, 'Sengo Nihon no Anzen Hoshō Seisaku no Keisei: 1943–1952—Nichi-Bei no Sengo Kōsō to sono Sōgo Sayō' [The formation of Japan's National Security Policy in the postwar era: 1943–1952—the postwar planning of Japan and the US and their reciprocal functioning], PhD diss., Kobe University, 2004.

8. WAR RESPONSIBILITY AND NONPARTISAN DIPLOMACY FOR PEACE

57   Yoshida Shigeru, Shidehara Kijūrō, Sato Naotake, Kojima Kazuo and Baba Tsunego, 'Kōwa no Toshi wo Mukaete' [Greeting the year of peace], *Yomiuri Shimbun*, 1 January 1950.

58   Summary Report by J. F. Dulles, 7 July 1950, 794.00/7-750, Decimal File 1950–54, Box 4229, Record Group 59, National Archives.

59   Baba Tsunego, *Jiden Tenbyō* [An autobiographical sketch] (Tokyo: Tōzai Bunmeisha, 1952), 203–04; Watanabe, *Tenno no Aru Kuni no Kenpo*, 2, 73, 166–67; Matsumura Masanao et al., eds, *Kakō Getsuen: Matsumura Kenzō Ibun Sho* [The flowers are beautiful, the moon is round: Excerpts from the writings of the late Matsumura Kenzō] (Tokyo: Seirin Shoin Shinsha, 1978), 168–69; Itō, *Zoku Shōwa-ki no Seiji*, 208–09.

60   Shidehara Kijūrō, 'Tōjin Okichi to Ochō Fujin' [Tōjin Okichi and Mrs Ochō], *Kaizō* 32, no. 1 (January 1951): 142.

61   Ibid.

62   Ibid., 142–143.

63   Shidehara Kijūrō, 'Gaikō 50 Nen' [Fifty years of diplomacy], *Yomiuri Shimbunsha*, 5 September – 14 November 1950; Shidehara Kijūrō, *Gaikō 50 Nen* [Fifty years of diplomacy] (Tokyo: Yomiuri Shimbun, 1951), 166–75. However, many parts of *Gaikō Gojūnen* [Fifty years of diplomacy] are incorrect.

64   Shidehara, 'A Frank Official Statement for Japan', 394–97.

65   John Gunther, *The Riddle of MacArthur: Japan, Korea, and the Far East* (New York: Harper and Brothers, 1951), 3, 104–05, 145.

66   Shidehara Kijūrō, 'Genesis of the Manchurian Incident of 1931', in 'Shidehara Heiwa Bunko', Reels 7 and 19.

67   Ibid.

68   Ibid.

69   Shidehara Kijūrō, 'Sensō no Yūrei: Manshū Jihen no Kiin' [The Ghosts of war: The cause of the Manchurian Incident], *Chūō Kōron* 66, no. 5 (May 1951): 68–70; Yoshida Shigeru, 'Japan and the Crisis in Asia', *Foreign Affairs* 29, no. 2 (1951): 171–81, doi.org/10.2307/20030825; statements by Dulles and Yoshida, 11 February 1951, Dulles Papers, Reel 20.

70   Nagai, 'Shidehara Danshaku no Omoide'.

71   Itō Nobufumi, 'Nihon no Shin-Gaikō to Shidehara-san' [Mr Shidehara and Japan's new diplomacy], date unknown, in 'Shidehara Heiwa Bunko', Reel 13.

9

A Legacy beyond War and Peace

A Peaceful Death

Until 8 March 1951, Shidehara had been attending the Diet in his capacity as speaker of the House of Representatives. However, according to his secretary Kishi Kuramatsu, on 9 March he was unable to rise for breakfast. On 10 March, as evening fell upon Setagaya, Shidehara quietly took his last breath. He died peacefully of a heart attack at the age of 78.[1] MacArthur promptly issued the following statement:

> I wish to express my deepest condolences at the passing of House Speaker Shidehara. Mr. Shidehara's insight and expansive knowledge has been of great service to Japan on its journey to recovery. With world affairs in their current tense state, Mr. Shidehara's passing will certainly be a significant blow.[2]

Shidehara had helped to build an era in prewar Japan. After the war he served as prime minister during the occupation before assuming the position of speaker of the House of Representatives. Though he had once detested political parties, he eventually served as president of the Progressive Party. In time, Shidehara's disagreements with Ashida led him to leave the Democratic Party and form the Dōshi Club. He would subsequently bring his supporters with him to merge with Yoshida Shigeru's Liberal Party, and he became chief adviser to the Democratic Liberal Party. As the Democratic Liberal Party had joined with the coalition faction of the Democratic Party and established the Liberal Party, it was expected that the former Dōshi Club's faction would be weakened by Shidehara's passing.[3]

Ultimately, however, in Shidehara's career, it is his time as foreign minister that looms the largest. When he passed away, it was seen, more than anything, as the loss of the Japanese diplomatic world's eldest statesman. Former prime minister Ashida Hitoshi remarked: 'In my opinion, the big stage upon which Mr. Shidehara strode as a diplomat was, more than anything else, the Washington Naval Conference on Disarmament of 1922'.[4] Similarly, President of the House of Councillors Satō Naotake immediately mentioned the London Naval Conference when discussing Shidehara's achievements. Satō added: 'Even at this age, I still cannot help but think of Shidehara as akin to my master; even in the Diet I was able to frankly ask for his advice'.[5]

On 12 March, two days after Shidehara's passing, a farewell service was held at his residence in Okamoto, Setagaya ward. On that occasion, a copy of some English-language correspondence that had been found in his bedside box of papers was brought out. The letter was addressed 'Dear Mr. Grew'. Its intended recipient was the former US ambassador to Japan, Joseph Grew. Grew had once agreed to a request from Shidehara that he write a message of hope for the youth of Japan, whose nation was now devastated. In response, Shidehara had written in English the following expression of thanks:

> May I thank you ever so much for your welcome letter of February 12, enclosing a message of encouragement to the youth of Japan? The message is as impressive as it is edifying, and exactly fits the need of the times. I have sent it to *the Tokyo Shimbun* (an influential Evening Daily) and *the Nippon Times* for publication.
>
> The article immediately arrested the attention of the public. Numbers of people, both aged and young, have expressed to me verbally or in writing their profound appreciation of the communication. They have been moved by the singleness of heart and of purpose which has actuated the advice contained in your utterance. Emerging from the depth of misery into which they had been precipitated by the War, they are now beginning to find a way of hope ahead, enlightened by your inspiring word.[6]

Shidehara's correspondence to Grew was shared with the successive mourners of various walks of life who visited the residence on that day. According to the *Tokyo Shimbun*:

> From this last piece of writing one has a sense of the friendship that [Shidehara] shared with Grew until his death, and of Mr. [Shidehara's] sympathy and hopes for the youth of Japan, whom he did not forget until the very end; it conveys to us a vision of the deceased.[7]

The mourners who paid their respects starting the day before included not only Prime Minister Yoshida but also Chamberlain Irie Sukemasa, who had been sent on behalf of the Shōwa emperor.

A House of Representatives Funeral

While a continuous stream of mourners visited the Shidehara residence for the farewell service, the House of Representatives—now missing its speaker—held a meeting of the Assembly Steering Committee. The topic of discussion was the holding of a state funeral, or, in this case, a 'House of Representatives funeral'. Until then there had only been three instances of a house speaker dying in office and none of them had a House of Representatives funeral. Indeed, for a precedent it was necessary to look instead to the passing of the president of the House of Councillors, Matsudaira Tsuneo. Matsudaira had died in office on 14 November 1949, and a 'House of Councillors funeral' was held the following day. Following this precedent, the committee decided to hold the first-ever House of Representatives funeral. The role of chairing the funeral organising committee went to the next speaker of the House of Representatives, while each of the Diet factions sent one person to assist as a committee member.

However, the ceremony differed from Matsudaira's in certain respects. While Matsudaira's House of Councillors funeral was held at the official residence of the president, this decision was unpopular due to the venue's small size. For Shidehara's funeral, even more mourners were expected. Taking into consideration matters such as the ongoing farewell service, it was decided to see if the funeral could be held at Tsukiji Honganji temple. After quickly confirming with the temple, it was determined that 16 March was the only full day available.[8] Thus, Shidehara's House of Representatives funeral was held on 16 March at 1 pm at Tsukiji Honganji temple. The chairman of the ceremony was Hayashi Jōji. Hayashi had been promoted by Prime Minister Yoshida and had only just been elevated from deputy prime minister to speaker of the House of Representatives following Shidehara's passing. The House of Representatives itself was adjourned for the day as an expression of mourning.[9]

Of the many distinguished men who attended the funeral, the one who garnered particular attention was Shigemitsu Mamoru, still on parole following his release from prison, and who had been tasked on this occasion with burning the ceremonial incense. When the incense-burning was concluded, Speaker Hayashi and the heads of the three branches of government each gave their messages of condolence. These three individuals were Satō, president of the House of Councillors; Prime Minister Yoshida; and Tanaka Kōtarō, the chief justice of Japan.[10]

What were Shidehara's last words as speaker of the House of Representatives? His last official statement was an address to the plenary session of the House of Representatives, held on 6 March. There were over 10 items on the day's agenda, including the nomination of members for the National Capital Construction Committee. The item that generated the most debate was related to the securing of emergency imports following the outbreak of the Korean War. As it happened, Shidehara's last official words as recorded in the session minutes were quite ordinary: 'Those standing are the majority. Therefore, all three proposals have been passed in accordance with the chairman's report. This concludes today's agenda. The session is now adjourned'.[11] Yet a close reading of the session minutes provides glimpses of Shidehara in his role as speaker, acting with his typical thoroughness. For example, when the Communist Party Diet member Kazahaya Yasoji opposed the resolution to secure emergency imports, Shidehara responded: 'If any inappropriate language has been used in Mr. Kazahaya's remarks, then I will take appropriate steps following an investigation of the stenographic records'.[12] Even during lengthy speeches, Shidehara did not let anything get past him; his mind remained as sharp as ever. This session took place on 6 March, only 10 days before the funeral.

After the plenary session for that day had ended, Shidehara headed towards the Imperial Palace together with the president of the House of Councillors, Satō Naotake. Satō later remarked:

> When we visited the palace together on March 6, which was Her Majesty the Empress's birthday, Mr. Shidehara quite easily consumed three or four of those red-lacquered cups worth of celebratory sake. I remember returning home and thinking to myself that he was still very much in good form.[13]

Satō continued:

> When I first met Mr. Shidehara, I was still a student at Hitotsubashi Commercial College. Mr. Shidehara was living on the same road, near [the present-day] Nogi Shrine in Akasaka. In the middle of the Russo-Japanese War, Mr. Shidehara was the director of the Telegraph Division [sic.] of the Ministry of Foreign Affairs. As such, he was very busy. I was up late at night myself those days, preparing for the diplomatic service exam, so I would hear when he returned from the ministry on a two-horse carriage. I still remember the sound of the driver's voice as he called out 'Welcome home' whenever they arrived.[14]

Satō also remarked that:

> It was surprising just how much he read. He also had a remarkable encyclopedic knowledge … I would frequently go to speak with him, and Mr. Shidehara would also sometimes casually drop by the president's office to pay me a visit.[15]

We have seen that Shidehara was in good health until just before his death. He had spent the coming of the new year of 1951 at his villa in the village of Kotsubo, in the Zushi region south of Yokohama. Shidehara would look forward to visits from old friends, and when guests arrived, he enjoyed regaling them with stories. He was always particularly talkative concerning the framed calligraphy of Saionji Kinmochi, which stated: 'Shūen Villa' (聚遠荘, Shūen-sō). Saionji's brushstrokes had an air of dignity about it. Those guests visiting the villa:

> Were able to entirely forget the outside world and the wretched state it was in. Even the passing of time would go unnoticed while they were enthralled by Shidehara's skillfully delivered stories.[16]

As he loquaciously spoke with his guests, Shidehara likely had little idea that his life was now nearing its end.

To identify Shidehara's last actions in the realm of diplomatic affairs, we need to return to when Dulles visited Japan in June 1950. At that time, Shidehara elaborated upon his long-held view that diplomacy ought to be kept separate from a nation's domestic politics. He would speak with a number of individuals in an effort to convince them of the need for nonpartisan diplomacy, including not only Prime Minister Yoshida but also opposition figures such as Tomabechi Gizō and Asanuma Inejirō. The *Yomiuri Shimbun* noted: 'It seemed as though Mr. Shidehara believed this work would be his last "public service" as the eldest statesman of [Japan's] diplomatic world'.[17] A Japanese saying notes 'the tenacity of old age'. Certainly, Shidehara was the very embodiment of this saying when it came to his efforts in those days.

Reactions, Domestic and Abroad

There is another saying in Japanese: it is only when the coffin is sealed that a person's worth can be assessed. Shidehara had continuously received both praise and censure while he was alive. But what did the various newspapers have to say after his passing? Of the editorials that appeared in the three major Japanese papers, the one with the most favourable assessment of Shidehara and his legacy was from the *Mainichi Shimbun*. This 11 March 1951, editorial stated:

> We had only recently lost another elder statesman of the nation's diplomatic world—Matsudaira, president of the House of Representatives. After all is said and done, however, Mr. Shidehara did not merely stand at the very peak of his field as it currently stands. As indicated by the term 'Shidehara diplomacy,' he also left a significant mark upon the landscape of Japan's diplomatic history in the form of his own systematic approach. Frankly, if Japanese diplomacy had proceeded along the course indicated by Mr. Shidehara, then this nation may well have managed to avoid ending up in its current miserable state. If we contemplate the fact that there is neither a 'Yoshida diplomacy' nor a 'Matsudaira diplomacy' but that there was a 'Shidehara diplomacy,' then we may be able to appreciate that we have lost more than merely the eldest statesman of that world.[18]

Meanwhile, although the 12 March editorial in the *Yomiuri Shimbun* praised Shidehara for his diplomatic efforts, it was quite harsh in critiquing his insufficient self-awareness as a politician:

> Mr. Shidehara's political and diplomatic contributions to our nation may be numerous. Yet what draws our attention above all is the manner in which he took charge of an extremely difficult

situation following the loss of the war, while at the same time bringing about the establishment of a 'new constitution' that is unprecedented worldwide in its intelligence and cultural refinement … When compared with his achievements as a diplomat, which were so significant that he actually defined a new era with his 'Shidehara diplomacy,' his work as a party politician, it must be admitted, was entirely ordinary … That Mr. Shidehara was more an individualist than a party man must be looked upon with some regret from the perspective of the development of our nation's party politics.[19]

Then there was the 11 March editorial of the *Asahi Shimbun*, which even attacked Shidehara's stance as a diplomat:

Mr. Shidehara was the very incarnation of a bureaucratic diplomat. He devoted his long life to diplomacy, and his achievements ought to be highly praised by the nation's citizens. However, now that Japan has been reborn as a democratic country, it is necessary to find a way towards a new national diplomacy. For this purpose, we must find new leaders of national diplomacy who can help show us the way forward.[20]

Although the *Asahi Shimbun* editorial recognised Shidehara's achievements as a 'bureaucratic diplomat', it looked forward to the coming of 'new leaders of national diplomacy', ones more suited to the democratic currents of the postwar era.

It should be remembered that Shidehara once made a name for himself on the international stage as well. It is worth examining how his passing was covered in the foreign press. First, let us look at the *New York Times*. An article on Shidehara's death, accompanied by a photograph, appeared in this paper on 11 March. It stated that Shidehara was 'among the few Japanese leaders who really understood the Western mind' and that he had spent his final few months helping with preparations for the coming peace settlement. This article was followed by another that served as a kind of corroboration. It was a message of condolence from Dulles. Having just returned from his visit to Japan, Dulles noted that he had 'met often with Mr. Shidehara and came personally to appreciate [his] liberal and anti-militarist spirit'.[21]

The *Washington Post* also included an obituary with a photograph on that day. Later, on 13 March, the paper ran a sympathetic piece on Shidehara's difficulties as foreign minister during the Manchurian Incident. A similar view was expressed in a 21 March letter to the editor by former US ambassador to Japan Joseph Grew. In it, Grew looked back on the period following the Russo-Japanese War, and the friendship between Shidehara and ministry adviser Denison. According to Grew, a young Shidehara had diligently studied international law under Denison while also polishing his English. Denison responded to this show of dedication, eventually bequeathing him 35 years' worth of diary entries and records of his official duties. Shidehara had also frequently written of Denison in his own diary. Tragically, both Shidehara's and Denison's diaries were destroyed in the bombing of Tokyo. As Grew recounted these anecdotes for the newspaper, he may well have been fondly reminiscing about the 'good old days' of Japan–US relations.

Grew was not the only one to pick up his pen upon seeing Shidehara's obituary. Another letter to the editor appeared in the *Washington Post* on 25 March, this time from Castle. Castle, it may be recalled, had served as US ambassador to Japan during the London Naval Conference on Disarmament. In his letter, he noted how impressed he had been by Shidehara's discernment. He further acknowledged that he had learned a great deal from Shidehara on the topic of China policy following the Northern Expedition. Castle concluded by noting that, in a postwar Japan where civil servants were now in control of politics, 'the influence of Shidehara will not die with him'.[22]

The San Francisco Peace Treaty and Shidehara's Legacy

History is concerned with facts, not counterfactuals. Yet it is hard not to wonder what might have happened if Shidehara had lived an extra half-year. For it was during this time that the San Francisco Peace Conference took place. In the newspapers published in Japan on 10 March 1951—the day of Shidehara's death—articles on Dulles made the front page. Having concluded his five-week tour of the Far East, Special Envoy Dulles had sent a report to the diplomatic committee of the US Senate. Dulles sought to obtain the support of the committee with an eye to bringing about an early conclusion to the peace accord negotiations with Japan. At the same time, Dulles had been making progress with a draft of the peace treaty itself, while taking pains not to forbid Japan from rearming.

However, it was not only the US that needed to be convinced. Australia had shown some resistance to the idea of signing a peace treaty permitting Japan's rearmament if there was no guarantee of a mutual defence treaty. In fact, the ANZUS treaty, signed later that year by Australia, New Zealand and the US, was just such a treaty. Nations such as the Philippines had also reacted negatively to Dulles's policy of not requesting Japan to pay reparations. The UK, meanwhile, apprehensive of a return to competing with Japan in the areas of shipping and textiles, sought a treaty that would limit the nation's economic activities. Then there was Yakov Aleksandrovich Malik, representative for the Soviet Union. Malik had told Dulles he would not even negotiate with him about a peace treaty with Japan.[23]

As a foreign minister, Shidehara had made a name for himself internationally. During the occupation, he had served as prime minister, and, at the time of his passing, he was still active as the speaker for the House of Representatives. If he had lived a little longer, therefore, he might have been a strong candidate as the plenipotentiary for Japan at the San Francisco Peace Conference. Indeed, the *Yomiuri Shimbun* noted that 'there was word Prime Minister Yoshida had sought to make Mr. Shidehara the peace plenipotentiary'.[24] After all, until just before his death, Shidehara remained healthy enough that he was still attending the House sessions.

Of course, as the *Asahi Shimbun* editorial pointed out, it was no longer the age of the 'bureaucratic diplomat'. Likewise, Shidehara struggled in his attempts at promoting nonpartisan diplomacy. Yoshida Shigeru, who, like Shidehara, was a former diplomat, would also struggle politically following the conclusion of the peace treaty. Yoshida had to deal with difficult problems such as rearmament; however, more fundamentally, he may have been unsuited to party politics. This was a time when 'leaders of national diplomacy' were desired, and Yoshida was a poor retail politician. He was also not the type to give speeches in public venues.

In many cases, the key to diplomacy in postwar Japan was the leadership of the prime minister. A fitting example was Prime Minister Hatoyama Ichirō's visit to the Soviet Union, which succeeded in normalising Japan–Soviet relations. The foreign minister in the Hatoyama cabinet was Shigemitsu Mamoru. As a member of the generation after Shidehara's, Shigemitsu was a representative diplomat of the Shōwa era. By contrast, Prime Minister Hatoyama was a party politician. As such, he was hardly likely to be as familiar with the practice of diplomacy as Shigemitsu. Nevertheless, it was Hatoyama's visit to the Soviet Union that secured the restoration of diplomatic relations. Simply put, it was Prime Minister Hatoyama who signed the Japan–Soviet Joint Declaration, not Foreign Minister Shigemitsu.

Other examples of diplomatic initiatives that were led by Japan's prime ministers include the amendment of the US–Japan Security Treaty carried out under Kishi Nobusuke, the reversion of Okinawa to Japan under Satō Eisaku[25] and the normalisation of the Sino-Japanese diplomatic relations under Tanaka Kakuei.[26] While Foreign Ministry diplomats had never received a great deal of attention, now even the foreign minister himself was increasingly becoming eclipsed. That said, prime ministers such as Kishi Nobusuke, Ikeda Hayato, Satō Eisaku, Fukuda Takeo and Ōhira Masayoshi were all originally bureaucrats. The difference was that their shared background was in economics rather than diplomacy.

Following the signing of the Treaty of San Francisco, Japanese diplomacy increasingly moved away from the ideals once promoted by Shidehara— those of centralisation under the Ministry of Foreign Affairs and nonpartisan diplomacy. That said, history is often full of ironies. It was under the occupation that former diplomats such as Shidehara, Yoshida and Ashida rose to the rank of prime minister. Even the posts of speaker and president of the two houses of the Diet were occupied by former diplomatic officials such as Shidehara, Matsudaira Tsuneo and Satō Naotake. However, once Japan regained its sovereignty, the authority of the Ministry of Foreign Affairs, its 'supreme power' over diplomatic affairs, appeared to wane. With his passing, only half a year before the conclusion of the peace treaty, it was almost as if Shidehara was alluding to this changing of the times. Most likely, there will never again be a figure whose own fate embodies the rise and fall of the Ministry of Foreign Affairs to the extent that Shidehara's did.

Endnotes

1   *Asahi Shimbun*, 11 March 1951. See also Hirano Saburō, *Heiwa Kenpō Hiwa: Shidehara Kijūrō Sono Hito to Shisō* [The secret story of the peace constitution: Shidehara Kijūrō, the man and his thought] (Tokyo: Kōdansha, 1972), 53; Shidehara Peace Foundation, *Shidehara Kijūrō*, 767–85. For further information on Kishi Kuramatsu, see Kajima Peace Research Center, ed., *Kaisō no Senji Gaikō* [Reflections on wartime diplomacy] (Tokyo: Bensei Shuppan, 2003), 67. This chapter is based on my previous work: Hattori Ryūji, 'Shidehara Botsugo' [After the death of Shidehara], *Sōbun*, no. 454 (June 2003): 16–20.

2   *Mainichi Shimbun*, 11 March 1951.

3   Ibid.
4   *Asahi Shimbun*, 11 March 1951.
5   *Mainichi Shimbun*, 11 March 1951.
6   Shidehara to Grew, 2 March 1951, in 'Shidehara Heiwa Bunko', Reel 17. This English correspondence was also translated into Japanese and printed in the *Tokyo Shimbun*, 13 March 1951.
7   *Tokyo Shimbun*, 13 March 1951.
8   'Dai Jukkai Kokkai Shūgiin Giin Unei Iinkai Giroku' [10th Diet House of Representatives Diet Operation Committee Minutes], no. 25, 20 March 1951.
9   'Zen-Gichō Shidehara Kijūrō-kun Shūgiin So Shikkō nitsuki Aitō no I wo Arawasuru tame Kyūkai Suru Koto wo Giketsu no Ken' [Matter of the resolution to adjourn in order to express our grief on the occasion of the House of Representatives funeral of former speaker of the House of Representatives Shidehara Kijūrō], 13 March 1951, 1-2A-028-04-rui-03527-100, National Archives of Japan.
10 *Asahi Shimbun*, 17 March 1951.
11 *Kanpō*, extra edition, 7 March 1951.
12 Ibid.
13 Satō Naotake, 'Shidehara-san wo Itamu' [Mourning Mr Shidehara], *Shūkan Asahi* 56, no. 12 (March 1951): 41.
14 Ibid.
15 Ibid.
16 Satō Junzō, 'Shidehara-san to Nihon-tō' [Mr Shidehara and the Japanese sword], *Kasumigaseki-kai Kaihō*, no. 179 (January 1961): 11–12.
17 *Yomiuri Shimbun*, 11 March 1951.
18 *Mainichi Shimbun*, 11 March 1951.
19 *Yomiuri Shimbun*, 12 March 1951.
20 *Asahi Shimbun*, 11 March 1951.
21 *New York Times*, 11 March 1951.
22 *Washington Post*, 11, 13, 21, 25 March 1951. A part was reprinted in Joseph C. Grew, 'Shidehara Kijūrō wo Itamu' [Mourning Shidehara Kijūrō], *Kaizō* 32, no. 6 (May 1951): 70–71.
23 *Asahi Shimbun*, 10 March 1951.
24 *Yomiuri Shimbun*, 11 March 1951.
25 Hattori Ryūji, *Eisaku Satō, Japanese Prime Minister, 1964—72: Okinawa, Foreign Relations, Domestic Politics and the Nobel Prize*, trans. Graham B. Leonard (London: Routledge, 2021), 150–204, doi.org/10.4324/9781003083306.
26 Hattori Ryūji, *Nicchū Kokkō Seijōka: Tanaka Kakuei, Ōhira Masayoshi, Kanryō Tachi no Chōsen* [The normalization of diplomatic relations between Japan and China: Tanaka Kakuei, Ohira Masayoshi, and bureaucrats' challenge] (Tokyo: Chūō Kōron Shinsha, 2011), 51–208. See also Hattori Ryūji, *Understanding History in Asia: What Diplomatic Documents Reveal*, trans. Tara Cannon (Tokyo: Japan Publish Industry Foundation for Culture, 2019), 23–28.

Conclusion: Diplomacy and Democracy

Life and Legacy

In this book I have traced some of the details of Shidehara Kijūrō's life alongside the currents of Japanese diplomatic history. I would like to conclude with a look back upon Shidehara's life and legacy.

Shidehara was born in Osaka, the second son of a wealthy farmer. Passing the diplomatic service exam, he began his career as a consular assistant in Incheon, Korea. He would subsequently move through positions such as consul in Busan, Telegram Division director, Investigation Bureau director-general, councillor at Japan's embassy in the US, councillor at Japan's embassy in the UK and minister to the Netherlands. In 1903, he would marry Masako, the youngest daughter of Iwasaki Yatarō, the founder of Mitsubishi, thereby becoming a brother-in-law to Katō Takaaki. The arrangement of his marriage to Masako was mediated by Ishii Kikujirō. Shidehara, who had been raised in fortunate circumstances, now also acquired influential connections. After Foreign Minister Katō ran into trouble with his issuing of the Twenty-One Demands to China during the Ōkuma cabinet, Katō was succeeded by Ishii. Under Foreign Minister Ishii, Shidehara became vice-minister for foreign affairs in 1915.

Shidehara would go on to serve as vice-minister for foreign affairs under Motono Ichirō, Gotō Shinpei and Uchida Yasuya. Later, with the formation of the Hara cabinet in 1919, Shidehara was selected for the important position of ambassador to the US. Representing Japan at the Washington Naval Conference as plenipotentiary representative, Shidehara succeeded in concluding a deal despite suffering at the time from kidney stones. Following his return to Japan, Shidehara would serve as foreign minister for a combined total of over five years, beginning in the Katō Takaaki cabinet. In the 1920s, Shidehara entered the best years of his career. In 1930, he helped guide the London Naval Conference on Disarmament to a successful conclusion. However, he left the Ministry of Foreign Affairs following the Manchurian Incident and, with increasing anguish, watched the country proceed towards the Pacific War. Yet defeat and occupation changed matters completely, with Shidehara becoming Japan's forty-fourth prime minister in October 1945. In his final years, he assumed the office of speaker of the House of Representatives in the Diet.

What did Shidehara seek to achieve through diplomacy in the prewar era? In general, Shidehara's diplomacy is considered to have been based on the ideal of international cooperation, with a corresponding emphasis upon maintaining an open door policy in East Asia. The reality is not so simple, however. While Shidehara accepted having an open door policy as a general principle, he sought to restrict its application in practice. Shidehara similarly had a narrow interpretation of the open door article included in the Nine-Power Treaty signed at the Washington Naval Conference. He saw it mainly in the context of equal opportunity—that is to say, the sense in which it was used in the first open door policy note. To put it another way, Shidehara was against other nations intervening in China's domestic politics. There was a certain policy goal that formed the background to this interpretation: the protection of Japan's interests in China. It was with an eye towards this goal that Shidehara wanted to recognise the 'open door policy' as a basic rule while also restricting its application. Japan was conscious of its special interests on the Asian continent, and, in his own way, Shidehara likewise wished to promote Japan's national interest.

Shidehara's guiding principle at this time was to respect the spirit of the Washington Naval Conference while also supporting China's unification. As seen with the example of the Beijing Special Conference on Tariffs, for the most part, Shidehara's conception of regional order remained within the framework established at the Washington Naval Conference. Shidehara's approach is exemplified in his response to the Northern Expedition, where he emphasised economic benefits such as trade and freedom of residence and defended them on the basis of the spirit of the Washington Naval Conference. Yet there were also occasions where he promoted the expansion of Japan's benefits in China, and not just their protection. We see this attitude in his approval of the construction of the Taoang Railway, despite the fact that this undertaking ran counter to the agreement reached with the New Four-Power Consortium. What this shows, I have suggested, is that even Shidehara was not free of the tradition of Japanese diplomacy.

What sets Shidehara apart from the above tradition most is that, following from his perspective that China's unification ought to be accepted, he implemented a policy of non-intervention in that nation's domestic affairs. Shidehara valued the promotion of political stability as well as economic diplomacy. In particular, when the Nanjing Incident of 1927 occurred during the Northern Expedition, Shidehara believed it had been orchestrated not by Chiang Kai-shek but by the 'communists'. To support political stability in China, Shidehara argued that 'peaceful and diplomatic methods' needed to be used to help 'a central figure such as Chiang Kai-shek' restore order. At the basis of this judgement was an understanding of national benefit that prioritised economic benefits. Shidehara demonstrated enthusiasm for enhanced trade with southern China and was also well informed on issues such as Japanese immigration to the US. As a principle, Shidehara believed in pursuing an 'honest diplomacy' based on building relationships of trust.

From a present-day perspective, one could conclude that Shidehara's policies were basically correct when viewed in the long-term. Yet, when viewed in the short-term, it is hard to see in them any concrete plans for protecting Japan's residents and interests in China. Thus, it seems unlikely that such policies could have convinced domestic audiences. The truth was that Shidehara operated within the framework of the Ministry of Foreign Affairs and did not pay much attention to the Japanese political context. If party politics in Japan had been more stable, then Shidehara might well have made an outstanding foreign minister. In this sense, his relationship with Prime Minister Hamaguchi represented the best-case scenario for Shidehara's career. With the London Naval Conference on Disarmament during the Hamaguchi cabinet, cooperative diplomacy reached its peak under Japanese party-based politics. However, the success of the London Naval Conference did not directly lead to improvements in other areas, such as Japan's relationship with the US. Instead, cooperation with the US on matters such as China policy and the revision of the Japanese Exclusion Act remained elusive.

Another side to Shidehara's career at this time, as the Manchurian Incident demonstrated, was that he showed himself to be inept at handling crises. During the First Sino-Japanese War and the Russo-Japanese War, Mutsu

Munemitsu and Komura Jutarō had earned renown. By contrast, the Manchurian Incident led to the collapse of Shidehara diplomacy. This is a decisive difference. Of course, it would be unjust to blame this failure on Shidehara alone. The Ministry of Foreign Affairs could not fully respond to overseas crises and domestic criticism at the same time. Even if it was at the beginning of the Goken Sanpa cabinet that Shidehara was entrusted with the nation's diplomacy, the next stage should have been for the political parties to seriously discuss the future direction of Japan's diplomatic efforts.

After leaving the Ministry of Foreign Affairs at the end of 1931, Shidehara was soon largely forgotten. While in political opposition, the only time that he directly engaged in diplomatic efforts was for the Japan–Soviet Fisheries Interim Agreement. Shidehara nevertheless retained a sharp mind, as evidenced by his cooperation with the compilation of historical documents for the ministry's Research Department. When World War II broke out, he also showed discernment when giving his views on how affairs might unfold. Yet Shidehara did not take the kind of decisive action that Yoshida Shigeru did. He argued for concluding an early peace when the Pacific War began, yet, in the maelstrom of the war's final days, he embraced the doctrine of bitter end resistance.

Shidehara enjoyed a reversal of fortunes with the coming of the Allied occupation. As prime minister, he endeavoured to secure the continued existence of the emperor system and was involved in the related undertaking of creating a new constitution. Shidehara further worked to rebuild the Ministry of Foreign Affairs, anticipating that it would be important once Japan had regained its sovereignty. He also protected his diplomat colleagues Shiratori Toshio and Shigemitsu Mamoru during the Tokyo Trial. Last, by establishing the Foreign Service Training Institute, Shidehara sought to help the ministry retain the pool of talented staffs that it required.

In his final years, during his term as speaker of the House of Representatives, Shidehara sought to utilise his experience to improve postwar Japan's foreign relations. Here, I refer first to his support for keeping Japan only lightly armed, so that more resources could be directed toward economically oriented diplomatic engagement with the surrounding region. Second, I refer to his promotion of cooperation with the UK and the US to foster political stability and development in East Asia. Shidehara was thus even more enthusiastic than Yoshida in wanting an ongoing US military presence in Japan, a fact that was conveyed to Dulles. In Shidehara's opinion, restoring trust between Japan and its foreign counterparts was essential, and for this he believed the promotion of nonpartisan diplomacy was indispensable.

In summary, Shidehara was an internationalist who most clearly embodied cooperative diplomacy with the US and UK at the time. The reason Shidehara became a prime minister during the occupation period was because of the reputation he had built as a foreign minister before the war. But Shidehara had a different face when it came to Asia. He took the annexation of Korea for granted and was reluctant to abolish China's unequal treaties, which had an imperialistic aspect from today's perspective. In this sense, Shidehara was an internationalist with an imperialist dimension.

Dilemma between Diplomacy and Democracy

Shidehara's trajectory highlights a certain dilemma with respect to conducting diplomacy in the age of party politics. I am speaking of the compatibility of democracy with stable (i.e. bureaucratically managed, nonpartisan) diplomacy. In a sense, this was a consistent theme in Shidehara's life work. Here 'democracy' has a broad meaning, referring to the presence not only of party-based cabinets but also of a political opposition, public opinion and the press. If that is the case, what kind of relationship should there be between democracy and diplomacy? These are difficult bedfellows in any era. If diplomacy ignores the will of the people, it is bound to fail. Yet diplomacy will also run into difficulty if it panders to the public.

From Shidehara's perspective, party-based politics was desirable. Yet he also believed that diplomatic continuity was essential. This was because diplomacy could affect a nation's dignity. Diplomatic policy therefore ought not to be significantly swayed by the changing of governments. This is why Shidehara sought the centralisation of diplomatic efforts under the control of the Ministry of Foreign Affairs. It was also why he was not overly concerned with domestic politics. This was orthodox Kasumigaseki-style (i.e. bureaucratic-style) diplomacy. In truth, Shidehara had his own way of considering domestic and foreign public opinion.

One clear example of his concern would be his publishing of diplomatic documents at the time of the enactment of the Japanese Exclusion Act. Nevertheless, he always kept his distance when it came to dealing with the press.

Meanwhile, when the Kenseikai entrusted Japan's diplomacy to Shidehara and thereby gained the trust of Saionji, the last of the *genrō* of the Meiji era, it gained recognition as a legitimate governing party. As a result, democratisation via a two-party system made considerable progress during the 1920s. As the successor to the Kenseikai, the Minseitō would eventually surpass the Seiyūkai. However, it should be noted that the Kenseikai cabinet's very dependency upon Shidehara entailed a certain eschewing of party-based guidance of diplomacy. While the party did gain Saionji's trust by leaving diplomatic decision-making to Shidehara, the next phase should have included a consideration of how political parties could involve themselves in this sphere. When Shidehara himself had a sense of impending crisis over the Tanaka cabinet's policies on China, he began to lean more openly towards supporting the Minseitō. While he never joined the party, he did participate in activities such as the making of public statements on Minseitō foreign policy. When Prime Minister Hamaguchi was shot, Shidehara even took the role of acting prime minister.

By all rights, as the political parties became increasingly influential in national politics, there should have been a concurrent expansion of their leadership into the sphere of foreign affairs. In practice, Prime Minister Hamaguchi welcomed this new stage of party politics at the time of the London Naval Conference on Disarmament. Yet, to a significant extent, this attitude was due to Hamaguchi's particular nature as a party politician. By comparison, Prime Minister Wakatsuki was quite powerless during the Manchurian Incident. Ultimately, the prewar party politics of Japan was unable to respond adequately to the aftermath of this incident, leading to its collapse. The greatest tragedy of 'Taishō democracy' is that, when the Manchurian Incident occurred, the political parties had yet to systematise the steering of diplomatic policy. For Shidehara as well, it was a time of continuous adversity.

Yet, eventually, Shidehara would become prime minister during the occupation and later serve as speaker of the House of Representatives. At this time, he further contemplated the nature of diplomacy and democracy, and the relationship between the two. In the prewar era,

Shidehara thought it only natural that the Ministry of Foreign Affairs should take the lead in foreign affairs. After the war, he began to recognise that the governing party had a role to play as well. Thus, Shidehara's stance gradually evolved. Indeed, Shidehara even participated directly in the rebirth of party politics. He had expressed pride in Japan's own prewar 'democratic currents' and had persuaded MacArthur that the nation should be allowed to further develop its own 'Japanese-style democracy'. As a party politician, he had also worked to help stabilise the domestic situation by promoting a 'conservative coalition'.

However, just as in the prewar era, the opposition continued to turn diplomatic affairs into political capital. Public opinion and mass media also played a role here. Vexed by this state of affairs, and with an eye towards the future conclusion of peace negotiations, Shidehara turned in his final years to championing nonpartisan diplomacy. What he meant by nonpartisan diplomacy was that parties would abstain from attempting to make political capital out of diplomatic problems. To promote this ideal, Shidehara spoke with, and tried to persuade, members of both ruling and opposition parties. Nonetheless, for opposition parties such as the Socialist Party, diplomatic problems were material to be used for criticising the ruling party. Such parties had no reason to readily abandon their involvement in diplomatic problems. In particular, the futility of asking the Socialist Party to embrace nonpartisan diplomacy revealed the limits of Shidehara's approach. Shidehara presumably felt the sting of this failure quite deeply. The mass media and public opinion were also quite critical of the foreign policy of the wider government and the ruling party, with deeply rooted support for a comprehensive peace treaty and for future demilitarised neutrality.

Therefore, the potential for realising the kind of nonpartisan diplomacy envisaged by Shidehara was actually extremely limited. This was because of the various assumptions that it depended upon. For example, a certain degree of maturity was required not only from the opposition party but also from the citizens of the nation and the mass media. The model for Shidehara's diplomatic ideals in this case was the UK. The reality, however, was that conditions in Japan remained a far cry from those in the UK. Indeed, far from embracing nonpartisan diplomacy, in postwar Japan the Socialist Party and other factions turned foreign policy into an ideological battleground. Shidehara's disappointment can well be imagined. What anguished him was the conflict that arose from attempting to reconcile diplomatic stability with democracy. This was the central dilemma of

Shidehara diplomacy. It should be noted that the Socialist Party would gradually move further away from becoming a potential ruling party, going in the opposite direction from the prewar Kenseikai. Perhaps ironically, this development would actually contribute to the stability of postwar diplomacy.

In the early spring of 1951, when he was 78, Shidehara's life ended peacefully. He did not live long enough to see Japanese politics reach maturity. Although Shidehara was unable to achieve nonpartisan diplomacy during his lifetime, his pursuit of nonpartisan diplomacy under party politics at the end of his life left a legacy worth considering in Japanese politics.

Appendix: Brief Chronology of Shidehara Kijūrō

1872	11 August	Born in Kadoma, Osaka
1895	July	Graduates from the School of Law, Imperial University of Tokyo
	November	Employed in the Bureau of Mining, Ministry of Agriculture and Commerce
1896	September	Passes diplomatic and consular official exam
	October	Appointed consular assistant; sent to the consulate in Incheon, Korea
1897	January	Arrives in Incheon
1899	May	Returns to Japan; sent to a posting in London
	August	Arrives in London
1900	December	Appointed consul, to serve in Antwerp
1901	September	Returns to Japan
		Appointed consul in Busan
1904	March	Returns to Japan
	April	Sent to provisionally assist with office work at the Ministry of Foreign Affairs
1905	November	Appointed foreign affairs secretary
		Sent to take over as director of the Telegraph Division, Minister's Secretariat
1908	October	Asked to be the concurrent director of the Investigation Division

1911	July	Assigned to the director-general of Investigation Bureau
		Concurrently foreign affairs secretary and Telegraph Division director
1912	May	Assigned to the position of embassy councillor, to attend posting in the US
	September	Arrives at posting in Washington
1913	November	Relieved of responsibilities in the US, transferred to the UK
1914	June	Sent to carry out the role of minister extraordinary and plenipotentiary
		Sent to posting in the Netherlands
		Concurrently responsible for diplomacy with Denmark
	July	Arrives at posting in The Hague
1915	October	Returns to Japan; given the position of vice-minister for foreign affairs
1919	September	Appointed ambassador extraordinary and plenipotentiary to the US
	November	Arrives in Washington, DC
1920	September	Made a baron
1922	April	Returns to Japan
	December	Relieved of ambassador extraordinary and plenipotentiary to the US to provisionally assist the ministry
1924	April	Relieved of provisional position; awaits new role
	June	Appointed foreign minister (until April 1927)
1926	January	Appointed member of the House of Peers by House of Peers Decree Article 1, no. 4
1929	July	Appointed foreign minister (until December 1931)
1930	November	Appointed acting deputy prime minister
1931	March	Relieved as acting deputy prime minister

1945	October	Appointed prime minister (until May 1946)
	December	Concurrently minister for First and Second Demobilization Ministries
1946	February	Appointed president of the War Research Institute
		Appointed chairperson of the Food Measures Deliberative Council
	May	Appointed minister of state
	June	Appointed director-general of the Demobilization Agency (until May 1947)
1947	April	Elected to the House of Representatives
1949	January	Elected to the House of Representatives
	February	Appointed speaker of the House of Representatives
1951	10 March	Death

Index

Note: Page numbers with 'n' indicate footnotes.

Abo Kiyokazu, 181, 195
Adachi Kenzō, 164, 197, 210
Adachi Mineichirō, 111, 160–61
Akamatsu Hiroyuki, 121–22, 124, 221n90
Alien Land Law (US, 1913 and 1920), 45–46, 67–68, 120
America–Japan Society, 68, 121, 192, 220n90, 221n92, 232
Anglo-Japanese Alliance, 22–23, 100n140
    Article 1, 27
    Article 2, 27
    Article 4, 81
    basis of war with Germany, 49
    First Anglo-Japanese Alliance, 71
    Second Anglo-Japanese Alliance, 28, 35, 71, 75
    termination, 70, 75–76, 79–80, 83, 85–86, 128–29, 132
    Third Anglo-Japanese Alliance, 71, 75
    threat to US interests, 73
anti-Japanese laws, *see* Alien Land Law
Aoki Shūzō, 63, 90n26
Aoki Tokuzō, 259–61, 285n24
Araki Sadao, 294, 298
Arita Hachirō, 84, 89n21, 182, 191–92, 228
    Asian Bureau, director-general, 104–05, 110, 127–28
    diplomatic service exam, 17
    foreign minister, 227, 230
    reformist, 168
Asanuma Inejirō, 310, 330
Ashida Hitoshi, 5, 40, 226, 238, 255, 260, 310, 326
    Ashida cabinet, 281, 309
    Democratic Party, president, 279
    disagreement with Shidehara, 278–80, 317, 325
    prime minister, 334

Baba Tsunego, 80, 122, 238, 244n19, 259, 313
Balfour, Arthur James, 75–77, 79, 100n140
Ballantine, Joseph W., 198, 215n43, 221n91
Bancroft, Edgar A., 125, 137–38, 155n84
Baty, Thomas, 48, 122
Beijing Special Conference on Tariffs, 106, 129, 132, 134, 140, 145–46, 175, 338
Bell, Edward Price, 124–26, 145
Black Chamber (US decoding room), 202–03
Blyth, R. H., 264–65
Boxer Protocol, 26
Boxer Rebellion, *see* Yihetuan Movement

349

Bryan, William J., 45, 67, 83, 86
Bryce, James, 5, 46–47, 83, 124, 283, 306
Byrnes, James F., 241, 252

Castle, William Richards, 5, 213n29, 218n72, 220n90, 221n95
    ambassador to Japan, 180–81, 217n66
    assistant secretary of state, 193, 199
    cooperative diplomacy, 196
    impression of Japan, 193
    improving US–Japan relations, 194
    relationship with Shidehara, 180, 182–87, 190–200, 215n41, 306, 332
    return to US, 192–93
Chamberlain, J. Austen, 131–33
Chiang Kai-shek, 119, 139–41, 160, 233, 307, 319, 339
Chinda Sutemi, 23, 33–34, 45, 49, 63, 67, 86, 89n21, 111, 121
Chinese Eastern Railway, 26, 30, 52, 57, 72, 84, 176, 219n74
Colby, Bainbridge, 66–67, 108, 120
Constitution of Japan (Meiji Constitution)
    Article 9, 4, 259, 269–76, 284n3, 313
Constitutional Democratic Party, see Rikken Minseitō
Constitutional Problems Investigation Committee, 267–68, 271–72, 276
Cotton, Joseph P., 181, 183
Craigie, Robert Leslie, 184, 232

Davis, Norman H., 24, 66
Debuchi Katsuji, 5, 120, 126–29, 211
    ambassador to the US, 168, 174, 181, 193–94, 207, 218n72
    Asian Bureau, director general, 107, 109–10, 116

chargé d'affaires (US), 63
    diplomatic service exam, 17
    family, 89n21
    member of Shidehara clique, 86, 105, 108, 144
    member of 'Western group', 104–05, 143
    non-intervention in China, 115–18, 144
    relationship with Shidehara, 86, 127, 198
    speech writing, 116–17
    transferred to Germany, 109
    vice-minister for foreign affairs, 110, 119, 126, 133, 200
    Washington Naval Conference, 109, 116
December Memorandum, 133, 139
Declaration of Humanity, 7, 264–67, 288n49
democracy
    Japanese-style, 180, 256, 257, 266, 343
    Taishō, 147, 342
Democratic Liberal Party (Minshu Jiyūtō), 281, 325
Democratic Party (Minshutō), 279–82, 310, 317, 325–26
Denison, Henry Willard, 5, 239, 241, 283
    death, 42, 48, 228
    friendship with Shidehara, 42, 228–29, 304, 332
    influence on Shidehara, 23, 31–32, 48, 50, 71, 78, 84–85
    instruction in diplomacy, 35–36, 41–42, 90n30, 234
    personal library, 42, 52, 82, 241
    will, 41–42
diplomacy, see also Komura Jutarō, Komura diplomacy; Mutsu Munemitsu, Mutsu diplomacy; Shidehara, Shidehara diplomacy; Tanaka Giichi, Tanaka diplomacy

British-style, 46–47, 83–85, 236, 306, 311
bureaucratic-style, 341
cooperative, 2, 3, 139, 179, 196, 339, 341
definition, 1
economic, 107, 120, 127, 129, 134, 145, 167, 339
gunboat, 85
honest, 78–80, 85, 211, 339
in a democracy, 1–2, 341–42
militaristic, 148
nonpartisan, 3, 7, 282, 309–11, 316–18, 322n52, 330, 333–34, 341, 343–44
propaganda, 81
Dohihara Kenji, 294, 299, 301–02
Dooman, Eugene H., 24, 79, 133, 183, 187, 193, 198, 200, 220n90
Dōshi Club, 280, 325–26
Dulles, John Foster, 309–10, 312, 317, 329, 331–33, 341

Egi Tasuku, 128, 164, 202
Eliot, Charles N. E., 79, 132
emperor system, 3, 9, 232, 251, 258, 262, 269–70, 272–76, 340
Enomoto Takeaki, 28
Extraordinary Foreign Diplomacy Investigation Committee, 60–61, 97n105

Far Eastern Commission, 206, 273–75, 306
February 26 Incident, 230
First Sino-Japanese War, 6, 8, 24–25, 29, 228–29, 339
First Trade Conference, *see* South Sea Trade Conference
Five Great Reforms, 257–58
Forbes, William Cameron, 193, 206–11, 218n68, 218n72, 232, 257, 306
Franco-Japanese Treaty, 22, 71, 84

Fukuda Takeo, 5, 334
Funakoshi Mitsunojō, 49–50, 95n79

Gaimushō Kakushin Dōshikai, 104, 120, 127–28
Goken Sanpa, 61, 103–04
    Goken cabinet, 104, 112, 277, 340
Gotō Shinpei, 41, 52, 56, 62, 86, 337
Great Kantō Earthquake, 81–82, 103, 117, 308, 315
    US aid, 82
Grew, Joseph C., 5, 240, 306, 310, 326–27
    ambassador to Japan, 199–200, 231–32
    emperor system, 232
    impression of Shidehara, 231, 295, 332
    Ten Years in Japan, 232, 256
    undersecretary of state, 240
    unrealistic expectations, 244n19
Grey, Edward, 5, 46–48, 83, 94n73, 133, 306
Gunther, John, 315–16
Guo Songling Incident, 119

Hagiwara Shuichi, 38
Hamaguchi Osachi, 181–87, 196–98, 214n37, 282, 339
    Castle's impressions, 182, 186–87, 197
    death, 202
    Hamaguchi cabinet, 104, 170, 173, 178–83, 185–89, 196, 202, 339
    Imperial University of Tokyo, 17
    Kellogg–Briand Pact, 164
    'lion prime minister', 202
    London Naval Treaty Conference, 147, 179, 339
    Osaka Middle School, 16
    prime minister, 110

recognition of Republic of China, 203
relationship with Shidehara, 173, 202, 339
Rikken Minseitō, president, 148, 160
Shidehara aligned, 6, 9
shooting incident, 194, 200–01, 209, 342
Hanihara Masanao, 75, 77, 128, 182, 192, 208
ambassador to the US, 44, 111, 121–23
diplomatic service exam, 17
Japanese Exclusion Act, 126, 220–21n90
vice-minister for foreign affairs, 59, 110
Washington Naval Conference, 43, 70
Hankou Incident, 141
Hara Takashi, 5, 7, 68, 140
director-general of the International Trade Bureau, 27
established diplomatic service exam, 17
Hara cabinet, 52, 56–58, 62, 64, 69, 142, 196, 202, 337
minister in Korea, 25
minister of home affairs, 37
prime minister, 41, 110
relationship with Shidehara, 23, 62, 86, 113
Rikken Seiyūkai, president, 2, 60
Harding, Warren G., 66
Harding administration, 66, 68–69
Hatoyama Ichirō, 121, 190, 277, 333–34
Hatoyama cabinet, 333
Hay, John, 71, 84
Hayashi Gonsuke, 25, 30, 49, 111, 132, 228–29, 308
Hayashi Kyūjirō, 204, 299–302

Hayashi Senjūrō, 204, 227, 231
Hayashi Tadasu, 5, 27–28, 37–38, 41, 63
Hibiya Incendiary Incident, 36
Hidaka Shinrokurō, 130
Higashikuni Naruhiko, 227, 239, 252, 254, 275, 306
Higashikuni cabinet, 252–54, 256
Hioki Eki, 130
Hiranuma Kiichirō, 227, 233, 254, 294
Hiranuma cabinet, 233, 235
Hirohito Shinno, 43, 68, 103, 109
see also Shōwa emperor
Hiroshi Saitō, 45, 70, 80
Hirota Kōki, 5, 63, 86, 110–11
ambassador to the Soviet Union, 201
diplomatic service exam, 17
foreign minister, 227, 229–33
member of 'anti-Shidehara clique', 40
member of 'Western group', 104–05, 143
politician-like behaviour, 129, 143
sentenced to death, 294
shunned by Shidehara, 128
Tokyo Trial, 296, 299
Hirota Yōji, 270–71
Honda Kumatarō, 17, 40, 117, 127, 164
Honjō Shigeru, 299
suicide, 320n18
Hoover, Herbert, 181–82, 196, 206, 215n41
Hori Teikichi, 181, 216n48, 218n70
Horikiri Zenjirō, 256, 273
Horinouchi Kensuke, 104, 127, 129, 175, 177, 310
Horiuchi Tateki, 120, 130
Hornbeck, Stanley K., 74–75, 87, 181, 191, 194, 199–200, 219n74, 221n91

Hoshi Tōru, 37, 63
Hotta Masaaki, 110, 129
Huang Fu, 131, 141
Huanggutun Incident, 160, 168
Hughes, Charles Evans, 122–23, 125, 133, 220n90, 283
    secretary of state, 24, 66
    Washington Naval Conference, 69–74, 76–78, 84
    Yap Island, 66

Ichiki Kitokurō, 38, 184, 189
Ijūin Hikokichi, 25, 110, 116–17
Inoue Junnosuke, 82, 173, 182, 193, 215n41, 225, 308
    assassination, 225
Inoue Kaoru, 5, 25, 27, 60, 89n21
Inoue Katsunosuke, 38, 47, 89n21
Institute of Pacific Relations, 177
International Military Tribunal for the Far East, *see* Tokyo Trial
Inukai Takeru, 278
Inukai Tsuyoshi, 60, 89n21, 190, 225–27
    assassination, 225
    Inukai cabinet, 89n21, 225
Ishibashi Tanzan, 15, 18n5, 238, 280
Ishiguro Takeshige, 267, 277
Ishii Itarō, 63, 78, 82, 124, 136, 233, 309, 314
Ishii Kikujirō, 42, 62, 111–13, 231, 304
    ambassador to US, 55, 58, 63
    consul, Incheon, 25
    family, 89n21
    foreign minister, 41, 51–55, 86
    Lansing–Ishii Agreement, 55, 59
    matchmaker, 29, 337
    missing after Great Tokyo Air Raid, 241
    relationship with Shidehara, 23, 112
    Telegraph Division, director, 31
    Treaty Revision Preparatory Committee, 38
    view on Intelligence Department, 80
    view on Korean annexation, 39
    view on League of Nations, 143
Itō Hirobumi, 5, 27, 28, 33–34, 37, 39, 41, 283
    Itō cabinet, 29, 61
Itō Masanori, 81, 238
Itō Miyoji, 60, 97n105
Itō Nobufumi, 38, 237
Iwasaki Hisaya, 88n21, 308
Iwasaki Masako, *see* Shidehara Masako
Iwasaki Yatarō, 29, 88n21, 308, 337
    Iwasaki family, 82, 88n21, 308, 337
Izawa Takio, 16–17, 147, 202, 226, 256

Japan
    'Great Power', 6
    surrender, WWII, 252–53
    universal suffrage for men, 104, 161
    universal suffrage for women, 276
    US occupation, 3, 9, 15
Japan–Korea Protocol, 31, 35
Japan–Soviet Fisheries Interim Agreement, 231, 234, 242, 340
Japan–US Commerce and Navigation Treaty, 39
Japan–US Gentlemen's Agreement, 45, 68
Japanese Communist Party, 257, 262, 328
    see also Tokuda Kyūichi
Japanese Exclusion Act (US), 114, 120–26, 192–94, 199, 220–21n90, 339, 342
    anti-US protest movements, 120, 123

Japanese immigration
  to Brazil, 124, 144
  to the US, 67, 108, 124, 144–145, 339
Jewel Voice Broadcast, 251, 253
Jinan Incident, 160, 165, 167
Johnson, Nelson Trusler, 24, 73, 75, 87, 99–100n134, 182, 194, 199

Kabayama Aisuke, 231, 310
Kadoma (Osaka), 13–15
  birthplace of Shidehara, 8, 13
Kakushin Club ('Reformist Club'), 6, 103–04
Kamiyama Mitsunoshin, 17
Kanamori Tokujirō, 276, 290n65
Kaneko Kentarō, 121, 144
Katayama Tetsu, 279
  Katayama cabinet, 279–81, 309
Katō Hiroharu, 69, 182, 196
Katō Takaaki, 5, 27, 59, 75, 77
  contrast with Shidehara, 61, 85–86
  death, 132
  foreign minister, 29, 37, 41, 49–50, 61
  Katō cabinet, 6, 61, 104, 112, 115, 117–18, 130, 138, 147, 179, 338
  Kenseikai, president, 103
  prime minister, 61, 110, 114, 118, 132, 138
  proponent of two-party system, 61
  relationship with Shidehara, 112–13
  Shidehara's brother-in-law, 23–24, 29
  Twenty-One Demands, 24, 50, 61, 85, 114
  view of Japan–US relations, 124–25
Katō Takayoshi, 182, 187–88, 190, 193

Katō Tomosaburō, 69–70
Katō Tsunetada, 57, 97n100
Katsura Tarō, 33–34, 36–38, 41, 91n32
  Katsura cabinet, 27, 29–30, 32, 37, 61
Kawashima Naniwa, 53
Kawashima Nobutarō, 38–40, 45, 128
Keenan, Joseph Berry, 293–95, 319n3
Kellogg, Frank B., 137, 139
Kellogg–Briand Pact, 164, 271
Kenseikai (party), 6, 29, 103–04, 114, 132, 146–47, 160, 165, 342, 344
Ketsumeidan (League of Blood), 225
Kido Kōichi, 230, 233, 237, 239, 254–55, 261, 263, 294
Kimura Eiichi, 38, 51, 110, 116, 127, 130, 142, 144, 168, 300
Kimura Seiichi, 119
Kishi Kuramatsu, 270, 290n65, 315–16, 325
Kishi Nobusuke, 5, 334
Kiyosawa Kiyoshi, 237–40, 242
Kiyoura Keigo, 103, 110
  Kiyoura cabinet, 103, 107, 117, 121–22
Kobayashi Seizō, 217n55, 239
Koike Chōzō, 17, 24, 51, 54
Koiso Kuniaki, 227, 240, 294, 301
  Koiso cabinet, 240
Komura Jutarō, 3, 5, 25, 63, 85–86, 92n51
  death, 34
  family, 89n21
  foreign minister, 27, 30, 32–33, 37–38, 42, 71, 85
  heroic diplomatic figure, 62, 340
  Komura diplomacy, 37, 40
  Korean annexation, 39
  prime minister, 41
  relationship with Shidehara, 23, 36–37, 40, 86

signed Boxer Protocol, 27
signed Treaty of Portsmouth, 36
Komura–Weber Memorandum, 26
Konoe Fumimaro, 227, 230, 236–37, 239, 241, 254, 268, 303
   Konoe cabinet, 232–33, 236
   suicide, 261
Korea, annexation by Japan, 3, 22–23, 31, 39–40, 84, 341
Korea Annexation Treaty, 35
Krupenskii, Vasilii N., 54, 56
Kurachi Tetsukichi, 38–39
Kurino Shinichirō, 32, 41, 229
Kwantung Army (Japanese), 33, 60–61, 119, 227, 296
   assassinated Zhang Zuolin, 6, 160
   Liutiaohu Incident, 204
   Manchurian Incident, 204–08, 243n2, 296, 298–302

Lamont, Thomas William, 81–82, 108–09
Lansing, Robert, 55, 58–59, 64–65, 67, 83, 108
Lansing–Ishii Agreement, 55, 59
League of Nations, 63, 65–66, 205, 207, 226, 229, 240, 302, 312, 316
   Japan's relationship, 143–44
   Shidehara's opposition to, 58–59
Liutiaohu Incident, 204, 296, 298–302, 315–16
London Naval Conference on Disarmament, 9, 147, 181, 183, 261, 342
   Castle's role, 190–91, 196, 198, 332
   high point in prewar Japanese democracy, 180
   Japanese Exclusion Act reform, 199
   Japan–US relations, 179–80, 194–96, 198, 200
   Second Naval Conference on Disarmament, 229–30
   Shidehara's role, 178, 180, 203, 326, 338–39
   split, 184
   views of Shōwa emperor, 188–89
London Naval Treaty Conference, *see* London Naval Conference on Disarmament
London Naval Treaty on Disarmament, 179, 189–96, 200, 226
Long, Breckinridge, 108–09

MacArthur, Douglas, 5, 254, 277, 290n65, 306
   Article 9 (Constitution of Japan), 269
   condolences on death of Shidehara, 325
   Declaration of Humanity, 265, 288n49
   Five Great Reforms, 257–58
   MacArthur Draft, 274
   meetings with Shōwa emperor, 262–64, 266, 276, 287n41, 287n42
   relationship with Shidehara, 257–58, 265, 267, 269–71, 274, 306, 343
   view on emperor system, 269, 273, 294
MacDonald, Claude M., 34
MacDonald, J. Ramsay, 182, 186
MacMurray, John Van Antwerp, 24, 65, 73, 74, 108, 192, 199, 220n90
Maeda Tamon, 256, 265, 267
Makino Nobuaki, 230–31, 235, 256, 259–60, 310
   Castle's impression, 197–98
   Denison memorial, 228–29
   Extraordinary Foreign Diplomacy Investigation Committee, 60
   family, 89n21
   foreign minister, 41, 51

lord keeper of the privy seal, 169, 184, 187, 197, 215n41
minister of the imperial household, 59
Manchurian Incident, 2, 6, 173–211, 257, 318, 342
   fallout, 3, 9, 104–05, 147
   'Genesis of the Manchurian Incident', 314–16
   Japan's relationship with the US, 206, 221n95
   Shidehara's actions, 168, 205, 242, 243n2, 295, 331, 338–40
   Tokyo Trial, 295–302, 319n1
Matsuda Michikazu, 110, 174, 201
Matsudaira Tsuneo, 184, 308, 312, 334
   ambassador to the UK, 110, 181–82
   ambassador to the US, 126
   American and European Bureau, director-general, 70, 110
   death, 327, 330
   diplomatic service exam, 17
   family, 89n21
   House of Councillors, president, 308
   Intelligence Department, director-general, 110
   relationship with Shidehara, 142, 144
   vice-minister, 116
Matsui Iwane, 119, 294, 297
Matsui Keishirō, 121–22, 228–29, 238
   ambassador to the UK, 111, 133
   foreign minister, 110, 113, 115–17, 134, 144
   Japanese Exclusion Act, 221n90
   Osaka Middle School, 16
   vice-minister for foreign affairs, 50–52
Matsumoto Jōji, 238, 256, 268, 270–71, 274–76
Matsumura Kenzō, 255–56, 267, 313
Matsuoka Yōsuke, 40, 142, 227, 236, 296
Matsushima Shikao, 134, 303–04
May 15 Incident, 6, 104, 179, 225–26
Minami Jirō, 204, 206, 208, 294, 296–302, 315–17, 319n1
Minseitō, *see* Rikken Minseitō
Mitsubishi, 29, 82, 135, 308, 337
Moore, Frederick, 80, 102n158, 256
Mori Tsutomu, 168, 195
Morishima Morito, 64
Moroi Rokurō, 24, 38–39, 86
Morris, Roland S., 56, 68, 124, 283
Motono Ichirō, 41, 52, 54–56, 86, 337
Mukden
   battle of, 29, 32–33, 43
Mushanokōji Kintomo, 40, 58, 90n32, 134, 314
Mutsu Munemitsu, 5, 27, 56, 62–63, 126
   heroic diplomatic figure, 62, 340
   Mutsu diplomacy, 3

Nagai Matsuzō, 144, 229
   ambassador to Belgium, 181
   impression of Shidehara, 52, 317
   International Trade Bureau, director-general, 110, 119, 121–22
   relationship with Shidehara, 113, 142
   Telegraph Division, director, 52
   vice minister for foreign affairs, 110, 174, 200–01
Nagai Ryūtarō, 164, 198
Nagano Osami, 64, 218n70
Nakasone Yasuhiro, 5
Nanbara Shigeru, 240–41, 247n50

Nanjing Incident, 139–41, 166, 169, 297, 339
Nara Takeji, 187–88, 218n70
Narahashi Wataru, 256, 262, 267–68, 277
National Revolutionary Army (of China), 119, 139, 160
Neville, Edwin L., 73, 182, 193, 209
New Four-Power Consortium, 22, 57–58, 81, 83, 108–09, 141, 146, 339
Nicolson, Harold, 1
Nippon Yusen (shipping company), 29, 135
Nishihara Kamezō, 60
Nishi–Rosen Agreement, 26
Nishiyama Takichi, 272–73
Nogi Maresuke, 22, 33
　Nogi, 42–44, 85
　suicide, 42, 92–93n56
Northern Expedition, 119, 133, 139–40, 145, 160, 332, 338–39

Obata Yūkichi, 127, 304, 315
　ambassador to Turkey, 134
　diplomatic service exam, 17
　expert on China, 54
　minister to China, 111, 116–17, 175–76
　Near East Trade Conference, chairman, 134
　Political Affairs Bureau, director-general, 57
　relationship with Shidehara, 142, 145
Ōdaira Komatsuchi, 243n2, 253, 269, 284n4
Ōhashi Chūichi, 64
Ōhira Masayoshi, 5, 334
Okabe Nagakage, 45, 47, 89n21, 185
Okada Keisuke, 184–85, 187, 214n36, 227, 230, 240, 295, 303
　Okada cabinet, 226, 229
Ōkubo Toshimichi, 5

Ōkuma Shigenobu, 41, 90n26
　Ōkuma cabinet, 29, 51–54, 61, 112, 337
Onozuka Kiheiji, 17, 247n50
Ōta Tamekichi, 45–46

Pacific War, 2–3, 9, 67, 89n21, 225–47, 253, 254, 261, 338, 340
　Shidehara residence damaged, 6
Paris Peace Conference, 6, 52, 58–59, 73, 83, 104, 106, 144, 175, 219n84
　Japanese mandated territory, 65, 72, 80
　Shidehara's reflections, 74, 118
Pearl Harbor, 232, 237
Phillips, William, 48, 55–56, 121
Polk, Frank Lyon, 67, 109
Poole, DeWitt Clinton, 24, 65
populism, 1
Potsdam Declaration, 242, 252, 293
Progressive Party (Nihon Shinpotō), 277–79, 282, 295, 317, 325

Reed, David A., 182, 184
Rehe Strategy, 227
Rikken Minseitō (Constitutional Democratic Party), 2, 162, 183, 196–98, 225–26, 255, 259, 342
　formation, 148, 160
　Hamaguchi Osachi, 160, 173, 197, 202
　Shidehara aligned, 9, 164–65
　Shidehara, policy development, 8, 164
　Wakatsuki Reijirō, 202
Rikken Seiyūkai, 118, 161–62, 164, 169, 179, 189, 210, 216–17n55, 226, 342
　Ashida Hitoshi, 255
　formation, 37
　'Goken Sanpa', 103–04
　Hara Takashi, 2, 37, 56, 60
　Inukai Tsuyoshi, 190, 225

Katō cabinet, 6
Mori Tsutomu, 168, 195
party-based politics, 2, 147
Saionji Kinmochi, 37
Tanaka Giichi, 6, 9, 148, 159, 256
Roosevelt, Franklin D., 33, 44, 231, 236–37
Roosevelt administration, 236
Root, Elihu, 24, 43
Russo-Japanese Agreement/s, 52, 54, 60, 142
Russo-Japanese War, 2, 6, 28–33, 41–44, 228–30, 234, 238, 329, 332
　Denison's reflections, 32, 78, 85, 234
　influence on Shidehara's career, 3, 8, 21, 23, 26, 85

Saburi Sadao, 5, 76–77, 110–11, 126, 133–34, 140, 142
　diplomatic services exam, 17
　embassy counsellor, 74, 81
　family, 89n21
　first secretary, 63–64, 66, 109
　International Trade Bureau, director-general, 123–24, 130–31
　member of Shidehara clique, 86, 105, 108, 144–45
　personality, 63
　Shidehara's right-hand man, 74, 86, 104–05, 119–21, 142, 145
　specialist on France, 109
　suicide, 174–75
Sainan Incident, *see* Jinan Incident
Saionji Kinmochi, 41, 114, 146, 159, 184, 227, 238, 283, 329, 342
　Saionji cabinet, 29, 37, 51, 56, 61
Saitō Hiroshi, 105, 110, 184, 310
Saitō Makoto, 185, 226–27, 230
　Saitō cabinet, 226, 256
Saitō Takao, 268, 278, 281

Saitō Yoshie, 110, 126, 135–36, 145
Sakatani Yoshirō, 121, 220–221n90
San Francisco Peace Conference, 332–33
　see also Treaty of San Francisco
Sansom, George, 79, 130, 193, 199, 268, 306–07
Satō Aimaro, 49, 55, 63, 89n21
Satō Eisaku, 5, 311, 334
Satō Naotake, 104, 143, 304, 306, 312–13
　ambassador to the Soviet Union, 111
　diplomatic service exam, 17
　family, 89n21
　foreign minister, 227, 231
　member of 'Western group', 104
　president of the house of councillors, 308, 326, 328
　reaction to Nogi's suicide, 92n56
Sawada Renzō, 88–89n21, 188–89, 240
Sawada Setsuzō, 47, 88n21, 128, 192, 221n90
Second Sino-Japanese War, 7, 225–47, 295, 297
Second Zhili–Fengtian War, 117–18
Seiyūkai, *see* Rikken Seiyūkai
Sensō Chōsa-kai (War Research Institute), 259–61
Shandong Peninsula, 6, 58, 65, 72, 74, 160
Shandong Treaty, 115
Shibusawa Eiichi, 29, 121
Shibusawa Keizō, 256, 266–67
Shidehara Kijūrō
　alumni association, the Nihachi-kai, 17–18
　anti-Shidehara clique, 40
　appendicitis, 159
　death, 316, 325, 328–29
　diplomatic service exam, 17, 24, 337
　English proficiency, 198

family, 14–16
Imperial University of Tokyo,
   16–17
impression of Washburn, 43–44
influenced by Sir Edward Grey,
   47–48
kidney problems, 67, 337
loss of Denison's books in fire, 82
marriage, 29
member of 'Western group',
   104–05
moderate, 323
neutral figure, 114
on British people, commonsense,
   48
on Japanese media, 23, 80
on public relations, 80
on rudeness of Americans, 69
open door policy, 22, 71–72, 84,
   86, 142, 338
Osaka Middle School, 16
rationalistic, 40, 44
reminiscences of Denison,
   257–58
Shidehara cabinet, 252–53, 255,
   258, 261–62, 264, 267,
   276–78, 283n3, 295, 304
Shidehara clique, 86, 105–08,
   127, 143–44, 279–80
Shidehara diplomacy, 3, 107,
   115, 147, 161, 206, 231–32,
   244n19, 330–31, 340, 344
Shidehara personnel, 173–74
strong will, 260
thiamine deficiency, 17
witness at Tokyo Trial, 295–303
Shidehara Masako, 29, 82, 182, 337
Shidehara Michitarō, 29
Shidehara Misao, 15–16
Shidehara Setsu, 15–16
Shidehara Shinjirō, 14, 16–17
Shidehara Shizu, 14
Shidehara Taira, 14–16, 18n5, 19n5,
   308

Shigemitsu Mamoru, 3, 5, 7, 84, 127,
   130, 145, 328, 334, 340
   ambassador to the Soviet Union,
      230–31
   diplomatic service exam, 17
   foreign minister, 227–28, 253, 333
   minister to China, 111, 177,
      203–04, 316
   reformist, 104–05, 168
   Tokyo Trial, 296, 298, 301–02,
      316–17, 340
   view on Saburi's death, 175
Shimooka Chūji, 17
Shinobu Junpei, 122, 238
Shiratori Toshio, 168, 290n65, 294
   family, 89n21
   Intelligence Department, director-
      general, 110, 210
   letter to Shidehara, 270–71
   reformist, 104–05
   sentenced to life imprisonment,
      294
   third secretary, 64
   Tokyo Trial, 296–98, 317, 340
Shōda Kazue, 60
Shōwa emperor, 5, 170, 187–90, 195,
   202, 208, 241, 303, 306
   classified as a moderate, 294, 303
   Declaration of Humanity, 7, 266
   divinity, 264–66
   'imperial decision', 242, 251–52
   Jewel Voice Broadcast, 251
   not prosecuted, 295
   pacifist, 232–33
   perceived as a war criminal,
      262–63
   relationship with Shidehara, 7,
      227, 253–54, 319n6
   Tanaka Memorial, 177
   see also Hirohito Shinno
Siberia
   US withdrawal, 64–65
Siberian Intervention, 6, 60, 64–65,
   67, 72, 83

Sino-Soviet conflict, 73, 176, 181, 219n74
South Manchuria Railway, 29, 50, 127, 146, 192, 306
    Kimura Eiichi, director, 306
    Kwantung Army, 204–06
    Liutiaohu Incident, 204
    Matsuoka Yōsuke, director, 142
    Treaty of Portsmouth (Article 6), 33
South Manchuria Railway Company, 61, 136, 141, 191, 253
South Pacific Mandate, 58
South Sea Trade Conference, 135–36, 154n79
Soviet Union
    relations with Japan, 137
Stimson, Henry L., 176, 181–82, 185–87, 191, 193–94, 199, 203, 206–11, 219n74
Suetsugu Nobumasa, 182, 185, 188, 214n37, 216n49, 218n70
Sugimura Yōtarō, 89n21, 128, 143
suicide, *see also* Honjō Shigeru; Konoe Fumimaro; Nogi Maresuke; Saburi Sadao
    as a form of protest, 121
Suzuki Kantarō, 184, 187, 216–17n55, 227, 241, 255, 275
    Suzuki cabinet, 252–53

Takahashi Korekiyo, 110, 118, 230
Takahira Kogorō, 33, 63
Takamatsu Nobuhito, 188–89, 239, 288n51
Takano Iwasaburō, 17
Takarabe Takeshi, 178, 181–82, 185, 218n70
Tanaka Giichi, 5, 9, 136, 138, 140, 145, 177
    foreign minister, 110, 143
    prime minister, 110
    Seiyukai party, president, 148, 159

Tanaka cabinet, 6–9, 148, 160–61, 163, 165–67, 169–70, 174, 180, 184, 256, 342
Tanaka diplomacy, 148, 165, 167, 318
Tanaka Memorial, 177, 294
vice chief of army general staff, 60
Tanaka Kakuei, 281, 334
Tanaka Kōtarō, 240, 328
Tanaka Seijirō, 17
Tanaka Tokichi, 17, 110–11, 127
Tani Masayuki, 50, 104–05, 110, 127–28, 130, 191, 227, 238
Taoang Railway, 141–42, 146, 338
Terauchi Masatake, 33, 41, 52, 54, 62, 86
    Terauchi cabinet, 41, 52, 54–56, 60
Tilley, John A. C., 132–33, 139–40, 186, 188–89, 192
Tōgō Heihachirō, 185, 218n70
Tōgō Shigenori, 5, 227–28, 237, 241, 296
Tōhō Kaigi (Eastern Summit), 169, 177
Tōjō Hideki, 227, 294, 262–63
    Tōjō cabinet, 237–38, 262
Tokuda Kyūichi, 256–57, 262
Tokugawa Iesato, 76–77, 81, 192
Tokyo Trial, 293, 319n1
    conclusion, 302
    Hirota Yōji, assistant counsel, 270
    Shidehara, witness, 3, 7, 9, 170, 295, 299, 316–317, 340
    Shiratori's letter, 271
    'victors' justice', 294
    view of history, 294, 319n2
Tomabechi Gizō, 310, 313, 330
Toranomon Incident, 103
Tōyō Bunko (Oriental Library), 307–08, 317
Treaty of Portsmouth, 32–33, 35–37, 39–40, 7, 84, 137, 228
Treaty of San Francisco, 9, 334

Treaty of Versailles, 58, 63, 72, 311
Treaty Revision Preparatory
    Committee, 37–38
Triple Intervention, 25, 27–28, 165
Truman, Harry S., 241, 257, 309
Tsugita Daisaburō, 254–56, 259,
    264, 267, 285n20
Twenty-One Demands, 24, 29,
    50–51, 61, 85, 114, 175–76, 318,
    337

Uchida Sadatsuchi, 49–50, 95n78
Uchida Yasuya, 41, 110, 121, 229,
    271, 337
    ambassador to the US, 63
    cautious, 72
    foreign minister, 51–52, 56,
        58, 66, 68, 77, 79, 83, 86,
        226–28
    Nagai Matsuzō's view of, 113
Uehara Etsujirō, 238, 240, 313
    Ugaki Initiative, 233
Ugaki Kazushige, 173, 227, 233, 241,
    245n24, 295, 303

Wakatsuki Reijirō, 133, 185, 206,
    215n38, 239, 240, 259, 295
    first Wakatsuki cabinet, 104, 147–
        48, 161–64, 202–05, 210,
        225, 242, 296–97, 301
    Kenseikai party, president, 132
    London Naval Conference, 178,
        181–82
    Manchurian Incident, 342
    Minseitō party, president, 202
    prime minister, 110, 204
    second Wakatsuki cabinet, 6, 104,
        147, 202, 204–05, 210, 225,
        242, 296–97, 310
    Tokyo Trial, 303
    vice-minister of finance, 38
Wang Rongbao, 51, 176, 197
Wang Zhengting, 116–17, 175
Washburn, Stanley, 24, 43

Washington Naval Conference, 6, 28,
    131, 133, 181, 205, 315
    Anglo-Japanese Alliance,
        termination, 85, 129
    Chinese Eastern Railway, 72
    diplomatic telegrams decoded,
        79, 202
    Five-Power Treaty, 69–70
    Four-Power Treaty, 69, 75–77,
        79–81, 128
    improved Sino-Japanese relations,
        163
    main topics of, 69
    Nine-Power Treaty, 69–71, 74,
        84, 100, 133, 220n90, 234,
        338
    precursor to London Naval
        Conference, 178
    Saburi's role, 119
    Shandong problem, 73
    Shidehara's role, 21–24, 59, 70,
        73, 83, 87, 163, 326, 337
    spirit of, 112, 115–17, 133,
        143–45, 147, 220n90, 338
    Washburn's role, 43
    Williams's role, 73
Washington System, 87, 132, 134,
    206
Webb, William Flood, 293, 296, 302
Wellington Koo, V. K., 205, 219n84
Western group, 104–05, 143
    see also Debuchi Katsuji; Hirota
        Kōki; Satō Naotake; Yoshida
        Shigeru
Williams, Edward Thomas, 24,
    73–75, 87, 219n84
Wilson, Woodrow, 45, 58, 83
    Fourteen Points, 58
    suspicious of Japan, 64
    Wilson administration, 45,
        55–57, 64–65, 67, 85, 94n73,
        108, 196
Whitney, Courtney, 273–74

Yamagata Aritomo, 1, 5, 7, 37, 54, 60, 62, 68, 89n21, 103, 113
Yamagata Isaburō, 89n21, 134
Yamagata–Lobanov Agreement, 25, 26
Yamakawa Tadao, 110, 304
Yamamoto Gonbē, 33–34, 36, 41, 51, 103, 110
    Yamamoto cabinet, 51, 82, 103, 116
Yamanashi Katsunoshin, 181, 184–85, 187, 190, 198, 218n70, 264–65
Yamaza Enjirō, 34
Yap Island
    problem of, 63–64, 66–67, 99n134
Yardley, Herbert O., 202–03
Yihetuan Movement (Boxer Rebellion), 26, 229
Yonai Mitsumasa, 227, 235, 256, 295
Yoshida Isaburō, 47–48, 125–26
Yoshida Shigeru, 3, 5, 7, 200, 228, 237, 262, 265, 273–75, 340
    Declaration of Humanity, 288n49
    diplomatic service exam, 17
    family, 89n21
    foreign minister, 227, 252, 254–55, 270
    Foreign Service Training Institute, 303–05
    intermediary for Shidehara, 197, 259–60, 277
    Liberal Party, 279, 281, 295, 317, 325
    London Naval Conference, 180, 184–87, 189, 191–92
    member of 'Western Group', 143, 180
    moderate, 231
    peace broker, 239, 242
    prime minister, 4, 14, 277, 304, 310–13, 327–28, 330, 333–34
    pro-British stance, 306
    relationship with Shidehara, 143, 168, 180, 197, 219n83, 256–57
    Tokyo Trial, 270–71,
    vice minister for foreign affairs, 110, 143, 168, 174, 182
    views on China, 84, 197, 227
    Yoshida cabinet, 9, 260, 277–78, 281, 290n65, 291n87, 293, 295, 305, 309
Yoshizawa Kenkichi, 40, 89n21, 110–11, 130, 225, 227–29, 310

Zhang Xueliang, 168–70, 205–06
Zhang Zuolin, 6, 117, 119, 127, 140, 142, 144, 160, 167–68, 170
    assassination, 170
    see also Guo Songling Incident
Zhang Zuolin Explosion Death Incident, *see* Huanggutun Incident

www.ingramcontent.com/pod-product-compliance
Lightning Source LLC
Chambersburg PA
CBHW061251230426
43664CB00025B/2920